A. E. BACKUS

to Patti
12-20-1979
Marian

INDIAN RIVER
CUISINE

FIRST EDITION
VOLUME I

Published by
INDIAN RIVER COMMUNITY COLLEGE
FOUNDATION
FORT PIERCE, FLORIDA

LIBRARY OF CONGRESS
NUMBER 79−67738

PRINTED AND BOUND BY
TAYLOR PUBLISHING COMPANY, INC.
DALLAS, TEXAS

INDIAN RIVER COMMUNITY COLLEGE FOUNDATION, INC.

BOARD OF DIRECTORS

Standish L. Crews
President

Samuel A. Block
Ben L. Bryan, Sr.
Mrs. T. R. Chambers
Edwin Colean
Guy N. Cromwell
Ben F. Dixon
Mrs. Juanita Geary

Robert H. Hazel
William L. Hendry
John M. Luther
Ira M. McAlpin, Jr.
Charles S. Miley
Vincent J. Montuoro
Mrs. Ida C. Morgan

Herman A. Heise, Ph.D., L.H.D.
President
INDIAN RIVER COMMUNITY COLLEGE

INTRODUCTION

Founded in 1959 through the Florida Legislature, Indian River Community College is a two year college conferring Associate in Arts, Associate in Science, and Associate in Applied Science degrees. Meeting the needs of over 20,-000 full-time and part-time students, the College has a main campus in Fort Pierce, Florida, Saint Lucie County; a center in Vero Beach, Florida, Indian River County; a site in Stuart, Florida, Martin County; and a site in Okeechobee, Florida, Okeechobee County. A number of classes are also held for citizens in the four-county area in various community and cultural centers.

The Vocational and Technical Departments along with the Division of Continuing Education are closely coordinated with the specific needs of the community at large as well as cultural programs, musical presentations, art exhibitions, and dramatic performances.

In July of 1965 the Indian River Community College Foundation, Inc., was formed to assist Indian River Community College by providing financial assistance for needed facilities, services, and programs for which public funds are not available; and providing academic scholarships for students of Indian River Community College for continuance of their education beyond two years of college.

The **Indian River Cuisine** has been compiled through a specially appointed Committee of Students, Faculty, Alumni, and Friends of Indian River Community College in association with the Indian River Community College Foundation, Inc. The proceeds will be used for furthering the goals of the Foundation by providing additional academic scholarships, programs, and services.

Welcome to the **Indian River Cuisine!** Within this unique volume of culinary treasures we offer you insights into the delights and traditions that make South Florida a place of gracious hospitality and fine cuisine.

This first edition of the **Indian River Cuisine** has brought together hundreds of select, time-tested heirloom recipes — specialties for every mood and season — of the most talented home chefs. Between its covers are traditional and contemporary South Florida recipes ranging from the Florida Key's conch dishes to the more cosmopolitan epicure, including international cuisine from around the world. Most of the traditional older recipes have been garnished with added ingredients to give them a more piquant flavor. Take full advantage of the interesting array of foods which this book has to offer.

We wish to acknowledge with deep appreciation the contributions made to this publication by the Committee of Students, Faculty, Alumni, and Friends of Indian River Community College. We are grateful, too, to each contributor who donated recipes for use in the book. Literally thousands of recipes to be considered for inclusion in the cookbook were donated by skilled South Floridian cooks. Unfortunately, lack of space prevented us from incorporating all of these prized recipes. Recipes were very carefully evaluated and tested and only those with the "par excellence" ratings were included.

You now have in your possession a collector's item, for the **Indian River Cuisine,** Volume I, is embellished with a lithographed reproduction of an original painting by the world-famed Florida landscape artist, A. E. Backus.

The Indian River Community College Foundation, Inc., is proud to share the **Indian River Cuisine** with you. We are confident it will soon become a treasured favorite.

Kathy Kirry Wockley, Ed.D.
Editor

INDIAN RIVER CUISINE

Editor
Dr. Kathy Kirry Wockley

SALES COMMITTEE

Mr. Robert Bielski and Mr. Timothy Selg, Co-Chairmen
Mrs. Betty Gene Hensick
Mrs. Fran Jaffe
Dr. John Kozma
Ms. Kim Nelson
Mr. Edward J. Rogers
Mr. R. Dale Trefelner

RECIPE COMMITTEE

Mrs. Nancy A. Bredemeyer, Chairman
Mrs. Gloria Bleck
Mrs. Audrey Cahill
Mr. Henry Christen
Mrs. Louisa Christen
Mr. Armand Della Volpe
Mrs. Dot Gortner
Mrs. Connie Montuoro
Mrs. Ethel Rosier
Mrs. June Carlton Vest
Mrs. Connie Wagers
Mrs. Sara Whitacre
Mr. Walter Wisnicky

PUBLICITY COMMITTEE

Mrs. Helen B. Keller, Chairman
Ms. Evelyn M. Fieseler
Mrs. Sheila Grose
Mrs. Jane B. Howard
Dr. Rudolph P. Widman
Mrs. Ada Coats Williams
Mr. Reginald M. Woodall

Cover by
Mr. A. E. Backus

CONTENTS

APPETIZERS

APPETIZERS

ARTICHOKE CANÂPES

OVEN: 350° 30 minutes

YIELD: 36 squares.

2 — 6 ounce jars marinated artichoke hearts
1 small onion, finely chopped
1 clove garlic, minced
4 eggs
¼ cup fine bread crumbs

¼ teaspoon salt
⅛ teaspoon pepper
⅛ teaspoon tabasco
½ pound shredded cheddar cheese
2 tablespoons minced parsley

Drain marinade from one jar of artichoke hearts into frying pan. Chop artichokes and set aside. Sauté onion and garlic in marinade about 5 minutes, until limp. In a bowl, beat eggs, add crumbs, salt, pepper and tabasco. Stir in
other ingredients. Turn into a greased 7" x 11" pan. Bake at 350° for 30 minutes. Let cool in pan and cut into 1" squares. Serve hot or cold.

Terese Burke

ARTICHOKE DIP

OVEN: 350° 15 minutes

1 cup mayonnaise
1 cup parmesan cheese

2 cans artichoke hearts, drained
and pulled apart
6 drops tabasco

Mix all ingredients 24 hours before using. Refrigerate. Bake at 350° for 15
minutes before serving in chafing dish with crackers.

Pamela B. Williams

ARTICHOKE SUPREME

OVEN: 350°

1 large can artichokes, cut up
1 cup Parmesan cheese

1 cup mayonnaise
dash of garlic salt

Mix all together, put into baking dish and bake at 350° until bubbly.
Serve with crackers that are not too salty.

Cindi McCarty

AVOCADO DIP I

1 avocado, mashed with fork
juice of ½ lemon
½ pound cottage cheese
2 tablespoons cream

2 teaspoons chopped onion OR
onion salt
2 tablespoons chopped parsley
½ cup chopped nuts
2 tablespoons mayonnaise

Thoroughly combine all ingredients. Serve with crackers.

Mary-Frazier Palmore

AVOCADO DIP II

YIELD: Approximately 1½ cups

2 ripe avocados
2 tablespoons mayonnaise
2 tablespoons fresh lemon OR lime
  juice

1 tablespoon grated
  onion
1 teaspoon Worcestershire sauce
½ teaspoon salt

Cut avocados in half, remove seeds, peel and mash avocados until smooth.
Add remaining ingredients, mixing thoroughly. Cover and chill for one hour.

The Committee

BLEU CHEESE PARTY BALL

1 — 8 ounce package cream cheese
1 — 4 ounce package Bleu cheese
¼ cup butter (½ stick)

⅔ cup ripe pitted olives, drained,
  finely chopped
1 package walnuts OR pecans

Let first three ingredients soften while olives are chopped. (Olives may be chopped in blender.) Mix cheeses and butter together by hand as the mixer makes it too runny. Add olives to mixture and refrigerate until fairly firm.
Form into a ball and press chopped nuts over all (give a generous coating). Refrigerate until firm.
Be sure to buy black pitted olives and chop very fine.

Ginger Doyle

BOURSIN CHEESE

8 ounces whipped unsalted butter
16 ounces cream cheese, softened
  to room temperature
2 cloves garlic, crushed
½ teaspoon oregano
¼ teaspoon marjoram
¼ teaspoon thyme

¼ teaspoon basil
¼ teaspoon dillweed
¼ teaspoon pepper
1 tablespoon chopped parsley,
  chopped very fine, and 1 tablespoon chopped chives may be
  substituted for dried spices.

Soften butter and cream cheese at room temperature. Beat together all ingredients with electric mixer, blend spices well.
Spread on small pieces of toasted bread, top with a piece of pimento or olive slice for canapes.

A.R. Trottier

An outstanding hostess makes notes in an address book of the special likes and dislikes of friends; then serves their likes when entertaining them.

CHEESE BALL I

1 large package cream cheese
1 stick butter
1 large can black pitted olives,
    drained and chopped

minced onion to taste
salt and pepper to taste
pecans, chopped

Soften cheese and butter. Mix olives, onion, salt & pepper and combine with cheese and butter. Roll into ball and coat with pecans. Keep refrigerated.
Serve with favorite crackers.
Soften cheese ball before serving. This may be frozen.

Susan Enns Stans

CHEESE BALL II

4 — 3 ounce packages cream
    cheese
1 — 5 ounce jar sharp cheese

1 — 4 ounce Roquefort OR Bleu
    cheese
½ teaspoon onion juice
½ teaspoon Worcestershire sauce
chopped nuts

Soften cream cheese. Add sharp cheese and other cheese, blend well. Add onion juice and Worcestershire sauce, shape into ball, coat with nuts and chill.

Sara R. Whitacre

CHEESE CRISPS

OVEN: 350° 20 minutes

2 cups sharp cheese, grated
2 cups flour
2 sticks oleo OR butter

½ teaspoon salt
¼ teaspoon red pepper
2 cups crisp rice cereal

Mix cheese, oleo, salt and pepper with hands. Add flour and work into dough. Cool in refrigerator. Roll and cut or pinch off small amount and pat out very thin. Bake in 350° oven about 20 minutes until light brown.

Carra Adams

CHEESE LOAF

1 large package cream cheese
¾ package Roquefort
1 tablespoon grated onion
1 tablespoon grated celery

1 tablespoon mayonnaise
pecans, finely chopped, enough to
    cover

Cream all ingredients thoroughly and place in refrigerator until set. Place on wax paper and form into roll, cover in finely chopped pecans.

Kathryn Woolford

CHEESE-MAYONNAISE PUFFS

1 egg white
½ cup mayonnaise
¼ cup grated Parmesan cheese

¼ teaspoon onion salt
1 teaspoon dry mustard
1 box Melba rounds

Beat egg white stiff, fold in mayonnaise, add cheese, salt and mustard. Spoon mixture onto Melba rounds. Place in broiler until puffy and golden brown.

Sara F. Haughton

CHEESE PUFF

OVEN: 375° 1 hour

2 eggs
2 cups whole milk
½ teaspoon dry mustard

1 teaspoon salt
½ pound (2 cups) sharp cheese
2 slices of bread

Butter a baking dish and break eggs into it. Add milk and mix mustard and salt. Add sharp cheese cut into small pieces. Generously butter bread and cut into small squares. Mix all ingredients together, dot with butter and place dish in a pan of warm water and bake at 375° for one hour.

Kathryn Woolford

CHEESE STRAWS

OVEN: 350° 10-15 minutes

2½ cups grated sharp cheese
2 sticks margarine

2 cups sifted flour
½ teaspoon cayenne pepper

Mix margarine and cheese together, add flour. Roll dough thin with wax paper covered roller. Cut into strips and bake 10-15 minutes in 350° oven.

Ivy H. Haynes

CHICKEN WINGS

OVEN: 350° 30 minutes; 450° 15 minutes   YIELD: 10 servings

1 cup oil
1 teaspoon ginger
4 cloves garlic, chopped
⅛ cup honey
½ cup soy sauce

1 tablespoon lemon juice
1 teaspoon monosodium glutamate
  (Accent)
⅓ can concentrated orange juice
4 pounds chicken wings

Combine all ingredients and marinate wings for several hours or overnight. Bake at 350° for 30 minutes; then at 450° for 15 minutes or more. To prepare wings, remove tip and discard, then disjoint wings to that you have two pieces from each wing.
Serves 10.

Mal Lowry

COCKTAIL COOKIES

OVEN: 350° 10-12 minutes   YIELD: 4-5 dozen

2 cups sifted all-purpose flour   1 cup butter OR margarine
⅛ cup sugar   2 cups grated cheddar cheese
1 teaspoon salt   1 cup pecans, finely chopped
dash of red pepper

Sift flour, sugar, salt and pepper. Cut in butter until particles are very fine. Add cheese, mixing with a fork. Stir in nuts. Press dough together in waxed paper to form rolls 1-½ inch in diameter. Chill or freeze. Cut into ⅛ inch slices. Bake on ungreased cookie sheet at 350° for 10-12 minutes.

Watch carefully to prevent scorching. A big hit!

Nilla Putnam

CRAB DIP

2 — 8 ounce packages cream   2 cans (6-8 ounces) crabmeat OR 1
    cheese   pound fresh crab
2 cans cream of mushroom soup   Worcestershire sauce to taste
                                    a little lemon juice or ¼ cup sherry
                                    may be added

Let cream cheese come to room temperature. Mash and add to the soup. Cook over boiling water in a double boiler until well blended. Add crabmeat, Worcestershire and lemon juice or sherry. Heat mixture thoroughly. Serve from a chafing dish with corn chips, toast points, or wafers.

May also be served as a lunch dish over toast.

The Committee

CRAB NEWBURG DIP

1 — 6 ounce package frozen crab-   1 can shrimp soup
    meat, thawed   ¼ cup sherry

Combine all ingredients and serve with toasted bread sticks.

Ty Fender

CRAB ROLLS

1 pound crabmeat   2 tablespoons butter
1 cup soft bread crumbs   ½ teaspoon salt
1 beaten egg   cracker meal
1 package frozen chopped onion   oil to deep fry

Mix crabmeat, bread crumbs, salt and egg. Melt butter in skillet. Add onions, simmer until soft, but not brown. Combine with crab mixture and shape into small rolls.

Chill about 2 hours then roll in cracker meal and deep fry at 375° until golden.

Jeanne Crutchfield

CRAB SWISS CANÂPES

OVEN: 375° 10 minutes   YIELD: 36

1 can crabmeat (6½ ounces),
  drained and flaked
1 cup grated Swiss cheese
½ cup mayonnaise
1 tablespoon finely chopped green
  onion
1 teaspoon lemon juice

½ teaspoon salt
¼ teaspoon curry powder
1 package butterflake refrigerator
  rolls (8 ounces)
1 can water chestnuts (5 ounces)
  sliced

Combine all ingredients except rolls and water chestnuts. Separate each roll into 3 layers. Place on ungreased cookie sheet. Spoon crab mixture on rolls. Top with a slice of water chestnut and bake at 375° approximately 10 minutes or until golden brown.

(Any leftover crab mixture may be used on triscuits and baked for about 5 minutes or until cheese bubbles.)

Carol I. Browder

CRABMEAT APPETIZERS

OVEN: 375° 20-25 minutes

1 jar Old English cheese
1 stick (real) butter
1 — 6½ ounce can Alaska Snow
  Crabmeat

1 tablespoon Worcestershire sauce
8 English muffins

Blend cheese and butter until well mixed. Add crabmeat and Worcestershire sauce. Spread on halved English muffins. Cut muffins into quarters. Place on cookie sheets, cover with foil and freeze.

When ready to use: remove quantity desired and place on baking sheet. Bake in pre-heated oven at 375° for 20-25 minutes. Serve hot.

Good when served with apple slices marinated in lemon juice.

Judy R. Jacobs

CRABMEAT DIP

OVEN: 350° 15-20 minutes

1 pound fresh crabmeat
2 — 8 ounce packages cream
  cheese, softened
⅓ to ½ cup cooking sherry OR
  white wine (sherry will make dip
  more salty)

10-12 drops tabasco
salt and pepper to taste
one small package sliced almonds

Mix first five ingredients well. Place in small casserole dish and sprinkle with almonds. Bake at 350° 15-20 minutes until heated throughout. Serve with party crackers.

This can also be reheated and enjoyed later.

Good for large cocktail parties because of the amount it yields.

Deedie Montgomery

CREAM CHEESE AND RED CAVIAR

1 — 8 ounce package cream cheese
¼ cup onion
½ cup sour cream

4 ounces red caviar
lemon juice
Melba toast

Chop onion very fine in food processor. Add cream cheese and sour cream. Add a few drops of lemon juice. When cheeses are mixed and soft, place in serving dish and fold in caviar throughout.

Serve with Melba toast.

This is also a good mixture for stuffing celery.

Shirley O'Haire

CURRIED CHEESE APPETIZERS

OVEN: Broil

YIELD: 5 dozen

1½ cups sharp cheddar cheese,
  shredded
½ cup mayonnaise
½ cup green onion, finely chopped
½ cup ripe olives, finely chopped

½ teaspoon curry powder
1 (6½ ounce) package whole wheat
  wafers
additional ripe olives, sliced

Combine first five ingredients, stir until well blended. Spread about 1 teaspoon of mixture on each wafer. Broil until cheese melts. Garnish with olive slices and serve hot.

Mrs. Noah Lybrand, Jr.

DEVILED EGGS

12 hard cooked eggs
1 teaspoon dry mustard
½ teaspoon horseradish
1 teaspoon salt
¼ teaspoon pepper

4 tablespoons mayonnaise
1 teaspoon butter
sliced olives
pimento
parsley

Bring eggs to boil on high heat then turn heat to low and simmer for 5 minutes. Turn off heat and let eggs stand in hot water for 10 minutes.

Remove yolks and mash through sieve. Add seasonings, butter and mayonnaise. Decorate with olive, pimento, parsley.

One-half teaspoon olive juice may be added if mixture seems a little thick. Small eggs will require slightly smaller amounts of ingredients.

Ethel Peery

Appetizers such as canapes and hors d'oeuvres provide an excellent method for use of left-overs.

DEVILED SHRIMP

2 level tablespoons butter
2 level tablespoons flour
1 cup milk
1 teaspoon salt
pepper to taste

1 tablespoon Worcestershire sauce
1 tablespoon prepared horseradish
2 teaspoons prepared mustard
1 pound shrimp
6 slices toast OR patty shells

Stir flour into melted butter over low heat. Gradually add milk until mixture becomes smooth and thick, but not lumpy. Add salt and pepper, constantly stirring. Remove from heat, add Worcestershire sauce, horseradish, and mustard. Boil shrimp, clean and devein and cut into small pieces. Mix shrimp into sauce. Serve on patty shells or on buttered toast. (Patties may be made from prepared pie crust mix.)

Recipe may be doubled or tripled for larger parties. Makes an unusual canape.

Mary-Frazier Palmore

DILL DIP

1 cup sour cream
1 cup mayonnaise
1 tablespoon dried parsley
1 tablespoon dried onion

1⅓ teaspoons beau monde (Spice Island)
1⅓ teaspoons ground dill

Combine all ingredients and mix well. Chill.

Great for parties where raw vegetables (carrots, celery, cucumbers and cauliflower) are served.

Rosemary Sowinski

DILLED GREEN OLIVES

YIELD: about 1½ cups

1 — 8 ounce jar unstuffed jumbo olives
1 clove garlic, split
1 small whole dried red pepper

1 teaspoon dill seed
¼ teaspoon black pepper
⅔ cup salad oil
⅓ cup cider vinegar

Drain olives and put in jar with tight lid. Add all other ingredients. Prepare several days ahead of serving and keep refrigerated turning jar upside down several times to distribute the marinade.

Pat DuBose

An appetizing and appealing decoration lovely enough to eat can be made by placing a small dwarfed kumquat tree on a table so that the guests may pick and eat as they desire.

DUTCH CHEESE FONDUE

1 pound Dutch Gouda cheese,
  coarsley grated (about 4 cups)
1 tablespoon cornstarch
2 cups dry white wine
1 medium garlic clove, peeled and
  bruised with flat of knife

2 tablespoons imported Kirsch Liqueur
⅛ teaspoon nutmeg, freshly grated
⅛ teaspoon salt
freshly grated black pepper
1 large loaf French OR Italian
  bread cut into 1-inch cubes, including crust

Toss cheese and cornstarch in large bowl until thoroughly combined. Pour wine into 2-quart fondue dish or flame-proof casserole, drop in garlic and bring to a boil over high heat. Boil wine briskly for 1-2 minutes, then with slotted spoon remove and discard garlic.

Reduce heat so wine barely simmers. Stir constantly with table fork and add cheese mixture one handful at a time. Let each addition melt before adding the next. When creamy and smooth, stir in Kirsch and taste; then add seasoning.

To serve, place dish over table burner on table. Regulate heat so fondue barely simmers. Serve with bread cubes.

June Carlton Vest

EGG SALAD MOLD

24 hard-cooked eggs, finely
  chopped
½ cup chopped green pepper
½ cup chopped pimento
½ cup chopped celery
1 tablespoon chopped fresh green
  onion
½ cup cream cheese

1 cup mayonnaise
4 teaspoons gelatin
⅓ cup cold water
½ pound bacon, fried and cut into
  fine pieces
2 teaspoons salt
whipped cream cheese

In separate bowl beat cream cheese until smooth. Then add to mayonnaise. Combine gelatin with cold water and let stand until thick, then melt over boiling water.

Add gelatin to cheese and mayonnaise mixture. Add this mixture to chopped eggs and other ingredients. Season with salt and bacon pieces. Let stand in refrigerator 7-8 hours until firm. Turn out onto platter and shape like an egg with hands. Chill again if mixture appears soft. When firm, spread entire egg with whipped cream cheese.

When ready to serve, use your own favorite garnish.

This recipe was given to me about 25 years ago in Chicago.

Jean Rusnak

When serving hors d'oeuvres and canapes, arrange the appetizers on a tray so that the darker colors face the outside. This will create a harmonious and artistic array.

GREEN CHILI CANÂPES

OVEN: Broil

1 stick margarine
1 — 4 ounce can chopped green
chili peppers
¼ pound grated Monterey Jack
cheese

½ cup mayonnaise
minced garlic to taste
slices of French bread OR small
rye

Combine margarine, green chili and garlic. Spread on bread.
Combine grated cheese and mayonnaise. Spread on top.
Broil until bubbly.

Gladys Baldwin

GREEN CHILI PIE

OVEN: 275° one hour

1 can green chilies, chopped
4 eggs, well beaten

1 — 10 ounce package Cheddar
cheese, grated

Lightly grease a 9 inch pie pan with butter. Spread chilies evenly over bottom of pan. Layer cheese evenly. Drizzle beaten eggs over cheese. Bake at 275° for one hour. Cut into bite-size pieces. For hotter pie, use 2 cans of green chilies.

Barbara Wells Steele

HAM MOUSSE

YIELD: 8 servings

1 envelope plain gelatin
¼ cup cold water
¼ cup vinegar
1 tablespoon sugar
1 tablespoon prepared mustard
¼ teaspoon salt

2 cups cooked ham, diced or
ground
1¼ cups celery, finely diced
½ cup bell pepper, finely diced
½ cup mayonnaise
1 cup cream, whipped

Soften gelatin in cold water. Dissolve over boiling water. Add sugar, salt, vinegar and mustard. Mix well, cool, and stir in ham, celery, pepper and mayonnaise. Fold in whipped cream. Pour into 6″ ring mold or in individual molds. Chill. Unmold on salad greens. Serve with more mayonnaise if desired.

The Committee

When serving appetizers before a meal, pour glasses of chilled white wine for the guests.

"HAPPY HOUR"

OVEN: 350° 40 minutes

1 — 6 ounce can crabmeat
1 can small shrimp
12 ounces cream cheese (use one 8 ounce package and half of a second package)

6 tablespoons mayonnaise
onion salt to taste
tabasco sauce OR Worcestershire sauce to taste

Soften cream cheese to room temperature. Drain crabmeat and shrimp, do not reserve liquid. Mix all ingredients well. Pre-heat oven to 350° and bake for 40 minutes. May be made in a loaf pan or in individual oven-proof ramekins. Cool for at least 20 minutes and serve.

Perfect when you have a group of people — it goes a long way.

Mae Stubbs

HEAVENLY CLAM-CRAB PUFFS

OVEN: 375° 40 minutes

Filling:
6 ounces cream cheese
4 tablespoons soft butter
¼ cup salad dressing (not mayonnaise)
1 — 10 ounce can minced, drained clams
1 — 6-½ ounce can crabmeat

1 teaspoon Worcestershire sauce
¼ teaspoon Tabasco sauce

Puffs:
½ cup plain flour
¼ cup butter
½ cup water
⅛ teaspoon salt
2 eggs

To make puffs, heat water to boiling, add butter, and heat until melted. Add flour, all at once, with salt, and stir until batter leaves side of pan and forms a ball. Remove from heat, stir in one egg at a time until each egg is blended. Drop by teaspoonfuls on greased cookie sheet. Bake at 375° for 40 minutes or until light brown.

To make filling, blend cream cheese, butter, salad dressing, Worcestershire sauce and Tabasco sauce until smooth. Fold in crabmeat and clams.

Pinch off tops of puffs and fill with the crabmeat and clam mixture.

Freeze on a cookie sheet and then package in freezer containers. To use, place on a cookie sheet and heat at 300° until filling is bubbly. You may have ½ cup of filling left after filling 36 puffs. This can be frozen for later.

Mrs. Winfield Brown

Cocktail appetizers consisting of fruit, vegetable, or seafood mixtures are served with a peppy sauce.

HOT BACON-CHEESE ROLL-UPS

OVEN: 400°

thin sliced bread   **bacon slices**
Old English cheese spread

Trim crusts from bread and cut each slice in half. Spread lightly with Old English cheese spread. Roll up bread and wrap with a half slice of bacon. Secure with toothpick and bake on a rack at 400° until bacon is crisp.

These may be half-cooked and frozen until needed. When ready to use, place on cookie sheet and bake.

Ty Fender

HOT CRAB COCKTAIL SPREAD

OVEN: 350° 15 minutes

1 — 8 ounce package cream cheese   **2 tablespoons chopped green onion**
1 tablespoon milk   **OR chives**
2 teaspoons Worcestershire sauce   **2 tablespoons toasted slivered al-**
1 — 7½ ounce can crabmeat   **monds**
                                              crackers

Combine cream cheese, milk and Worcestershire sauce. Drain crabmeat and add to cream cheese mixture along with chives OR onion.

Turn into a greased 8 inch pie plate or small baking dish. Top with slivered almonds.

Bake in 350° oven for 15 minutes or until heated through. Keep warm over candle warmer.

Serve with crackers.

Dottie Flora

HOT CRABMEAT DIP

OVEN: 350°   YIELD: serves 50

1 pound crabmeat   **3 tablespoons Worcestershire**
2 pounds cream cheese   **sauce**
⅓ cup milk   **onion salt to taste**
½ cup chopped onion   **garlic salt to taste**

Combine all ingredients and place in a greased casserole. Sprinkle top with slivered almonds. Bake in 350° oven until heated through.

Will serve approximately 50 persons.

Kathy Goodwin

Garnishes used as appetizers should be delicate and colorful, and kept in harmony with the appetizer.

HOT CURRIED CHEESE DIP

OVEN: 350° 20 minutes

1 — 8 ounce package cream cheese
2 tablespoons milk
½ cup sour cream
1 jar (2½ ounce) dried beef,
   chopped
2 tablespoons finely chopped onion

2 tablespoons finely chopped green
   pepper
⅛ teaspoon ground black pepper
1½ teaspoons curry powder
⅓ cup chopped walnuts OR pecans

In medium bowl blend cream cheese and milk until smooth. Add sour cream and mix well. Add dried beef, onion, green pepper, black pepper, and curry powder. Beat at low speed.

Spoon mixture into shallow (2 cup) baking dish. Sprinkle with chopped nuts. Cover and refrigerate. Just before serving, uncover and heat in preheated 350° oven for 20 minutes.

Serve with Melba toast, crackers or vegetables.

June Carlton Vest

HOT SHRIMP DIP

OVEN: 325° 20 minutes

1 can baby shrimp
2 small packages cream cheese
grated onion to taste

lemon juice to taste
2 tablespoons mayonnaise

Thoroughly combine all ingredients and place in a baking dish. Bake in 325° oven for 20 minutes.

Sprinkle top with paprika before serving.

Marge Dunklee

ISABELLE'S BLEU CHEESE DIP

1 cup mayonnaise minus one tablespoon
½ cup crumbled Bleu cheese
2 hard-cooked eggs, chopped
2 tablespoons chopped pimento

4 small sweet pickles, chopped
1 teaspoon capers (optional)
1 teaspoon dry mustard
few drops of Tabasco sauce

Cream mayonnaise and cheese until smooth. Add remaining ingredients, mix gently but well.

Let stand in refrigerator about four hours to season and mix flavors.

Delicious dip for cauliflower, carrot sticks, green onions, celery, and radishes. A positive favorite.

Isabelle Dorland McClintock

JEZABEL SAUCE

1 — 18 ounce jar pineapple preserves
1 — 18 ounce jar apple jelly

1 small jar creamed horseradish
1 small can dry mustard

Mix all ingredients together. Refrigerate. The longer it sets the better it is.
To serve, pour 1 cup over an 8 ounce block of cream cheese and spread on
crackers.

Mrs. B.Q. Waddell

JOHN'S FAVORITE PÂTÉ de FOIE

¼ pound butter (1 stick)
1 large onion, chopped
4 sprigs parsley, stems removed
1 leaf basil, fresh or dried
⅛ teaspoon mace
3 ounces dry white wine
salt and pepper to taste
1 pound chicken livers
1 clove garlic, crushed

2 sprigs rosemary, fresh or dried
1 bay leaf
pinch of curry powder
2 ounces medium sherry
monosodium glutamate
1 ounce brandy
1 ounce water
1 package unflavored gelatin

In large sautéing pan simmer all ingredients except brandy, water, and gelatin, until livers lose their pinkness; (cut large livers in half) approximately
20-30 minutes. Remove from heat.
Meanwhile, soften gelatin in the water and brandy. When soft, add to
warm liver mixture. Stir well. When almost cooled remove bay leaf and place
mixture in blender all at one time. Puree well. Taste for seasoning. Saltiness
will disappear after refrigerating. Pour into small serving crocks. Let cool
thoroughly in refrigerator and when really set, cover with Saran Wrap right
to the surface.
The crocks may be double wrapped and refrigerated for one week or frozen
for several months.
If frozen, defrost the day before using, in refrigerator.

Gloria Grimyser

LIVER PÂTÉ

2 tablespoons butter, melted
½ pound chicken livers, well-done,
chopped fine
1 can mushrooms, chopped fine
2 tablespoons chives

¼ cup parsley
¼ cup mayonnaise
salt and pepper to taste
bay leaf

Boil chicken livers in salted water with bay leaf until well-done. (About ½
hour.) Chop fine with mushrooms. Add melted butter and remaining ingredients. Mix well and season to taste. Refrigerate or freeze. Serve at room temperature with crackers.
This recipe improves with age. Make it several days in advance of serving.
Watch the salt when flavoring at the end.

Mrs. John S. Stobbelaar

LOBSTER CHEESE PÂTÉ

1 — 8 ounce package cream cheese
¼ cup white wine
¼ teaspoon onion salt

½ teaspoon salt
⅛ teaspoon dill
1½ cups sliced lobster

Soften cream cheese and beat in wine. Blend in onion and other salt and dill. Stir in the lobster and refrigerate overnight or for a few hours.

If you wish to use this as a dip, add some milk and blend to a softer consistency. Serve with saltines or other crackers. Very good served with champagne.

Grace Barrie

MUSSELS FOR APPETIZERS

1 can smoked mussels

¼ pound sweet butter

Soften butter. Open can of mussels and pour over butter. Mash mussels thoroughly with butter and place mixture in serving dish. Chill.

This is so simple to make, but it is delicious!

Lyle Gustavsson

PARTY BARBECUE BEEF

OVEN: 300° one hour per pound

1 — 6 pound brisket
2 tablespoons celery salt
2 tablespoons onion salt
2 tablespoons garlic salt

2 tablespoons liquid smoke
2 teaspoons Worcestershire sauce
1 tablespoon liquid smoke
1 teaspoon salt

Mix together 2 tablespoons each of celery salt, onion salt, garlic salt, and liquid smoke. Rub mixture in brisket. Wrap brisket tightly in foil and refrigerate overnight. Before baking, unwrap and add Worcestershire, 1 tablespoon liquid smoke, and salt. Place in 300° oven and cook one hour for each pound of brisket. Let cool and slice real thin. Reheat in foil or in pan covered with foil just before serving.

Doris Coxe

PARTY DIP

8 ounces Braunschweiger
8 ounces sour cream
1 envelope onion soup mix

1 tablespoon Worcestershire sauce
1 dash tabasco

Place all ingredients in blender and blend well. Chill.

June Pierce

PARTY MEATBALLS

8 pounds ground beef 1 large bottle ketchup
1 pound apple jelly ½ stick oleo

Form ground beef into small balls. Melt oleo in skillet and brown meatballs. When browned, add jelly and ketchup to form sauce. Heat thoroughly.

Betty Lane Hockett

PECAN-BACON HORS D'OEUVRES

OVEN: 350°

bacon strips pecan halves

Cut bacon strips into thirds. Wrap pecan halves with bacon and secure with toothpick. Bake in shallow pan at 350° until bacon is brown and crisp. Drain on paper towels and serve while warm.
Can be made ahead and reheated just before serving.

Nancy Carlton

"PLAINS SPECIAL" CHEESE RING

1 pound grated sharp cheese black pepper to taste
1 cup finely chopped nuts dash cayenne
1 cup mayonnaise strawberry preserves (optional)
1 small onion, finely grated

Combine all ingredients except preserves and season to taste with pepper. Mix well and place in a 5-6 cup lightly greased ring mold. Refrigerate until firm for several hours or overnight.
To serve, unmold and if desired, fill center with strawberry preserves, or serve with plain crackers.

Rosalynn Carter
The White House

QUICK PARTY SPREAD

1 — 8 ounce package cream cheese Pickapeppa sauce*

Place cream cheese in serving plate and pour sauce over to cover and run down sides. Spread on crackers for a party snack.

*You will find Pickapeppa sauce in the grocery store near the Worcestershire sauce.

Hilda Perkins

When entertaining with a wine-tasting party, plan on one-fourth to one-half pound of cheese per person and one-half bottle of wine per person.

REUBEN BALLS

OVEN: 350° 20 minutes

1 — 8 ounce package cream cheese	flour
1 — 12 ounce can corned beef	eggs
1 pound sauerkraut	bread crumbs

Soften cream cheese, add corned beef and snipped and drained sauerkraut. Mix thoroughly. Form into 1"-1½" balls, roll in flour and refrigerate until firm. When firm, dip in egg and bread crumbs. Fry in deep fat for a few minutes until brown. Cool a bit then place in plastic bag and freeze. To serve, bake for 20 minutes at 350°.

Mrs. E.E. Jones

SALAMI ROLL

OVEN: 350° 45 minutes

1 package hot roll mix	½ pound Swiss cheese
½ pound Genoa salami, sliced thin	½ pound Provolone cheese
1 stick pepperoni, sliced thin	beaten egg yolk

Prepare roll mix according to package directions and allow to rise. Divide in half and roll each out to ⅛ inch thick. Slice cheeses very thin. Divide meats and cheeses in half and spread over dough. Roll up like a jelly roll and place on a greased cookie sheet. Brush tops with beaten egg yolk and bake at 350° for 45 minutes. May be eaten hot or cold and can also be frozen.

Mrs. G. Catenaci

SALMON PARTY LOG

1 — 1 pound can salmon	1 teaspoon prepared horseradish
1 — 8 ounce package cream cheese, softened	¼ teaspoon salt
	¼ teaspoon liquid smoke
1 tablespoon lemon juice	½ cup chopped pecans
2 teaspoons grated onion	3 tablespoons snipped parsley

Drain and flake salmon removing skin and bones. Combine with all ingredients except nuts and parsley. Mix thoroughly. Chill several hours or overnight. Combine nuts and parsley. Shape salmon into log. Roll in nut and parsley mixture. Chill well.

Serve with crackers.

Other nuts can be tastefully added to or substituted for pecans — especially almonds.

Paul J. Hall

For another easy canape, cut out rounds of thinly-sliced white bread. Dip the bread in melted butter, sprinkle with a dash of Parmesan cheese, and bake at 400 degrees for a few minutes.

SAUERKRAUT BALLS

YIELD: 50 balls

4 tablespoons butter
1 chopped onion
1⅓ cups chopped ham
½ clove minced garlic
4 tablespoons flour
½ cup boullion
1 tablespoon chopped parsley

3 cups drained, chopped sauerkraut
1 egg, slightly beaten
2 cups milk
bread crumbs
flour

Brown garlic and onions in butter. Stir in flour and cook well. Add broth, kraut, ham, parsley and cook a few minutes more. Ingredients should form a stiff paste.

Place mixture in refrigerator. When cool, form into balls.

Beat one egg and milk. Dip balls into flour, then egg mixture and coat with bread crumbs. Fry in deep fat.

Can be frozen after cooking and reheated later in oven. Just eat plain, needs no sauce.

Eileen Schiavone

SEVICHÉ

YIELD: 8 appetizer servings

1 pound any white fish fillets
½ pound shrimp, shelled and deveined
½ pound scallops
¾ teaspoon salt
2 medium onions, sliced thin

1 cup lime and/or lemon juice
1 clove garlic, chopped fine
2-3 hot peppers, seeded and diced
1-2 medium tomatoes, diced shredded lettuce
cocktail sauce, optional

Cut fish into ¼″ slices. Cut shrimp on bias into thin slices. Cut scallops into thin slices.

In large glass or ceramic bowl combine fish, shrimp, scallops, onions, salt, lime juice, garlic and peppers. Stir to coat. Refrigerate 8 hours or more.

At serving time, add tomatoes and serve on bed of shredded lettuce with cocktail sauce if desired.

Gloria Bleck

SHRIMP SPREAD

2 cans medium shrimp, drained
8 ounces cream cheese
2 green onions, use tops also
1 stalk celery, cut fine

2 tablespoons mayonnaise
1 teaspoon lemon juice
salt to taste

Combine all ingredients and mix well. Serve with crackers

Tastes even better if prepared a day before and refrigerated until needed.

Judy Gooding

SPINACH BALLS

OVEN: 325° 15-20 minutes

YIELD: 11 dozen

2 — 10 ounce packages frozen
  chopped spinach
3 cups herb-seasoned stuffing mix
1 large onion, finely chopped
6 eggs, well beaten

¾ cup melted butter OR margarine
½ cup grated Parmesan cheese
1 tablespoon pepper
1½ teaspoons garlic salt
½ teaspoon thyme

Cook spinach according to package directions. Drain well and squeeze to remove excess moisture. Combine spinach and remaining ingredients. Mix well. Shape spinach mixture into ¾ inch balls and place on lightly greased cookie sheets. Bake at 325° for 15 to 20 minutes.

Connie Montuoro

SPINACH HORS D'OEUVRE

1 pound breakfast bacon
2 packages frozen spinach
1 scallion or green onion

hot sauce
mayonnaise

Fry bacon and crumble. Drain well. Cook spinach. Drain well. Combine spinach, bacon, finely chopped scallion, sprinkle hot sauce and small amount of mayonnaise.

Use cold with crackers, toast squares, or rye bread.

Use hot as a vegetable.

My son Dick created this recipe and it has been well received at parties.

Ruth Davis

SPINACH SPREAD

1 package vegetable soup mix
1 cup yogurt
1 cup mayonnaise
3 green onions, chopped

1 can sliced water chestnuts,
  drained
1 package frozen spinach drained,
  chopped, thawed
1 loaf pumpernickel round bread

Mix first six ingredients together making sure that spinach is well drained. Chill at least 5 hours. Scoop out pumpernickel bread.

Pour spinach spread into bread shell just before serving. Cut top portion of bread and scooped out part into small pieces for serving spread.

Mrs. Robert DeCarlo

Green olives will have a more pleasing flavor if the brine is emptied and the container filled about one-fourth full with olive oil. Shake well and allow to stand for an hour before using.

STUFFED MUSHROOMS

2 ounces Swiss cheese, (½ cup
  shredded)
1 hard cooked egg, finely chopped
3 tablespoons bread crumbs
½ clove garlic, minced

2 tablespoons butter, softened
1 pound fresh mushrooms, 1"-1½"
  in diameter
4 tablespoons melted butter

In mixing bowl, combine cheese, egg, crumbs, garlic, and softened butter. Blend thoroughly. Remove stems from mushrooms and place unfilled mushroom, round side up, on baking sheet. Brush tops with melted butter and broil ¾" from broiling element for 2-3 minutes, or until light brown. Remove from oven and fill with mixture. Return stuffed mushrooms to oven and broil for 1 to 2 minutes.

Mushrooms can be frozen after filling, then taken from freezer to broiler when ready to use and broil for 7-9 minutes.

JoAnn Staszewski

STUFFED MUSHROOMS ITALIENNE

OVEN: 425° 10 minutes

1 pound, medium to large mushrooms
2 tablespoons oleo
1 medium onion, chopped fine
¼ cup green peppers, chopped fine
1 tablespoon parsley, chopped fine
mushroom stems, chopped fine

3 tablespoons Parmesan cheese
½ teaspoon salt
dash of pepper
3 slices fresh bread, crumbed
chicken broth
2 tablespoons pepperoni, chopped
  fine

Wipe mushrooms with damp cloth and separate stems from the caps. Saute onion, green pepper and mushroom stems in oleo for 5 minutes. Add salt, pepper, garlic powder, parsley, pepperoni, cheese and bread crumbs. Mix well. If dry add a small amount of chicken broth. Pile mushroom caps high with this mixture.

Place 2 tablespoons of water and cooking oil in a shallow baking pan and arrange mushrooms in the pan. Bake in hot oven at 425° for 10 minutes.

Emily Gasper

STUFFED SNAILS

OVEN: 350°   YIELD: 2-4 servings

1 can snails with shells, approximately 24 per can
2 cloves garlic, squeezed through a
  press OR chopped fine

½ pound sweet butter
2 tablespoons chopped shallots OR
  onions
white wine

Mix shallots or onions with garlic and butter. Place a little of this mixture in each snail shell. Place snail in each shell, and top with more of butter mixture. Place snails in a baking pan and cook in 350° oven until shells are hot and butter is bubbly. Baste, while cooking, with wine.

Hutchie Altobello

SWEET AND SOUR MEATBALLS

¾ pound ground beef
¼ pound ground pork
¾ cup quick rolled oats
½ cup milk
¼ cup finely chopped pecans OR
  walnuts
½ teaspoon salt
½ teaspoon garlic powder
1 tablespoon Worcestershire sauce

1 or 2 dashes Tabasco
Sauce:
1 cup granulated sugar
¾ cup vinegar
¾ cup water
1 teaspoon paprika
½ teaspoon salt
1 tablespoon water
2 tablespoons cornstarch

Mix all ingredients as you would for a meat loaf and form into small balls and brown in butter until done. (Browned on all sides.)

For sauce, cook sugar, vinegar, water and paprika and salt for 5 minutes; then add 1 tablespoon water and 2 tablespoons cornstarch that have been mixed together in a cup. Cook mixture until almost clear, the paprika will add some color. If freezing, cool sauce before pouring over meatballs.

This recipe freezes well and is very easy to double or triple. Defrost slowly at room temperature. When heating, do not heat large quantities at a time. If necessary, use two pans at a time and the meatballs will keep their shape.

Connie Wagers

TANGY CRAB APPETIZER

OVEN: 325° 15-20 minutes

1 pound crabmeat
1 cup sour cream
2 cups mayonnaise
1 teaspoon lemon juice
2 tablespoons grated onion
½ teaspoon salt

dash of Tabasco
2 cups soft bread crumbs or cubes
3 hard-boiled eggs, sieved
Parmesan cheese
paprika

Remove any shell or cartilage from crabmeat. Combine mayonnaise, sour cream, lemon juice, onion, salt, tabasco, and eggs. Fold in crumbs and crabmeat, mixing lightly. Place in well greased shells and sprinkle with cheese and paprika. Bake in 325° oven until browned, approximately 15-20 minutes.

Betty Dezzutti

Trays of assorted hors d'oeuvres may be charmingly decorated by using frosted grapes. Grapes are frosted by dipping in slightly beaten egg whites, coating with granulated sugar, and placing on waxed paper until dry.

TOASTED SHRIMP

YIELD: Approximately 3 dozen

1 loaf sliced bread
1 pound fresh shrimp, chopped
2 tablespoons green onions,
  chopped
1 dozen water chestnuts, chopped

1 egg, unbeaten
1 tablespoon soy sauce
½ teaspoon salt
1 tablespoon sherry
1 tablespoon cornstarch

Mix all ingredients together, except bread. Cut bread slices into quarters. Place shrimp mixture on quartered sections and deep fat fry with mixture side down. When browned, turn over and brown other side. Drain on paper towels. Serve hot.

The Committee

VEGETABLE CURRY DIP

1 cup mayonnaise
3 tablespoons ketchup
1 tablespoon Worcestershire sauce
3 teaspoons curry powder

¼ tablespoon grated onion, optional
salt and pepper to taste

Mix together all ingredients. Use with raw vegetables — carrots, celery, cucumbers, yellow squash, zucchini, cauliflower, broccoli.

Great for cocktail parties and can be made and stored in refrigerator indefinitely.

Deedie Montgomery

BEVERAGES

BEVERAGES

APPLE TODDY

12 winesap apples
juice of 12 lemons
1½ cups sugar
1 quart boiling water

1 quart dark rum
1 quart apple brandy
1 quart good bourbon

Roast apples until skins break in 375° oven. Watch carefully. Combine juice of lemons, sugar and boiling water together then pour over apples.

Add rum, brandy, and bourbon. Stir a bit and cover for two months. When ready, throw away apples, strain, chill and serve.

Mrs. Thomas Smythe

AUNT EMMA'S SPICED TEA

⅔ cup instant tea
2 cups sugar (scant)
2 packages lemonade mix

14 ounce jar orange breakfast
  drink mix
2 teaspoons cinnamon
2 teaspoons cloves

Mix dry ingredients and store.
When ready to use, use 2 teaspoons for each one cup of tea.
Pour boiling water over mixture.

Elouise Padrick

BLACKBERRY WINE I

ripe blackberries
water (1 gallon for each gallon of
  fruit)

brown sugar (3 pounds per gallon)

Select ripe blackberries. Wash and measure. To one gallon of fruit add one gallon of water and let stand for 24 hours uncovered to ferment. Strain. To one gallon of liquid add 3 pounds of brown sugar (enough to "bear an egg" as the old books say) and strain mixture again. Put in cask. Leave cask open a few days until fermentation begins, then close tightly. This is the hardest part of all — let stand for 6 months. Then draw off and bottle.

Blackberry wine — as made by a decendant of Savannah's most famous connoisseur. If you leave it long enough, it is as mellow as good old port. This recipe was given to me by dear friends, the Franklin Tylers.

George Gortner

Before dinner, sip a dry sherry, a cold sparkling white wine, or have a glass of champagne.

BLACKBERRY WINE II

blackberries   sugar
water

Crush berries. To each quart of berries add 2 quarts of water. Let stand for 36 hours. Add sugar to float an egg (size of quarter above water). Let ferment 7 to 10 days, skimming each day. Keep lightly covered. Strain through flannel bag. Put in bottles. Cork very lightly and leave in a dark place until bubbles stop. When bubbles stop, put in corks tightly, then dip tops of bottles in liquid paraffin. Cool and store. Do not use for at least six months.

A.L. Raulerson

BRIDE'S PINK PUNCH BOWL

YIELD: about 100 small glasses

6 bottles champagne   1 bottle burgundy
2 bottles sauterne   2 quarts sparkling water

Combine all ingredients. Chill.
Makes about 100 small glasses.
Less expensive champagne is fine for this.

The Committee

CAPUCINO

YIELD: 7-8 servings

5 cups strong coffee   nutmeg
2½ cups milk   additional chocolate for grating
5 ounces semi-sweet chocolate   brandy OR Coffee Liqueur
3 cups sweetened whipped cream

Pour 4 cups of prepared coffee into a very clean, preferably enameled pot. Scald milk and add to the coffee. Keep the mixture hot, but do not boil. Melt the chocolate in 1 cup of coffee, and add to the milk mixture; blend well. Serve in coffee cups, topped with whipped cream, sprinkled with a little nutmeg and grated chocolate. Some people may want more sugar, serve sugar on the side. Also, serve a decanter of brandy or a bottle of Coffee Liqueur with the beverage; ½ tablespoon of brandy or liqueur per cup makes it completely delicious.

The Committee

Freeze small pieces of fruit — maraschino cherries, oranges, grape-fruit — in ice cube trays to add color to iced drinks.

CHAMPAGNE PUNCH

YIELD: 20-30 glasses depending on size

1 quart pink pineapple juice
1 quart grapefruit and orange
  juice
16 ounces orange concentrate
1 quart ginger ale

1 quart pineapple grapefruit juice
2 quarts champagne
2 quarts strawberries
2-3 oranges

Chill all ingredients before mixing. Combine all juices in a punch bowl. Add the ginger ale. Add champagne and mix thoroughly.

If using fresh fruit, wash strawberries. Add fresh fruit or frozen fruit, floating them in the punch. Slice oranges and add them to punch.

A delicious and very potent punch. If you want to use more champagne, substitute a magnum for the 2 quarts.

Sharon Smith

CITRUS SANGRIA

1 orange
4-6 tablespoons sugar
2 cups orange juice

1 bottle (4/5 quart) rosé wine (a
  claret or Italian red type)
¼ cup lemon juice
2 cups ice cubes
1 lemon sliced thin and halved

Peel orange in one continuous spiral, then cut into short spirals. Drop spirals into punch bowl with sugar. Add orange juice and lemon juice. Pour in wine and stir. Add ice cubes.

When chilled, add lemon slices and serve.

Sunny Gates

CLASSIC EGGNOG

YIELD: about 18 cups

12 eggs, separated
1 cup sugar
1½ cups bourbon
½ cup brandy

6 cups milk
ground nutmeg
1 cup whipping cream

In a large bowl, beat egg yolks and sugar until blended at low speed. Beat for 15 minutes at high speed until lemon colored. Add bourbon and brandy a tablespoon at a time. Egg yolk mixture may curdle if liquors are beaten in too quickly. Refrigerate.

About 30 minutes before serving, stir egg yolk mixture, milk and 1-¼ teaspoons nutmeg until blended.

In large bowl at high speed, beat egg whites until soft peaks form. In small bowl at medium speed beat heavy whipping cream. Fold egg whites and whipped cream into egg yolk mixture until just blended.

Sprinkle nutmeg lightly over punch bowl and punch cups when ready to serve.

The Committee

COFFEE FRAPPÉ

YIELD: 200-250 servings

3 pounds ground coffee
6 gallons boiling water
6 quarts milk
3 pounds (6 cups) sugar

2½ gallons coffee OR vanilla ice
cream
6 quarts heavy whipped cream

Place coffee in large container. Add water and cover tightly. Let stand 5 minutes then strain through a fine strainer. Cool. Add milk and sugar and stir. Pour into a punch bowl. Add ice cream and whipped cream.

Dot Gortner

COFFEE PUNCH

1 quart coffee made the night before OR 5 tablespoons instant
coffee

½ gallon ice cream
2 quarts milk
1 quart coffee cream

Place coffee, milk and cream in punch bowl. Add ice cream and serve.

Betty Bleech

FANTASTIC RUM PUNCH

1 — 6 ounce can orange juice
1 — 5½ ounce can apricot, peach
OR pear nectar

1 package instant Mai-Tai mix
light run

Mix orange juice according to directions on can. In blender, place nectar and add packaged Mai-Tai mix and one orange juice can of light rum (more or less to taste). Blend. Mix blender contents with orange juice. Serve on the rocks. Cheers.

Carol I. Browder

GEORGE WASHINGTON'S FAVORITE EGGNOG

1 quart cream
1 quart milk
1 dozen eggs
12 tablespoons sugar

1 pint brandy
½ pint rye whiskey
¼ pint dark Jamacian rum
¼ pint sherry

Mix liquor first. Separate eggs and add sugar to beaten egg yolks and mix well. Add liquor to egg yolk/sugar mixture drop by drop at first while slowly beating. Add milk and cream and continue to slowly beat mixture. Beat egg whites until stiff in a separate bowl. Slowly fold into mixture. Let set in a cool place for several days and taste frequently. If nothing else, the recipe is guaranteed to produce a genial host.

Bourbon is usually substituted for the rye.

Thomas Wagers

GOOMBAY SMASH

YIELD: 1-¼ gallons

46 ounces Hawaiian Very Berry
   fruit drink
46 ounces pineapple juice, unsweetened

12 ounces frozen orange concentrate
12 ounces grapefruit concentrate
12 ounces lime concentrate
1 quart white rum

Combine all ingredients and mix well.
Serve over ice.

Jim Foster

HOT BUTTERED CRANBERRY PUNCH

1 tablespoon whole cloves
⅓ cup brown sugar
½ teaspoon whole allspice
3 — 2 inch cinnamon sticks

1 pint cranberry juice cocktail
1 — #2 can unsweetened pineapple juice
1 tablespoon butter

Combine first four ingredients and place in percolator basket. In bottom of
percolator pour the cranberry juice and pineapple juice. Perk for 5-10 minutes. Remove basket. Add butter to hot liquid. Serve hot.
   Especially good served at Christmas-time.

Reda Larson

INSTANT RUSSIAN TEA

1 package lemonade mix, 2 quart
   size
1½ cups instant orange breakfast
   drink

½ cup instant tea
1 teaspoon ground cloves
1 teaspoon ground cinnamon

Combine all ingredients. Stir thoroughly. Store in air-tight container.
When ready to use, mix 2 teaspoons in tall glass with water and ice.
This is even better as a hot tea.

Debbie Jameson

ORANGE BLOSSOM PUNCH

3 cups sugar
3 cups water
6 cups grapefruit juice

6 cups orange juice
1½ cups lime juice
1½ quarts ginger ale

Combine sugar and water; heat and stir until sugar is dissolved. Bring to a
boil and boil for 5 minutes without stirring. Chill. Add juices and ginger ale.
Serve over ice.

The Committee

PARTY PUNCH
(ROSE COLOR)

YIELD: 30 servings

1 can (46 ounces) Hawaiian Punch
fruit drink

1 can (6 ounces) frozen lemonade
diluted
2 bottles (26 ounces) ginger ale

Combine Hawaiian Punch and lemonade, add ginger ale just before serving and serve over ice.

The Committee

PEACH CORDIAL

YIELD: 1½ quarts

3 pounds fresh peaches
4 cups bourbon whiskey
2½ cups sugar

4 strips lemon peel, each piece 2″
long
2 cinnamon sticks
6 whole cloves

Pit and quarter peaches. In a gallon screw top jar, mix all ingredients. Cover tightly; invert jar and let stand for 24 hours. Turn jar upright and let stand for 24 hours. Repeat turning jar every 24 hours until sugar is dissolved. Store in cool, dark place for at least 2 months. Strain through cheesecloth into decanters. Cover.

The Committee

PUNCH

YIELD: 2 gallons, about 50 servings

2 ounces citric acid (ground up,
from pharmacy)
6 quarts water

1 can frozen orange juice
1 large can pineapple juice
4-6 cups sugar (to taste)

Mix all ingredients and chill well. Serves about 50 persons. Ginger ale can also be added just before serving.

An inexpensive punch. It can be colored for the holidays. You can also add sherbet, ice cream or vodka.

Eileen Schiavone

To add an exotic touch to punch, thinly slice carambola (star fruit) and float in punch bowl.

SLUSH

1 large can frozen orange juice
1 large can frozen lemonade
9 cups water

2 cups vodka
1 cup sugar
7-Up

Thaw frozen juices. Combine all ingredients and freeze.
To serve, fill glasses ½ full with slush and then fill glasses to the top with 7-Up.

Helen Riggle

SPICED TEA

YIELD: 16 cups

2-3 oranges, sliced
1 lemon, sliced
whole cloves
4 sticks cinnamon (in half)

1½ cups sugar (2 teaspoons per cup)
tea bags (4 family size OR 16 individual bags)

Place whole cloves in orange and lemon slices. Place clove studded slices and stick cinnamon into cold water. Bring to a boil and allow to simmer ½ hour. Add tea bags and steep 5-8 minutes. Add sugar, stir and serve.

Nancy Bredemeyer

TEA BASE FRUIT PUNCH

2 cups sugar
1 quart water
juice of three lemons
1 teaspoon vanilla
lemon rind

1 large can pineapple juice (optional)
2 cups very strong tea
1 teaspoon almond extract
1 large bottle ginger ale

Boil sugar and water with lemon rind for 5 minutes and cool. Combine all other ingredients and serve chilled.

Celia Bonds

TEA LIQUEUR

YIELD: 1 quart — 70-proof

½ cup boiling water
2 tablespoons instant tea
½ cup honey

2½ cups 80-proof vodka
¾ cup 80-proof brandy

Add boiling water to the tea and honey; stir vigorously to dissolve; cool. Stir in vodka and brandy to cooled mixture. Store in a tightly covered decanter or bottle at room temperature. Before serving, shake vigorously; foam will quickly subside.
The liqueur may be offered as an after-dinner drink to guests. It is also delightful added to hot or iced tea.

The Committee

TEA SLUSE

7 cups water
1 large can orange juice
1 large can lemonade
2 cups strong tea (4-5 tea bags)

1½ cups sugar
1 cup whiskey
1 cup rum
7-Up

Mix all ingredients together and freeze. To serve, mix ½ glass of sluse and ½ glass of 7-Up.

Jane DuBois

BREADS

BREADS

SPREADS

ANGEL BISCUITS I

OVEN: 450° 10-12 minutes   YIELD: 24-30 biscuits

6 cups self-rising flour
⅓ cup sugar
¼ teaspoon salt
1 teaspoon soda

1 cup shortening
2 packages dry yeast, dissolved in
¼ cup lukewarm water
2 cups buttermilk

Preheat oven to 450°. Sift flour, sugar, salt, and soda together. Cut in shortening. Add yeast and buttermilk. Knead well. It may be necessary to knead in more flour. Cut out biscuits and bake 10-12 minutes. Dough may be covered and refrigerated for a week.

This dough does not have to rise before baking. Biscuits may be baked immediately.

Connie Wagers

ANGEL BISCUITS II

OVEN: 400° 12-15 minutes   YIELD: about 2½ dozen

1 package dry yeast
2 tablespoons very warm water
5 cups all purpose flour
1 teaspoon soda
3 teaspoons baking powder

2 tablespoons sugar
1½ teaspoons salt
1 cup vegetable shortening
2 cups buttermilk
melted butter

Dissolve yeast in warm water. Sift dry ingredients into a large bowl. Cut in shortening with a pastry blender. Add buttermilk and yeast mixture; stir until thoroughly moistened.

Turn dough out onto floured board and knead 1 or 2 minutes. (No rising is required.) Roll dough out to ½ inch thick, and cut with a 2 inch biscuit cutter. Place on ungreased baking sheets, brush with melted butter. Bake at 400° for 12-15 minutes or until lightly browned.

Dough may be refrigerated in a plastic bag or covered bowl until ready to use. It keeps well for several days. Biscuits may be prepared for baking the day before and refrigerated. Just remove them from refrigerator one hour before baking to allow them to reach room temperature.

Jewell Hoyt

A substitute for one cup of buttermilk is one cup of milk plus one tablespoon of lemon juice. Allow to stand for five minutes; beat well.

ANGEL BISCUITS III

OVEN: 400° 15 minutes

2½ cups unsifted flour
1½ teaspoons baking powder
½ cup shortening
1 tablespoon warm water
½ teaspoon soda

⅛ cup sugar
½ teaspoon salt
1 teaspoon dry yeast
1 cup buttermilk

Sift together flour, sugar, baking powder, soda and salt. Stir in shortening. Meanwhile, dissolve yeast in warm water and add with buttermilk and flour to mix. Mix well. Turn out on floured board, knead a little. Roll out to ¼ inch thick, cut with round cutter. Dip in melted butter, fold over to make a pocket and bake 15 minutes at 400°.

Pearl Wolfe

APPLE-CARROT BREAD

OVEN: 350° one hour

1 stick margarine
1 cup sugar
1 egg
2 cups flour (I like to use 1½ cups whole wheat flour and ½ cup all-purpose flour)
1 teaspoon baking soda
1 teaspoon cinnamon
½ teaspoon ground cloves

½ teaspoon nutmeg
¼ teaspoon mace
½ teaspoon salt
⅔ cup chopped nuts (pecans or walnuts are best)
1 cup shredded carrots
1 cup cored, but not peeled, shredded apples

Preheat oven to 350°. Grease one loaf pan. Cream together first three ingredients until light. Sift together all dry ingredients. Blend dry ingredients with creamed ingredients. The batter will be very stiff and sticky. Add shredded ingredients and nuts. Bake for one hour.

Cool for ten minutes and wrap tightly in aluminum foil. For best shelf life (up to two weeks) store in refrigerator. It may also be frozen with good results for an indefinite period of time.

Don't leave out the mace! This is the secret ingredient that made your grandmother's pound cake so moist and rich, and it does the same here. Also, I have quit hand mixing this recipe since I got a food processor. Place all ingredients in processor (shred fruits and chop nuts ahead, of course), process, and spatula out into pan. This is primarily a breakfast delight; it may be sprinkled with confectioner's sugar and served as a dessert or it may grace any light buffet table.

Elaine Kromhout

One pat equals one teaspoon; one dot equals one-half teaspoon.

APPLE KUCHEN

OVEN: 350° 35 minutes total time

½ cup margarine
1 package yellow cake mix
½ cup flaked coconut
1 can sliced pie apples

½ cup sugar
1 teaspoon cinnamon
1 cup sour cream
2 egg yolks (OR 1 egg)

Heat oven to 350°. Cut butter into cake mix until crumbly. Mix in coconut, and pat mixture lightly into ungreased 9x13 pan. Bake for 10 minutes. Arrange apple slices on warm crust. Mix sugar and cinnamon. Sprinkle on apples. Blend sour cream and egg yolks and drizzle over apples. Bake for 25 minutes or until light brown on edges.

One can of sliced peaches, drained, may be substituted for the apples. Use a white cake mix with the peaches instead of the yellow cake mix. Company always loves this.

Mary Hardee

APRICOT CRANBERRY LOAF

OVEN: 350° 60-65 minutes

2 cups unsifted flour
¾ cup sugar
1 tablespoon baking powder
½ teaspoon salt
1 cup diced dried apricots
1 cup chopped fresh or frozen
  cranberries

½ cup chopped almonds
2 eggs
1 cup milk
¼ cup butter OR margarine,
  melted
1 teaspoon grated lemon peel

Sift flour, sugar, baking powder and salt together in large bowl. Add apricots, cranberries and almonds. Toss lightly until fruits are coated. Beat eggs, milk, butter and peel in small bowl. Pour over dry ingredients. Stir until dry ingredients are moistened. Pour into greased 9x5 loaf pan. Bake at 350° for 60-65 minutes or until done. Cool in pan for 10 minutes.

Mrs. Karl Keller

When only baking a few muffins, place a small amount of water in the unused muffin cups. This procedure will eliminate warped pans.

BAKING POWDER COFFEE CAKE

OVEN: Moderate heat 20-25 minutes

3 cups flour
5 tablespoons sugar
1 egg
1¼ teaspoon salt
3 tablespoons baking powder

½ to ¾ cup milk
3 tablespoons shortening
½ cup chopped nuts
1 cup raisins

Sift dry ingredients together. Add raisins. To milk, add sugar, melted shortening, and beaten egg. Mix thoroughly and add to dry ingredients. Add extra milk if needed to make dough soft. Roll dough out lightly to ½ inch thick. Place in greased pan and sprinkle with sugar and nuts. Allow dough to rise in pan for 15 minutes. Bake in moderate oven 20-25 minutes.

Sheila Grose

BANANA BREAD

OVEN: 325° one hour   YIELD: one 5x9 loaf

3 ripe bananas
¾ cup sugar
1 teaspoon salt
1 teaspoon baking soda

2 eggs
2 cups flour
½ cup nuts, chopped

Crush bananas with a fork. Beat the eggs well with a fork and add to the bananas. Sift flour and combine it with sugar, salt and soda, then add dry ingredients to the banana mixture. Mix well. Add nuts. Bake one hour in 325° oven.

A good way to use up aged bananas.

Millie Cook

BEER BREAD

OVEN: 350° 1¼ hours

3 cups self-rising flour
12 ounces beer, room temperature

2 tablespoons sugar

Stir together flour and sugar. Stir in beer. Beat 25 strokes. Place in buttered bread pan and bake at 350° for 1¼ hours. Cool and wrap in foil overnight.

Variations include adding yogurt for sour dough taste.

Lynne Christen

One dash equals eight drops; one pinch equals one/eighth teaspoon; and one teaspoon equals sixty drops.

BISCUIT SUPREME

OVEN: 400° 15 minutes

2 cups flour
4 teaspoons baking powder
½ teaspoon cream of tartar
1 teaspoon salt

2 tablespoons sugar
½ cup shortening
⅔ cup milk

Blend together all ingredients. Roll dough and cut with biscuit cutter. Bake for 15 minutes in 400° oven.

Dot Gortner

BLUEBERRY COFFEE CAKE

1 package blueberry muffin mix
½ cup sour cream
1 egg
¼ cup milk

Streusel mixture:
½ cup brown sugar
⅓ cup flour
¼ cup cold butter
½ teaspoon cinnamon

Mix sour cream and egg, stir in milk. Add blueberry muffin mix, and stir until blended. Pour one-half of batter into pan. Combine struesel mixture in small bowl with fork or fingers. Sprinkle one-half of streusel mixture on batter. Pour other half of batter on top and sprinkle with remaining streusel mixture.
Easy and delicious!

Mary Hardee

BLUEBERRY MUFFINS

OVEN: 425° 20 minutes

½ cup melted butter
1 cup sugar
2 cups sifted flour
½ cup milk

2 eggs, well beaten
2 teaspoons baking powder
1½ cups blueberries

Mix ingredients well in order given, making sure to add blueberries last. Bake in 425° oven for 20 minutes, filling muffin cups ¾ full.
Frozen blueberries may be used.

Anita Smith

When mixing cold shortening, heat the blades of an electric mixer in hot water just before using. This prevents clogging.

BRAN-OATMEAL BREAD

OVEN: 375° 35-45 minutes   YIELD: 2 5x9 loaves

1 cup oatmeal, quick or regular
1 cup whole bran cereal
⅓ cup brown sugar
¼ cup salad oil
2 teaspoons salt

1 envelope dry yeast
4 cups all purpose flour, more if
  needed
2 cups boiling water
½ cup warm water

Place first five ingredients in large bowl and pour boiling water over them. Let them stand until lukewarm. Dissolve yeast in warm water and add to cooled mixture in bowl. Add enough flour to make a dough that can be kneaded. Turn out on a floured surface and knead until smooth and well mixed. Dough will be sticky, so use enough flour to knead. Place dough in greased bowl and let rise until it is doubled in size, about 2 hours. Keep dough warm while rising. Shape into loaves and let rise again until doubled in size. Bake at 375° for 35-45 minutes or until done. Cool on rack.

Mrs. Charles Proctor

CARROT BREAD

OVEN: 325° 55 minutes

1 cup sugar
¾ cup salad oil
2 eggs
1½ cups flour
1 teaspoon cinnamon

1 teaspoon soda
¼ teaspoon salt
1 cup carrots, grated
½ cup nuts, chopped

Mix together sugar and oil, add eggs and beat well. Sift together flour, soda and salt and add to mixture. Mix well. Add carrots and nuts. Blend. Bake in greased loaf pan for 55 minutes at 325° or until done.

Jane Howard

Before baking bread, brush the top with a beaten egg plus one tablespoon of water and the loaf will have a glossy crust. If a soft crust is desired, brush the top with melted butter when bread is removed from the oven.

CHALLA — YELLOW BRAIDED EGG BREAD

OVEN: 375° 25-30 minutes   YIELD: 4 loaves

2 packages granulated yeast
2½ cups warm water
6 tablespoons sugar
2 teaspoons salt
⅓ cup salad oil, not olive oil
4 eggs

8⅔ cups all-purpose flour
Glaze:
1 egg yolk
1 teaspoon water
4 teaspoons poppy seeds

Using a large mixing bowl, dissolve yeast in the warm water in the bowl. Add sugar, salt, oil and slightly beaten eggs and 6 cups flour. Beat thoroughly with wooden spoon. Place remaining flour on pastry board, add dough and knead until smooth and all flour is absorbed. If dough is still sticky add a little more flour to the dough until right consistency is obtained.

Place dough in bowl used to mix ingredients and let rise in a warm place for 1½ hours or until triple in bulk. Punch down and divide into 12 portions. Shape each portion into a rope about 1" wide. Braid three ropes together and place in well-greased bread pans and let rise in warm place for ¾ hour or until triple in bulk. Brush tops with egg and water mixture and sprinkle with poppy seeds. Bake at 375° for 25-30 minutes or until golden brown.

This is a variation of the braided egg bread which our Jewish neighbors and friends use during their holidays. My mother came to this country from Austria in 1914 and her specialty was yeast breads. This recipe comes very close to the braided bread she used to make when we were growing up. I like it because it makes 4 loaves at one time and conserves energy when it comes to heating an oven. This freezes well, too.

Mrs. Richard O. Burkhardt

To substitute one cup self-rising flour, use one cup all-purpose flour plus one and one/half teaspoons baking powder and one-fourth teaspoon salt.

CHEESE BISCUITS

OVEN: 325° 15 minutes   YIELD: about 4 dozen

1 cup sharp cheese, shredded
½ cup oleo
1 cup crisp rice cereal
1 cup plain flour

⅛ teaspoon salt
½ teaspoon hot pepper, Tabasco or
  cayenne pepper

Have all ingredients at room temperature. Mix together well. Pinch off marble sized pieces and place on lightly greased cookie sheets. Flatten with fork. Bake at 325° about 15 minutes.

Aerline Shippey

CHICKEN OR TURKEY STUFFING

OVEN: 300° 1 hour

your favorite cornbread
saltines
½ cup celery, finely chopped
½ cup onion, finely chopped
salt to taste

pepper to taste
chicken OR turkey stock
½ stick butter
6 boiled eggs

Bake your favorite cornbread. (This can be done the day before.) Crumble cornbread and add an equal amount of saltines, broken. Add celery and onion. Salt and pepper to taste. Stir in a mixture of chicken OR turkey stock and the butter. Then mash the boiled eggs. Add enough stock to make a paste. Spread over dressing mixture and bake for 1 hour at 300°. Serve with giblet gravy.

Lois Kinsaul

COCOA WAFFLES

1 cup unsifted all purpose flour
¾ cup sugar
½ cup cocoa
½ teaspoon baking powder
½ teaspoon baking soda
¼ teaspoon salt

2 eggs
1 cup buttermilk OR sour milk
¼ cup butter OR margarine,
  melted
1 teaspoon vanilla

Combine flour, sugar, cocoa, baking powder, baking soda and salt in mixing bowl. Add eggs and buttermilk, beat just until well blended. Gradually add melted butter while beating to keep batter smooth.

Bake in a waffle iron according to manufacturer's directions. Serve warm with butter and syrup, sausages, or bacon if desired.

Mrs. Richard Keefe

For a toasted flavor, use fine bread crumbs to thicken cream sauces used in casseroles.

COFFEE CAKE I

OVEN: 350° 20-25 minutes

¾ cup sugar
¼ cup shortening
1 egg
½ cup milk
1½ cups flour
½ teaspoon salt

2 teaspoons baking powder
Topping:
2 tablespoons melted butter
2 tablespoons flour
2 teaspoons cinnamon
½ cup brown sugar

Cream sugar and shortening. Add egg and cream again. Sift together flour, salt, and baking powder. Add flour mixture alternately with milk and mix well.

Topping: Mix together flour, cinnamon, and brown sugar. Add melted butter and mix well. Spread half of batter mixture into a square layer cake pan, spread half of topping mixture over this. Repeat with remaining batter and topping. (Pan should be greased and floured.) Bake at 350° for 20-25 minutes or until cake tester comes out clean.

Serve cake warm with butter and coffee. Chopped nuts may also be added to the topping if desired. Mix dry ingredients the night before you plan to make the cake. This makes less work in the morning so you can sleep in.

Mary Sowinski

COFFEE CAKE II

OVEN: 350° 40-45 minutes

½ pound margarine
1½ cups sugar
3 eggs
2½ cups sifted flour
3 teaspoons baking powder
¾ teaspoon baking soda
1½ teaspoons vanilla

1 cup sour cream
½ teaspoon salt
Topping:
1 cup chopped nuts
½ cup sugar
1 teaspoon cinnamon

Cream together margarine and sugar. Add eggs one at a time, mixing well after each addition. Mix together flour, baking powder, and baking soda. Combine vanilla and salt in separate bowl with sour cream. Alternate sour cream mixture and dry ingredients to creamed mixture. In separate bowl combine topping ingredients. Spread one half of batter in 13x9 pan then sprinkle on one half of the topping. Repeat with remaining batter and topping. Bake at 350° 40-45 minutes.

Gertrude Weh

An alternate for scalded milk is canned evaporated milk diluted with equal parts of hot water — a huge time saver.

COFFEE CAKE III

OVEN: 300° 40 minutes

1 stick butter OR oleo
1 cup sugar
dash of salt
2 eggs
2 cups flour
1 teaspoon baking powder
½ teaspoon soda

½ pint sour cream
1 teaspoon vanilla
Topping:
¼ cup sugar
1 tablespoon brown sugar
1 teaspoon cinnamon

Cream together first four ingredients. Mix well. Add remaining ingredients and mix well. Grease and flour a 9x12 inch baking pan. Pour mix into pan and set aside.

Mix together topping ingredients in a small bowl. Sprinkle topping mixture over batter in pan. With a fork, lightly swirl the very top of mixture. Bake in 300° oven for 40 minutes.

Mrs. Jesse Horne

CORN BREAD

OVEN: 400° 30 minutes   YIELD: serves 8-10

2 cups biscuit mix
1 cup yellow cornmeal
2 eggs
½ cup cheese
1 teaspoon salt
1 can Mexicana corn

1 green pepper
1 yellow pepper
1 medium yellow onion
1 cup milk
¾ cup oil

Preheat oven to 400°. Pour oil into glass baking dish, 9x5 inch size. Place in oven until hot. Mix dry ingredients together with eggs, salt, chopped peppers and onion. Mix in cheese, cornmeal and milk. Check oil, be sure it is very hot. (Almost smoking hot.) Pour mixture into baking dish and bake 30 minutes or until golden brown. Serve with fish or beef.

Deborah VonJoshua

CORN BREAD — LIGHT AND KRISPY

OVEN: 450° 20-25 minutes

1 cup water-ground meal
½ cup flour
2 rounded teaspoons baking powder, fresh

1 teaspoon salt
1 egg, slightly beaten
2 tablespoons cooking oil
⅞ cup whole milk

Preheat oven to 450°. Sift together dry ingredients in a bowl. When oven reaches 450°, place oil in a shallow baking pan (11x7 inch), and place in oven. Add egg and milk to meal mixture gradually. Beat well. Mixture will be thin. When oil is hot, add to mixture, leaving a little in pan. Pour immediately into hot pan and bake 20-25 minutes.

Mabel Burry

CORN DOGGERS

1½ cups white water-ground corn-
    meal
½ teaspoon baking soda

½ teaspoon salt
1 tablespoon lard OR shortening
1 cup boiling water

Combine ingredients in order listed, adding boiling water last. Make small patties or balls and drop into pot of boiling turnip greens or collards.

These patties can be fried and served as bread.

This was a recipe my mother served to the family during my early life-time. Carrie Roberts Holmes (Feb. 20, 1867-Oct. 20, 1967).

Addie Holmes Emerson

DATE AND NUT BREAD

OVEN: 275°-300° 2 hours

¼ cup butter
1 cup sugar
½ teaspoon salt
2 teaspoons baking powder
1 cup all purpose flour

4 eggs, separated
1½ teaspoons vanilla
1½ pounds pitted dates
2 pounds English walnuts

Cream butter and sugar. Add egg yolks and vanilla. Beat well. Add sifted dry ingredients. Batter will be very stiff. Add dates and nuts, using large fork and heavy spoon. Add stiffly beaten egg whites. Bake for about 2 hours at 275°-300°. Cool in pan, well covered with wax paper. (Use 6½x10½ pan.) Store in tight can, well wrapped.

This makes an excellent holiday treat and keeps for months.

Kathryn Woolford

DATE NUT BREAD

OVEN: 325° one hour

1 egg, well beaten
1½ cups sugar
1 tablespoon melted butter
2¾ cups flour
2 teaspoons soda

1 teaspoon salt
1 cup dates, cut
1½ cups boiling water
1 cup chopped nuts
1½ teaspoons vanilla

Pour water over dates. Set aside. Mix sugar, beaten egg and butter. Beat well. Sift flour, soda and salt. Add to egg mixture alternately with water from dates. Add dates and nuts and vanilla. Bake in loaf pan at 325° for about one hour.

Celia Bonds

To plump raisins boil two cups of water; soak raisins in the boiled water for five minutes in a covered container.

DILL BREAD

OVEN: 350° 35 minutes

1 package active dry yeast	1 tablespoon butter OR margarine
¼ cup warm water	1 teaspoon salt
2 tablespoons sugar	¼ teaspoon soda
1 cup cottage cheese	1 egg, beaten
1 tablespoon instant minced onion	2½ to 3 cups all purpose flour
2 teaspoons dill seed	

Soften yeast in warm water. In saucepan, heat cottage cheese to lukewarm. Stir in shortening, sugar, onion, dill seed, salt and softened yeast. Beat in egg. Add flour a little at a time to make a soft dough. Knead on lightly floured surface till smooth and elastic — about 5 minutes. Place in greased bowl, turning once to grease surface. Cover and let rise in a warm place for one hour. Punch down, cover, and let rest for 10 minutes. Shape into loaf and place in greased 9x5x3 loaf pan. Turn once on greased pan surface when placing in pan. Cover, let rise again until almost double, about 30-45 minutes. Bake in 350° oven for 35 minutes. Remove from pan and brush with melted butter or margarine.

Freezes beautifully. Serve with warm seafoods or beef.

Pearl Wyse

ENGLISH MUFFIN LOAF

OVEN: 400° 40-50 minutes

2 packages dry yeast	2 tablespoons sugar
5-6 cups sifted flour	1 teaspoon salt
2½ cups water	cornmeal

In large mixing bowl combine yeast and 2 cups flour. In medium saucepan heat water with sugar and salt until just warm. Add water to dry flour and yeast mixture. Blend, then beat at high speed for 3 minutes. By hand stir in enough of the remaining 3-4 cups of flour to make a soft dough. Place in lightly greased bowl, cover and let rise to double its size. Punch down and let rise for 10 minutes. Grease 2 bread pans and sprinkle with cornmeal. Turn dough into pans and let rise until doubled. Bake at 400° for 40-50 minutes. Cover tops loosely with foil if loaves brown too fast. After slicing to desired thickness, place under broiler and toast both sides. May be toasted in toaster, toasting two times to achieve desired doneness. Butter while hot.

R.M. Croghan

To make delectable French bread, melt one-half stick butter, add one-fourth teaspoon garlic powder and one-eighth teaspoon each of basil, oregano, and thyme. Simmer twenty minutes and brush mixture on bread.

FLORIDA ORANGE BREAD

OVEN: 325° 1¼ hours   YIELD: 15 servings

3 medium juice oranges
½ cup sugar
¼ cup water
1 tablespoon butter
1 cup orange juice

1 egg, well beaten
2½ cups all purpose flour
2½ teaspoons baking powder
¼ teaspoon soda
½ teaspoon salt

Grease a 9x5x3 inch loaf pan. Start oven 10 minutes before baking and set at 325°. Wash and dry oranges. Pare off thin rind with sharp knife, cutting around orange, then cut yellow rind in very thin slivers with scissors to yield ½ cup. Combine sugar and water, add rind and stir constantly over heat until sugar dissolves. Boil gently for 5 minutes. Measure ⅔ cup of this peel/syrup. Add butter to this and stir until melted. Sift flour, measure, and then resift 3 times with baking powder, soda and salt. Combine peel/syrup mixture, orange juice and egg, then add to dry ingredients all at once. Mix just enough to moisten. Batter should be lumpy. Turn into pan and bake 1¼ hours or until done.

Ethel Rosier

FRENCH COFFEE CAKE

OVEN: 325° 55 minutes

½ pound butter
1 cup sugar
3 cups flour
4 eggs
4 teaspoons baking powder
1 cup sour cream
1 teaspoon baking soda

vanilla
Mixture:
½ cup brown sugar
½ cup granulated sugar
1 cup chopped nuts
cinnamon

Cream together butter and sugar. Add eggs, one at a time, beating well after each addition. Add sifted flour with baking powder, alternating with sour cream and soda. Blend well. Add vanilla. Pour half of batter into 10″ tube pan (greased). Sprinkle with ¾ of crumb mixture which has been combined in a separate bowl. Cover with remaining batter and sprinkle with rest of mixture. Bake at 325° for 55 minutes.

Mary Culbreth

When baking with honey, use low moderate oven temperatures. Honey carmelizes at a low temperature and causes baked products to brown quickly.

FRENCH TOAST

1 quart milk
3 eggs, beaten lightly
⅛ cup brandy
nutmeg to taste
pinch of salt
1 loaf French bread
deep fat for frying, add ½ cup bacon drippings to vegetable oil to brown.

Sauce:
1 can milk, carmelized
12 maraschino cherries, chopped fine
2 tablespoons cherry juice
2 tablespoons brandy OR enough to spread easily

Beat eggs until foamy, add milk and beat well. Cut French bread straight across into 1¼ inch pieces. Dip bread into milk mixture until soaked. Drain and squeeze to get moisture out. Fry in deep fat (preferably oil) 350° until light brown. Serve with honey, sauce or syrup, Drain on paper towel and keep in 200° oven until ready to serve.

To caramelize the large can of canned milk, bring milk to boiling and simmer one hour.

Carra Adams

FRIED CORN BREAD

2 cups cornmeal, water-ground
½ cup flour
½ tablespoon salt

2 cups water (more if you prefer thin, crisp bread)
bacon drippings

Combine all ingredients and mix well. Fry in deep fat. I add bacon drippings to oil for flavor and it browns more easily. Drain on paper towels.

Carra Adams

FRUIT KUCHEN
(Apple, Peach or Plum)

OVEN: 350° 30-45 minutes

1¼ cups flour
1 heaping teaspoon baking powder
⅛ pound butter, melted
1 tablespoon sugar
pinch of salt

⅛ cup milk
fruit of your choice, sliced
lemon juice
sugar
cinnamon

Blend dry ingredients together, add melted butter, then add milk. Mix well. This will form a mealy dough. Press dough into 9″ greased (bottom and sides) pan. Place sliced fruit in rows and sprinkle with lemon juice, sugar and cinnamon. Dot with bits of butter. Bake in 350° oven 30-45 minutes.

Mrs. James W. Moses

GRAHAM MUFFINS

OVEN: 375° 20 minutes

YIELD: 1 dozen

1½ cups graham cracker crumbs
2 teaspoons baking powder
⅓ cup butter, melted
1 egg, beaten

¼ cup light corn syrup
½ cup milk
½ cup chopped pecans

Add all ingredients to mixing bowl, stir to mix well. Mixture will be thick. Fill greased muffin pans or paper baking cups ⅔ full. Bake in moderate oven, 375°, for 20 minutes or until nicely browned.

18 graham crackers, crushed fine may be substituted for packaged crumbs.

Helen George

HARVEST BREAD

OVEN: 350° 55-60 minutes

3 eggs
1½ cups sugar
1½ cups salad oil
1 teaspoon vanilla
2 cups chopped OR shredded vegetables OR fruit*
3⅓ cups flour
2 teaspoons soda
1 teaspoon salt
⅔ cup chopped nuts
1 teaspoon cinnamon
1 teaspoon cloves
1 teaspoon baking powder
*You may also add any ONE of the following COMBINATIONS:
2 cups chopped apples AND

⅔ cup raisins
OR
2 cups chopped rhubarb AND 2 teaspoons grated lemon peel
OR
2 cups chopped zucchini, not peeled
OR
2 cups grated squash
OR
2 cups coarsely grated carrots
OR
2 cups shredded sweet potatoes plus ½ cup flaked coconut and ¼ cup water

Beat eggs, oil, sugar, vanilla, and vegetables OR fruit for one minute at medium speed. Add dry ingredients and beat at low speed for 15 seconds. Fold in nuts and pour into 2 greased and floured bread pans (9x5x3) and bake for 55-60 minutes at 350°.

The sweet potato, coconut mixture is the only one with added water.

If you use whole wheat flour you will need to add ¼ cup water to each combination.

Marie Mann

One pound of bread equals twelve to sixteen slices.

HOLIDAY FRUIT BREAD

OVEN: 350° 1 hour

2½ cups sifted all purpose flour
4 teaspoons baking powder
¾ teaspoon salt
¾ cup chopped nuts
1½ cups chopped, mixed, candied
   fruit

⅓ cup white OR dark raisins
½ cup shortening
¾ cup sugar
3 eggs
½ cup mashed ripe banana
½ cup orange juice

Sift together flour, baking powder, and salt. Stir in chopped nuts, candied fruit and raisins. Cream shortening. Add sugar and beat until light and fluffy. Add eggs, one at a time, beating after each addition. Combine mashed banana and orange juice. Add to creamed mixture alternately with flour mixture, beginning and ending with dry ingredients. Turn into a waxed paper lined and greased 9x5 inch loaf pan. Bake at 350° for one hour. Cool 15-20 minutes, turn out on rack and cool completely.

Connie Wagers

HOMEMADE GRANOLA

OVEN: 300° 40-50 minutes   YIELD: 6½ cups

2½ cups old-fashioned rolled oats
1 cup shredded coconut
½ cup coarsley chopped almonds
½ cup sesame seeds
½ cup shelled sunflower seeds

½ cup unsweetened wheat germ
½ cup honey
¼ cup cooking oil
½ cup dried apricots, chopped
¼ cup raisins

In large bowl, combine oats, coconut, almonds, sesame seeds, sunflower seeds, and wheat germ. Combine honey and oil. Stir into oat mixture. Spread out in 13x9x2 inch baking pan. Bake in 300° oven until light golden brown, approximately 40-50 minutes. Stir every 15 minutes while baking. Remove from oven, stir in apricots and raisins. Remove to another pan to cool. Stir occasionally during cooling to prevent lumping. Store in lightly covered jars or plastic bags.

To store more than two weeks, seal in plastic bags and freeze.

Edith Abbey

HUSH PUPPIES I

YIELD: 8-10 servings

2 cups sifted cornmeal
1 cup sifted flour
1 teaspoon baking powder
½ teaspoon salt
½ teaspoon sugar

1 tablespoon melted butter
½ cup chopped onions
½ cup buttermilk
¾ cup water
1 whole egg

Mix together dry ingredients. Add onions, milk, water, butter, and egg. Roll mixture into balls about ¾ inch thick. Cook in deep fat at 350° for 5-7 minutes.

The Committee

HUSH PUPPIES II

½ cup all purpose flour
1 cup cornmeal
3 teaspoons baking powder
2 tablespoons sugar
½ teaspoon black pepper

1 teaspoon Lowry's seasoning
1 egg
1 medium size onion, chopped very
  fine
milk

Mix all dry ingredients with the chopped onion. Add beaten egg and enough milk to make a rather heavy batter. Drop by teaspoon into hot fat until golden brown. Drain well. Serve with fried fish — a must. These hush puppies are always light and they have a great flavor.

Mildred Brown Garrett

INDIAN CORNBREAD

OVEN: 450° 30 minutes

1 pound ground sausage, chopped
1 bell pepper, chopped fine
1 or 2 onions, chopped fine
1 cup buttermilk

1 cup water-ground cornmeal
½ cup flour
½ teaspoon soda
2 teaspoons baking powder

Mix first four ingredients well. Add sifted dry ingredients. Bake in heavy pan for 30 minutes at 450°.

Florrie Chandler

IRISH SODA BREAD

OVEN: 375° 1 hour

4 cups flour
¼ cup sugar
3 teaspoons baking powder
1 teaspoon salt
2 tablespoons caraway seeds
¼ cup butter
2 cups raisins

1⅓ cups buttermilk OR 1⅓ tablespoons lemon juice and 1⅓ cup
  milk
1 egg
1 teaspoon baking soda
1 egg yolk and 1 teaspoon water
  (to brush on top of bread)

Preheat oven to 375°. Grease pan with unsalted shortening. Sift flour, sugar, baking powder, and salt together. Stir caraway seeds in last. Add butter, cutting in with pastry blender or two knives. Stir in raisins. Blend buttermilk, egg and baking soda. Add dry ingredients to liquid. Turn out on a floured surface and knead lightly till dough is smooth. Shape into a ball and place in pan. Cut an X with a sharp knife ½ inch deep on top of loaf. Brush egg yolk/water mixture on top. Bake for one hour at 375°.

This recipe came directly from Ireland. It was given to me by my mother who received it from a friend who got it while visiting her cousin.

Kathy Sayers

LEMON BREAD

1 cup sugar
6 tablespoons shortening
1 tablespoon grated lemon rind
2 eggs
1½ cups sifted all purpose flour
½ teaspoon salt

1 teaspoon baking powder
½ cup milk
½ cup nuts, chopped
¼ cup sugar (scant)
3 tablespoons lemon juice

In medium bowl with electric mixer, cream sugar with shortening. Add lemon rind. Beat in eggs. Sift flour, salt and powder. Add milk and flour mixture alternately. Begin and end with flour. Stir in nuts. Pour into greased 9x5x3 loaf pan. Bake until toothpick inserted comes out clean.

In small saucepan, heat ¼ cup sugar in lemon juice. Pour over hot bread. Allow bread to cool in pan. When cold, remove from pan.

Gladys M. Smith

LEMON MUFFINS

OVEN: 375° 25 minutes   YIELD: 2 dozen

1 cup butter
1 cup sugar
4 egg yolks, well beaten
2 cups flour
2 teaspoons baking powder

1 teaspoon salt
½ cup lemon juice
4 egg whites
2 teaspoons grated lemon rind

Cream butter and sugar. Add yolks and beat mixture until light. Add baking powder and salt to flour and add to yolk mixture alternately with lemon juice. Do not overbeat. Beat egg whites until stiff but not dry and fold into the batter with the lemon rind. Pour into buttered muffin tins, filling each ¾ full. Bake in 375° oven for 25 minutes.

The Committee

LIGHT BREAD

OVEN: 400°

2 cups hot liquid, milk OR water
2 tablespoons sugar
2 tablespoons shortening

1 package dry yeast
2 teaspoons salt
6-8 cups flour

Add shortening, sugar and salt to one half of the liquid. Cool remaining liquid to lukewarm and dissolve yeast in it. Pour liquids together in a large bowl and beat in enough flour to make a soft dough. Turn out on floured board and knead until smooth. Cover with bowl and let rise until doubled in bulk. Punch down. Repeat. Knead and shape into loaves. Allow to rise in greased pans. Bake in 400° oven.

Mrs. G. C. Brown

MAMA'S GINGERBREAD

OVEN: 350°

2 sticks oleo OR butter
1 cup sugar
3 eggs, well beaten
1½ cups pure cane syrup
¾ cup coffee OR buttermilk to
  which 1 teaspoon soda has been
  added

3 cups all purpose flour
2 teaspoons ginger
2 teaspoons vanilla
a pinch of salt if desired

Have all ingredients at room temperature. Cream together butter and sugar. Add eggs, beat well. Mix in syrup. Sift together flour and ginger. Alternately add flour mixture and coffee OR buttermilk to creamed mixture. Add vanilla and a pinch of salt if desired. Pour into a greased and floured tube pan and bake at 350° until done.

This is a delicious, moist gingerbread and keeps well.

Olive Peterson

MANGO NUT BREAD

OVEN: 350°

½ cup shortening OR butter
¾ cup sugar
2 eggs
⅔ cup raw mango, cut fine
2 cups flour, sifted

1 teaspoon soda
1 tablespoon lime juice
¼ teaspoon salt
½ cup chopped nuts

Cream together shortening and sugar. Add eggs. Stir in dry ingredients, mango, lime juice, and nuts. Mix together well. Bake in 350° oven.

Dot Gortner

MARMEE'S BUTTERSCOTCH BISCUITS

OVEN: 425°   YIELD: 2 dozen

2 cups flour
4 teaspoons baking powder
1 teaspoon salt
4 tablespoons shortening

⅔ cup milk
1 cup brown sugar
¼ cup butter

Sift dry ingredients. Cut in shortening, then add milk gradually. Roll dough into ¼″ thickness. Mix together brown sugar and butter. Spread mixture on dough. Roll up dough. Cut dough into 1″ pieces and bake in greased muffin tins until brown at 425°.

Mrs. E. J. Minton

MAYONNAISE QUICK BISCUITS

OVEN: 400°   YIELD: 6 large or 12 small rolls

1 cup self-rising flour OR any bis-   3 tablespoons mayonnaise
  cuit mix   ½ cup milk

Combine all three ingredients until smooth. Pour into a cupcake tin. Bake in 400° oven until golden brown.

Julia Hall

MEXICAN CORNBREAD

OVEN: 375°   YIELD: serves 8

3 cups cornmeal mix   1 large can cream style corn
3 beaten eggs   1½ cups grated sharp Cheddar
1⅓ cups milk   cheese
½ cup cooking oil   2 hot banana peppers, grated
1 teaspoon sugar   1 large onion, grated

Combine all ingredients, mixing well. Preheat oven to 375° and pour batter into pan. Bake until golden brown.

Sgt. James E. Parsley

MOIST OYSTER DRESSING

1 large pan cornbread, crumbled   2 large onions, chopped
1 tube saltines, crushed   4 pieces celery, chopped
3 slices toast, cubed   6 raw eggs
6 boiled eggs, chopped   ½ pint oysters
½ stick butter   salt, pepper
1 quart liquid, turkey OR chicken   sage
  broth

Use salt, pepper, and sage to taste; mix together and combine with other ingredients.

This will yield enough for a medium size covered dish. Saltines keep dressing from being sticky.

Joyce Frier

Croutons can be made very easily by sautéing one cup of bread crumbs in six tablespoons of melted butter and one-half teaspoon of seasoned salt. When lightly browned on all sides remove the croutons from sauté pan and place on a paper towel to drain.

MOTHER'S CINNAMON COFFEE CAKE

OVEN: 370° 40 minutes

½ cup butter OR margarine
1 cup sugar
3 eggs
1 teaspoon baking soda
1 teaspoon baking powder
2 cups sifted flour
1 cup sour cream

1 teaspoon vanilla
¾ cup raisins, optional

Mixture:
½ cup sugar
2 teaspoons cinnamon
½ cup chopped walnuts

Cream together butter and sugar. Add eggs, blend well. Add sifted dry ingredients then sour cream and vanilla. If using raisins, add last. Mix sugar, cinnamon and nuts.

In greased and floured tube pan alternate layers of batter and cinnamon/sugar/nut mixture beginning with batter and ending with mixture. Do NOT stir.

Bake at 370° for 40 minutes. Cool and remove from pan.

This cake freezes well. It is very good served warm.

Diana Dukes

MOTHER'S FAVORITE ROLLS

OVEN: 400°

1 cup shortening
1½ teaspoons salt
½ cup sugar
2 eggs, beaten

1 cup boiling water
2 packages yeast
1 cup warm water
6 cups flour

Place shortening, sugar and salt in mixing bowl. Pour boiling water over ingredients, blend and cool. Add eggs. Let yeast dissolve in warm water 5 minutes. Add yeast to mixture and then add flour. Place in refrigerator at once. Use as needed, allowing to rise 3 hours. Bake at 400° until light brown.

Joe and Jack Wolff

For savory-tasting biscuits, crumble fried bacon bits into the dry ingredients of a biscuit recipe; mix and bake as recipe directs; then serve hot with a teaspoon of honey poured on top.

MRS. RHODA CARLTON'S DRESSING

OVEN: 325° 2 hours

2 pounds ground round
1 pound sausage
2-3 packages dry bread cubes
2 cups diced celery
2 medium onions, chopped
2 green peppers, diced

6-8 hard boiled eggs, chopped
2 cups diced cooked potatoes
1 cup or more chicken broth
salt, pepper and sage to taste
¼ cup butter

Mix bread cubes with hot chicken broth and add meat. Sauté onions, celery and green peppers in ¼ cup butter until translucent. Add sautéed items to bread-meat mixture and season with salt, pepper, and sage. With a fork, lightly add cooked potatoes and chopped eggs. Stuff turkey loosely. Place leftover dressing in a casserole. Cover with foil and bake at 325° for 2 hours.

This dressing was used in wild turkeys, and is also delicious in domestic turkeys.

Marilyn Carlton

MRS. WATSON'S BUTTERHORN ROLLS

OVEN: 450° 10 minutes

1 cake yeast
1 teaspoon sugar
1 cup lukewarm water
½ cup butter, scant

½ cup sugar, scant
¾ teaspoon salt
3 well beaten eggs
4 cups unsifted flour

Crumble yeast cake and add sugar. Stir until liquid forms. Add lukewarm water and let yeast stand for a few minutes. Then stir until dissolved. Cut butter into pieces in a bowl. Add the ½ cup sugar, salt, and well beaten eggs to the butter. Mix well. Add yeast mixture into the bowl. Blend. Stir in 2 cups of the flour and beat until smooth. Then add the other 2 cups of flour stirring until the dough leaves the side of the bowl. More flour may be added if needed to make a soft dough that is easy to handle.

Divide the finished dough into 3 parts. Roll each part in a circle on lightly floured surface. Cut into fourths then cut each fourth into fourths. Roll each triangle starting at widest end, ending with tip. Roll into crescent shape. Let rise until double in bulk. Bake at 450° for 10 minutes or until golden.

Carol Ann Gollnick

One cup of honey is equal to one cup of sugar. Since one cup of honey contains one-fourth cup of liquid, deduct one-fourth of liquid from the recipe when substituting honey for sugar.

NUT BREAD

OVEN: 350° 45 minutes

4 cups flour, sifted	1 teaspoon salt
4 teaspoons baking powder	2 cups nut meats
2 eggs	1 cup sugar
2 cups milk	

Combine all ingredients together. Mix thoroughly. Pour into 2 greased loaf pans approximately 5x10 inches. Bake in 350° oven for 45 minutes or until done.

Very easy and very good.

Irene Baker

OATMEAL BREAD

OVEN: 350° 45 minutes

1½ cups boiling water	2 teaspoons salt
1 cup rolled oats	1 tablespoon dry yeast
¾ cup molasses	2 cups warm water
3 tablespoons soft butter	8 or more cups flour

Pour boiling water over oats and let stand 30 minutes. Add molasses, butter, salt, yeast, and warm water. Beat at low speed one-half minute, then beat 3 minutes at high speed. Work in enough flour to make soft dough. Turn onto floured surface and knead till smooth and elastic (about 10 minutes). Place in a greased bowl, turning once to put greased surface of dough on top. Let dough rise until double, about 1½ hours. Punch down. Let rise for 10 minutes. Divide and shape into 2 loaves. Place in greased pans. Cover and let rise until double in bulk, about 1 hour. Bake in 350° oven 45 minutes.

You may brush loaves with egg and milk and sprinkle with oats before baking.

Jeanette R. White

OATMEAL PANCAKES

YIELD: 12-14 pancakes

1 cup flour	1½ cups buttermilk (approxi-
1 cup quick oats	mately)
2 teaspoons baking powder	2 eggs, beaten
1 teaspoon salt	¼ cup margarine, melted
½ teaspoon baking soda	

Combine flour, oats, baking powder, salt and soda. Stir in buttermilk, eggs, and margarine. Mix until smooth. Use ¼ cup of batter for each pancake and bake until golden. (Stir in a little bit more buttermilk if necessary.)

Edith Boynton

OLD FASHIONED ALL-BRAN MUFFINS

OVEN: 400° 25 minutes

1½ cups flour
3 teaspoons baking powder
pinch of salt
½ cup honey

1½ cups all-bran
1¼ cups milk OR cream
⅓ cup oil
1 egg

Sift together flour, baking powder, salt and sugar and set aside.
Place all-bran in a bowl and add milk OR cream. Let it set for about 2 minutes, then add the egg and oil. Mix well and add dry ingredients to the cereal mix. Blend all ingredients well and fill muffin tins about half full. Bake at 400° for about 25 minutes.

You may use a little more than ½ cup honey. Be careful and watch when you blend ingredients. Slice walnuts may also be added to the mixture. The muffins are delicious. I hope you enjoy them as much as I.

Grace Barrie

OLD FASHIONED SPOON BREAD

OVEN: 400° 20-30 minutes   YIELD: 5-6 servings

¾ cup yellow cornmeal
2 cups milk
½ teaspoon salt

½ stick butter or margarine
5 egg yolks, beaten
5 stiffly beaten egg whites

Bring milk to a boil and add butter. Sift cornmeal and salt into the milk. Cook until thick, stirring constantly. Remove from heat. Stir in egg yolks. Fold in stiffly beaten egg whites. Pour into a well greased 2 quart casserole. Bake at 400 degrees for 20 to 30 minutes. Serve immediately. Makes five to six servings.

Peggy Hoskins

ORANGE BISCUITS

OVEN: 425° 15-20 minutes   YIELD: about 18 tiny biscuits

1¾ cups sifted flour
3½ teaspoons baking powder
1 tablespoon sugar
2 tablespoons shortening

¾ cup rich milk
grated rind of one orange
orange marmalade

Combine flour, baking powder and sugar. Cut in shortening with pastry blender or two knives until mixture resembles coarse crumbs. Add milk and orange rind and mix until dough forms a ball. Turn out on lightly floured board. Knead lightly. Pat or roll out ¾" thick. Cut with a very small cutter which has been floured. Make a small indentation in top of each biscuit. Fill indentation with ¼ teaspoon of orange marmalade. Bake in 425° oven, until lightly brown, about 15-20 minutes.

The Committee

POPOVERS I

OVEN: 450° 20 min./350° 15 min.   YIELD: 8

1 cup sifted flour
¼ teaspoon salt
2 eggs

1 cup milk
1 tablespoon melted shortening

Sift flour and salt together. Beat eggs and add milk, shortening and sifted dry ingredients. Beat until smooth with rotary beater.

Fill greased muffin pans (preferably iron) one-half full and bake in very hot oven 450° for 20 minutes. Reduce temperature to 350° and bake 15 minutes longer.

Beatrice D. Coffman

POPOVERS II

OVEN: 375° 45 minutes   YIELD: 8

¾ cup flour, sifted
1 teaspoon salt

2 eggs
¾ cup skim milk

Preheat oven to 375°. Grease 8 custard dishes. Sift flour and salt into bowl. In small bowl, beat eggs, then beat in milk. Pour into flour mixture, beat smooth with egg beater. Bake 45 minutes. Cut slit in each to let steam out.

Mrs. Robert Matthews, Jr.

POTATO LATKES
(Pancakes)

6 medium potatoes
1 small onion
1 teaspoon salt

1 egg
3 tablespoons flour OR matzo meal
oil

Wash and grate potatoes; drain. Grate onion and add to potatoes with salt and egg. Beat well. Mix remaining ingredients, except oil, into potatoes. Drop by spoonfuls into hot oil and brown on both sides, drain.

If you are lucky enough to have a food processor, simply cut potatoes and onions into pieces, place in processor bowl with other ingredients and using pulse button mix until batter is of right consistency. This takes practice with the processor, but it is worth it for the saving of time involved.

Peggy Berg

Combine ½ teaspoon crumbled, dry sage or minced, fresh sage to the grated rind of one lemon in 1 cup of honey for a delicious sweet-tasting spread to use on fresh-baked muffins.

PRONTO PIZZA

OVEN: 350° 20 minutes

1 package yeast
1 cup warm water
2 tablespoons shortening
3 cups flour
1½ teaspoons salt

Sauce:
1 medium can tomato sauce
1 medium can tomato paste
⅛ teaspoon garlic powder

⅛ teaspoon red pepper
½ cup finely chopped onions

Topping:
8 ounces mozzarella cheese
3 ounces grated Romano OR Parmesan cheese
¼ pound raw hamburger
2 teaspoons oregano

Put yeast in warm water and let stand for 5 minutes. Add one-half of flour and stir, add salt, shortening, and remainder of flour. Stir, cover, and let sit.

Mix sauce ingredients together. Pat out dough. Spread with sauce — using a round pizza pan.

Grate cheeses and crumble meat. Place on top of sauce on dough. Sprinkle on oregano. Bake at 350° for about 20 minutes or until done.

Debbie Jameson

PRUNE BREAD

OVEN: 350° 50 minutes

1 cup oil
1½ cups sugar
3 eggs
1 cup cooked, chopped prunes
1 teaspoon salt
1 teaspoon soda

1 cup buttermilk
1 teaspoon cinnamon
1 teaspoon nutmeg
2 cups flour
1 cup chopped nuts

Chop nuts very fine. Beat eggs a little; cream oil and sugar together. Add eggs and beat until light. Add buttermilk and chopped prunes. Mix. Add dry ingredients after they have been sifted together. Add nuts last. Turn batter into 2 small loaf pans or one tube pan. Bake at 350° for 50 minutes.

One-half teaspoon cloves may also be added if desired.

Marie Mann

PUMPKIN BREAD I

OVEN: 350° 1 hour

3 cups sugar
1 cup oil
1½ teaspoons salt
1 teaspoon cinnamon
1 teaspoon nutmeg
2 teaspoons soda in ⅔ cup water

1 teaspoon vinegar
2 cups pumpkin (#2 can)
3½ cups flour, unsifted
4 eggs (5 if eggs are small)
½ (or more) cups chopped nuts

Grease bottom and sides of 3 loaf pans. Combine all ingredients and mix at high speed. Pour into pans. Bake at 350° for 1 hour.

LeVan N. Fee

PUMPKIN BREAD II

OVEN: 325° 1 hour   YIELD: 4 round loaves OR 3 bread loaves

3 cups sugar
4 eggs, beaten
1 cup oil
1 — 16 ounce can pumpkin
3⅓ cups flour
1 teaspoon salt
2 teaspoons soda

2 teaspoons nutmeg
3 teaspoons cinnamon
½ teaspoon mace
1 cup raisins
1 cup chopped pecans
⅔ cup water

Sift together flour, salt and soda. Mix all ingredients together well. Pour batter into four 1 pound greased and floured coffee cans. Fill each can one-half full. Bake for 1 hour at 325°.

This freezes very well and can be sliced very thin while frozen. Will also make 3 loaves if baked in pans.

Linda E. Boudet

QUICK HERB BREAD

OVEN: 350° 45-50 minutes

3 cups biscuit mix
½ cup sharp cheddar cheese, grated
1 tablespoon sugar
1¼ cups milk

1 egg
1 tablespoon oil
2 teaspoons chives
1 teaspoon sweet basil

Mix together biscuit mix, cheese, and sugar. In a small bowl mix milk, egg, oil, chives and basil. Add liquids to dry mixture and stir only until blended. Bake in a well-greased 9x5 inch pan in a 350° oven for 45-50 minutes. Serve hot.

This is especially good with fowl and pork.

Joyce Emmi

REFRIGERATOR BRAN MUFFINS I

OVEN: 350° 20 minutes   YIELD: 5½ dozen

1 — 15 ounce box wheat bran flakes cereal with raisins
5 cups all purpose flour
2½ cups sugar
5 teaspoons soda

2 teaspoons salt
4 eggs, beaten
1 quart buttermilk
1 cup shortening, melted

Combine first 5 ingredients in large bowl. Make a well in center of mixture. Add remaining ingredients and stir just enough to moisten. Cover and store in refrigerator until ready to bake. Will keep as long as 5-6 weeks.

When ready to bake, spoon batter into greased muffin tin filling ⅔ full. Bake at 350° for 20 minutes.

Nancy Davis

REFRIGERATOR BRAN MUFFINS II

OVEN: 375° 20 minutes

1½ cups sugar
½ cup shortening
2 eggs
2 cups Bran Buds
1 cup All Bran

1 cup boiling water
2½ cups flour
1½ teaspoons salt
2½ teaspoons soda
2 cups buttermilk

Soak brans in water. Mix soda in buttermilk. Cream together sugar, shortening and eggs. Add dry ingredients alternately with the buttermilk. Fold in bran mixture. Bake in muffin tins in 375° oven for 20 minutes.

Mixture may be kept in refrigerator for 3-4 weeks. Recipe may also be doubled.

If you wish, raisins may be added to mixture. Boil one cup of raisins in one cup of water for five minutes. Add to mixture any time before baking. I often add the raisins after the mixture has been in the refrigerator a week.

Harriet Walting

RYE BREAD

OVEN: 350° 40-50 minutes

1 tablespoon salt
1 tablespoon dark syrup
2 tablespoons molasses
4 cups rye flour
4 cups boiling water

2 tablespoons lard
1 cup sugar
¾ cup lukewarm water
2 yeast cakes
6 cups white flour (approximately)

Place all ingredients in large, heat-proof bowl, and pour water over all. Let stand until warm then mix in lukewarm water, yeast, and white flour to stiffen. Knead. When light, form into loaves and bake in 350° oven for 40-50 minutes.

Mrs. L. Segerstrom

When baking plain muffins, add a surprise. Roll sugar cubes in cinnamon, then in grated orange rind. Place each in the middle of the muffins and bake.

SCOTCH SCONES

OVEN: 350° until brown

2 cups sifted flour
3 teaspoons baking powder
2 tablespoons shortening OR bacon fat

2 tablespoons sugar
1 teaspoon salt
1 cup milk
1 egg

Combine ingredients and mix into a soft dough. Do not overmix. Divide dough into 2 balls. Lightly roll or pat each to about ¾". Shape into a round with hands. Fit dough into layer cake pans and cut each round into pie slices, keeping slices together while baking. Bake in 350° oven until tops appear brown.

For tea scones, add either currants or raisins; a little more sugar and a tiny bit of vanilla to taste. The vanilla is not traditional.

For molasses scones, use molasses instead of sugar to taste and color. These are called Treacle Scones.

For soda scones, use up any sour milk and use soda instead of baking powder (2 teaspoons soda or it will taste strong).

If time is short, biscuit mix may be substituted.

Isabel Gordon McElroy

SIX WEEK BRAN MUFFINS

OVEN: 400° 15 minutes

1 — 15 ounce box raisin bran cereal
3 cups sugar
5 cups flour
5 teaspoons soda

2 teaspoons salt
4 beaten eggs
1 quart buttermilk
1 cup vegetable oil

Mix cereal, sugar, flour, soda and salt. Add eggs, buttermilk, and oil. Mix well. Store in covered container in refrigerator and use as needed. Fill muffin tins ⅔ full and bake for 15 minutes at 400°. This mixture will keep well for 6 weeks.

Theresa Haisley

Stir baking powder or baking soda into bread batters but do not beat the mixture. If the batter is over-mixed the bread may be tough or develop large holes.

SOFT GINGERBREAD

OVEN: 350° cake pan — 60 min.; cupcakes — 25 min.

3¾ cups flour
1 cup butter
2 cups brown sugar, lightly packed
4 eggs
1 cup New Orleans molasses
1 cup sour milk OR buttermilk

1 teaspoon baking soda
1 teaspoon cream of tartar
3 tablespoons ground ginger
¼ teaspoon ground cloves
1 tablespoon ground cinnamon

Sift all dry ingredients and set aside. Cream butter in a large bowl, stir sugar into butter and beat well. Stir eggs in and beat well. Add molasses and mix well. Beginning and ending with flour, add milk alternately to creamed ingredients, stirring each in well. Pour dough ⅓ full into an 8x8″ pan and 12 cup cake molds. Bake at 350° for about 60 and 25 minutes respectively.

My grandmother often made a big crockful of gingerbread drop cakes by adding another cup of flour.

These large, spicy discs and a batch of crisp, browned sugar cookies were always available in the cool, shuttered pantry during our childhood summer visits.

The fragrant, light gingerbread cake, fresh from the huge cast-iron oven fueled by ½ coal and ½ wood needed no icing. Often, grandmother would dust it with powdered sugar or cover it with a boiled white frosting, swirled and crunchy and soft inside. It was marvelous, too, with a touch of her lemon butter.

Caroline Bassett Haman

SOUR CREAM COFFEE CAKE

OVEN: 350° 40-45 minutes

2 sticks butter
1½ cups sugar
3 eggs
1 cup sour cream
1 tablespoon vanilla
3 cups flour

½ teaspoon salt
2½ teaspoons baking powder
½ teaspoon soda

Topping:
½ cup sugar
1 tablespoon cinnamon

Cream together butter and sugar. Add eggs, one at a time, beating well after each addition. Sift together flour, salt, baking powder and soda. Add to creamed mixture, beating well. Combine ingredients for topping in a small bowl. Put half of batter in greased 9x13x2 inch pan. Sprinkle with half of topping. Add remaining batter and sprinkle with remaining topping. Bake 40-45 minutes at 350°.

Blanche A. Hunt

Add a new flavor to gingerbread by substituting 1 teaspoon fresh gingerroot for the 1 or 2 teaspooons of ground ginger.

SOUTHERN MOLASSES MUFFINS

OVEN: 400° 18-20 minutes

6 ounces softened butter OR margarine
½ cup sugar
2 eggs
¼ cup molasses
1 teaspoon soda

½ cup buttermilk
2 cups self-rising flour
¼ teaspoon cinnamon
¼ teaspoon ginger
½ cup plump raisins

Cream together butter and sugar. Add eggs one at a time, beating well after each addition. Add molasses. Combine soda and buttermilk and add to molasses mixture and blend. Combine flour and spices. Add to molasses mixture. Dry raisins, dust with a little flour, fold into batter. Fill greased muffin tin ⅔ full and bake at 400° for 18-20 minutes.

These molasses muffins should be served warm, with butter as a bread. These muffins are not as sweet as old fashioned gingerbread that is served with whipped cream or ice cream and used as a dessert.

Mildred Brown Garrett

SOUTHERN SPOON BREAD

OVEN: 375° 30 minutes

3 cups milk
1¼ cups cornmeal
3 eggs

2 tablespoons butter
1¾ teaspoons baking powder
1 teaspoon salt

Stir meal into rapidly boiling milk. Cook until very thick, stirring constantly to prevent scorching. Remove from heat and allow to cool. The mixture will be cold and very stiff. Add well beaten eggs, salt, baking powder and melted butter. Beat with electric mixer 15 minutes. Pour into well greased 1½ quart casserole. Bake 30 minutes at 375°. Serve from casserole by spoonfuls.

Ivy H. Haynes

One tablespoon dried marigold petals added with the flour to your bread recipe will give the bread a beautiful pale-yellow color and add a mild, slightly peppery flavor.

STREUSEL FILLED COFFEE CAKE

OVEN: 350° 45 minutes

Streusel:
½ cup brown sugar
2 tablespoons flour
2 teaspoons cinnamon
2 tablespoons butter, melted
½ cup nuts, chopped

Cake:
1⅔ cups flour
1 cup sugar
¼ teaspoon salt
2½ teaspoons baking powder
⅔ cup milk
⅓ cup shortening (approximately)
1 egg
1 teaspoon vanilla

To prepare streusel topping, mix sugar, flour and cinnamon together. Blend in melted butter and stir in chopped nuts. Mix well. Set aside.

Sift together flour, sugar, salt and baking powder. Measure milk into measuring cup and add shortening to bring milk up to one cup level. Add milk/shortening, unbeaten egg, and flovoring all at once. Beat all ingredients for 2 minutes or until batter is smooth.

Pour half of batter into well greased and floured tube pan or 11x7x1½ inch pan. Sprinkle with half of streusel filling. Add remaining batter and sprinkle remaining topping over top. Bake at 350° for 45 minutes.

Mrs. John D. Perdue

SUNSHINE LOAF

OVEN: 350° 1 hour, 10 minutes

3 cups biscuit mix
½ cup sugar
1 tablespoon grated orange peel
½ cup orange juice

1 package, 8 ounces, pitted dates, cut up
2 large bananas, mashed

Heat oven to 350°. Blend all ingredients in large bowl on low speed ½ minute. Scrape bowl frequently, then beat 2 minutes at medium speed. Pour batter into loaf pan. Bake for 1 hour, 10 minutes at 350°. Cool for 10 minutes and remove from pan. Cool thoroughly before slicing.

This is a homey banana bread with dates and fresh orange juice added for extra vitamins. Delectable when served with orange pekoe tea.

Saundra H. Rohn

SWEET POTATO BISCUITS I

OVEN: 425° 15 minutes

YIELD: 12-14 biscuits

2 cups sifted, all purpose flour
1 tablespoon baking powder
½ teaspoon salt
¼ cup shortening

¾ cup milk
2 large baked sweet potatoes, mashed

Mix all ingredients together until they have consistency of biscuit dough. Add potatoes and mix thoroughly. Bake at 425° for 15 minutes.

Butter heavily as soon as they come out of the oven and serve immediately. This recipe is one my mother used to make.

Harold Ray

SWEET POTATO BISCUITS II

OVEN: 450°

2 cups sweet potatoes
1 cup sugar
3 cups flour
1 cup shortening

3 tablespoons buttermilk
1 tablespoon soda
4 teaspoons baking powder
1¼ teaspoons salt

Boil potatoes until tender. Mash well and add sugar while hot. Let stand in refrigerator until cold. Cut shortening into sifted dry ingredients. Add potatoes and milk to make a stiff dough. Roll on floured board to about ½″ thick and cut. Bake at 450°. If using canned potatoes, heat them in syrup, drain juice, mash and add sugar. Serve with fried ham or sausage, grits and scrambled eggs.

Kitty Brown

TREASURE COAST HUSH PUPPIES

YIELD: 6 servings

1 pound (4 cups) fine white corn
  meal
1 egg
1 tablespoon salt

1 tablespoon sugar
pinch of baking soda
1 cup buttermilk

Mix all ingredients together; add water, about 1 cup, stirring well, until mixture is a thick consistency. To make the hush puppies into finger shapes, push the back of a large metal spoon forward into the batter, bring the spoon forward taking up just enough batter to cover about ¼ of the spoon lengthwise.

Drop the finger shapes into deep fat, 375°, and let fry until they are golden brown.

If fish are served, dip the fish in cracker crumbs, to which paprika has been added, so they will become golden brown with very little cooking. The biggest mistake cooks can make is to overcook fish, and without paprika they do not brown enough.

Helen B. Keller

TURKEY STUFFING

2 loaves of bread, crumbed
1 quart finely chopped celery
1 cup chopped onion
½ pound butter

salt and pepper to taste
1 cup boiling water
parsley

Crumb bread loaves two days in advance of use. Prepare chopped celery and onion one day in advance. Heat together, slowly, butter and celery and onions, until celery is soft. Sprinkle salt, pepper and parsley on bread. Mix. Slowly pour boiling water into bread crumbs. Stir. Add celery mixture. Mix well.

Mrs. John Hostetter

WAFFLES

YIELD: 8 large squares

2 cups flour
4 teaspoons baking powder
½ teaspoon salt
2 teaspoons sugar

2 eggs, separated
1¾ cups milk
½ cup butter, melted

Sift dry ingredients together. Mix well. Add milk mixed with egg yolks and melted butter. Fold in beaten egg whites.
Bake in waffle iron.

Dot Gortner

WHOLE WHEAT BREAD

OVEN: 350° 50-60 minutes

YIELD: 2 loaves

1 package dry yeast
¼ cup warm water
½ cup unsulphured molasses
3 tablespoons lard
1 tablespoon salt

1 cup boiling water
¾ cup cold water
4 cups whole wheat flour
1-2 cups unbleached flour
1 cup wheat germ

Soften yeast in warm water. Combine molasses, lard, salt and hot water. Add cold tap water and cool mixture to lukewarm. When lukewarm, add yeast mixture. Add wheat germ. Mix well. Gradually add whole wheat and unbleached flour to form a stiff dough. Knead on floured surface until smooth and satiny; about 7-10 minutes. Place in greased bowl and cover with a damp towel. Let rise until double. Punch down and let rise for 30 minutes. Divide dough in half. Shape and place in loaf pans. Let rise again and bake at 350° for 50-60 minutes.

Mae Zuver

ZUCCHINI BREAD

OVEN: 325° 1 hour

3 eggs, beaten
1 cup cooking oil
2 cups sugar
2 cups zucchini, grated
2 teaspoons vanilla
3 cups flour

1 teaspoon soda
½ teaspoon baking powder
1 teaspoon salt
2 teaspoons cinnamon
½ cup nuts, chopped

Beat eggs. Add oil, sugar, zucchini and vanilla to eggs. Beat until smooth. Add flour with salt, soda, cinnamon and baking powder. Mix well and add nuts. Bake in 2 greased and floured loaf pans at 325° for 1 hour.
Can be frozen and used anytime.

Rosemary Sowinski

ZUCCHINI PANCAKES

YIELD: 12

3 cups zucchini (1½ pounds)
½ cup flour, sifted
1 teaspoon baking powder, sifted
salt
pepper

1 egg, beaten
oil for frying
butter, melted
Parmesan cheese

Grate zucchini and combine with flour, baking powder, salt and pepper in a large bowl. Add egg and stir to blend ingredients. Drop mixture by large spoonfuls onto a smoking, oiled frying pan and cook until brown on both sides. Serve with melted butter and grated cheese.

An interesting and unusual addition to the meal. It takes the place of potato pancakes.

Mary-Frazier Palmore

GARLIC BUTTER

2 pounds butter
2 pounds oleo
2 cloves fresh garlic, chopped fine
2 tablespoons garlic powder
2 ounces fresh shallots

2 ounces Worcestershire sauce
1 teaspoon white pepper
1 teaspoon nutmeg
1 tablespoon lemon juice
1 ounce sherry

Mix all ingredients together and blend until very smooth.

**Peter A. White
Brass Sandpiper**

HERB BUTTER

YIELD: ½ cup

½ cup butter, softened
2 teaspoons parsley, chopped
1 teaspoon chives, chopped

½ teaspoon oregano
2 tablespoons Parmesan cheese
⅛ teaspoon garlic salt

Beat butter in a small bowl until creamy. Add remaining ingredients and beat until smooth.

Very good spread on any knid of bread, especially French or Italian, and placed under broiler for a couple of minutes.

Debbie Jameson

Breads can be baked in all types of pans; the most common are the 9x5x3 inch and 5x3x2 inch loaf pans. Casseroles, baking sheets, round pans, and other utensils can be used creatively. Be sure to grease the utensils with oil or butter and then shape the dough into the pan. Do not fill the utensil more than half-full.

ORANGE HONEY

grated yellow rind from 2 oranges
2 pounds strained honey

juice and pulp from 12 oranges (to equal 1 quart)

Grate yellow rind from 2 oranges and add to honey. Add the quart of juice to honey. Place all ingredients into preserving kettle and boil carefully for ½ hour. Pour into pots. When cool, cover with paraffin or oiled paper.

Sheila Grose

WHIPPED FLORIDA SUNSHINE BUTTER

1 pound butter
1 box confectionery XXXX powdered sugar

1 small can orange juice concentrate

Whip butter until light and fluffy, then gradually add sugar and beat until smooth. Add slightly thawed concentrate very gradually so it does not curdle. Chill in refrigerator a few hours and serve with piping hot homemade biscuits.

This makes enough for a large luncheon or dinner party, but plan to pass the biscuits and butter several times.

Mrs. O. R. Minton

CAKES AND FROSTINGS

CAKES

FROSTINGS

ALSACIEN-KUGELHOPF

OVEN: 350° 1 hour

375 grams flour (3¼ cups)
25 grams yeast (1 ounce)
160 grams unsalted, sweet country
    butter (¾ cup)
3 eggs
2 tablespoons powdered sugar

pinch of salt
½ cup raisins, light or golden
½ cup chopped walnuts
¾ cup milk (¼ cup condensed)
1 jigger cognac
halved walnuts for garnish

Plump raisins and soak in cognac. To well-sifted flour, add yeast which has been mixed with tepid milk; butter, eggs, powdered sugar and salt. Knead carefully; add raisins and cognac; knead again; then place the dough in a Kugelhopf mold.

The mold should be buttered and garnished with walnuts and should be filled only half full. Let the dough rise in a warm place. When the mold is full, put it in the oven and cook at a moderate temperature, about 350°, for about 1 hour.

If desired, more raisins and chopped walnuts may be added. Good served on the same day as baked, but even better on the day after. Especially delicious when served with freshly brewed coffee at breakfast.

Kugelhopf is the traditional cake of Alsace.

Kathy Kirry Wockley, Ed.D.

APPLE CAKE

OVEN: 350° 1¼ to 1½ hours

3 cups all purpose flour
2 cups sugar
½ cup cooking oil
4 eggs
3 teaspoons baking powder

½ cup orange juice
5 large apples
2 teaspoons cinnamon
5 tablespoons sugar

Use a large tube pan, 10", greased well, and dusted with flour.

Measure the first six ingredients into a large bowl and mix well. Peel and slice apples and sprinkle them with cinnamon that has been mixed with the sugar. Place half of the mixture in the prepared tube pan and cover with half of the apple mixture. Add remainder of the batter and top with remaining apples.

Bake in preheated 350° oven for 1¼ to 1½ hours.

This cake has excellent keeping qualities and freezes well.

Miriam Nugent

One pound of whole apples equals three cups pared and sliced apples.

APPLE NUT CAKE

OVEN: 325° 45 minutes

1 cup oil
3 eggs, beaten
1 cup chopped nuts
3 cups plain flour
1 teaspoon soda

2 cups sugar
3-4 apples, peeled and diced
1 teaspoon salt
2 teaspoons vanilla

Mix oil and sugar. Beat in eggs. Add remaining ingredients to make a stiff batter. Pour into ungreased 9x13x2 inch pan and place in cold oven set to 325°. Bake for 45 minutes.

This is a moist cake that keeps well and improves as it keeps.

Idell Pearce

APPLE WALNUT SUPREME CAKE

OVEN: 350° 45-50 minutes

4 cups coarsely chopped and
  peeled apples
1¾ cups sugar
2 eggs
½ cup oil
2 teaspoons vanilla

2 cups sifted flour
2 teaspoons baking soda
1 teaspoon salt
2 teaspoons cinnamon
½ cup chopped walnuts

Preheat oven to 350°. Combine apples and sugar and set aside. In a large mixing bowl mix eggs, oil and vanilla. Beat one minute at medium speed. Mix dry ingredients together. Add dry ingredients alternately with apple mixture to creamed mixture. Stir in walnuts. Bake in a greased and floured 13 x 9 x 2 inch pan at 350° for 45-50 minutes or until cake tests done with toothpick. Do not underbake.

If desired, drizzle top of cooled cake with lemon glaze: blend 1 cup confectioners sugar, 1½ tablespoons lemon juice, ½ teaspoon vanilla and 1 tablespoon corn syrup until smooth.

Peg Beaudoin

APPLESAUCE CAKE I

OVEN: 350° 45-50 minutes

½ cup soft shortening
2 cups sugar
1 large egg
½ cup applesauce
2½ cups sifted flour
1½ teaspoons baking soda
1½ teaspoons salt

¾ teaspoon cinnamon
½ teaspoon cloves
½ teaspoon allspice
½ cup water
½ cup walnuts, chopped
1 cup seedless raisins

Cream together shortening and sugar. Add egg and applesauce and set aside. In a large bowl, mix flour, soda, salt and spices. Add dry ingredients to creamed mixture. Blend well, add water, then fold in walnuts and raisins. Bake in a 13 x 9 oblong pan for 45-50 minutes at 350°.

Sofia Bagley

APPLESAUCE CAKE II

OVEN: 300° 1 hour

1 cup butter	1 pound raisins
2 cups sugar	1 cup chopped nuts
3 eggs	½ teaspoon cloves
2 cups flour	½ teaspoon cinnamon
2 cups cold applesauce	½ teaspoon nutmeg
1 teaspoon soda	

Sift soda and spices with flour. Cream butter and sugar together. Beat in eggs, one at a time. Dissolve soda in applesauce. Beat in flour mixture and applesauce to creamed mixture alternately, ending with flour. Add nuts and raisins. Mix well. Bake in ring pan in slow oven, 300°, about one hour.

Mrs. George Cave

APRICOT BRANDY POUND CAKE

OVEN: 325° 1 hour

1 cup butter (no substitute)	½ cup apricot brandy
3 cups sugar	½ teaspoon rum flavoring
6 eggs	1 teaspoon orange flavoring
3 cups flour, all purpose	¼ teaspoon almond flavoring
¼ teaspoon soda	½ teaspoon lemon flavoring
½ teaspoon salt	1 teaspoon vanilla
1 cup sour cream	

Grease and flour tube or Bundt pan. In large bowl, cream butter and sugar. Add eggs, one at a time. Beat well after adding each egg. Sift flour then measure quantity needed. Sift together flour, salt and soda, THREE TIMES (this is important). Combine sour cream, flavorings and brandy. Add dry ingredients alternately with sour cream mixture, beginning and ending with dry ingredients (this is important). Bake at 325° one hour or until done (test).

Shirley Morgan

Cut the paper lining for a cake pan a little smaller than the bottom of the pan so that the lining can be removed easily.

AUNT CARRIE'S CAKE

OVEN: 325° 30 minutes

½ cup butter OR margarine
½ cup sugar
1 cup all purpose flour
4 eggs, separated
1 teaspoon baking powder
5 tablespoons milk

½ teaspoon vanilla
1 cup sugar
½ pint whipped cream
1 teaspoon sugar
frozen strawberries
chopped nuts

Cream ½ cup sugar with shortening and beaten egg yolks, and vanilla. Add dry ingredients alternately with milk. Spread mixture into two eight inch cake tins. Batter will look very scant, but don't worry. Beat egg whites and add 1 cup sugar. Beat until stiff but not dry. Spread meringue mixture over batter in pans. Sprinkle with chopped nuts. Bake for 30 minutes at 325°.

While cake is baking, mix whipped cream with 1 teaspoon sugar. Drain frozen strawberries very well and fold into whipped cream.

To assemble cake, place one layer with meringue and nut side down on plate. Place filling on top. Place other meringue layer on top with meringue side up.

Leona DeWolff

AUNT SADE'S CHEESECAKE

OVEN: 350° 40 minutes total

Filling:
1½ pounds cream cheese
4 eggs
1⅓ cups sugar
1 teaspoon vanilla

Crust:
1½ cups graham cracker crumbs
¼ cup melted butter

Topping:
1 pint sour cream
1 teaspoon vanilla
¼ cup sugar

Soften cream cheese, add sugar, eggs, and vanilla into a large bowl. Beat 20 minutes until smooth. Prepare pie crust by melting butter and blending into crumbs. Grease a spring-form pan and mash crumb mixture into bottom and sides. Pour cream cheese filling onto crumb crust. Bake at 350° for 30 minutes.

Mix topping ingredients together and pour over filling after it has been baked for 30 minutes. Return cake to oven and bake for 10 minutes more. Refrigerate at least overnight.

If you have a food processor, simply cut cream cheese into 1" pieces and add ½ pound at a time to the processor with one egg and process until smooth. Repeat with each 8 ounces of cream cheese adding one egg each time. Add last egg with other ingredients and process until smooth. Bake as directed. Super quick.

Peggy Berg

BACARDI RUM CAKE

OVEN: 325° 1 hour

Cake:
1 cup chopped pecans OR walnuts
1 - 18½ ounce package yellow cake
   mix
1 - 3¾ ounce package instant vanilla pudding mix
4 eggs
½ cup cold water

½ cup oil
½ cup Bacardi dark rum

Glaze:
¼ pound butter
¼ cup water
1 cup granulated sugar
½ cup Bacardi dark rum

Preheat oven to 325°. Grease and flour 10 inch tube pan or 12 cup Bundt pan. Sprinkle nuts over bottom of pan. Mix all cake ingredients together. Pour batter over nuts. Bake one hour. Set on rack to cool. Invert on serving plate, prick top. Drizzle and brush glaze evenly over top and sides.

For glaze, melt butter in saucepan. Stir in water and sugar. Boil for 5 minutes, stirring constantly. Stir in rum.

Optional: Decorate with border of sugar frosting or whipped cream. Serve with seedless green grapes dusted with powdered sugar and whole maraschino cherries.

The Committee

BANANA CUPCAKES

OVEN: 350° 25-30 minutes

½ cup butter
1½ cups sugar
2 beaten eggs
2 cups flour
½ teaspoon salt

1 teaspoon baking powder
¾ teaspoon soda
1 cup mashed bananas
1 teaspoon vanilla
¼ cup sour milk

Cream butter and sugar. Add eggs. Sift together flour, salt, baking powder and soda. Add alternately with sour milk. Add bananas and vanilla. Bake at 350° for 25-30 minutes or until done.

Mildred Jones

Oven temperatures should be lowered twenty-five degrees when using glass, enamel, and dark metal pans as they absorb more heat than shiny pans.

BANANA SPLIT CAKE I

Crust:
2 cups vanilla wafer crumbs
1 stick oleo, softened
Filling:
1 — 8 ounce package cream cheese
1 stick oleo, softened
2 cups confectioners sugar

Topping:
3 bananas, sliced crosswise
1 large can crushed pineapple, well
  drained
1 large container Cool Whip
1 cup chopped pecans
maraschino cherries

Mix together vanilla wafer crumbs and oleo. Press in bottom of 9 x 13 pan.
Blend together cream cheese, oleo, and confectioners sugar. Spread on top of wafer mixture.
Next, distribute evenly over cream cheese mixture ingredients in the order listed: bananas, pineapple, Cool Whip, pecans. Garnish each piece as it is served with cherries.
Keep refrigerated.

Drusilla Powell

BANANA SPLIT CAKE II

Crust:
1 stick oleo
2 cups graham cracker crumbs
Filling:
2 cups powdered sugar
2 eggs
2 sticks oleo

Topping:
2-3 bananas, sliced lengthwise
1 large can crushed pineapple,
  drained
1 large container Cool Whip
black walnuts
maraschino cherries, cut in half

Melt oleo and combine with crumbs then pat into 9 x 13 inch pan.
Beat powdered sugar, eggs, and oleo for 15 minutes and spread on crumbs.
Layer ingredients in order listed, bananas, pineapple, Cool Whip, walnuts, cherries.
Make the night before and refrigerate.

Cindy Doyle Shultz

BEER AND SAUERKRAUT CAKE

OVEN: 350° 30 minutes

½ cup cocoa
½ pound butter, melted
1 cup beer
2 cups sugar
2 cups flour

2 eggs
½ teaspoon soda
½ cup sour milk OR sour cream
½ cup sauerkraut, chopped and
  drained

Mix together sugar and butter. Blend in flour. Combine beer and cocoa. Slowly blend beer and cocoa mixture to flour mixture alternating with the eggs. Add sour milk, soda and sauerkraut last. Pour batter into two 8 x 8 square pans, oiled and floured. Bake at 350° for 30 minutes.
The sauerkraut tastes like coconut. This is a very rich cake.

Theresa Haisley

BEER SPICE CAKE

OVEN: 375°

½ cup butter OR margarine
1 cup brown sugar
1 egg, slightly beaten
1½ cups sifted flour
1 teaspoon baking powder
1 teaspoon cloves
1 teaspoon cinnamon

1 teaspoon allspice
¼ teaspoon soda
¼ teaspoon salt
1 cup chopped walnuts
1 cup chopped dates
1 cup beer

Cream together butter and brown sugar until light and fluffy. Stir in lightly beaten egg. Sift together flour, baking powder, cloves, cinnamon, allspice, soda and salt. Sift dry ingredients over chopped walnuts and dates. Add to creamed mixture alternately with beer. Pour into greased 9x5x3 loaf pan. Bake at 375° until done.

Joanne W. Bolton

BOB'S FAVORITE CHOCOLATE COCONUT MACAROON CAKE

OVEN: 350° 30-35 minutes

⅔ cup butter OR margarine, softened
1¾ cups sugar
1 teaspoon vanilla
2 eggs
3 - 1 ounce squares, unsweetened chocolate, melted and cooled
2½ cups sifted flour
1¼ teaspoons soda

½ teaspoon salt
1¼ cups ice cold water
1 — 7 or 8 ounce package flaked coconut
1 cup broken walnuts (more if desired)
½ cup light corn syrup
½ teaspoon vanilla
1 teaspoon water

Cream butter and slowly add sugar; continue creaming until very light. Add vanilla and eggs, one at a time, beating well after each addition. Blend in chocolate. Sift flour, soda, and salt together. Add to creamed ingredients alternating with water. Beat well after each addition. Bake in greased and floured 9x13x2 pan at 350° for 30-35 minutes.

While cake is baking, combine remaining ingredients in a small bowl. Mix well. Cover and set aside. When cake is done, preheat broiler, carefully spread coconut mixture on top of hot cake. Broil 5-7 minutes until coconut is golden brown. Cool on wire rack.

A package dark chocolate cake mix with ⅓ cup oil can be used to make this faster.

Diana Dukes

BROWN SUGAR POUND CAKE

OVEN: 350° 1 hour, 15 minutes

1 stick butter &
2 sticks margarine, softened
1 box (1 pound) light brown sugar
1 cup white sugar
6 eggs
3 cups plain flour, unsifted
½ teaspoon salt

1 teaspoon baking powder
1 cup (scant) milk
1 teaspoon lemon juice
1 teaspoon vanilla

Glaze:
1 cup confectioners sugar
¼ cup lemon juice

Grease and flour 10″ tube pan or large Bundt pan. In LARGE mixing bowl, cream butter, margarine, and both sugars. Add eggs, one at a time, beating between additions. Add salt and baking powder to sifted flour. Add flour mixture and milk alternately to creamed batter. Add lemon and vanilla. Beat about 2 minutes. Pour into prepared pans and bake at 350° for approximately 1 hour, 15 minutes. (Begin checking after 1 hour as ovens vary.) Let cool 10 minutes, then turn out onto cake plate. While still warm, top with lemon glaze.

Mix together sugar and lemon juice. Sugar should be measured then sifted to remove lumps. Add more juice for a tarter taste. Pierce cake with fork or toothpick so glaze will soak into cake.

Juanita Geary

BUTTER CAKE

OVEN: 325° 1 hour

2 sticks butter
4 eggs

1½ cups flour
1½ cups sugar

Have butter and eggs at room temperature. Beat butter and sugar until creamy, add eggs, one at a time. Sift in flour. Beat until smooth. Pour into lightly greased Bundt pan. Bake at 325° for 1 hour or until done.

Do not substitute the butter with margarine. This cake does not need to be frosted.

Marilyn Carlton

Grease pans and dust with cocoa instead of flour when baking chocolate cakes; substitute powdered sugar for flour when baking white or yellow cakes.

BUTTERMILK SPICE CAKE

OVEN: 325° 25-40 minutes

¼ cup shortening
1 cup sugar
1 teaspoon vanilla extract
1 teaspoon baking powder
1 teaspoon salt
¾ teaspoon ground cinnamon
1 cup buttermilk

¾ cup firmly packed brown sugar
3 eggs
2¼ cups all purpose flour
¾ teaspoon soda
¾ teaspoon ground cloves
dash of pepper

Cream shortening and brown sugar until light and fluffy. Gradually add sugar and continue beating. Add eggs, one at a time, beating well after each addition. Add vanilla extract. Combine flour, baking powder, soda, salt, cloves, cinnamon, and pepper. Add to creamed mixture alternately with buttermilk, beginning and ending with flour, beat well. Grease two 9" round cake pans, line with greased wax paper. Pour batter into prepared pans and bake at 325° for 25 to 40 minutes. Cool in pans 5 minutes before turning out on wire racks to finish cooling. Frost with frosting of your choice.

Mrs. W. P. Sutton

CALAMONDIN SUPREME CAKE

OVEN: 350° 40 minutes

1 package lemon flavored cake mix
1 package lemon Jello
⅓ cup milk
½ cup calamondin puree
4 large eggs
¾ cup cooking oil

1 teaspoon lemon extract

Glaze:
½ cup calamondin puree
4 tablespoons soft margarine
2 teaspoons lemon extract
2 cups powdered sugar

Make calamondin puree by cutting fruit in quarters, removing seeds and grinding in blender. Mix together cake mix, dry jello, milk, calamondin puree. Beat eggs, oil, and lemon extract. Add egg mixture to cake mix mixture and mix well. Pour batter into oiled and floured 10x4½ angel food pan or a 13 x 9 x 2 flat pan. Bake in preheated oven at 350° for approximately 40 minutes or until sharp knife comes out clean when inserted in center.

While cake is still warm spread with glaze. Combine all ingredients for glaze and mix well. Spread glaze over cake after puncturing lightly with fork tines.

Elsie Kauffmann

Course-grained cakes are the result of using an over abundance of leavening ingredients or insufficient creaming and beating of ingredients.

CAN'T BE BEET CAKE

OVEN: 350° 40 minutes

2 teaspoons lemon juice
1 cup grated cooked beets
2½ cups all purpose flour
1 teaspoon salt
2 teaspoons soda
2 cups sugar
½ cup cocoa

1½ cups melted butter
4 beaten eggs
2 tablespoons honey
½ cup milk
2 teaspoons vanilla extract
(cream cheese frosting)

Sprinkle lemon juice over beets. Set aside. Combine next ten ingredients in a large mixing bowl. Stir in beets. Beat for 2 minutes with electric mixer at medium speed. Pour into greased 13 x 9 x 2 pan and bake at 350° for 40 minutes. Cool. Then frost with your favorite cream cheese frosting.

John O'Neil

CARAMEL NUT CAKE

OVEN: 325° 90 minutes

1 cup butter
½ cup oil
1 box light brown sugar
1 cup granulated sugar
½ teaspoon salt

½ teaspoon baking powder
3 cups all purpose flour
1 cup milk
1 teaspoon vanilla
1 cup chopped pecans

Cream together until smooth butter, oil, brown and white sugars. Add eggs, one at a time, beating well after each. Sift together flour, salt, and baking powder. Alternate flour mixture with milk in thirds, beginning and ending with flour. Blend in vanilla and pecans. Grease and flour tube pan and pour batter into pan. Bake at 325° for 90 minutes. Check after 1 hour, 15 minutes, with a toothpick. Cool cake in pan for 15 minutes.

For variation, sour cream or evaporated milk can be substituted for regular milk.

Mrs. Orlando Brown

CHEESECAKE I

OVEN: 375° 20 minutes; 500° 5 minutes

1 package shortbread cookies
½ stick butter OR oleo, melted
3 — 8 ounce packages cream cheese
1 cup sugar
3 eggs

½ teaspoon vanilla

Topping:
1 pint sour cream
3 tablespoons sugar
½ teaspoon vanilla

Roll cookies into crumbs and mix with butter. Pat on sides and bottom of a 9 inch spring-form pan. Beat cheese thoroughly, add sugar gradually, then eggs, one at a time, beating after each addition. Blend in vanilla. Pour into crust carefully and bake 20 minutes at 375°. While cake is baking, whip sour cream and add sugar and vanilla. Remove cake from oven and pour topping over cake. Return to oven and bake at 500° for 5 minutes. Cool and keep in refrigerator. Let stand overnight before using and it will keep for several days.

Jean Huck

CHEESECAKE II

OVEN: 350° 1 hour

2 pounds ricotta cheese	2 tablespoons lemon juice
1 pound cream cheese	1 tablespoon vanilla
6 tablespoons flour	6 large eggs
1½ cups sugar	1 pint sour cream

Preheat oven to 350°. Cream together ricotta cheese and cream cheese. Add flour and sugar, lemon juice and vanilla. Beat well. Blend in eggs, one at a time, using low speed of mixer. Slowly mix in sour cream. Butter and flour a 9″ spring-form cake pan. Pour mixture into pan and bake for one hour. Turn oven off after one hour and leave cake in oven for several hours. This cake must be left in oven for several hours to prevent cracking.

Grace Redmer

CHEESECAKE III

OVEN: 375° 20 minutes; 475° 10 minutes

Filling:
2 — 8 ounce packages cream cheese
3 whole eggs
½ cup sugar
1 teaspoon vanilla

Crust:
3 cups graham cracker crumbs

¼ pound butter, melted
¼ cup sugar

Topping:
1 pint sour cream
¼ cup sugar
1 teaspoon vanilla

Crust: Mix ingredients well and line bottom and sides of a 12x7x2 pan. Reserve some for top.
Filling: Beat well all ingredients in a large bowl. Pour mixture over crust. Bake for 20 minutes at 375°. Cool for at least 45 minutes.
Topping: Beat together all ingredients until blended. Spread on cooled cake. Cover with reserved crumbs. Bake for 10 minutes at 475°. Refrigerate overnight.

Seems like a lot of trouble, and it is, but it is well worth it. Lots of compliments.

Ann McPadden

Entertaining with a special occasion cake? An adornment of tiny flowers can be attractive. Simply place short pieces of macaroni into the icing as vases to hold the flowers.

CHEESECAKE BAVARIAN STYLE

OVEN: 325° 45-60 minutes

Pastry:
1 stick softened unsalted sweet
  butter
1 cup sugar
1 medium size egg
2 cups all-purpose flour
2 teaspoons baking powder
1 teaspoon rum
1 teaspoon fresh lemon juice
1 teaspoon canned milk

Filling:
16 ounces whipped cream cheese
16 ounces sour cream
3 tablespoons sugar
2 medium size egg yolks
2 beaten egg whites
1 grated peel of whole lemon
1 tablespoon fresh lemon juice
¾ cup seedless white or golden raisins
1 cup apple cider
⅓ cup rum

For Pastry: Cream butter and sugar; add egg and beat well. Blend in with spoon the rum, fresh lemon juice, and canned milk alternately with flour; add baking powder and work dough just enough to form ball consistency. Grease 15½x10½x1 inch cookie pan with butter; work prepared dough onto center of pan and spread out evenly to cover bottom of pan and all sides.

For Filling: Plump raisins in heated rum and apple cider for five minutes. Mix together cream cheese, egg yolks, sugar, grated lemon peel, and lemon juice; add sour cream, stirring lightly. Fold in beaten egg whites. Pour mixture over dough. Sprinkle evenly with rum and apple cider-soaked raisins; and bake in pre-heated 350° oven for 45 to 60 minutes.

Sprinkle lightly with powdered sugar, if desired, cool, and cut into serving squares.

Now a Floridian, Anneliese brought this heirloom dessert recipe with her from her native Bavaria, Germany.

Anneliese von der Cron

CHERRY CAKE

OVEN: 350° 1 hour

2 cups sugar
2 eggs
2½ cups plain flour
¾ cup buttermilk OR sour milk
1 teaspoon soda
½ cup melted butter, cooled
½ cup drained sour pitted canned
  cherries
½ cup cherry juice

1 cup nut meats
1 teaspoon nutmeg
1 teaspoon allspice
1 teaspoon cinnamon
1 tablespoon cocoa
pinch of salt
½ teaspoon lemon extract
½ teaspoon vanilla extract

If not using buttermilk, sour regular milk by mixing 1 tablespoon vinegar to 1 cup of milk. Dissolve soda in milk. Mix all ingredients together. Blend well. Bake in tube pan for one hour at 350°. Let stand for 10 minutes in pan and then turn out onto plate.

This cake keeps well and is very good. This recipe has been handed down in the family for three or more generations.

Loretta W. Scott

CHOCOLATE FUDGE CAKE

OVEN: 400° 20 minutes

2 cups flour
2 cups sugar
1 stick oleo
½ cup liquid shortening
4 tablespoons cocoa
1 cup water
½ cup buttermilk
2 eggs
½ teaspoon soda
½ teaspoon cinnamon

½ teaspoon vanilla
½ teaspoon salt

Icing:
1 stick oleo
6 tablespoons milk
4 tablespoons cocoa
1 box powdered sugar
1 teaspoon vanilla
1 cup chopped nuts

Sift flour and sugar together. In saucepan, heat to boiling point the oleo, liquid shortening, cocoa, and water. Pour liquids over dry ingredients and stir well. Add remaining ingredients. Beat well. Pour batter into 15"x16" well-greased pan. Bake 20 minutes at 400°.

When cake has baked 15 minutes, begin to prepare icing. Slowly bring just to a boil the oleo, milk, and cocoa. Stir in powdered sugar, vanilla, and nuts. Spread at once over hot cake. Cool in pan and cut into squares.

Louise A. Roadman

CHOCOLATE POUND CAKE

OVEN: 325° 80 minutes

½ pound butter
½ cup shortening
3 cups sugar
5 eggs
1 teaspoon vanilla

3 cups cake flour
½ teaspoon salt
½ teaspoon baking powder
1 cup milk
4 tablespoons cocoa

Cream butter and shortening, add sugar. Beat in eggs, one at a time, and vanilla. Sift flour, salt, baking powder and cocoa. Beat in flour mixture alternately with milk ending with flour. Pour into greased and floured tube pan. Bake 80 minutes at 325°.

Perilie White

When an over abundance of sugar or shortening is used in baking a cake the resultant cake will be quite heavy.

COCA COLA CAKE AND FROSTING

OVEN: 350° 40-45 minutes

1 cup butter OR margarine, softened
2 cups sifted all purpose flour
1¾ cups sugar
3 tablespoons cocoa
1 teaspoon soda
1 teaspoon vanilla
2 eggs

½ cup buttermilk
1 cup carbonated cola drink
1½ cups tiny marshmallows

Frosting:
½ cup butter, softened
⅓ cup cola drink
4 cups confectioners sugar
1 cup chopped walnuts OR pecans

Combine all ingredients except cola and marshmallows. Blend on low speed of electric mixer, then beat 1 minute at medium speed. Add cola and blend well. Remove mixer from bowl and stir marshmallows in by hand. Pour batter into a greased and floured 13x9x2 cake pan. Bake at 350° for 40-45 minutes or until toothpick inserted will come out clean. Cool on rack at least 30 minutes before frosting with cola frosting.

To make frosting, combine butter, cola drink, confectioners sugar, and beat smooth. Stir in chopped nuts.

This cake is easy to make since all ingredients except cola and marshmallows are placed into bowl at once. Cola is best stirred in and then marshmallows folded in carefully.

Polly Crowell

COCONUT POUND CAKE

OVEN: 350° 30 minutes

3 sticks butter
3 cups sugar
6 eggs
3 cups plain flour
8 ounces sour cream

¼ teaspoon salt
¼ teaspoon soda
1 package frozen coconut
1 teaspoon vanilla flavoring

Before preparing cake, defrost coconut and have eggs at room temperature to avoid cake failures. Preheat oven to 350°. Grease a tube pan. Using electric mixer, cream butter and sugar well. Add eggs, one at a time, mixing well after each addition. Add all other ingredients except coconut. Beat well. Stir or fold in coconut. Pour batter into pan. Bake for about 30 minutes at 350°.

Ruby Scott

Add 1 teaspoon of fresh or dried marigold leaves to your next basic pound cake recipe for a delightful change.

DATE CAKE

OVEN: 350° 1 hour

2 cups dates, cut up
2 cups boiling water
2 teaspoons baking soda, rounded
2 cups sugar, granulated
2 eggs

1 cup shortening
1 teaspoon salt
1 teaspoon vanilla
3 cups all purpose flour

Pour boiling water over cut dates. Add baking soda and mix well. Let stand. Cream sugar, shortening, and vanilla. Add eggs and beat well. Add flour and salt and date mixture. Mix well. Pour batter into a 9 x 13 inch pan. Bake at 350° for 1 hour.

Kim Nelson

DEVIL'S FOOD CAKE

OVEN: 350° 25-30 minutes

½ cake chocolate
1 cup milk
½ cup sugar

1 cup sugar
½ cup butter
2 eggs, well beaten
½ cup milk

1 teaspoon soda, dissolved in 3 tablespoons hot water
2 cups flour
pinch of salt
2 teaspoons baking powder
1 — 4½ ounce package vanilla pudding

Boil chocolate, milk and sugar until thick. Remove from heat. Cream butter and sugar; add other ingredients and mix well. Add chocolate mixture; blend thoroughly. Bake in layers of loaf pan in 350° oven for 25-30 minutes or until cake tests done.

Margaret Enns and Florence Gladwin

EARLY SETTLERS' CARROT CAKE

OVEN: 325° 1 hour

2 cups flour
2 cups sugar
2 teaspoons soda
¾ teaspoon salt
1½ teaspoons cinnamon
1½ cups vegetable oil
4 eggs
3 cups grated carrots

1 cup chopped pecans
a little coconut, if you like

Icing:
1 box powdered sugar
8 ounces cream cheese
1 stick margarine, softened
1 teaspoon vanilla

Sift dry ingredients together. Add oil and eggs and beat well. Add carrots, pecans, and coconut last. Bake in 13 x 9 greased pan at 325° for about 1 hour or until cake draws away from side of pan, and springs back when touched lightly.

To prepare icing, cream the margarine and cream cheese. Add vanilla, then the powdered sugar. This is a lot of icing. If you leave the cake in the pan to ice it, you can use about half of this amount.

Beverly Lush Traub

Swedish country-style home of
Miss Ruth Hallstrom
Indian River County, Florida

Pool and cabana at "GRACEWOOD"
home of Mrs. John M. Hopwood
Indian River County, Florida

EASY CARROT CAKE

OVEN: 325° 1 hour

3 cups grated carrots
1½ cups salad oil
2 cups sugar
4 eggs
2 cups self-rising flour
1 teaspoon cinnamon
1 cup chopped walnuts

1 tablespoon vanilla

Icing:
1 cup sugar
½ cup buttermilk
dash of salt
¼ teaspoon baking soda

Cream together sugar and salad oil. Add eggs, one at a time. Add carrots, flour and nuts. Roll nuts in flour before mixing. Add cinnamon and vanilla. Cook in tube pan at 325° for 1 hour.

For icing, mix together in a sauce pan all ingredients. Let boil for 5-6 minutes over low heat. Pour over cake while it is still warm.

Deedie Montgomery

ELLA MAE'S CARROT CAKE

OVEN: 350° approximately 1 hour

2 cups flour
2½ cups sugar
2 teaspoons soda
½ teaspoon salt
2 teaspoons cinnamon
3 eggs, beaten

1 cup vegetable oil
3 cups carrots grated fine
1 teaspoon vanilla
1 cup chopped dates
1 cup chopped nuts
1 cup crushed pineapple, drained

Sift dry ingredients together, make a well in center of dry ingredients and add beaten eggs, vegetable oil and vanilla. Mix together and add dates, nuts, carrots and pineapple. Bake at 350° for a little over an hour.

Mixture will be very stiff at first, but will get thinner after carrots are added. Grease an oblong pan and line with greased wax paper on bottom and sides.

Penelope B. Holland

EVA'S CHOCOLATE ROLL

OVEN: 325°-350° 30 minutes

5 eggs
1 cup powdered sugar
2 tablespoons cocoa

1 pint whipping cream
chocolate sauce

Separate eggs. Beat egg whites very stiff. To yolks add sugar and cocoa then fold in egg whites. Grease oblong pan lightly, but flour pan heavily. Pour batter into pan and cook at 325° or 350° about 30 minutes. Turn out on large piece of wax paper powdered heavily with 4X sugar. Knife around the sides and turn over. Roll up (wax paper too) immediately until ready to use. Unroll when ready to use and spread with whipped cream, then roll back up. Pour chocolate sauce over top.

Penelope B. Holland

EXPENSIVE SHEET CAKE

OVEN: 400° 20 minutes OR 350° 30 minutes

2 cups flour
2 cups sugar
2 sticks butter
1 cup water
1 teaspoon vanilla

1 teaspoon cinnamon
3½ tablespoons cocoa
½ cup buttermilk
2 eggs

Boil butter, water, cocoa, and pour over other ingredients. Don't use mixer. Pour batter into 9 x 13 buttered pan and bake 20 minutes at 400° or 30 minutes at 350°.

Pamela B. Williams

FAIRMONT MANOR WHITE CHOCOLATE CAKE

OVEN: 350° 30 minutes — layers; 75 minutes — tube pan

¼ pound WHITE chocolate, melted
over hot water
1 cup butter (do not substitute)
2 cups sugar
4 eggs
1 teaspoon vanilla
dash of salt
2½ cups cake flour
1 teaspoon baking powder

1 cup buttermilk
1 cup chopped pecans
1 cup flaked coconut

Icing:
2 cups sugar
2 sticks butter
1 teaspoon vanilla
dash of salt
1 small can condensed milk

Cream butter and chocolate. Add eggs, one at a time, blend well. Add vanilla and salt. Sift baking powder with flour. Blend in flour, baking powder, and buttermilk. Stir in coconut and nuts. Bake at 350° for 30 minutes in layer pans, or 75 minutes for tube pan. Pans should be greased and floured before use.

Icing: Combine all ingredients and let stand one hour (stir occasionally). Then cook until soft ball forms when dropped in cold water. Beat until creamy. Spread on cake.

When buying white chocolate, make sure it has NO wax in it.

Our home was named Fairmont Manor in 1920 by the Jones Family from Fairmont, WV. This recipe was given to me in May 1964 when we purchased Fairmont Manor.

Beverly Cambron

Instead of one square (one ounce) of unsweetened chocolate use three tablespoons unsweetened cocoa plus one tablespoon butter or margarine.

FAMOUS KENTUCKY WHISKEY CAKE

OVEN: 300° 3-4 hours

1 pound candied red cherries	½ pound light raisins, cut in half
1 pint Kentucky Bourbon	1 cup brown sugar
2 cups granulated sugar	6 eggs separated
¾ pound butter	1 teaspoon baking powder
5 cups sifted all purpose flour	4 cups pecans
2 teaspoons grated nutmeg	

Soak cherries and raisins in whiskey overnight. Cream butter and sugar until fluffy. Beat in egg yolks. Add soaked fruit and remaining whiskey. Reserve a small amount of flour for dredging nuts. Sift remaining flour, baking powder and nutmeg. Add to creamed mixture. Beat egg whites and fold in. Add pecans dredged with flour.

Bake in large greased tube pan or two 4 x 8 x 2 inch loaf pans. (Line bottom of pans with greased paper.) Bake at 300° for 3 or 4 hours depending on pan size, in 2 or 3 inches of water.

Peach or apricot brandy or rum may be substituted for whiskey.

Mrs. Robert Terry

FANCY CHOCOLATE CAKE

OVEN: 350° 25-30 minutes

1 package chocolate cake mix	½ cup cooking oil
1 — 3¾ ounce instant chocolate pudding	apricot preserves
	apricot liqueur
1 cup water	whipped cream
4-5 eggs (to equal 1 cup)	

Stir instant pudding with cake mix. Add water and eggs. Beat until well mixed. Add oil and beat. Line layer pans with greased wax paper. Bake at 350° until done, about 25-30 minutes. Split layers when thoroughly cooled. Pour liqueur into each layer and stack cake with preserves in between. Ice cake with whipped cream. Keep refrigerated.

Any fruit jelly or marmalade and liqueur may be substituted.

Kathryn Scott

When whipping egg whites, wait until the whites stand in soft peaks before adding sugar. If the sugar is added too soon the mixture will not thicken.

FARMER'S FRUIT BUNDT

OVEN: 350° 1 hour, 15 minutes

3 cups flour
2 cups sugar
3 teaspoons baking powder
1 teaspoon salt
1 cup salad oil
4 eggs
¼ cup orange juice

1 tablespoon vanilla
6 cups pared, cored, and sliced apples, peaches, OR plums, fresh only
⅓ cup sugar
1½ teaspoons cinnamon
¾ teaspoon nutmeg

Preheat oven to 350°. Grease large Bundt or angel food pan. Mix fruit with sugar, cinnamon and nutmeg and set aside. Sift together flour, 2 cups sugar, baking powder, and salt in large bowl. Make a well in center of dry ingredients and pour in oil, eggs, orange juice, and vanilla. Beat with spoon or electric mixer until thick and well blended. Spoon into pan, alternating layers of batter with layers of fruit, ending with batter, if possible. Bake at 350° for 1 hour, 15 minutes. Cool to lukewarm before removing from pan.

Excellent served warm with whipped cream or lemon sauce.

Betty Morse Hendershott

FRESH APPLE CAKE

OVEN: 325° 45 minutes

¼ cup oil
2 cups sugar
3 cups flour
3 eggs
½ teaspoon baking soda

1 teaspoon salt
4 medium cooking apples, diced
1 cup chopped nuts
2 teaspoons vanilla

Grease tube pan. Cream oil and sugar in large bowl. Add eggs. Beat well. Add flour, salt and soda and vanilla. Fold in nuts and apples. Bake in cold oven at 325° for 45 minutes or until well done. Top with your own choice of frosting, or powdered sugar is excellent.

Kay Nergard

A stand-in for one teaspoon baking powder is one-fourth teaspoon baking soda plus one-half teaspoon cream of tartar.

FRUIT CAKE

OVEN: 275° until done

1 pound butter
12 eggs
1½ pounds brown sugar
2 cups flour
4½ teaspoons baking powder
2 teaspoons nutmeg
3 teaspoons cloves
3 teaspoons cinnamon
4 cups flour
4 pounds mixed fruit

3 pounds pineapple
2 boxes raisins
3 pounds pecans
2 pounds chopped dates
3 pounds cherries, red and green
2 pounds citron
1 can applesauce
1 pound black walnuts
1 pint sherry

Combine butter, eggs, and brown sugar. Add 2 cups of flour mixed with baking powder, nutmeg, cloves and cinnamon. Blend well.

In a separate bowl mix well with 4 cups of flour the mixed fruit, pineapple, raisins, pecans, dates, cherries, citron, applesauce and walnuts. Add fruit and nut mixture to batter with 1 pint of sherry. Mix well. Bake at 275° until done.

Mrs. Forest Pearce

FRUIT COCKTAIL CAKE

OVEN: 350° 30-40 minutes   YIELD: 18 servings

Cake:
2 cups sugar
2 cups self-rising flour
1 egg
1 — 16 ounce can fruit cocktail

Topping:
1 stick oleo
1 cup sugar
1 can evaporated milk
1 cup coconut, shredded
1 cup walnuts, chopped
1 teaspoon vanilla

Preheat oven to 350°. Grease 9 x 13 pan.

Mix sugar, flour, egg and fruit cocktail together. Pour into prepared pan. Bake for 30-40 minutes or until done.

For topping, melt oleo, add sugar and evaporated milk. Bring mixture to a boil and boil for 10 minutes stirring constantly. Add coconut and walnuts. When cake is cool, put topping on cake.

Joan Kite

FUDGE BROWNIE RING CAKE

OVEN: 325° 60-70 minutes

1 package family size brownie mix
1 package coconut pecan frosting
   mix
1 cup sour cream

⅔ cup milk
2 eggs
powdered sugar

Preheat oven to 325°. Grease and flour a 10 inch tube pan. In a large bowl, combine all ingredients except powdered sugar. Stir well. Pour batter into prepared pan. Bake 60-70 minutes or until toothpick inserted in center comes out clean.

Sprinkle with powdered sugar or serve with whipped cream.

Brenda Campbell

FUNNY CAKE

OVEN: 350° 30-35 minutes

1½ cups flour
1 cup white sugar
¼ cup cocoa
½ teaspoon salt
1 teaspoon soda

1 cup cold water
⅓ cup cooking oil
1 teaspoon vanilla
1 teaspoon vinegar

Put all ingredients in a bowl and mix. Pour batter into ungreased 8 x 8 x 2 inch pan. Bake at 350° for 30-35 minutes.

Edie Stretch

GRAHAM TORTE

OVEN: 350° 20-25 minutes

3 eggs, separated
1 cup sugar
1 cup graham cracker crumbs
1 teaspoon baking powder
1 cup chopped pecans
1 teaspoon vanilla

Cream Filling:
1 cup milk

1½ tablespoons cornstarch
1 whole egg OR egg yolk
1 teaspoon vanilla
⅓ cup sugar

Topping:
1 carton whipping cream, sweetened
vanilla

Beat egg yolks and ¾ of the cup of sugar until light and fluffy. Add and mix by hand the vanilla, graham cracker crumbs, baking powder and nuts. Beat egg whites and remaining ¼ cup sugar until stiff but not dry. Fold beaten egg whites into egg yolk mixture. Divide batter into two greased 8″ loose bottom cake pans. Bake for 20-25 minutes in 350° oven. Let sit about 5 minutes (no more) and remove from pans.
Combine ingredients for filling and cook in saucepan until filling starts to thicken. Pour filling into shells that have been removed from pans. Frost with 1 cup of whipped cream that has been sweetened and blended with a touch of vanilla.
Refrigerate.

Shirley Morgan

Removing the shell from a fresh coconut will be easier if heated in a warm oven for a few minutes.

HALF POUND CAKE

OVEN: 300° 1 hour

2 sticks butter OR margarine　　　**2 cups plain flour**
2 cups sugar　　　　　　　　　　**2 tablespoons bourbon whiskey**
6 eggs

Cream together butter and sugar. Add eggs, one at a time, beating well after each addition. Add flour, beat well. Then add bourbon. Pour batter into greased and floured tube pan and place in COLD oven. Bake at 300° for 1 hour or until done.

This is not a large, fine-texture pound cake. It is quick and easy and is excellent to use with strawberries and whipped cream or thick lemon sauce to pour over.

This is a pretty company dessert. I like to serve it in a cut glass bowl with a spoon and let everyone serve themselves. You can use dessert plates or small bowls on plates and serve with a light, crisp cookie.

Ty Fender

HARVEY WALLBANGER CAKE

OVEN: 350° 45 minutes

1 package orange cake mix (for 2　　**½ cup orange juice**
layer cake)
1 package vanilla pudding mix　　　*Glaze:*
4 eggs　　　　　　　　　　　　　**1 cup sifted confectioners sugar**
½ cup oil　　　　　　　　　　　　**1 tablespoon orange juice**
½ cup Galliano　　　　　　　　　　**1 tablespoon Galliano**
2 tablespoons vodka　　　　　　　**1 teaspoon vodka**

Combine cake mix and pudding in large bowl. Add orange juice, oil, Galliano and vodka. Beat at low speed for one-half minute. Beat at medium speed for 5 minutes, scraping bowl frequently. Pour into greased and floured Bundt pan. Bake at 350° for 45 minutes. Cool in pan 10 minutes. Remove to rack and pour on glaze while still warm.

Elizabeth Vaughn

Never fill a pan more than two-thirds full with batter. When baking, the batter may overflow. Make cupcakes or mini-cakes from the remaining batter.

HAWAIIAN PINEAPPLE COCONUT CAKE

OVEN: 350° 35-40 minutes

2 cups sugar
½ cup butter OR margarine,
  melted
1 tablespoon fresh lemon juice
½ teaspoon salt
4 eggs
½ teaspoon baking soda
1½ cups flour
3 small cans crushed pineapple,
  well drained

1 cup coconut
1 cup coarsely chopped walnuts

Frosting:
8 ounces cream cheese
1 box confectioners sugar
½ teaspoon salt
1 tablespoon fresh lemon juice
2 tablespoons condensed milk
1 teaspoon vanilla

Combine sugar and butter. Add eggs, one at a time, beating well after each addition. Add lemon juice. Sift dry ingredients and add to batter alternately with pineapple and coconut. Add nuts and mix well. Pour batter into an oiled and floured 9 x 13″ pan. Bake at 350° for 35-40 minutes. Cool. Frosh and sprinkle with additional coconut.

The Committee

HEATH CANDY BAR CAKE

OVEN: 350° 30-35 minutes

2 cups light brown sugar
2 cups flour
½ cup margarine
1 cup buttermilk
1 teaspoon soda

1 egg
1 teaspoon vanilla
½ teaspoon salt
8 Heath Candy Bars

Mix together sugar, flour and margarine. Batter will be like pie crust dough. Reserve one cup of batter for top of cake.

Mix soda in buttermilk and add to other ingredients. Add egg, vanilla and salt. Mix. Pour batter into 9 x 13 inch pan. Sprinkle reserved crumb batter on top. Crush candy bars and put on top of crumbs.

Bake at 350° for 30-35 minutes.

Pat Sawusch

In place of one cup of cake flour use one cup all-purpose flour minus two tablespoons.

HOBO CAKE

OVEN: 350° 45 minutes

2 sticks butter
1 cup water
2 tablespoons cocoa
2 cups flour
2 cups sugar
2 eggs
1 teaspoon baking soda
½ cup sour cream

Frosting:
½ stick butter
2 tablespoons cocoa
2 tablespoons milk
½ box confectioner's sugar
1 teaspoon vanilla
crushed nuts

Preheat oven to 350°. In a saucepan melt butter with water and cocoa. Mix the remaining ingredients. Pour batter into greased oblong baking pan. Bake about 45 minutes or until toothpick comes clean. Frost with fudge frosting.

Frosting: Melt first four ingredients in a small saucepan. Remove from heat and add vanilla and sugar. Beat and add remaining ingredients. Pour on cake while cake is still warm. (If frosting is too runny, add more sugar.)

Top with crushed nuts.

Jeanne Powell

HUNGARIAN WALNUT TORTE

OVEN: 350° 25-30 minutes

½ cup sifted flour
½ teaspoon concentrated coffee
½ teaspoon cocoa
2 cups chopped walnuts
6 eggs, separated

1 cup sugar
1 teaspoon grated lemon peel
1 teaspoon rum
⅓ teaspoon vanilla

Grease bottoms of two 9″ round layer cake pans. Sift together flour, coffee, and cocoa. Thoroughly combine chopped walnuts with flour. Divide into four portions. Beat egg yolks until thick and lemon-colored with ½ cup sugar. Add grated lemon peel, rum and vanilla. Set aside. Beat egg whites until frothy, gradually adding ½ cup sugar while beating until rounded peaks form. Gently spread egg yolk mixture over egg whites. Spoon one portion of flour-nut mixture over egg mixture. Fold gently (only partially blend). Repeat until all is blended. DO NOT OVER MIX. Gently turn batter into pans and spread to edges. Bake at 350° for 25-30 minutes. Cool. Remove.

Helen Bullock

Vanilla beans are more economical to use than vanilla extract. They also yield better flavoring results.

JAN'S TEA CAKE

OVEN: 350° 25-30 minutes

1 egg, well beaten	1 cup cake flour
3 tablespoons butter, melted	¼ teaspoon salt
2 teaspoons baking powder	1 teaspoon vanilla
½ cup milk	cinnamon
½ cup sugar	sugar

Assemble dry ingredients in a large bowl. Pour liquid ingredients all at once into dry ingredients. Beat until smooth and glossy. Pour into greased and floured one-layer cake pan. Cover with a mixture of cinnamon and sugar and bake at 350°, about 25-30 minutes. Test for doneness.

Janice G. Louks

JAVA ANGEL CAKE

OVEN: as package directs   YIELD: 16

Cake:
1 package angel food cake mix
1 tablespoon instant coffee
1 teaspoon vanilla

Icing:
2 packages whipped topping mix
6 tablespoons sugar
5 teaspoons coffee OR 4½ teaspoons Tia Maria liqueur
½ cup instant cocoa
1½ teaspoons vanilla

Prepare cake according to directions dissolving coffee in the water. Add vanilla. Pour into tube pan and bake according to package directions.
Combine icing ingredients and spread on cake and chill.
Make topping while cake is baking. Refrigerate icing until ready to frost cake.
Preparation time, 45 minutes. Must do ahead. A nice dessert after a heavy meal.

Celeta Arden

JIFFY FRUIT CAKE

OVEN: 300° 3 hours

½ pound candied cherries	2 cups sugar
6 rings of candied pineapple	4 eggs
1 pound dates	2 cups flour
1 pound walnuts	½ teaspoon salt
1 pound pecans	1 teaspoon baking soda
1 cup flour	1 cup dairy sour cream
1 cup margarine	

Cut cherries in half and pineapple into eighths. Chop dates and nuts coarsely. Dredge with 1 cup flour. Cream butter and sugar with electric mixer until light and fluffy. Add eggs, one at a time, and beat well after each addition. Add sifted flour, salt, and baking soda alternately with cream, beating until smooth after each addition. Mix in fruits and nuts. Turn into a 10" tube pan, well greased, lined with heavy brown paper (on bottom and sides), and greased again. Bake in 300° oven for 3 hours.

Pat Sawusch

KENTUCKY BLACKBERRY CAKE

OVEN: 350° 35 minutes

20 ounces frozen blackberries
¼ cup flour
1 cup margarine
2 cups sugar
5 egg yolks
1 whole egg
3 cups flour
3 teaspoons baking powder
2 teaspoons grated nutmeg
2 teaspoons cinnamon

1 teaspoon soda
1 cup buttermilk
1 teaspoon vanilla

Frosting:
5 egg whites, stiffly beaten
1 cup sugar
1 cup light corn syrup
½ cup water
1 teaspoon vanilla
4 ounces shredded coconut

Dissolve soda in buttermilk. Spread frozen blackberries on a paper towel on a cookie sheet. Thaw for 2 hours at room temperature. Sift ¼ cup flour lightly over berries just before adding them to batter. Cream together margarine and sugar. Beat in eggs; sift flour, spices and baking powder together. Add buttermilk and dry ingredients to batter alternately. Add vanilla. Spoon the lightly floured berries into the mixture, a few at a time, being careful not to crush them. Pour batter into 3 greased and floured 9" pans and bake in 350° oven for 35 minutes.

For frosting, boil sugar and water on medium high heat until it "hairs", approximately 14 minutes. Pour syrup mixture, slowly, into egg whites. Add vanilla. For each layer, sprinkle coconut generously on top of layer. Do not mix coconut with the frosting.

Ethel Peery

LEMON COCONUT CAKE

OVEN: 350° 50-60 minutes

1 — 8 ounce (2⅔ cups) package
   shredded coconut
1 — 18½ ounce package lemon cake
   mix
1 — 3¾ ounce box instant lemon
   pudding

4 large eggs
½ cup canned coconut cream
½ cup fresh lemon juice
¼ cup oil
¼ cup dark rum
powdered sugar

Preheat oven to 350°. Generously grease 10" tube pan and sprinkle bottom with one-half of coconut. Place remaining coconut on baking sheet and toast until golden, stirring frequently, about 8 minutes.

Combine remaining ingredients except powdered sugar in large bowl. Using electric mixer, beat at medium speed 3-4 minutes. Stir in toasted coconut. Pour batter into prepared pan and bake 50-60 minutes or until cake tests done. Place pan on rack and cool completely. Remove from pan, invert onto serving plate and sprinkle with powdered sugar.

Connie Wagers

LEMON JELLO POUND CAKE

OVEN: 300° 1 hour

1 package yellow cake mix
1 cup water
½ cup cooking oil

1 box instant lemon pudding mix
4 eggs

Mix water and cake mix. Add pudding and mix. Add oil and beat. Add eggs, one at a time, beating well after each addition. Bake 1 hour in 300° oven.

Thelma Bell

LEMON-PECAN CAKE

OVEN: 350° 1 hour

1½ cups sifted flour
1 teaspoon baking powder
1 teaspoon salt
1 cup sugar
½ cup butter OR margarine
2 eggs

½ cup milk
4 teaspoons grated lemon rind
1 cup finely chopped pecans

Glaze:
¾ cup sugar
3 tablespoons lemon juice

Onto a piece of wax paper or foil sift flour, baking powder, and salt. Set aside. In large bowl, cream sugar and butter or margarine. Beat in eggs. Add milk and flour mixture alternately, beating after each addition. Stir in rind and pecans. Pour into greased 10″ loaf pan. Bake at 350° for about 1 hour. Meantime, in small saucepan, blend sugar and lemon juice. Cook and stir over low heat until sugar is melted. As soon as cake is done, remove from pan to sheet of foil. Place on wire rack. Gradually spoon glaze over cake so that loaf absorbs mixture. Allow to cool thoroughly before serving.

Barbara Matuszewski

LITTLE FRUIT CAKES

OVEN: 275° 1 hour

11 ounces pitted dates
8 ounces candied cherries
1 teaspoon baking powder
2 eggs
4 cups pecans

8 ounces candied pineapple
1 cup all-purpose flour
¼ teaspoon salt
½ cup sugar

Grease small muffin cups (small, bite size). Set oven at 275°. Cut into small pieces, dates, pineapple, and cherries. Place in a large bowl. Sift together flour, baking powder and salt. Pour over fruit. Separate pieces so all will be coated with flour. With electric mixer, beat eggs until fluffy, gradually adding sugar to eggs. Pour egg mixture over fruit mixture. Add pecans that have been chopped, and mix well. Fill muffin cups ½ full packing down well with fingers. Place pecan half on top of each cake. Bake for 1 hour.

Jane Christopher

MANDARIN ORANGE CAKE

OVEN: 350° 35 minutes

1 cup flour
1 cup sugar
1 egg
1½ teaspoons soda
¼ teaspoon vanilla

1 small can mandarin oranges,
  drained

Topping:
¾ cup brown sugar
3 tablespoons butter
3 tablespoons milk

Put ingredients in bowl and mix well with mixer. Bake in a square pan at 350° for 35 minutes.

After cake bakes, spoon on topping mixture, while cake is hot.

To make topping, boil all ingredients and blend well.

Serve cake with whipped cream.

Donna Williford

MANGO SHORTCAKE

OVEN: 375° 30-35 minutes

Cake base:
2 cups prepared biscuit mix
3 eggs
½ cup sugar
1 medium size ripe mango

Mango filling:
2 medium size ripe, diced mangos
3 egg yolks
2 tablespoons cornstarch
½ cup sugar
¼ cup water

Peel and slice mango, roll slices in biscuit mix and add to beaten eggs and sugar. Pour batter into well greased 9" square cake pan. Bake in 375° oven for 30-35 minutes. Cool and cut in squares and slice through middle and spread with mango custard.*

Put slices together like a layer cake and spread more filling on top. Garnish with whipped cream.

*Mango filling: Put mangos through ricer. Beat egg yolks and add cornstarch mixed with sugar and water. Strain and add to mango pulp. Cook slowly until thick and smooth. Remove from heat and add butter. Chill for 2 hours before spreading on cake.

Dot Gortner

Ten minutes before cup cakes are finished baking, place a marshmallow on top of each cup cake. When baked the cup cakes are covered with a luscious topping.

MANGO UPSIDE-DOWN CAKE

OVEN: 350° 45 minutes to 1 hour

½ cup butter
1 cup brown sugar
1 mango, sliced
3 egg yolks
1 cup sugar, granulated

5 tablespoons mango juice
1 cup flour
1 teaspoon baking powder
3 egg whites

Melt butter in heavy frying pan. Add brown sugar and spread evenly. Remove from stove.

Arrange sliced arcs of mango in a circle in the pan and place halves of maraschino cherries in between the fruit.

Make a sponge batter by beating the egg yolks, adding the sugar and mango juice. Sift in flour and baking powder. Fold into stiffly beaten egg whites. Pour over fruit in pan. Bake at 350° 45 minutes to 1 hour. Cool for 10 minutes. Invert a pretty dish on the pan and turn the whole thing over. Remove pan gently.

Cut mango into slices on one side. Then slice under them to release slices. Then do other side. Catch juice as mangos are cut. When in season, I prepare and freeze enough slices for a cake on a paper plate.

Margaret Goodman

MILKY WAY CAKE WITH CARAMEL ICING

OVEN: 350° 25-30 minutes

8 Milky Way bars
1 stick margarine
1 cup pecans
2 cups sugar
4 eggs
1¼ cups buttermilk
2½ cups plain flour
½ teaspoon soda

2 teaspoons vanilla

Icing:
2 cups sugar
½ cup milk
1 stick margarine
1 teaspoon vanilla
½ cup sugar to caramelize

Combine Milky Way bars, margarine and pecans in saucepan and heat until melted. Cool. Combine remaining ingredients and fold in candy mixture. Pour into 3 or 4 cake pans. Bake at 350° for 25-30 minutes.

Icing: Place sugar, milk, and margarine in a large saucepan. In another pan place ½ cup sugar to caramelize. Start cooking both at the same time. When the sugar is a golden brown, turn the large pan on low and pour in caramelized sugar very slowly, stirring all the time. Remove from stove and beat until thick. Spread on cake.

Mrs. A. K. Hockaday

One square of chocolate equals one ounce.

MOCHA CAKE

OVEN: 350° 40 minutes

¾ cup sugar
1 cup sifted flour
2 teaspoons baking powder
⅛ teaspoon salt
1 square unsweetened chocolate (1 ounce)
2 tablespoons butter

½ cup milk
1 teaspoon vanilla
½ cup brown sugar
½ cup sugar
4 tablespoons cocoa
1 cup cold, double strength coffee

Sift first four ingredients together. Melt chocolate and butter together over hot water in double boiler. Add chocolate to sifted mixture, blend well. Combine milk and vanilla, add to flour mixture, blend well. Pour into greased 9″ square pan. Combine brown sugar, ½ cup sugar and cocoa; sprinkle over batter. Pour coffee over top. Bake in 350° oven for 40 minutes.
Serve with whipped cream or ice cream.

Mrs. Conrad Hardie, Jr.

NON-SWEET CAKE

OVEN: 350° 50-60 minutes

¼ cup sugar
½ teaspoon cinnamon
½ cup finely chopped pecans
1 package yellow cake mix
1 package butter pecan pudding mix
4 eggs

¼ cup oil
½ pint sour cream

Glaze:
2 teaspoons pancake syrup
1 teaspoon water
1 cup confectioners sugar

Mix sugar, cinnamon and pecans well and set aside. Blend cake mix, pudding mix, eggs, oil, and sour cream at medium speed for 4 minutes. Pour ⅔ of batter into greased Bundt pan. Sprinkle with nut mixture. Add remaining batter. Bake at 350° for 50-60 minutes.
For glaze, mix ingredients well and pour on hot cake.

Gladys Baldwin

ONE-HALF POUND CAKE

OVEN: 350° 45 minutes

1⅔ cups sugar
2 cups cake flour
1 pinch of salt

1 cup butter OR margarine
5 eggs

Cream butter and sugar. Beat in eggs, one at a time. Sift flour and salt together. Add to creamed mixture. Put in warm oven and bake at 350° for 45 minutes.

Lee Anita Williams

1-2-3-4 CAKE

OVEN: 375° 30 minutes

3 cups flour
3 tablespoons baking powder
½ teaspoon salt
1 cup shortening

2 cups sugar
4 eggs, separated
1 teaspoon vanilla
1 cup milk

Grease and flour 3 nine-inch cake pans. Preheat oven to 375°.
Sift together flour, baking powder and salt. Cream sugar, shortening, and vanilla together until fluffy. Add beaten egg yolks to mixture. Beat well.
Add flour alternating with milk. Beat well after each addition. Beat egg whites until stiff but not dry. Fold into batter.
Pour batter into 3 cake pans and bake at 375° for 30 minutes. Cool completely and frost with Dorothy's Coconut Frosting. (See recipe.)

Dorothy Koske

ORANGE CAKE I

OVEN: 350° 45 minutes

6 egg yolks
1 cup butter OR oleo
2 cups sugar
½ teaspoon soda
½ teaspoon salt
3 cups flour
2 teaspoons baking powder
1 cup buttermilk

3 egg whites

Filling:
1 box or can coconut
grated rind of 1 orange
1 cup orange juice
3 egg whites
3 tablespoons sugar

Cream butter, sugar and egg yolks. Sift flour, salt, baking powder and soda. Add flour mixture alternately with buttermilk to creamed mixture. Beat 3 egg whites, and fold into batter. Pour in greased 9 x 13 pan and bake at 350° for about 45 minutes.
While cake is baking, combine coconut, orange rind, and orange juice. Let mixture soak. Beat remaining 3 egg whites until stiff and gradually add in sugar. Beat well and stir into coconut and orange juice. Spread on cake while cake is warm.

Ethel Peery

Grated lemon or orange rind combined with a bit of lemon juice can be used in place of vanilla extract. Other substitutes include ¼ teaspoon nutmeg for each teaspoon of vanilla, or a dusting of cinnamon.

ORANGE CAKE II

OVEN: 350° 1 hour

1 box yellow cake mix
½ cup sugar
1 cup fresh orange juice
¾ cup cooking oil

4 eggs

Glaze:
¾ cup orange juice
1 cup sugar

Combine cake mix, sugar, orange juice, and oil together. Add one egg at a time, beating 1 minute for each egg. Pour batter into greased and floured tube pan. Bake for 1 hour at 350° or until done.

Meanwhile, mix orange juice and add sugar until dissolved. When cake is done, turn out on towel. Have large plate wrapped in tin foil, big enough to come up on sides of cake. Pour orange juice and sugar over top.

Cake is better if it sits overnight.

Other juices may be substituted for orange juice.

Loretta Hunter

ORANGE CAKE III

OVEN: 350° 30-40 minutes

juice of one orange
1 cup brown sugar
1 cup seedless raisins
1 orange peel
1 cup white sugar
½ cup shortening
2 cups flour, sifted

2 eggs
¼ teaspoon salt
1 teaspoon soda
⅔ cup buttermilk
½ cup chopped pecans
orange juice
brown sugar

Combine white sugar and shortening; add flour and salt. Mix soda with buttermilk. Add to mixture. Beat eggs and add to mixture. Mix well. Next add pecans, rind and raisins (last). Mix well and pour in 9 x 14 pan and bake 30-40 minutes at 350°. When done, pour orange juice and brown sugar that have been mixed together, over cake. Cool and cut in squares.

Margaret Matthews

Honey cakes and cookies will remain moist longer than those made with sugar since honey retains moisture to a greater extent than does sugar.

ORANGE CANDY CAKE

OVEN: 250° 3 hours

1 cup butter
2 cups granulated sugar
4 eggs
1 teaspoon baking soda
½ cup buttermilk
4 cups unsifted flour

1 — 14 ounce box dates OR 2 cups
  raisins
1 pound candied orange slices
2 cups chopped nuts
1 cup flaked coconut
1 cup fresh OR frozen orange juice
1 cup unsifted confectioners sugar

Cream butter and sugar. Add eggs one at a time, creaming after each addition. Dissolve soda in buttermilk. Alternately add buttermilk to creamed mixture with 3½ cups of flour. Add rest of flour to dates and candy, etc. Add coconut. Pour into 10″ greased and floured tube pan. Bake at 250° for 3 hours, until cake springs back when touched.

Combine orange juice and confectioners sugar and mix well. Pour over hot cake when it is done. Let stand overnight in pan. Remove from pan and slice to serve.

This is the perfect holiday cake for those who do not care for fruit cake. It freezes well and can be taken out, thawed and eaten at any time.

Mary Sowinski

ORANGE POUND CAKE

OVEN: 350° 1 hour

1 cup shortening
4 eggs
1 teaspoon vanilla
½ teaspoon baking powder
1 cup buttermilk
2 cups sugar
2 teaspoons lemon extract
½ teaspoon soda

½ teaspoon salt
3 cups flour

Frosting:
grated rind of 1 orange
6 tablespoons orange juice
grated rind of 2 lemons
1½ cups powdered sugar

Cream shortening and sugar. Beat in eggs, one at a time. Add flavorings. Beat in sifted ingredients alternately with milk. Pour in a greased and floured tube pan. Bake at 350° for 1 hour.

For frosting, mix all ingredients together and pour over hot cake.

Betty Bleech

Tough cakes may result if the batter is over-beaten after the flour has been added.

ORANGE RUM CAKE

OVEN: 350° 1 hour

YIELD: 12-16 servings

1 cup butter OR margarine
2 cups sugar
grated rind of 2 large oranges
grated rind of 1 lemon
2 eggs
2½ cups sifted, all-purpose flour

2 teaspoons salt
1 cup buttermilk
1 cup chopped English walnuts OR
  pecans
juice of 2 large oranges
2 tablespoons rum

Cream butter until light. Add 1 cup of sugar gradually. Beat until light and fluffy. Add orange and lemon rinds. Add eggs, one at a time, beating well after each addition. Sift dry ingredients together and add to creamed mixture alternately with buttermilk. Beat until smooth. Fold in walnuts. Pour into 9-10″ tube pan or 2 quart Bundt pan. Bake at 350° for 1 hour or until done. Strain juices into saucepan. Add remaining sugar and rum. Bring liquids to a boil. Pour mixture over hot cake in pan and let stand at least one day before serving.

Mary Butler

ORANGE SLICE CAKE

OVEN: 250° 2½ to 3 hours

1 cup butter OR shortening
2 cups sugar
4 eggs
1 teaspoon soda
½ cup buttermilk
3½ cups plain flour
1 pound dates, chopped

1 pound candy orange slices,
  chopped
2 cups nuts, chopped
1 can coconut
1 can frozen orange juice
2 cups powdered sugar

Cream shortening and sugar. Add eggs, one at a time, and beat well after each addition. Dissolve soda in buttermilk and add to creamed mixture. Place flour in a large bowl and add dates, orange slices, nuts and coconut. Stir to coat each piece. Add this to creamed mixture. This makes a very stiff dough and should be mixed with hands. Put dough in greased and floured 9 x 13 x 2 pan. Bake at 250° for 2½ to 3 hours.
Combine orange juice and powdered sugar and pour over hot cake. Let stand in pan overnight.

Mrs. Jake Evans

To keep your bowl from sliding when mixing ingredients, place a crumpled towel or sponge-type cloth under the bowl.

PARTY CAKE

OVEN: 350° 15-20 minutes   YIELD: 12-16 servings

1 package yellow cake mix
1 package (small size) instant
  vanilla pudding
1 cup milk
8 ounces cream cheese

9 ounces frozen whipped topping,
  thawed
1 — 20 ounce can crushed pineapple,
  drained
1 can coconut
  nutmeats

Make cake according to directions and place in floured and greased jelly roll pan (15½"x10½"x1"). Bake at 350° for 15-20 minutes. Cool 5 minutes. Invert on foil covered cardboard.

Dissolve pudding with milk and set aside. Cream the cheese and add whipped topping. Beat. Add pudding to creamed mixture and beat. Mixture should resemble whipped cream. Spread over cake. Put drained pineapple over icing. Sprinkle with coconut and then nuts.

Mrs. Richard Keefe

PATTI'S CARROT CAKE

OVEN: 300° 25 minutes

2 cups flour
2 cups sugar
2 teaspoons cinnamon
1 teaspoon salt

1½ cups oil
4 eggs
3 cups grated carrots
1 cup chopped nuts

Sift flour, sugar, cinnamon and salt together and mix well. Add oil and mix well again. Add eggs, one at a time, and mix well after each addition. Add carrots and nuts; blend into mixture. Bake in 2 greased and floured 9" cake pans in 300° oven for 25 minutes.

Annie Parker
Villa Capri

Honey should be kept in a warm dry place tightly covered. It loses its aroma and flavor and absorbs moisture when exposed to the air. If honey granulates, place container in hot water until it liquifies.

PAVLOVA CAKE

OVEN: 250° 1½ to 2 hours

6 egg whites
12 ounces superfine, granulated
   sugar
2 teaspoons white vinegar

1 teaspoon vanilla essence
½ teaspoon salt
¾ pint whipped cream
sliced strawberries OR peaches

Heat oven to 250°. Beat egg whites to a soft foam, preferably with an electric beater. Add salt, vanilla and vinegar. Continue beating for a short time until a moderately stiff foam is formed. Add ¼ of the sugar and beat. Repeat the addition of about ¼ of the sugar and beat as before. When all the sugar has been added in this way, finish beating until mixture forms standing peaks. Heap onto baking tray or oven proof dish. The cake should measure about 9″ in diameter. Bake for 1½ to 2 hours. When cooked, color will be very pale fawn and center texture will be marshmallowy. Leave cake to cool in oven with door open.

Cover with ¾ pint whipped cream and decorate with sliced strawberries or peaches, etc. For a typical New Zealand dish, serve with kiwi fruit or passion fruit.

Nyra Harriman

PEAR CRUMB CAKE

OVEN: 325° 45 minutes

1½ cups graham cracker crumbs
3 tablespoons butter OR margarine, melted
1 teaspoon grated lemon rind
¾ cup sugar
1 — 8 ounce package cream cheese
juice of 1 lemon

2 eggs
1 teaspoon vanilla
tart red jelly
1 cup sour cream
1 can (1 pound, 13 ounces) pear
   halves, drained

Mix crumbs, 2 tablespoons of sugar and melted butter together. Set aside 2 tablespoons of this mixture. Press remaining crumbs evenly over bottom and sides of 9 or 10″ spring form pan, or pie pan. Blend cream cheese, ½ cup sugar, lemon rind and juice. Beat in eggs, one at a time. Carefully pour into crumb crust. Bake at 325° for 45 minutes.

Blend sour cream, vanilla and 2 tablespoons of sugar together. Spread over cream cheese layer. Sprinkle with reserved crumb mixture. Arrange pears cut side up in sour cream. Bake at 325° for about 15 minutes. Let cool. Chill. Fill center of each pear with jelly.

May be baked without pears and topped instead with a fruit glaze.

Hutchie Altobello

Fresh eggs yield more volume and should be used in pound cakes, angel food cakes and sponge cakes.

PECAN DATE CAKE

OVEN: 300° 1 hour

1 quart shelled pecans, do not chop
1 cup sugar
1 cup flour
3 large OR 4 small eggs

3 rounded teaspoons baking powder
1 teaspoon vanilla
15 ounces dates, cut up

Beat eggs, one at a time, into sugar. Sift baking powder and flour. Add to egg and sugar mixture. Mix well. Add remaining ingredients. Fold in. Bake in tube pan or loaf pan for 1 hour at 300°. Pan should be greased and floured lightly.

For use during pecan season — especially for those who are not fond of traditional fruit cake. Slices well. Keeps for months.

Adelaide R. Snyder

PINEAPPLE COOKIE SHEET CAKE

OVEN: 350° 25 minutes

2 cups flour
2 cups sugar
2 eggs
2 teaspoons soda
1 — #2 can crushed pineapple, use
juice too

Frosting:
8 ounces cream cheese
½ stick oleo
1 cup powdered sugar
1 teaspoon vanilla

Mix together all ingredients. Blend well. Bake in oblong pan at 350° for 25 minutes. Pan should be greased and floured.

Blend cream cheese, oleo, sugar and vanilla together. Frost cake when cool. Refrigerate.

Marybelle Funnell

Confectioner's sugar will give a cake a fine-grained texture, but the cake will dry out sooner. Always sift confectioner's sugar before using; moisture absorbed by the cornstarch in it may cause lumps.

PIONEER ORANGE CAKE (1892)

OVEN: 350°

2 cups fresh Indian River orange
  juice
2 cups sugar
1 teaspoon grated fresh orange
  peel

Cake:
1 cup butter
2 cups sugar

6 eggs
3 cups all-purpose flour
½ teaspoon salt
2 teaspoons baking powder
1 cup milk
1 teaspoon vanilla
1 teaspoon grated fresh orange
  peel

Combine orange juice, sugar, and orange peel. Stir until all sugar is dissolved. DO NOT HEAT. Set aside.

Cream butter and sugar in a large bowl. Add eggs, one at a time, beating well after each addition. Mix flour, salt and baking powder together. Add flour and milk alternately to creamed batter, starting and ending with flour. Add vanilla and orange peel. Blend. Pour batter into a greased sheet pan 14 x 18 and bake in 350° oven. Test with cake tester.

Remove cake from oven when done and spoon orange juice mixture over hot cake at once. When cold, dust top of cake with 10X sugar very lightly. This 10X sugar forms a thin glaze.

This cake recipe was developed by my mother, Mrs. R. L. Brown, Sr. in 1892, when she was 20 years old. The glaze was added to the original recipe several years ago.

Mildred Brown Garrett

PISTACHIO CAKE

OVEN: 350° 45 minutes

1 box yellow cake mix
2 boxes pistachio pudding mix
½ cup oil
4 eggs

1 cup club soda
½ cup chopped cherries
½ cup chopped pecans
1 teaspoon almond extract

Combine all ingredients and mix well. Pour into greased and floured tube or Bundt pan.

Bake at 350° for 45 minutes or more.

Pamela B. Williams

In an emergency, ⅞ cup of solid vegetable shortening plus ½ teaspoon of salt can be substituted for butter. To measure the shortening, measure 1 cup, then remove 2 tablespoons; ⅞ cup will remain.

POPPY SEED CAKE

OVEN: 350° 50-55 minutes

2 bottles poppy seeds
⅔ cup evaporated milk
4 eggs
1½ cups cooking oil
1 teaspoon vanilla

3 cups flour
1½ teaspoons baking powder
1 teaspoon salt
2 cups sugar

Soak poppy seeds overnight in evaporated milk. Beat together eggs and sugar until creamy. Add oil and stir. Add poppy seed mixture and vanilla and mix well.

Blend flour, salt and baking powder together then add to above ingredients. Mix well. Bake at 350° for 50-55 minutes. Cake should be slightly underdone.

Jeanie Fowler

POT CHEESE CAKES

OVEN: 350° 30 minutes

YIELD: 8

Filling:
1 cup pot style cottage cheese
2 eggs, slightly beaten
⅓ cup milk
⅓ cup sugar
¼ teaspoon pure vanilla extract
¼ teaspoon ground coriander
⅔ cup currant jelly, melted

Dough:
½ cup sweet butter
1 cup sugar
1 tablespoon vegetable shortening
3 eggs
2 cups flour
1 teaspoon baking powder
½ teaspoon nutmeg

To prepare filling, combine all ingredients except jelly and beat with mixer until smooth. Set aside.

To prepare dough, cream butter, sugar and vegetable shortening. Add 2 eggs, one at a time. Add flour, baking powder and nutmeg; mix until blended. Grease eight 4½″ tartlet pans. Pat dough into pans making a depression in center. Fill hole with filling. Brush dough edge with one beaten egg. Bake for 30 minutes. Pour jelly into center.

An unusual cake of Russian origin.

The Committee

POUND CAKE

OVEN: 325° 1 hour

2 sticks butter OR margarine
2 cups sugar
2 cups flour
4 eggs

1 small can evaporated milk
1 teaspoon almond extract
1 teaspoon vanilla extract

Cream butter and sugar; add eggs and beat fairly well. Add flour and milk alternately to creamed mixture. Mix well. Add flavorings and blend. Bake at 325° for 1 hour.

Substitute almond flavoring with lemon if preferred.

Martha W. Rogers

PRUNE CAKE I

OVEN: moderate

1 cup sugar
3 tablespoons buttermilk
3 eggs
1 teaspoon soda

½ cup butter
1 cup nuts
1½ cups flour
1 cup cooked prunes, cut up

Combine all ingredients, adding prunes last. Blend well. Bake in a moderate oven, until done.

This cake can be iced with caramel or served with hard sauce or whipped cream.

Elizabeth Leonard

PRUNE CAKE II

OVEN: 300° 45-50 minutes

1 cup prunes, cooked and chopped
1 cup oil
2 cups sugar
3 eggs
1 cup buttermilk
1 teaspoon vanilla
2 cups flour
1 teaspoon soda
1 teaspoon cinnamon

½ teaspoon allspice
pinch of salt

Sauce:
½ cup buttermilk
½ teaspoon soda
1 cup sugar
2 teaspoons white corn syrup
1 stick butter
½ teaspoon vanilla

Cream sugar and oil, add eggs which have already been beaten. Blend. Add buttermilk, prunes and vanilla. Sift all dry ingredients together and add to mixture. Pour batter into greased 9 x 13 pan and bake 45-50 minutes at 300°.

For sauce, mix all ingredients except vanilla. Boil for 2 minutes and add vanilla. When cake is done, immediately pour over cake.

Peggy Prange

Never beat egg whites until they are dry. Whip only until the egg whites will stand high with a slight bend. Over-beaten dry egg whites are characterized by loss of shine, and stiff stright peaks.

PRUNE CAKE III

OVEN: 350° 40 minutes

Cake:
1½ cups sugar
¾ cup oil
3 whole eggs
1 cup buttermilk
1 teaspoon vanilla
2 cups self-rising flour
1 teaspoon salt
1¼ teaspoons soda
1 teaspoon nutmeg

1 teaspoon allspice
1 teaspoon cinnamon
1 cup cooked prunes, chopped
1 cup chopped nuts

Glaze:
1 cup sugar
1 tablespoon white corn syrup
½ cup buttermilk
1 stick margarine

Grease and flour one oblong pan or two 8″ square pans. Heat oven to 350°.
Measure all ingredients. Sift dry ingredients together. Mix ingredients in order given. Turn batter into pan and bake 40 minutes. While cake is baking, make glaze.
Glaze: combine all ingredients in saucepan and bring to a boil. Pour over cake in pan while cake is hot, and serve.

Carrie Sue Ray

PRUNELLA CAKE

OVEN: 350° 25 minutes

½ cup shortening
1⅔ cups flour
1 cup sugar
⅔ cup sour milk
⅔ cup stewed prunes
3 eggs
½ teaspoon soda
½ teaspoon salt
½ teaspoon cinnamon
½ teaspoon nutmeg

½ teaspoon allspice
½ teaspoon baking powder

Icing:
2 cups confectioners sugar
½ teaspoon cinnamon
¼ teaspoon salt
2 tablespoons butter
2 tablespoons prune juice
1 tablespoon lemon juice

Cream shortening and sugar. Add eggs, chopped prunes and stir in. Add milk to sifted dry ingredients. Blend with creamed mixture. Pour batter into 2 greased layer pans. Bake in moderate oven 350° about 25 minutes.
Icing: combine 1 cup of the sugar with butter. Blend. Add remaining sugar to mixture along with prune juice and lemon juice. Beat till creamy. Frost cake when cool.

Margaret McSwain

Butter can be softened quickly by inverting a small, heated pan over it or by grating it.

PUMPKIN CAKE I

OVEN: 325° 35-40 minutes

2 cups sugar
1 cup cooking oil
2 teaspoons soda
2 teaspoons cinnamon
½ teaspoon nutmeg
2 cups pumpkin
¾ cup raisins
1 cup nuts
½ teaspoon salt

2 eggs
2 cups all-purpose flour

Icing:
1 stick oleo
1 cup brown sugar
6 tablespoons cream
1 cup coconut
1 teaspoon vanilla

Cream together oil and sugar. Add eggs, one at a time. Blend well. Add sifted dry ingredients and beat. Add pumpkin. Beat. Dust raisins and nuts with flour and add to mixture. Bake in 13 x 9 x 2 pan at 325° for 35-40 minutes.

Mix icing ingredients in saucepan. Bring to a boil. Boil for 1 minute. Remove from heat and beat until mixture thickens. Cool and ice cake.

Virginia Cravens

PUMPKIN CAKE II

OVEN: 350° 30-35 minutes

2 cups sugar
2 cups canned pumpkin
4 eggs
1¼ cups oil
2 cups sifted, plain flour
2 teaspoons soda
2 teaspoons cinnamon
2 teaspoons baking powder
1 teaspoon salt

½ cup nuts, chopped
½ cup flaked coconut

Frosting:
1 stick butter
8 ounces cream cheese
1 box confectionery sugar
1 teaspoon vanilla
½ cup nuts, chopped
½ cup flaked coconut

Mix sugar, oil, pumpkin, and eggs. Blend well. Add remaining ingredients and blend. Pour batter into three greased and floured layer pans. Bake at 350° for 30-35 minutes. Test for doneness. Cool and frost.

For frosting, cream butter and cheese with remaining ingredients. Frost cool cake.

Jane DuBois

The shape of a pan specified in a recipe is not important, but the surface area of the pan is. Different pans may be substituted as long as the total surface area is about the same. The substituted pan may be deeper than the pan originally called for, but never shallower.

RED VELVET CAKE

OVEN: 350° 30 minutes

½ cup shortening
2 eggs
2 ounces red food coloring
1 teaspoon vanilla
2½ cups sifted cake flour
1 teaspoon soda, level
1½ cups sugar
2 teaspoons cocoa
1 teaspoon salt

1 cup buttermilk
1½ teaspoons vinegar

Frosting:
¼ cup butter
8 ounces cream cheese
1 pound powdered sugar
vanilla
pecans, optional

Cream together shortening and sugar. Add eggs, blend well. Make paste of cocoa and food coloring and add to creamed mixture. Mix salt and vanilla with buttermilk and add alternately with flour to creamed mixture. Mix soda and vinegar together and fold into mixture. DO NOT BEAT. Bake in two 9" layer pans for 30 minutes at 350°.

You may substitute 1 cup sweet milk mixed with 1 tablespoon vinegar for the buttermilk.

Frosting: blend butter and cheese together. Fold in sugar and beat until smooth. Add vanilla and blend.

Gwen Hale

RED VELVET CAKE
(WALDORF)

OVEN: 350° 30 minutes

½ cup shortening
1½ cups sugar
2 eggs
2 ounces red food coloring
2¼ cups plain flour
1 teaspoon salt, scant
2 tablespoons cocoa
1 teaspoon vanilla
1 teaspoon soda
1 cup buttermilk

1 tablespoon vinegar
1 teaspoon butter flavoring (optional)

Frosting:
3 tablespoons flour
1 cup butter, oleo OR shortening
1 teaspoon vanilla
1 cup milk
1 cup granulated sugar

Cream shortening, sugar and eggs. Make a paste with coloring and cocoa and add to mixture. Add salt and flour with buttermilk and vanilla. Alternately add soda and vinegar and don't beat hard, just blend. Bake 30 minutes at 350°, using greased and floured 8" pans (2). Layers may be split to make four layers.

Frosting: cook flour and milk on low heat until thick. Cool. Cream sugar and butter and vanilla until fluffy. Add to flour/milk mixture. Beat until like whipped cream. Spread on layers. Sprinkle with coconut or nuts if desired. Keep cake cool.

The Committee

ROBERT E. LEE CAKE

OVEN: 350° 30 minutes

1 cup shortening
2 cups sugar
1 teaspoon vanilla
4 egg yolks
3 cups flour
¼ teaspoon salt
3 teaspoons baking powder
1 cup milk
4 stiffly beaten egg whites

Frosting:
3 egg whites, unbeaten
2¼ cups white corn syrup
1½ teaspoons vanilla
pinch of salt
meat of 2 coconuts, shredded
½ cup lemon juice
½ cup orange juice

Thoroughly cream shortening and sugar. Add egg yolks and vanilla. Beat well. Add sifted dry ingredients alternately with milk. Fold in egg whites. Bake in three wax-paper lined 8″ round cake pans at 350° for 30 minutes. Beforehand, shred coconut. Also squeeze lemon and orange juices. Do not mix; set aside.

For frosting, combine egg whites, corn syrup and salt in top of double boiler. Place over rapidly boiling water (turned to low) and beat with mixer until it stands in stiff peaks (5-7 minutes). Remove from boiling water, add vanilla, and beat until thick enough to spread.

To assemble, place bottom layer on plate. Spread with lemon juice and orange juice generously. Then spread a layer of frosting. Sprinkle fresh coconut on top of frosting. Repeat with each layer. Do not move cake until set as it is approximately 8″ high.

Dolly Markham

RUBY SLIPPER

OVEN: 350° 45-50 minutes

1 package, 2-layer size, yellow cake mix
1 cup (½ pint) sour cream
¼ cup water

2 eggs
1 package (3 ounce) raspberry flavored gelatin mix

Combine cake mix, sour cream, water and eggs in large bowl. Blend, then beat at medium speed for 2 minutes; until creamy. Spoon ⅓ of batter into well-greased and floured 10″ fluted tube pan. Sprinkle with ½ of gelatin. Repeat layers, spreading the last ⅓ cake mix over gelatin. Bake at 350° for 45-50 minutes, or until cake springs back when lightly pressed. Cool in pan for 5 minutes. Remove from pan and cool on rack. Sprinkle with confectioners sugar if desired.

Dorothy Bateman

Condensed milk is whole milk, sweetened, then evaporated. Evaporated milk is whole milk with about one-half of the water content removed. No sweetening is added to evaporated milk.

SOCK-IT-TO-ME CAKE

OVEN: 375° 1 hour

1 box butter yellow cake mix
4 eggs
½ pint sour cream
¾ cup oil
1 cup chopped pecans

½ cup sugar
1 teaspoon vanilla
4 tablespoons brown sugar
2 teaspoons cinnamon

Combine cake mix, sugar, eggs, sour cream, oil, pecans and vanilla together. Blend well. Grease and flour tube pan. Pour half of batter into pan. Mix brown sugar and cinnamon together. Sprinkle over batter in pan, then pour remainder of batter into pan. Bake 1 hour at 375°.

Mrs. Winfield Brown

SOUR CREAM COCONUT CAKE

OVEN: as package directs

1 package yellow cake mix
2 cups sugar
1 — 16 ounce container sour cream

12 ounces coconut
1½ cups whipped topping

Bake cake as package directs using 2 layer pans. When cake is cool, split layers.

Combine sugar, sour cream and coconut and blend well. Chill. Reserve 1 cup of this mixture.

To assemble cake, spread coconut mixture between layers.

Take cup of reserved mixture and mix with whipped topping. Spread this mixture on top and sides of cake. Place cake in airtight container and refrigerate for 3 days.

Ann Tedder

SOUR CREAM POUND CAKE

OVEN: 300° 1½ hours

2 sticks butter
3 cups sugar
6 large eggs
1 teaspoon vanilla
¼ teaspoon almond extract

1 teaspoon lemon extract
3 cups plain flour
¼ teaspoon salt
¼ teaspoon soda
1 cup sour cream

Cream together butter and sugar. Beat in eggs, two at a time. Add vanilla, almond and lemon. Sift flour salt and soda together. Beat in alternately with 1 cup sour cream. Pour into greased and floured tube pan and bake at 300° for about 1½ hours.

This cake will be very thick and it will make a large cake.

Blanche A. Hunt

SOUTHERN GEORGIA CHOCOLATE POUND CAKE

OVEN: 325° 1½ hours

3 cups flour
3 cups sugar
1 cup cocoa
3 teaspoons baking powder
1 teaspoon salt

2 sticks butter OR margarine (1 cup)
1½ cups milk
3 teaspoons vanilla
3 eggs
¼ cup light cream

Sift dry ingredients together in the bowl with electric mixer. Make a well in the center of the ingredients and add butter, milk, and vanilla. Beat the mixture for 5 minutes. Add the eggs, one at a time, and add the cream; beating mixture thoroughly after each addition. Pour batter into a well oiled 10" tube pan and bake at 325° for 1½ hours, or until the cake tests done. Cool cake completely on a wire rack and remove it from the pan.

Lucy Willey

SPANISH SHERRY CAKE

OVEN: 350° 1 hour   YIELD: 1 cake, about 8 servings

1½ cups sugar
¾ cup water
¾ cup cream sherry
1½ quarts pound cake cubes (one 12 ounce cake)

¾ cup pecan halves
4 egg yolks
1 teaspoon almond extract (optional)
¼ teaspoon salt

Combine sugar and water in a saucepan. Bring to a boil. Reduce heat and simmer, uncovered, for 10 minutes. Cool. Combine half the syrup with sherry and cake cubes, tossing lightly just to mix. Grind pecans in electric blender or nut grinder. Add pecans, egg yolks, almond extract and salt to remaining half of syrup. Heat, stirring often over medium heat just until it begins to bubble, about 5 minutes.

To assemble cake, layer cube mixture in bottom of buttered 1 quart fancy mold. Top with ⅓ of pecan mixture. Repeat layering twice. Bake at 350° for 1 hour or until top is golden and crusty. Cool ½ hour, loosen sides with knife and invert onto plate. Cover. This cake should be aged in the refrigerator for a day or two, wrapped in aluminum foil. The flavor develops better that way. Serve with puffs of whipped cream, additional pecans and some chocolate curls if desired.

The Committee

Recipes calling for a 9 or 10 inch tube pan can be baked in a flat 13x9x2 pan. If in doubt about the pan size, measure from the inside edges. Measure volume by filling the pan with water, using an 8-ounce measuring cup.

STRAWBERRY GLAZED CHEESECAKE

OVEN: 350° 25 minutes

1 pound cream cheese
½ teaspoon vanilla
⅔ cup sugar
3 eggs
graham cracker crumbs OR prepared graham cracker crust
1 cup sour cream
1 teaspoon vanilla

4 tablespoons sugar

Glaze:
1 pint strawberries
¼ cup water
½ cup sugar
1½ tablespoons cornstarch
¼ cup water

Cream cheese, beat in sugar and vanilla and eggs, one at a time. Pour into pan which has been greased and dusted with Zwieback crumbs or graham cracker crumbs. (Or prepared crust.) Bake at 350° for 25 minutes.

Mix together sour cream, vanilla, and 4 tablespoons sugar. Spread on top of baked cheese cake and return cake to oven for 5-10 minutes. Remove and let cake cool.

Mash ½ cup of the strawberries. Boil mashed berries with water and sugar. Then add cornstarch which has been mixed in water. Cook, stirring constantly until thick. Cool. Add remaining berries. Spread over cheesecake and chill.

Betty Bleech

STRAWBERRY SPICE CAKE

OVEN: 350° 35 minutes

⅓ cup shortening
1 cup dark brown sugar
2 eggs
1 teaspoon salt
1¾ cups self-rising flour
1 teaspoon cinnamon

½ teaspoon cloves
¼ teaspoon nutmeg
¼ teaspoon ginger
¾ cup milk
1 cup strawberry preserves

Blend shortening with sugar, salt and eggs. Beat well. Sift flour with spices and add to egg mixture. Add milk and preserves. Beat until well blended. Pour into greased, shallow 8½" square pan. Bake in preheated oven at 350° for about 35 minutes, or until silver knife inserted into cake comes out clean.

Peggy Hoskins

Cardamon, the dried ripe fruit of a large herb, can be combined with lemon rind or almonds to make a delicious pound cake.

SURPRISE CAKE

OVEN: 350° 25-30 minutes

1 package yellow, butter cake mix
   (no substitute)
½ cup oil
4 eggs
1 can mandarin oranges, use juice
   and oranges

Frosting:
1 — 20 ounce can sweetened crushed
   pineapple, undrained
1 package instant vanilla pudding
1 — 9 ounce carton whipped topping

Mix ingredients in large bowl. Beat at medium speed until well blended, about 5 minutes. Bake in three 9″ cake pans at 350° for 25-30 minutes. Cool

Combine crushed pineapple and pudding mix, blend well. Add whipped topping and fold in well. Spread frosting between cooled layers of cake. Also, cover top and sides of cake. Refrigerate overnight, then serve.

Eddie B. Bishop

SYRUP CAKE

OVEN: 350° 55 minutes

¼ cup butter
1 cup sugar
3 eggs
1 cup milk
2 cups cane syrup

4 cups plain flour
2 teaspoons soda
1 teaspoon cinnamon
1 teaspoon allspice

Combine all ingredients in large bowl. Mix well. Pour batter into 13x9x2 greased pan which has been lined with greased wax paper. Bake at 350° for 55 minutes.

Delma Nettles

TEXAS CAKE

OVEN: 350° 25 minutes

2 cups plain flour
2 cups sugar
½ teaspoon salt
1 teaspoon baking soda
2 eggs
½ cup sour cream
4 tablespoons cocoa
2 sticks oleo

1 cup water

Icing:
6 tablespoons milk
4 tablespoons cocoa
1 stick oleo
1 box powdered sugar
1 cup chopped pecans
1 teaspoon vanilla

In large bowl combine flour, sugar, salt, soda, eggs and sour cream. Mix together. In saucepan boil cocoa, oleo and water, stirring constantly. Add boiled mixture to other ingredients. Batter will be thin. Bake in greased 9x13 pan for 25 minutes at 350°. Ice cake while warm.

Icing: In saucepan, mix milk, cocoa and oleo. Boil for 1 minute, watch and stir! Remove from heat and mix in powdered sugar, pecans and vanilla.

This is a very moist cake. Icing tastes like cooked fudge.

Eileen Schiavone

TEXAS SHEET CAKE

OVEN: 350° 20 minutes

2 cups flour
2 cups sugar
1 teaspoon baking soda
⅛ teaspoon salt
1 cup water
4 tablespoons unsweetened cocoa
2 sticks margarine
2 eggs
½ cup + 1 tablespoon buttermilk

1 teaspoon vanilla

Frosting:
1 stick margarine
3 tablespoons cocoa
6 tablespoons buttermilk
1 teaspoon vanilla
¾ to 1 pound powdered sugar
¼ to ½ cup chopped nuts

Sift together flour, sugar, soda and salt. In saucepan, boil rapidly water, cocoa, and margarine. Add wet mixture to dry ingredients. Beat in eggs. Add buttermilk and vanilla. Bake in greased and floured cookie sheet for 20 minutes at 350°.

For frosting, place margarine, cocoa, and buttermilk in a saucepan and bring to a rapid boil. Add vanilla, powdered sugar and chopped nuts. Blend well.

Pour frosting over cake while still warm.

If refrigerated, cake will last longer. A little goes a long way.

Ann Broom

VALENTINE PARTY CAKE

YIELD: 16 servings

1 large, store bought, angel cake
  ring
1 — 6 ounce package strawberry gelatin

2 cups boiling water
1 pound package frozen strawberries
1 pint whipping cream

Break cake into pieces and place in large bowl. In another bowl, put gelatin. Pour boiling water in and stir to dissolve gelatin. Stir in frozen strawberries in hot gelatine mixture. As strawberries melt, mixture will thicken. Place bowl with strawberry/gelatin mixture in refrigerator to thicken. When mixture reaches jam-like stage, pour over cake pieces and mix well. Fold in beaten cream (sweetened). Oil or spray large angel cake pan with salad oil and put cake into pan. Refrigerate for 24 hours. Remove from pan and slice.

Peg Beaudoin

VANILLA WAFER STACK CAKE

1 large box vanilla wafers
2 cups whipping cream

4 tablespoons liquid chocolate
2 tablespoons sugar

Whip the cream until light and fluffy. Add sugar and chocolate and dip wafers, one by one into the cream. Stack wafers, making a round, square, or oval cake. Let stand in refrigerator overnight, or make early in the morning for dinner party that evening. When sliced, it looks like many tiny layers of cake. The layers soften to make a very interesting cake.

This may be served with a scoop of chocolate ice cream.

Aggie Counts

WACKY CAKE

OVEN: 350° 35-40 minutes

3 cups flour, sifted
2 cups sugar
1 tablespoon salt
2 tablespoons soda
⅔ cup cocoa

2 teaspoons vanilla
2 teaspoons vinegar
⅔ cup salad oil
2 cups water

Mix ingredients any way you care to; that's what is "wacky" about this recipe. Bake in 3 round cake pans or one 12x18 oblong pan at 350° for 35-40 minutes. Use touch method to test for doneness.

Frost with your favorite icing or serve with ice cream and fudge sauce.

I like this cake recipe because you can make half of the recipe if you are on a diet.

Jesse Backus Guhse

WHITE FRUIT CAKE I

OVEN: 250° 3 hours

5 eggs
½ pound butter
1 cup sugar
1¾ cups flour
½ teaspoon baking powder

¾ pound candied cherries
1 pound candied pineapple
4 cups pecans
1 tablespoon vanilla
1 teaspoon lemon extract

Chop nuts and fruit to medium size pieces. Dredge fruit and nuts with a small part of the flour.

Cream butter and sugar together until light and fluffy. Add well beaten eggs and blend well. Sift remaining flour and baking powder together. Fold into creamed mixture. Add fruit and nuts and blend. Pour batter into greased, paper lined 10" tube pan. Place in cold oven and bake at 250° for 3 hours. Cool in pan on cake rack. Wrap in foil.

Thelma Glatz

WHITE FRUIT CAKE II

OVEN: 250° 3 hours

5 large eggs
½ pound butter
1 cup white sugar
1¾ cups all-purpose flour
½ teaspoon baking powder
1 pound candied cherries

1 pound candied pineapple
4 cups shelled pecans
1½ fluid ounces pure vanilla extract
1½ fluid ounces pure lemon extract

Cream butter well and add sugar, creaming until light and fluffy. Add eggs, which have been beaten by rotary egg-beater. Chop nuts and fruit, mix with a portion of the flour. Sift remaining flour and baking powder together and add to butter and egg mixture. Add fruit and nuts and flavoring. Pour into greased and paper lined tube pan. Place in cold oven and bake at 250° for 3 hours.

This cake weighs 5 pounds when baked.

Marie C. Box

ZUCCHINI CAKE

OVEN: 350° 1 hour

3 large eggs
2 cups sugar
1 cup vegetable oil
2 cups grated, peeled, raw zucchini
2 teaspoons vanilla
3 cups flour

1 teaspoon salt
¼ teaspoon baking powder
¼ teaspoon baking soda
3 teaspoons cinnamon
1 cup chopped walnuts OR pecans

In large bowl combine eggs, sugar, oil, zucchini and vanilla. Mix all ingredients well. In separate bowl, blend flour, salt, baking powder and soda and cinnamon. Add dry ingredients to zucchini mixture. Mix well. Add nuts and pour batter into well greased loaf pans. Bake at 350° for 1 hour.

Carol R. Lyons

BUTTER FLUFF FROSTING

1½ cups butter
1½ cups sugar
1½ teaspoons vanilla

1½ cups milk
6 tablespoons flour

Mix milk and flour and cook over medium heat, stirring constantly until thickened. Cool completely. Beat butter and sugar until fluffy. Add vanilla and milk mixture to butter and sugar. Beat on high speed for 10 minutes.

This frosting is delicious on any flavor cake or cupcakes. It never fails to bring a compliment because it is light and not too sweet. It also freezes well.

Nancy Maxwell

BUTTER ICING

1 cup butter
2½ cups powdered sugar
1 egg yolk

coffee extract, to taste
¼ cup black coffee, if needed

Wash butter in cold water to free it from salt. Pat it to remove all water, then beat it into a cream. Add egg yolk and gradually blend in powdered sugar. Add enough coffee extract to give desired flavor. The tint of frosting should be that of strong coffee with cream. Add black coffee if needed.

One or two squares of melted chocolate may be used instead of coffee.

This recipe came from my great-grandmother, Mamie Oliver. Approximate date — 1875.

Sheila Grose

Poppy seeds, blended with honey and a bit of lemon juice into a paste form makes a quick tart or cake filling.

DOROTHY'S COCONUT FROSTING

3 egg whites, unbeaten
2¼ cups sugar
7½ tablespoons cold water

2¼ teaspoons light corn syrup
1½ teaspoons vanilla
1 can coconut

Beat egg whites, sugar, water and corn syrup in upper part of double boiler. Beat with rotary egg beater until mixed thoroughly. Place over rapidly boiling water and beat constantly with egg beater. Cook for 7 minutes or until frosting stands in peaks.

Remove from heat, add vanilla and beat until thick enough to spread. Fold in ½ can of coconut. Spread on cooled cake. Sprinkle remainder of coconut on cake while frosting is still soft.

Makes enough frosting to frost the tops and sides of 3 layers.

Dorothy Koske

FAVORITE FUDGE FROSTING

¼ cup cocoa
½ cup milk
1 cup sugar

2 tablespoons butter
⅛ teaspoon salt
1 teaspoon vanilla

Cook to a rolling boil. When a soft ball forms in cold water remove from heat. Add butter and vanilla.

This also makes a very good candy recipe.

Natalie Myers

ICING FOR HUNGARIAN WALNUT TORTE
(MOCHA ICING)

1⅔ cups confectioners sugar
1-2 tablespoons cocoa
¼-½ cup butter

¼ teaspoon salt
3 tablespoons strong, hot coffee
1 teaspoon vanilla OR rum

Sift together sugar and cocoa. Beat butter until creamy, adding sugar mixture gradually. Blend until creamy. Add salt and hot coffee. Beat for 2 minutes. Add flavoring and let stand for 5 minutes. Beat well and spread.

Helen Bullock

MOTHER'S CARAMEL ICING

2 cups light brown sugar
½ cup butter

½ cup canned milk

Mix ingredients in saucepan and stir until mixture starts to cook. Cook for 5 minutes. Remove from heat and beat until it is the proper consistency to spread. If icing should get too thick to spread, add a little more milk.

Ginger Doyle

NEVER-FAIL FROSTING

1 cup sugar
¼ teaspoon cream of tartar
2 egg whites

⅓ cup boiling water
1 teaspoon vanilla

In large mixing bowl combine sugar, cream of tartar and egg whites. Beat well and add boiling water. Beat mixture until stiff and add vanilla. Blend well.

Mrs. Forest Pearce

TOPPINGS FOR CHEESECAKE
(CHERRY, PINEAPPLE)

for cherry glaze:
1 pound can red cherries
½ cup sugar
2 tablespoons cornstarch
4 drops red food coloring
1 cup liquid (see directions)

for pineapple glaze:
1 small can crushed pineapple
  (about 2 cups)
dash of salt
¼ cup sugar
2 tablespoons butter
4 tablespoons cornstarch (approximately)
½ cup water

Reserve cherry liquid and add enough water to make 1 cup. Mix sugar and cornstarch, add to liquid. Cook in saucepan until thickened. Remove from heat and stir in food coloring and cherries. Pour over cool cheesecake.

Mix together all ingredients using just enough cornstarch to thicken mixture. Pour on top of cooled cheesecake.

Gladys Grammer

WHIPPED CREAM ICING

1½ cups cold milk
3 tablespoons cornstarch
½ cup sugar

1 stick margarine
½ cup shortening
1 teaspoon vanilla

Stir cornstarch into milk. Blend well. Cook in saucepan until thick. Place in refrigerator until very cold (about 2 hours or overnight). Cream together margarine, shortening and sugar. Add vanilla. Then add cold milk and cornstarch mixture. Beat until fluffy.

Great on spice cake, devilsfood cake, or strawberry shortcake.

Gladys Grammer

COOKIES AND CANDIES

COOKIES

CANDIES

ALMOND CHRISTMAS COOKIES

OVEN: 350° 8 minutes

1 pound sweet butter, unsalted
¾ cup granulated sugar
2 tablespoons vanilla
3½ cups flour

½ pound ground almonds, about 2
cups
confectioners sugar

Let butter stand out until soft. Cream softened butter and sugar. Add vanilla, then flour and nuts. Roll into ¼" thick dough or put through a cookie press. Bake in 350° oven until slightly brown, about 8 minutes. When cool, sprinkle with confectioners sugar.

I prefer to use a cookie press with these delicate cookies. This recipe can be cut in half.

Nanci Miller

ANNA'S SWEDISH COOKIES

OVEN: 350° 8-10 minutes

1 cup butter, softened
2 cups flour
⅓ cup heavy cream

Filling:
1 egg yolk

¾ cup confectioners sugar
¼ cup butter
vanilla, a drop or two
flour
granulated sugar

Place butter, flour and heavy cream in a bowl and mix until it forms a dough. Chill. Roll dough out to ⅛" thickness on floured surface. Cut out with a small round cookie cutter. Drop each cookie, one side only, in granulated sugar. Place cookies on cookie sheet and prick with a fork. Bake in 350° oven about 8-10 minutes. They burn easily, so watch closely. Blend filling ingredients and place between two cookies at a time.

Carol I. Browder

APPLE HERMITS

OVEN: 350° 12-15 minutes

1 cup seedless raisins
1 cup shortening
1½ cups brown sugar
¼ cup molasses
3 unbeaten eggs
3½ cups sifted flour
1 cup chopped, peeled apples

½ teaspoon salt
1 teaspoon baking soda
3 teaspoons cinnamon
½ teaspoon ground cloves
½ teaspoon nutmeg
1 cup walnut meats

Rinse raisins in hot water and drain on paper towel. Cream shortening with brown sugar until mixture is light and fluffy. Add molasses, blend. Add unbeaten eggs, one at a time, beating after each addition. Sift together flour, salt, baking soda and spices. Add flour mixture to molasses mixture; mix lightly. Stir in walnuts, apples and raisins. Mix well. Drop by spoonfuls on greased cookie sheet and bake in moderate oven, 350°, for 12-15 minutes.

Elizabeth Leonard

BACK TO NATURE COOKIES

OVEN: 350° 8-10 minutes

1⅔ cups whole wheat flour
¾ teaspoon baking soda
¾ teaspoon cinnamon
¼ teaspoon salt
¼ teaspoon nutmeg
¼ cup oil
¼ cup honey

¼ cup black molasses
1 egg
1 mashed banana
1 cup oats
1 cup mixture millet, wheat germ, bran, sesame seeds, sunflower seeds and raisins

Combine all ingredients. Bake on greased cookie sheet for 8-10 minutes in 350° oven.

Jerrie Faircloth

BLONDE BROWNIES

OVEN: 350° 20-25 minutes   YIELD: 2 dozen

1 cup sifted flour
½ teaspoon baking powder
⅛ teaspoon soda
½ teaspoon salt
½ cup chopped nuts

⅓ cup melted butter
1 cup brown sugar, firmly packed
1 slightly beaten egg
1 teaspoon vanilla
½ cup chocolate chips

Measure sifted flour, baking powder, soda and salt; sift again. Add nuts, mix well and set aside.

Add brown sugar to melted butter, mix well and cool slightly. Add beaten egg and vanilla to butter-sugar mixture; blend. Add the flour mixture, a small amount at a time to the butter-sugar-egg mixture, mixing well after each addition.

Spread batter in a greased 9 x 9 x 2″ pan and sprinkle chocolate chips over the top. Bake in 350° oven for 20-25 minutes. Cool and cut into bars.

Joyce Money

BOILED COOKIES

YIELD: about 4 dozen

4 cups sugar
2 sticks oleo
1 cup milk
5 cups quick oats
5 tablespoons cocoa

1 teaspoon vanilla flavoring
1 pinch salt
peanut butter OR
coconut OR
chopped nuts

Mix sugar and cocoa in large boiler. Add milk and melted oleo. Stir, then add salt and vanilla. Boil for 1½ minutes while stirring. Remove from heat and add oats and other desired ingredients. Drop cookies onto wax paper and let cool.

Never stir the sides of the boiler while boiling. I prefer using crunchy peanut butter.

Rhonda K. Myrick

BROWNIES

OVEN: 350° 20 minutes

4 eggs
2 cups sugar
1 cup butter
2 cups flour

4 tablespoons cocoa, heaping
1 cup nuts
2 teaspoons vanilla

Beat eggs, sugar and butter. Add flour, cocoa, nuts and vanilla. Bake for 20 minutes in 350° oven.

James Padgett

BROWNIES DELUXE

OVEN: 325° 25-30 minutes   YIELD: 6 dozen

1 cup butter OR margarine
4 — 1 ounce squares unsweetened chocolate
4 eggs
2 cup granulated sugar
1 cup brown sugar
1½ cups all-purpose flour
1 teaspoon baking powder
2 teaspoons vanilla extract
1 cup chopped pecans OR walnuts OR combination of both

5 ounces miniature marshmallows

Frosting:
½ cup butter OR margarine
1 cup sugar
3 — 1 ounce squares unsweetened chocolate
⅔ cup evaporated milk (one small can)
1 — 1 pound box powdered sugar
1 teaspoon vanilla extract

Melt chocolate and butter over warm water in top of double boiler. Beat eggs; add granulated and brown sugars, then flour sifted with baking powder. Stir in flavoring and nuts; then chocolate mixture. Turn into greased and lightly floured 15 x 10 x 1" pan and bake at 325° for about 25-30 minutes. Remove from oven, immediately spread marshmallows over top. While brownies are baking, prepare frosting.

Do not wash chocolate pot used in preparing brownies. Add to this pot, butter or margarine, sugar, chocolate squares and evaporated milk. Cook over boiling water until well blended. Beat in powdered sugar and vanilla. Pour immediately over hot marshmallow-covered brownies. Let set for 24 hours before cutting into 1" squares.

These will freeze beautifully, and may be prepared ahead of time.

Pat DuBose

BROWNIES, FUDGE

OVEN: 325° 30-35 minutes

½ cup butter
1 cup brown sugar
1 teaspoon vanilla
2 eggs

2 — 1 ounce squares unsweetened chocolate, melted
½ cup sifted flour
½ cup walnuts, chopped

Cream first three ingredients. Add eggs, beat. Blend in chocolate then stir in flour and nuts. Bake in greased 8 x 8 x 2" pan at 325° for 30-35 minutes. Cool. Frost with Fudge Frosting and top with nuts. Cut into squares.

Whole walnuts may be used on top.

Linda Brown

BUTTERBALLS

OVEN: 400° 14-16 minutes

1 cup margarine
½ cup powdered sugar
2¼ cups flour

1 teaspoon vanilla
¾ cup chopped pecans OR walnuts

Cream butter and sugar; add flour, vanilla and pecans. Mix well. Put in refrigerator for 2-3 hours. Roll into balls and bake on ungreased cookie sheet in 400° oven for 14-16 minutes until light brown. Roll in powdered sugar and store in tin container.

Nina Rogers

BUTTERSCOTCH OATIES

OVEN: 350° 10 minutes
YIELD: 5 dozen

1 — 6 ounce package butterscotch
   morsels
¾ cup butter OR margarine
2 tablespoons boiling water
1 teaspoon baking soda

2 cups quick cooking oats
1 cup sifted flour
¾ cup sugar
dash of salt

Preheat oven to 350°. Combine butterscotch bits and butter and melt over boiling water. Mix the 2 tablespoons boiling water with soda and add to butterscotch mixture. Gradually blend in remaining ingredients. Drop by slightly rounded teaspoonfuls onto cookie sheet. Bake at 350° for 10 minutes.

Helen George

CEREAL PEANUT BUTTER BARS

½ cup light corn syrup
¼ cup brown sugar
dash of salt
1 cup peanut butter
1 teaspoon vanilla
2 cups rice cereal

2 cup flaked corn cereal, lightly
   crushed
1 — 6 ounce package semi-sweet
   chocolate pieces OR butterscotch
   pieces

Combine sugar, syrup and salt in saucepan and bring to a boil. Stir in peanut butter. Remove from heat and add vanilla and cereals and chocolate or butterscotch pieces. Press mixture into a buttered 9 x 9 x 2" pan. Chill for at least 1 hour. Cut into squares.

Carra Adams

Cookies are best baked on buttered cookie sheets. Chill the dough first for easier handling.

CHOCOLATE CHIP COOKIES

OVEN: 350° 10-15 minutes

YIELD: 2 dozen

1¼ cups flour
1 teaspoon baking powder
½ teaspoon baking soda
¾ teaspoon salt
½ cup shortening

6 tablespoons sugar
6 tablespoons brown sugar
½ teaspoon vanilla
1 egg
½ to 1 cup chocolate chips

Sift flour, baking powder, soda and salt together in one bowl. Cream shortening; add vanilla and sugars; lastly, add egg. Mix creamed ingredients with dry ingredients. Add chocolate chips. Bake in 350° oven for 10-15 minutes or until light brown. Cookie sheets should be ungreased.

Melody Streeter

CHOCOLATE CREAM CHEESE BROWNIES

OVEN: 350° 40-45 minutes

YIELD: 16 squares

1 — 4 ounce package sweet cooking chocolate
2 tablespoons butter OR margarine
3 eggs
1½ teaspoons vanilla

1 cup sugar
½ cup all-purpose flour
½ teaspoon baking powder
½ cup chopped nuts
1 — 3 ounce package cream cheese, softened

Melt chocolate and butter, cool. In a bowl, beat together 2 eggs and 1 teaspoon vanilla; gradually add ¾ cup sugar. Continue beating until thick and lemon colored. Stir together flour, baking powder, and ¼ teaspoon salt; add to egg mixture. Beat well. Blend in chocolate mixture and nuts; set aside. Cream together cream cheese and ¼ cup sugar until fluffy. Blend in remaining egg and vanilla. Spread half of the chocolate mixture in a greased and floured 8 x 8 x 2″ baking pan. Pour cheese mixture over and top with remaining chocolate mixture. Swirl layers to marble. Bake in 350° oven for 40-45 minutes. Cool and cut into squares.

Mrs. Dale Cassens

Substitute two squares (two ounces) unsweetened chocolate plus two tablespoons sugar or one-third cup unsweetened cocoa plus two tablespoons sugar and two tablespoons butter or margarine for three ounces semi-sweet chocolate.

CHOCOLATE DELIGHT

OVEN: 325° 20 minutes

1 stick butter, softened
1 cup flour
1 cup chopped pecans
8 ounces cream cheese, at room
  temperature
1 cup confectioners sugar
1 small container whipped topping

2 small boxes instant chocolate
  pudding mix
3½ cups milk
2 small almond Hershey bars;
  shredded OR grated
1 large container whipped topping

Combine butter, flour and chopped pecans; press mixture on the bottom of a 9 x 13 pan. Bake in 325° oven approximately 20 minutes, until light golden brown.

Combine cream cheese, confectioners sugar, and small container whipped topping. Spread mixture on top of cooled crust.

Add milk to pudding mix, blend well; spread on top of cream cheese layer. Cover pudding with whipped topping from large container. Shred or grate candy bars and sprinkle over top. Refrigerate.

This is too good to be true.

Kathy McPadden

CHRISTMAS COOKIES

OVEN: 300°-325° 25 minutes

3 cups flour
1 teaspoon cinnamon
1 teaspoon cloves
1 teaspoon allspice
½ cup butter
1 cup brown sugar, firmly packed
4 eggs
5 tablespoons milk OR buttermilk

1 tablespoon soda, scant
⅔ cup whiskey
1 pound pineapple, candied
1 pound candied cherries, cut up
½ pound white raisins
¼ pound candied lemon peel
¼ pound candied orange peel
2 pounds broken pecans

Measure dry ingredients; re-shift 2½ cups flour with cinnamon, cloves and allspice. Cream butter and sugar; add eggs, one at a time, beating well after each addition. Add flour and liquids alternately to creamed mixture. Dissolve soda in milk, before adding liquids. Mix ½ cup flour with cut candied fruits and raisins. Add fruits to mixture and mix well. Add pecans; drop by teaspoons on greased cookie sheet. Bake at 300° to 325° for about 25 minutes.

Jean Finger

To keep cookies soft, just place a piece of bread in the cookie container.

CHRISTMAS ICE BOX COOKIES

OVEN: 350° 12 minutes

YIELD: about 5 dozen

1 cup butter OR margarine, softened
1 cup sugar
2 tablespoons milk
1 teaspoon vanilla OR rum extract

2½ cups sifted all-purpose flour
½ cup red candied cherries, chopped
½ cup finely chopped pecans
¾ cup flaked coconut

Cream together butter or margarine and sugar; blend in milk and vanilla. Stir in flour and mix well. Add candied cherries and nuts. Form mixture into 2 rolls approximately 2″ in diameter and 8″ long. Roll in coconut. Wrap in wax paper and chill overnight. Slice ¼″ thick. Place on ungreased cookie sheet and bake in 350° oven for 12 minutes or until edges are golden. Let stand for 5 minutes and remove to cooling rack. Store in air-tight containers.

Ruth Huggins

COCONUT COOKIES

OVEN: 350° 15 minutes

1 cup sugar
1 cup shredded coconut

3 egg whites, whipped until stiff

Mix sugar and coconut; add beaten egg whites and mix. On wax paper-lined cookie sheet, drop by teaspoonfuls about 2″ apart. Bake at 350° for approximately 15 minutes.

Mrs. F. Keller

CONGO SQUARES

OVEN: 300° 25-30 minutes

YIELD: 50 servings

⅔ cup shortening OR butter
1 box light brown sugar
3 eggs
2¾ cups sifted flour, self-rising

1 teaspoon vanilla flavoring
2 tablespoons water
1 cup nuts
1 large package chocolate chips

Melt shortening and add brown sugar. Stir until well mixed. Add one egg at a time and beat well. Add remaining ingredients and mix well. Pour into greased pan and bake in 300° oven for 25-30 minutes. Cool and cut into squares. Baking time may take longer than 30 minutes.

Kim Hood

A basic cookie dough can be varied by cutting and shaping a number of different designs and by adding various fruits and nuts to the dough mixture.

CRESCENT COOKIES

OVEN: 350° 10-12 minutes

1 cup soft butter
¼ cup powdered sugar
1½ teaspoons water

2 teaspoons vanilla
2 cups flour
1 cup chopped pecans

Cream butter and powdered sugar until light and fluffy. Add water and vanilla; add flour and pecans, mixing well. Mixture will be soft. Form into small balls and bake in a 350° oven for 10-12 minutes. Roll in powdered sugar while still warm.

Barbara Kammeraad

CRESCENTS

OVEN: 250°

1½ sticks butter
2 teaspoons vanilla
¾ cup nuts

6 tablespoons confectioners sugar
2 cups sifted all purpose flour

Combine all ingredients and mix well. Shape as crescents on a greased pan. Bake in slow oven (about 250°) and let brown slightly. Roll when cool in confectioners sugar.

Blanche Hunt

CUPCAKE BROWNIES

OVEN: 325° 25 minutes

YIELD: 24 cupcakes

2 sticks oleo OR butter
1¾ cups granulated sugar
3 large eggs

4 — 1 ounce squares semi-sweet
  chocolate
1 cup plain flour
1 teaspoon vanilla
2 cups chopped pecans

Melt butter and chocolate. Mix sugar and flour together; add eggs, then add melted mixture. Add vanilla and pecans. Mix all ingredients together well and spoon into lined muffin tins. Bake in 325° oven for no longer than 25 minutes. Cool.

Glenda H. Shelfer

Melt chocolate with a bit of butter over very low heat or in a double boiler to keep the chocolate from burning. Your pan will also be easier to clean.

DATE BALLS

YIELD: 40-50 balls

½ cup oleo OR butter
1 cup light brown sugar
1 — 7½ ounce package dates, cut in
  small pieces
1 cup pecans OR walnuts, chopped

1 cup canned coconut
2 cups dry rice cereal
1 teaspoon vanilla
⅛ teaspoon salt
sifted powdered sugar

Mix first three ingredients and cook over low heat until mixture barely simmers. Simmer for 5 minutes; stir constantly. Remove from heat and add the next 5 ingredients. Mixture will be thick. Roll into small walnut-size balls, and roll in powdered sugar to coat.
I like using ½ light brown sugar and ½ dark brown sugar or all dark brown sugar may be used if desired.

Connie Wagers

DATE BARS

OVEN: 350° 20-25 minutes

1 cup nuts
1 cup pitted dates
1 cup powdered sugar
2 eggs, beaten

1 tablespoon lemon juice
¼ cup flour
1 tablespoon melted butter
½ teaspoon salt

Combine all ingredients and mix thoroughly. Turn into greased shallow pan to approximately ¼″ thick. Bake in moderate, 350° oven for 20-25 minutes. While hot, cut into strips and roll strips in powdered sugar.

N. Rogers

DATE FINGERS

1 egg
¾ cup sugar
¼ pound butter
1 cup chopped dates
2 cups rice cereal

½ cup broken pecans
dash of salt
1 teaspoon vanilla
flaked coconut

Cook egg, sugar, butter and dates until mixture is thick; then cool. Fold in rice cereal, nuts, vanilla and salt. Work all together and shape into fingers; roll in coconut. Cover and store in refrigerator.

Elizabeth Leonard

Recipes for cookies, fruit desserts, and cakes usually call for salt since salt improves the flavor a sweet dish. The same is true of sugar when added to salted dishes.

DATE NUT BARS I

OVEN: 350° 30 minutes

½ cup flour
¼ teaspoon salt
1 teaspoon baking powder
3 eggs
1 tablespoon butter
1 cup sugar

½ cup quick oatmeal
1 teaspoon vanilla
1½ cups dates, approximately 8 ounces
1 cup nuts

Sift flour, salt and baking powder together. Beat eggs with butter and sugar. Add flour mixture to egg mixture and beat well. Add oatmeal, vanilla, dates and nuts. Blend. Bake in jelly roll pan in 350° oven about 30 minutes. Cut while warm and sprinkle with powdered sugar if desired.

Mrs. Forest Pearce

DATE NUT BARS II

OVEN: 350° 25-30 minutes

¾ cup sifted flour
½ teaspoon baking powder
½ teaspoon salt
1 cup packed brown sugar

2 well-beaten eggs
2 tablespoons butter, melted
1 cup walnuts OR pecans, chopped
1 cup dates, chopped

Sift together flour, powder and salt into a large bowl. Add brown sugar and mix well. Blend in eggs and butter; mix thoroughly. Stir in nuts and dates.

Spread batter in well-greased 11 x 7" or 9 x 9" pan and bake in moderate, 350°, oven for 25-30 minutes. While warm, cut into bars. If desired, roll in confectioners sugar before serving, or sift confectioners sugar lightly over the top.

Ethel Peery

DATE SQUARES

OVEN: 325° - 350° 30 minutes

1 pound pitted dates
1 cup water
½ cup sugar
2 cups rolled oats
1 cup flour

1 cup brown sugar
1 teaspoon soda
½ teaspoon salt
¾ cup shortening OR margarine

Boil dates, water and sugar for 5 minutes or until soft. Cool.

Cut shortening into oats, flour, brown sugar, soda and salt. Spread ½ of shortening mixture in bottom of a 13 x 9" baking pan. Add a layer of the cooled date mixture then top with the balance of the dry mixture. Bake in 325° to 350° oven for about 30 minutes. Cut into small squares when cool. They keep well — if you hide them.

This is a very good recipe, and it is at least 75 years old.

Loretta W. Scott

DATE STICKS

OVEN: 250° 1 hour

3 egg yolks, beaten
1 teaspoon vanilla
1 cup sugar
1 cup flour
1 teaspoon baking powder

1 package dates, quartered
salt
1 cup nuts
3 egg whites, beaten stiff
confectioners sugar

Cut up nuts and mix in a large bowl with quartered dates. Separate eggs; place yolks in a large bowl and whites in another bowl. Add flour, baking powder and salt to the bowl with nuts and dates. Blend vanilla and sugar with egg yolks in the separate bowl. Beat egg whites until stiff. Add flour, nut, date mixture and egg whites alternately to the creamed egg yolk mixture.

Line a 9 x 9" baking pan with heavy brown paper and add mixture. Bake in a slow oven, approximately 250° for about 1 hour. Cut in rectangular shape and roll in confectioners sugar.

Mrs. Bruce E. Mills

DATE STRIPS

OVEN: 350° 30-40 minutes

3 eggs
1 cup sugar
1 cup flour
1 cup nuts, walnuts OR pecans

8 ounces dates, cut up
2 teaspoons baking powder
¼ teaspoon soda
1 teaspoon vanilla

Mix ingredients well in the order given. Grease brownie pan and add mixture. Bake in 350° oven for 30-40 minutes. Let cool on wire rack and cut into lengthy strips and roll each strip into powdered sugar.

Anita Smith

DREAM BARS

OVEN: 350° 30-35 minutes

YIELD: 24 bars

Crumb mixture:
½ cup butter
½ cup brown sugar
1 cup flour
Bar mixture:
1 cup brown sugar
1 teaspoon vanilla

½ teaspoon baking powder
1 cup coconut
2 tablespoons flour
2 eggs
¼ teaspoon salt
1 cup pecans, chopped

Combine butter, sugar, and flour until the mixture is the texture of coarse meal. Pat mixture into a buttered 9 x 9" pan. Bake for 10 minutes at 350° or until slightly browned.

Mix all bar ingredients together and pour over baked crumb layer. Return pan to oven and bake at 350° for 20-25 minutes or until brown. Cool and cut into bars.

This can be prepared ahead of time and frozen.

Celeta Arden

DIABETIC COOKIES

OVEN: 400° 10-15 minutes OR 425° 25 minutes

1½ cups quick cooking oatmeal, uncooked
1½ cups flour, whole wheat if preferred
⅔ cup melted butter OR margarine OR cooking oil
2 eggs, beaten

9 envelopes artificial sweetener
½ teaspoon salt
2 teaspoons baking powder
½ cup skim milk
1 teaspoon vanilla
¼ to ¾ cup raisins OR currants
1 teaspoon cinnamon
walnuts, optional

Dissolve sweetener in milk. Combine remaining ingredients and mix together with milk. Place dough on cookie sheets in small spoonfuls. Place a piece of walnut on top of each cookie, optional. Bake in 400° oven for 10-15 minutes. If you like crisp cookies, bake in 425° oven for 25 minutes.

The Committee

EASY BROWNIES

OVEN: 350° 20 minutes

2 cups sugar
½ cup butter
2 cups flour
½ cup milk
4 eggs
½ cup cocoa
½ teaspoon salt

1 teaspoon vanilla
½ cup chopped walnuts

Frosting:
½ cup cream (half & half)
1½ cups sugar
3 generous tablespoons butter

Place all of the brownie ingredients in a large mixing bowl and mix well. Grease a jelly roll pan approximately 10″ x 16″ and add batter. Bake for 20 minutes at 350°. Be careful not to overbake.
Prepare frosting. Bring ingredients to a boil and boil until they reach the soft-ball stage. Stir constantly. Cool.
When brownies are cool, frost.

Sheila M. Bielski

EASY DATE BARS

OVEN: 375° 20-25 minutes

½ cup biscuit mix
½ cup brown sugar
¼ teaspoon baking powder
1 egg

1 tablespoon milk
1 teaspoon vanilla
1 cup chopped dates
1 cup chopped nuts

Stir together biscuit mix, brown sugar, and baking powder. Add and mix thoroughly, egg, milk, vanilla; stir in dates and nuts. Blend well. Pour into 8 x 8″ greased pan and bake in 375° oven for 20-25 minutes.
Dough will be quite thick; you will probably have to pat it into the pan with your hands. This is a very easy recipe and always gets compliments.

Betty Dezzutti

EASY GINGERSNAPS

OVEN: 350° 10-12 minutes   YIELD: about 60 cookies

1 cup sugar
¾ cup liquid shortening
1 egg
4 tablespoons molasses
¾ teaspoon ginger

¾ teaspoon cinnamon
2 cups flour
2 teaspoons soda
½ teaspoon salt

Combine all ingredients and mix well. Refrigerate batter overnight.
Pull off small piece of dough, about the size of a walnut and roll ball in granulated sugar. Place on baking sheet and bake for 10-12 minutes at 350°. Cookies will flatten as they bake.

Dorothy E. Richwine

EBBA'S RASPBERRY SQUARES

OVEN: 350° 40 minutes

1 egg
1 cup flour
1 teaspoon baking powder
½ cup butter OR margarine
1 tablespoon milk
8 tablespoons raspberry jam

Topping:
1 egg, beaten
4 tablespoons butter OR margarine, melted
½ cup sugar
2 cups coconut
1 teaspoon vanilla

Beat egg; sift flour and baking powder into a bowl and work butter into flour mixture until it becomes mealy. Stir in beaten egg and milk. Mix well and spread over an 8″ square pan. Cover with jam. Spread topping over jam. Topping ingredients need only be mixed together to blend. Bake in 350° oven for 40 minutes. Cool, then refrigerate for better slicing.

Carol I. Browder

ELLA'S SWEDISH YUM YUM GEMS

OVEN: 350° 15-20 minutes

½ cup shortening
1 cup light brown sugar
1 egg
1 cup sour milk
2 cups flour
1 teaspoon soda

½ teaspoon salt
1 teaspoon cinnamon
1 teaspoon nutmeg
1 teaspoon cloves
1 cup raisins
½ cup chopped nuts

Blend shortening, brown sugar, egg and sour milk together. Sift dry ingredients and add to blended mixture. Stir in raisins and nuts. Drop by teaspoonfuls on greased cookie sheet. Bake in 350° oven for 15-20 minutes. Watch closely after 15 minutes.

Carol I. Browder

FILLED ICE BOX COOKIES

1 pound dates, chopped
½ cup sugar
1 cup nut meats
½ cup water
2 cups brown sugar
4 cups flour
1 cup shortening OR butter

3 eggs
½ teaspoon cinnamon
½ teaspoon salt
1 teaspoon soda
1 teaspoon baking powder
1 teaspoon vanilla

Cream brown sugar and shortening; add eggs and cinnamon, salt, soda, baking powder, vanilla and flour to form dough. Blend well. Divide dough and roll out into ⅛" thickness. Combine dates, ½ cup sugar, nut meats and water to make filling. Heat mixture until smooth. When cooled, spread filling over dough. Roll up like jelly roll. Wrap in wax paper. Store in refrigerator. When ready to bake, slice thin.

Esther Crist

FRESH LEMON CAKE BARS

OVEN: 350° 20-25 minutes

1 medium lemon
1 cup water
½ cup softened margarine

1 egg
1 package yellow cake mix
½ cup flaked coconut, optional

Cut a thin slice from each end of unpeeled lemon. Cut lemon in quarters lengthwise. With a sharp knife, remove white core. Remove all seeds and cut lemon into chunks. Place chunks and water in blender and puree. Add margarine and egg; whirl until blended. In a large bowl, combine cake mix and lemon mixture; beat with wooden spoon until well blended. Turn into greased 15 x 10 x 2 pan and spread evenly to edges; sprinkle with coconut. Bake in preheated oven at 350° for 20-25 minutes. Cool on a rack and cut into bars.

If desired, omit coconut and sift confectioners sugar over the top lightly.

Pearl M. Wyse

One splash equals one tablespoon; one dollop equals one tablespoon; and one lacing equals one tablespoon per one cup.

GERMAN CHOCOLATE BROWNIES

OVEN: 350° 35-40 minutes

YIELD: 16-20

1 — 4 ounce package German sweet
  chocolate
5 tablespoons butter
1 — 3 ounce package cream cheese
1 cup sugar
3 eggs
1 tablespoon flour

1½ teaspoons vanilla
½ teaspoon baking powder
¼ teaspoon salt
½ cup unsifted all-purpose flour
¼ teaspoon almond extract
½ cup chopped nuts

Melt chocolate with 3 tablespoons butter over low heat, stirring constantly. Cool. Cream remaining butter and cheese. Gradually add ¼ cup sugar; cream well after each addition. Blend in 1 egg, 1 tablespoon flour and ½ teaspoon vanilla. Set aside. Beat 2 eggs until thick and light in color. Gradually add ¾ cup sugar, beating until thickened. Add baking powder, salt and ½ cup flour. Blend in chocolate mixture, nuts, 1 teaspoon vanilla and almond extract. Spread about half of batter in greased 8 or 9″ square pan. Spread cheese mixture over top of batter; spoon on remaining chocolate batter. Zig-zag through batters with spatula to marble. Bake at 350° for 35-40 minutes. Cool, then cut.

Jean Ueltschi

GIUGUILENI COOKIES
(Italian)

OVEN: 350° 10 minutes

1 pound flour
1¼ teaspoons baking powder
¼ teaspoon salt
½ teaspoon vanilla
1 cup sugar

¼ cup milk
1 egg
½ pound shortening
sesame seeds

Add shortening to sifted flour, salt and baking powder. Add sugar, beaten egg, milk, and vanilla. Work dough until all ingredients are well mixed. Roll dough into strips and cover with sesame seeds. Cut into desired sizes and bake on a greased cookie sheet in 350° oven for 10 minutes or until golden brown.

These are good with coffee after dinner, or at mid-morning coffee break.

Mary M. Hardee

Recipes requiring a bit, a touch, or a pinch of salt are equal to 1/16 teaspoon.

GRANDMA'S OATMEAL COOKIES

OVEN: 325° 10-15 minutes

2 cups oatmeal	4 tablespoons milk
2 cups flour	2 eggs
1 cup sugar	pinch of salt
1 cup shortening	1 heaping teaspoon cinnamon
1 cup raisins	1 teaspoon vanilla
1 teaspoon soda	½ cup nuts, chopped

Cream butter and sugar. Add eggs, beating well after each addition. Sift flour and spices together thoroughly. Add milk and vanilla; blend. Then add flour mixture. Add oatmeal and nuts. Drop by teaspoonfuls onto buttered baking sheet and bake at 325° for about 10-15 minutes.

Sunny Gates

GRANDMOTHER'S OLD FASHIONED TEA CAKES

1 cup butter	2 teaspoons nutmeg
1 cup brown sugar	4½ to 5 cups plain flour
1 cup nut meats	1 teaspoon soda
3 eggs	1 teaspoon baking powder
¼ cup buttermilk	

Cream together butter and sugar. Add eggs and cream again, well. Add milk and other ingredients; roll as thin as desired and bake in moderate oven until golden brown and done.

Jane B. Howard

GRANDMOTHER'S SOFT GINGER COOKIES

1 cup molasses	1 cup sugar
1 cup shortening	1 tablespoon ginger
3 eggs	1 tablespoon cinnamon
1 cup boiling water	salt
5½ cups flour	cloves
1 tablespoon soda	

Mix all ingredients thoroughly and let stand for 30 minutes. Drop from teaspoon onto ungreased cookie sheet and bake in moderate oven until golden brown.

Jane B. Howard

Before measuring sticky liquids such as honey or syrup, oil the measuring cup and rinse it in hot water.

GREEK PECAN BARS

OVEN: 350° 35 minutes

1 pound sweet butter	2 tablespoons vanilla
8 tablespoons powdered sugar	2 tablespoons ice water
4 cups chopped pecans	1 pound powdered sugar
4 cups flour	

Cream butter thoroughly; add 8 tablespoons powdered sugar and continue creaming until all is blended. Mix nuts and flour and then add to creamed mixture gradually until well blended. Add vanilla and ice water and mix. Roll pieces of dough with palms of hand into 1" rolls or shaped like half moons. Bake on cookie sheet for 35 minutes in 350° oven or until golden brown. Put 1 pound powdered sugar on wax paper; place bars on sugar and sprinkle more on top.

Carol R. Lyons

HELLO DOLLIES

OVEN: 350° 25-35 minutes

1 cup graham cracker crumbs	1 — 6 ounce package butterscotch
1 stick butter, melted	chips
1 — 6 ounce package chocolate	1 can flaked coconut
chips	1 cup chopped pecans
	1 can condensed milk

Mix melted butter and graham cracker crumbs in the bottom of a 9" square pan to form crust. Mix all other ingredients together and pour on top of crust. Bake in 350° oven for 25-35 minutes.

Mrs. Winfield Brown

JERRY'S BARS

OVEN: 350° 20 minutes   YIELD: 18 bars

1 cup chopped pecans	⅛ teaspoon baking soda
2 tablespoons melted butter	2 eggs
1 cup brown sugar	1 teaspoon vanilla
5 tablespoons flour	

Melt butter in 8" square baking pan. In a small bowl, mix brown sugar, flour, baking soda and pecans. In a mixing bowl, beat eggs; stir in brown sugar mixture and vanilla. Pour mixture over melted butter in pan. Do not stir. Bake in 350° oven for 20 minutes. Remove from oven and let cool slightly. Cut into bars and sprinkle with powdered sugar.

These are simple to make. My sister and I started to bake these when we were about 9 years old.

Mary K. Montuoro

KOULOURAKIA
(Greek Butter Cookies)

OVEN: 350° 20-25 minutes

3 cups flour
½ teaspoon salt
¼ teaspoon nutmeg
¼ cup shortening
2 eggs
¼ cup whipping cream OR evaporated milk

2 tablespoons milk
2 teaspoons baking powder
¼ teaspoon cinnamon
1 stick butter
½ cup sugar
1 teaspoon vanilla
2 small boxes sesame seeds

Combine flour, baking powder, salt, cinnamon, and nutmeg; set aside. Cream butter and shortening; gradually add sugar and cream well. Set creamed mixture aside. Combine one egg and vanilla, add to creamed mixture and set aside.

Alternately add the ¼ cup whipping cream (or evaporated milk) and dry ingredients to the creamed mixture, blending well after each addition.

Grease a cookie sheet. Beat remaining egg and add 2 tablespoons milk and beat again. Place sesame seeds in a dish. Dip shaped cookies into egg and then into seeds. Place on cookie sheet with sesame seeds on top. Cookies should be about ½″ apart. Preheat oven to 350° and bake for 20-25 minutes.

Sophie Reeves

LEMON BARS

OVEN: 350° 45-50 minutes   YIELD: 30 small bars

2 cups sifted flour
½ cup sifted confectioners sugar
1 cup margarine
4 beaten eggs

2 cups granulated sugar
⅓ cup lemon juice
¼ cup sifted flour
½ teaspoon baking powder

Sift together flour and confectioners sugar; cut in melted butter until mixture clings together. Press mixture into a 13 x 9 x 2 greased pan. Bake at 350° for 20-25 minutes. Beat eggs, granulated sugar and lemon juice together. Sift together ¼ cup flour and baking powder; stir into egg mixture. Pour over baked crust, still hot from oven. Return pan to oven and bake for 25 minutes. Sprinkle with confectioners sugar. Cool, then cut into bars. Store in sealed container.

Mrs. Harold R. Runte

One-half cup evaporated whole milk and one-half cup water will substitute for 1 cup of fresh milk.

LIZZIES

OVEN: 275°-300° 25-30 minutes

YIELD: about 100

½ cup butter
1 cup brown sugar
4 large eggs
3 tablespoons milk
1 teaspoon soda
3 cups sifted flour
½ cup brandy OR rum
1 teaspoon nutmeg
1 teaspoon cloves

1 teaspoon cinnamon
1½ pounds chopped pecans
1 pound candied red and green cherries
1 pound candied pineapple
¼ pound citron, orange and lemon peel
1 pound golden OR white raisins

Dissolve soda in milk; set aside. Cream butter and sugar; add eggs, one at a time and beat well until mixed; blend in milk and soda mixture. Sift flour and spices together and add to creamed mixture, reserving ½ cup of mixture to flour cut fruit. Alternate sifted mixture with brandy, adding flour last. Fold in floured fruit. Drop mixture by teaspoonfuls onto greased cookie sheet and bake in slow oven, 275° to 300° for about 25-30 minutes.

Mixture freezes well. Store in tightly covered tin or cookie jar.

These may be served with hard sauce put on with cake decorator. I always freeze 1 pint of mixture and bake in July.

Mrs. T. N. McMullan

LOVE LACE COOKIES

OVEN: 350° 8 minutes

YIELD: 4-5 dozen

½ cup light brown sugar
½ cup corn syrup
1 stick oleo
1 cup sifted flour

1½ cups pecans OR walnuts, chopped
½ - 1 teaspoon vanilla

Combine brown sugar, syrup and oleo in saucepan and bring to a boil. Allow mixture to cool. Mix flour, pecans, and vanilla into cooled syrup mixture.

Line a cookie sheet with aluminum foil. Drop ½ teaspoon of dough at a time; 12 cookies to a cookie sheet and bake in 350° oven for about 8 minutes.

The Committee

Dip scissors in hot water while cutting sticky ingredients.

MADELEINES

OVEN: 350° 12-15 minutes

YIELD: 3 dozen cookies

1¼ cups sifted cake flour
½ teaspoon baking powder
¼ teaspoon salt
3 eggs
1 teaspoon vanilla extract

⅔ cup sugar
2 teaspoons finely grated lemon
rind
¾ cup butter, melted and cooled
confectioners sugar

Sift flour with baking powder and salt; set aside. Beat eggs until light; add vanilla; gradually add ⅔ cup of sugar; beat. Continue beating until volume has increased to about 4-times the original. Fold in lemon rind; gradually fold in flour mixture. Stir in butter. Brush pans with additional melted butter and spoon about 1 tablespoon of batter into each shell, filling each about ¾ full. Bake in a preheated 350° oven for 12-15 minutes, or until golden-brown. Remove cookies to wire rack and sift confectioners sugar over the tops.

Special madeleine pans are available for a few dollars in most gourmet shops or larger department stores. Each pan makes 12 cookies.

Connie Wagers

OATMEAL AND COCONUT COOKIES

OVEN: 350° 10-12 minutes

1 cup shortening
1 cup white sugar
1 cup brown sugar
2 eggs
1 teaspoon vanilla
2 cups flour

½ teaspoon baking powder
1 teaspoon soda
½ teaspoon salt
2 cups rice type cereal
2 cups quick rolled oats
1 cup coconut

Cream together shortening and sugars; add eggs, vanilla, and blend well. Add flour, baking powder and soda and salt to mixture and mix well. Add rice cereal, oats and coconut and blend in with spoon.

Mold mixture into balls the size of walnuts; press down with a fork. Bake at 350° for 10-12 minutes.

Helen Schulz

OATMEAL AND RAISIN COOKIES

OVEN: 400° 10-12 minutes

½ cup shortening
1¼ cups sugar
2 eggs
6 tablespoons molasses
1¾ cups sifted flour
1 teaspoon soda

1 teaspoon salt
1 teaspoon cinnamon
2 cups oats
½ cup nuts
1 cup raisins

Beat together sugar, shortening, eggs and molasses. Sift dry ingredients together and add to molasses mixture. Add oats, nuts and raisins. Mix all ingredients well and drop on cookie sheet by rounded teaspoonfuls. Bake at 400° for 10-12 minutes.

Joan Schroeder

OATMEAL-CHIP COOKIES

OVEN: 350° 8-10 minutes

½ cup oleo
1 cup light brown sugar
1 teaspoon vanilla
1 egg
1¼ cups flour
1 teaspoon soda

½ teaspoon salt
1 cup oatmeal
1 cup rice cereal
¾ cup chocolate chips
½ cup nuts

Beat oleo, sugar, vanilla and egg together well. Add flour, soda, baking powder and salt. Use electric mixer and beat again. Add oatmeal, cereal, and nuts; fold in with a spoon. Add chocolate chips. Place batter on cookie sheet in small teaspoonsful, flatten. Bake at 350° for 8-10 minutes.

Peggy Boudrias

OATMEAL COOKIES

YIELD: 5 dozen

OVEN: 350° 10 minutes

1 cup shortening OR butter
1 cup brown sugar
1 cup granulated sugar
3 eggs
1 teaspoon vanilla
⅓ cup peanut butter, plain OR crunchy
1½ cups all-purpose flour

1 teaspoon salt
1 teaspoon soda
2 cups quick cooking oatmeal
2 cups bran flake cereal OR 3 cups vitamin fortified similar-type cereal
½ cup raisins

Cream shortening and sugars; add eggs and vanilla; blend. Add peanut butter. Sift and add flour, salt and soda. Stir in cereal and raisins. Roll batter into 1-½" rolls on waxed paper. Chill, or freeze and use later. Slice ¼" thick and bake in 350° oven for 10 minutes.

Any stale cereals may be used. You may also add ½ cup chopped nuts and wheat germ for flavor and nutrition.

Gail Smith

ONE-TWO-THREE COOKIES

2 sticks oleo, melted
1 box confectioners sugar
1 can flaked coconut
1 cup nuts

4-5 tablespoons peanut butter
2 cups graham cracker crumbs
1 small cake paraffin
1 — 12 ounce package chocolate bits

Mix oleo, sugar, coconut, nuts, peanut butter and graham crumbs together. Form batter into balls. Melt paraffin in boiler, then dissolve chocolate bits in it. Dip cookies in paraffin/chocolate mixture until well covered. Drain and harden on wax paper.

Adjust quantity of crumbs to get the mixture to right consistency to make balls.

Ruth Davis

ORANGE DATE COOKIES

OVEN: 375° 12 minutes

YIELD: 4 dozen

1 cup white all-purpose flour
1 cup whole wheat flour
1 teaspoon cinnamon
½ teaspoon salt
½ teaspoon baking soda
1 stick butter OR margarine
1 cup brown sugar

1 teaspoon vanilla
2 eggs
1½ cups chopped dates, about 8
  ounces
½ cup chopped nuts
½ cup orange juice
grated rind of 1 small orange

Sift together flours, cinnamon, soda and salt. Cream butter and sugar until light and fluffy; add eggs and vanilla, mixing well. Stir in flour mixture alternately with orange juice. Stir in orange rind, dates and nuts. Blend. Drop by tablespoonfuls on greased baking sheets. Bake at 375° for about 12 minutes or until done; lightly browned.
Store in closed container in refrigerator or freezer.

Mrs. Charles A. Proctor

ORANGE GUMDROP COOKIES

OVEN: 325° 10-12 minutes

YIELD: 6-8 dozen

1 cup shortening
1 cup granulated sugar
1 cup brown sugar
2 eggs
1 teaspoon vanilla
2 cups flour
1 teaspoon baking powder

1 teaspoon baking soda
½ teaspoon salt
2 cups quick cooking oatmeal
1 cup chopped pecans
1 cup flaked coconut
1 cup chopped orange slices OR
  gumdrops

Cream shortening and sugar together. Add eggs, one at a time, blending well after each addition. Add vanilla. Add sifted dry ingredients. Add remaining ingredients and mix well. Drop mixture by teaspoonfuls on greased cookie sheet. Bake at 325° for 10-12 minutes. Let cool slightly before removing from cookie sheet.

Tabithia Purvis

PEANUT BUTTER COOKIES

OVEN: 350° 10-12 minutes

1 package yellow cake mix
1 cup peanut butter
½ cup cooking oil

2 tablespoons water
2 eggs

Combine all ingredients in a large bowl. Mix well, and drop from teaspoon onto ungreased cookie sheet. Criss-cross cookies with fork dipped in water, to flatten dough. Bake at 350° for 10-12 minutes. Cool on sheet for 1 minute; remove from sheet and finish cooling.

Alice Dibo

PECAN CRUNCH COOKIES

OVEN: 350° 15 minutes   YIELD: 3-½ dozen

1 cup butter OR margarine
½ cup sugar
1 teaspoon vanilla

½ cup crushed potato chips
½ cup chopped pecans
2 cups flour

Cream together butter, sugar and vanilla. Add potato chips, and pecans. Stir in flour. Form into small balls about 1 teaspoon each. Place on ungreased cookie sheet. Press balls flat with the bottom of a glass dipped in sugar. Bake at 350° for about 15 minutes or until lightly browned.

If desired, sprinkle with colored sugar, or top each cookie with a half of pecan, or candied cherry.

Helen George

PECAN PUFFS

OVEN: 325° 30 minutes   YIELD: 32 balls

1 cup pecans, cut up
¼ pound butter OR margarine
1 cup cake flour

2 tablespoons sugar
1 teaspoon vanilla
powdered sugar

Combine pecans, butter, flour, sugar and vanilla; blend well and form into balls. Bake in 325° oven for 30 minutes. Roll in powdered sugar when cold.

Mrs. James W. Mueller

POLLY'S BROWNIES

OVEN: 350° 30-40 minutes

1 stick butter OR oleo
1 cup sugar
2 eggs, beaten well

½ cup chopped pecans
2 cups crushed graham crackers
1 teaspoon vanilla

Melt butter in saucepan; add sugar, eggs, nuts and crushed graham crackers and vanilla. Pour into a square pan that has been greased and bake at 350° for 30-40 minutes. When cool, sprinkle with powdered sugar and cut.

May be baked in a pie pan and served warm with whipped cream.

Mrs. John McCarty

POTATO CHIP COOKIES I

OVEN: 350° 10-12 minutes   YIELD: 3¼ dozen

1 cup butter OR margarine
½ cup sugar
1 teaspoon vanilla

½ cup crushed potato chips
½ cup chopped pecans
2 cups sifted all-purpose flour

Cream together butter or margarine, sugar and vanilla. Add crushed potato chips and pecans; stir in flour. Form into small balls, using about 1 teaspoon of dough for each. Place on ungreased cookie sheet and press flat with bottom of tumbler dipped in sugar. Bake in 350° oven for 10-12 minutes or until lightly brown.

Estelle King

POTATO CHIP COOKIES II

OVEN: 350° 11-12 minutes   YIELD: 100

2 sticks margarine
½ cup sugar
1 teaspoon vanilla

½ cup chopped nuts
⅔ cup crushed potato chips
1½ cups flour

Mix all ingredients together and drop by spoonfuls onto ungreased cookie sheet. Press with fork, or glass covered with wet cloth. Dip fork in water to keep batter from sticking. Bake at 350° for 11-12 minutes.

Oven temperatures vary — you may have to bake at 350° for longer time or reduce heat and bake for shorter time. Experiment.

Helen Leedy

ROCKS — CHRISTMAS COOKIES

OVEN: 350° 10 minutes

1½ cups brown sugar
½ pound butter
3 eggs
1 cup raisins
1 pound date pieces

2½ cups flour
1 teaspoon soda, dissolved in a little water
1 pound walnut pieces
pinch of salt

Combine all dry ingredients. Add other ingredients to dry ingredients. Mix well. Drop by teaspoonfuls on greased cookie sheet. Bake at 350° for 10 minutes.

Keep spoonfuls small and don't crowd too many on one sheet.

This recipe is one my wife's mother used each year during the Christmas holidays. It must be close to 100 years old.

Bob Palmer

SCOTCH SHORTBREAD I

OVEN: 300°-325° 1 hour

1 pound soft butter (no substitute)   5 cups all-purpose flour
1 cup confectionary sugar

Place butter in a large bowl and let it sit until very soft. Add sifted sugar to the butter. Gradually add flour. At first you can mix batter with a fork; as it thickens you will have to mix with your hands. Line a cookie sheet, approximately 9″ x 15″ with three layers of paper towels. Pat the dough evenly over the sheet, leaving it about 1″ thick. Prick all over with a fork. Bake in a slow oven, 300°-325° for one hour or until golden brown. Cut into squares while still warm. You make these two or three weeks ahead and store in a tightly sealed tin or container.

My great grandfather was a piper in the castle Glen Caladh in the Kyles of Bute up in the highlands of Scotland. As a girl, my grandmother spent many hours playing in the kitchen. She brought this recipe to Glasgow and my mother brought it with her when she came to America. It is a traditional Christmas treat and is always on the table at wedding receptions.

Rita Avril

SCOTCH SHORTBREAD II

OVEN: 310° 10 minutes; 275° 1 hour

**2 sticks butter, at room tempera-
ture**

**2 sticks margarine, at room temp-
erature
1 generous cup powdered sugar
4 cups flour**

Mix butter and sugar together on low speed of electric beater. Sift in 3 cups of the flour, one cup at a time, continuing to beat between each cup. Place 4th cup of flour on a pastry cloth or clean counter. Dump entire mix on top of flour. Knead flour into mix with corner of the cloth or hands until all the flour disappears. Place all of the mix on a cookie sheet, 10" x 16", and pat down until it is fairly level. Turn oven on to 310°. Prick dough at 1" intervals, completely to the bottom of the pan. Then cut dough into fingers. Dough will bake together, but it will cut more easily when completed. I like a little granulated sugar on top.

Cook for 10 minutes at 310°, then reduce heat to 275° and continue cooking for about 1 hour.

Sometimes it may take longer to cook; if so, reduce heat a little more. Oven temperatures vary. When cool, store in an air-tight container. They are better if they age a week or two, but this is not necessary. Will keep for weeks.

Isabel Gordon McElroy

SPRINGERLE

OVEN: 300°   YIELD: about 5 dozen

**1 pound powdered sugar
4 eggs
1 pound cake flour**

**¼ teaspoon baking soda
½ teaspoon baking powder
1 tablespoon anise seed**

Have all ingredients at room temperature. Beat eggs slightly; add sugar gradually and beat with electric mixer on medium speed until mixture is lemon colored or foamy. Add anise seed; then add flour gradually. It will make a stiff dough.

Let dough rest for about 1-2 hours in a covered bowl in a cool place. Then roll dough out to about ½" thick; press with Springerle mold or cut out with cookie-cutter. Place cookies on well buttered or greased cookie sheet, ½" apart. Let stand overnight in a warm room. Bake in 300° oven until yellow or light brown on the bottom. Remove from cookie sheet and cool on a rack.

These are traditional German Christmas cookies.

Louise Beerhalter

Run hard candy through a food chopper and sprinkle tiny bits on frosted cookies. These dainty and delectable cookies are a very nice compliment with dessert and with tea.

SYRUP COOKIES

OVEN: 350° 15-18 minutes

7-8 cups flour
2 cups cane syrup
1 egg
1 cup melted shortening
1 tablespoon baking powder

1 teaspoon baking soda
½ teaspoon salt
½ teaspoon cinnamon
½ teaspoon allspice

Combine all ingredients and blend well. Bake on cookie sheet in 350° oven for 15-18 minutes.

Delma Nettles

TOP-OF-STOVE COOKIES

YIELD: about 3 dozen

2 cups granulated sugar
½ cup cocoa
½ cup corn oil
½ cup milk

1 teaspoon vanilla
pinch of salt
3 cups quick cooking oats

Combine sugar, cocoa, salad oil and milk in a saucepan; boil for 3 minutes. Quickly stir in salt, vanilla and oats. Blend all thoroughly; batter will start to stiffen. Drop by tablespoons on waxed paper. Cool thoroughly.

These are easy to make on a hot day, and they do not get messy for a picnic lunch on the beach.

Mrs. C. L. Elias

YUMMY COOKIES

OVEN: 350° 25 minutes

½ cup shortening
1 cup sugar
2 egg yolks, well beaten
1 teaspoon vanilla
1½ cups sifted flour
½ teaspoon salt
1 teaspoon baking powder

⅔ cup milk

Topping:
2 egg whites
½ cup brown sugar
½ cup nuts, optional
powdered sugar

Cream shortening and add sugar; mix well. Add eggs and vanilla. Sift flour, salt and baking powder together. Add alternately with milk to creamed mixture. Place on a greased cookie sheet.

Prepare topping. Beat egg whites stiff. Add brown sugar and blend well. Add nuts, and spread over mixture on cookie sheet. Bake for 25 minutes at 350°. Sprinkle with powdered sugar and cut into squares.

This is a sure hit for any bake sale.

Rita Sowinski

AFTER DINNER MINTS

1 box powdered sugar
1 egg white, unbeaten
1 tablespoon cream
1 teaspoon vanilla

1 heaping teaspoon soft butter OR
white shortening for pure white
mints
3 drops oil flavoring of your
choice; peppermint, cinnamon,
lemon, etc.
food coloring, for pastel mints

Combine egg white, cream, vanilla, oil flavoring, and coloring. Stir well. Add sugar all at once; mix thoroughly. Add butter or shortening and more sugar if necessary to make the mixture the right consistency to roll into a firm ball. Arrange the balls on wax paper and press each ball with tines of a fork dipped in powdered sugar or cornstarch. When mixing in the sugar, you may need to add a bit more cream. Cream will give white mints a creamy white color. Let stand overnight to form a crust, then pack in tins with wax paper between each layer. May be frozen and kept for several months.

The Committee

BOOTS' CHRISTMAS CANDY

1 package butterscotch chips
½ cup salted peanuts

1 cup Chinese noodles

Melt chips in double boiler. Add peanuts and noodles; mix well. Drop in very small amounts on wax paper. Chill.

Eleanor Colean

BOURBON BALLS

YIELD: about 4-½ dozen

1 stick butter
1½ ounces bourbon
1 cup broken pecan pieces

1 — 6 ounce package semi-sweet
chocolate, melted
confectioners sugar

Using all the ingredients, make a moist dough. Use enough powdered sugar to hold dough together. Form dough in small balls and roll in more powdered sugar.

Ann Hitt

Grease the cooking utensil one inch inside of top rim to prevent candy mixture from boiling over.

BUTTER CRUNCH

YIELD: 1 pound

1 cup butter
1 cup sugar
2 tablespoons water

2 tablespoons light corn syrup
¾ cup ground nuts
4 ounces semi-sweet chocolate

Melt butter in a 2 quart saucepan. Remove from heat and add sugar. Stir with wooden spoon until mixture is well blended. Return to low heat; stir fast until thoroughly mixed and beginning to bubble. Add water and corn syrup; mix well. Put candy thermometer into mixture; keep heat low, stirring frequently until thermometer reaches 290°. Remove at once from heat. Sprinkle nuts over surface and quickly mix in. Pour batter on lightly greased cookie sheet. Cool to room temperature. Loosen mixture 2-3 times. Melt chocolate over hot water and spread on candy; turn mixture over and frost the other side. Break into pieces when cool.

A candy thermometer is a must for this recipe.

Helen Leedy

CANDIED ORANGE AND GRAPEFRUIT PEEL

oranges
grapefruit

water
granulated sugar

Prepare fruit by pulling out all dividing membranes and cutting into strips about ¼″ wide. For a mild-flavored peel, thick-skinned fruit should be used. For a bitter-flavored peel, preferred by some people, choose thin-skinned fruit, or cut away the inner white portion of the rind.

Cover peel with cold water and bring to a boil, drain. Repeat, using fresh water each time, 4 times for orange peel and 6 times for grapefruit peel, or until peel is only slightly bitter. After last draining, add equal amount of sugar to peel. Place over low heat and toss gently until sugar is dissolved. Continue simmering until syrup reaches soft ball stage, 238°. Turn into strainer and drain thoroughly. Roll each piece in granulated sugar. Spread on a plate to cool and dry. Store in a covered metal box.

Ethel Rosier

CANDIED ORANGE NUTS

2 cups sugar
1 tablespoon flour
⅝ cup milk, not canned milk
½ tablespoon butter

3 cups pecans
juice of 1 orange
grated rind of 1 orange

Sift sugar and flour together. Add milk and butter; cook mixture to soft ball stage. Add juice and rind and cook to firm ball stage. Pour mixture over pecans in a large bowl and beat until creamy and pecans fall apart. Turn out on paper and separate any nuts that stick together.

Mildred Staton

CHRISTMAS STRAWBERRIES

YIELD: 1 pound, 3 ounces

2-3 ounce packages strawberry flavored gelatin
1 cup ground pecans
1 cup flaked coconut

¾ cup condensed milk
½ teaspoon vanilla
red decorator sugar
blanched, sliced almonds

Combine gelatin, pecans and coconut. Stir in milk and vanilla; mix well. Chill for 1 hour. Shape into strawberries and roll in red sugar.

If you wish, tint almonds green with food coloring and stick in tops to form leaves.

The 15 ounce can of condensed milk equals 1½ cups.

Christmas is not official if these elegant confections are not presented.

Charlotte Sparling

COCOA BOURBON BALLS

YIELD: 3 dozen

1 cup finely crushed vanilla wafers
2 tablespoons cocoa
¼ cup bourbon
chocolate shot

1 cup sifted confectioners sugar
1 cup pecans, chopped
2 tablespoons light corn syrup
fine granulated sugar

Combine wafer crumbs, powdered sugar, 1 cup pecans and 2 tablespoons of cocoa. Add corn syrup and bourbon. Mix well. Shape into 1″ balls. Roll some in granulated sugar and others in chopped pecans, cocoa or chocolate shot. Store in air-tight container.

Mrs. Lester Jennings

CREOLE DATE ROLL

YIELD: about 2 pounds

3 cups sugar
2 cups sliced dates

1½ cups nut meats, broken small
1 cup evaporated milk

Place sugar and milk in a saucepan. Stir over low flame until sugar is dissolved. Increase heat and boil to a soft ball stage; add dates and cook for 2½ minutes. Remove from stove and cool, beat until candy begins to thicken. Continue to beat until it is firm enough to form into a roll. Wrap in a damp cloth until cold. Then cut into slices.

Marjorie Rehak

To insure smoothness, always allow candy to cool to lukewarm before beating.

EASY FUDGE

YIELD: 2-½ pounds

1 - 8 ounce Hershey bar, chopped
6 ounces chocolate tidbits
½ pint marshmallow creme
¼ cube oleo

1 teaspoon vanilla
6½ ounces evaporated milk
2¼ cups sugar
1 cup nuts

Bring milk and sugar to a boil in saucepan, stir constantly and boil for 5 minutes. Add remaining ingredients and stir until melted and well mixed. Pour into 9″ x 13″ baking dish which has been heavily buttered. Work quickly.

Mary K. Jones

KENTUCKY COLONEL CANDY

½ pound butter
2 pounds powdered sugar
8 tablespoons whiskey
2 cups nuts

lemon juice, if desired

Dip:
7 squares semi-sweet chocolate
1 tablespoon paraffin

Soften butter and add 1 pound of sugar. Add whiskey, then 2nd pound of sugar; nuts, and lemon juice. Blend until all mixed. Roll into balls and let cool overnight. Melt chocolate and paraffin in top of double boiler; blend well. Remove from heat and cool slightly. Dip candy in chocolate/paraffin mixture.
Candy dips better when dark chocolate is used.

H. B. Kennedy

KIM'S PECAN PRALINES

2 cups brown sugar
1 cup white granulated sugar
1 cup water

1 cup evaporated milk
3 cups pecans

Combine sugar, milk and water in a saucepan and cook to soft ball stage, 238°. Remove from heat and beat until creamy. Add nuts and drop by spoonfuls onto waxed paper or aluminum foil.

Kim Lybrand

Add one teaspoon cornstarch per cup of sugar for a creamier fudge.

MERINGUE KISSES

OVEN: 275° 30 minutes

YIELD: 3 dozen

3 egg whites
1 teaspoon vanilla
¼ teaspoon cream of tartar
¼ teaspoon peppermint extract,
  optional

dash of salt
1 cup sugar
3 dozen milk chocolate candy
  kisses

In small mixer bowl, combine egg whites, vanilla, cream of tartar, extract, if used, and salt. Beat to soft peaks. Very gradually add sugar, beating until very stiff peaks form. Meringue will be glossy.

Drop from tablespoon onto ungreased cookie sheet about 1½″ apart. Press 1 piece of candy into each meringue. Bring meringue up and over sides of candy with a knife or narrow spatula, swirling top. Sprinkle with red or green sugar crystals. Bake in 275° oven for 30 minutes. Immediately remove from baking sheet and cool.

Wayne Whitson

MILLION DOLLAR FUDGE

YIELD: 4½ - 5 pounds

4½ cups sugar
1 tall can evaporated milk
2 large Hershey bars

nuts, if desired
2 packages chocolate bits
1 pint marshmallow creme

Combine sugar and milk; mix thoroughly and bring mixture to a boil for 8 minutes, stirring constantly. Remove from heat and add candy bars, nuts, chocolate bits and marshmallow creme. Stir mixture until chocolate is melted. Pour batter into buttered pans. No beating is necessary.

Annie Raulerson

MRS. N. BUCHANAN'S PRALINES

3 cups brown sugar
½ stick margarine
1 cup evaporated milk OR cream

grated rind of 1 orange
½ teaspoon mabelene flavoring
½ cup pecans

Combine all ingredients except orange rind and mabelene. Bring ingredients to a boil, stirring constantly until soft ball stage is reached. Remove from heat and add orange rind and mabelene. Place pan in cold water until mixture cools. Beat until stiff and add nuts. Drop by teaspoon onto wax paper. Store in tin box.

Nina B. Rogers

Packed brown sugar, either light or dark, can be substituted for granulated sugar, measure for measure. A light molasses flavor will result.

NEVER-FAIL FUDGE

4½ cups sugar
¼ pound butter OR margarine
1 large can evaporated milk
1 large Hershey bar

semi-sweet chocolate bits, large
  bag
1 teaspoon vanilla, optional
1 cup nuts, optional

Place sugar, butter and milk in large kettle. Boil for 5 minutes. Time begins when mixture starts to boil. Remove from heat; batter will be thin.

Add candy bar and chocolate bits. Stir until chocolate is melted. Pour batter into greased pan and cool; then cut into squares.

Vanilla and nuts are optional. If used, add them with candy bar and chocolate bits.

Janiece Sumner

OKEECHOBEE SNOWBALLS

OVEN: 325° 30 minutes

1 cup butter
2 cups flour
1 cup chopped pecans

¾ cup powdered sugar
1 teaspoon vanilla

Mix ingredients together and roll by hand into small balls. Place on a baking sheet and bake in 325° oven about 30 minutes. Roll in powdered sugar while warm and roll again in sugar when cool.

Lee Christopher

ONE-TWO-THREE FUDGE

2½ cups sugar
¼ cup butter OR margarine
6 ounces marshmallow creme

¾ cup evaporated milk
1 cup walnuts
6 ounces semi-sweet chocolate

Place sugar, butter, creme and milk in a large saucepan. Cook and stir mixture to a full, all-over boil. Mixture will be bubbly. Boil over medium heat for 5 minutes. Remove from stove and add chocolate bits and walnuts. Pour hot mixture into a buttered square or oblong pan. Place pan in refrigerator until mixture is cool.

May be served cool from refrigerator or at room temperature.

Linda Gagnon

Homemade candy will retain its freshness for days by adding a few drops of glycerine to the mixture. The glycerine also prevents graining.

PEANUT BRITTLE

2 cups shelled peanuts, leave the
red outsides on
½ cup water

½ cup white corn syrup
1 cup sugar
1 teaspoon soda

Prepare a long strip of wax paper for mixture to be placed on. Butter paper and set aside.

Boil sugar, syrup and water until it forms a thread. Add peanuts and cook until they quit popping. They will pop as cranberries pop. Remove mixture from heat and add soda and stir.

Quickly pour mixture onto buttered wax paper and spread as thin as possible. Work quickly. Let mixture cool then break into pieces.

Jane B. Howard

PEANUT BUTTER CANDY I

1 box 10X powdered sugar
1 stick butter

1 small can evaporated milk
½ - 1 jar peanut butter

Cream sugar and butter together. Add milk a little at a time. Dust a piece of wax paper with flour and roll out mixture, shaping into a square. Spread on ½ to 1 jar of peanut butter on the dough. Roll dough into roll. If mushy, place in freezer for about 1 hour; then cut into thin slices. Refrigerate until ready to eat.

Alice Dibo

PEANUT BUTTER CANDY II

1 box powdered sugar
2 sticks oleo
1 cup peanut butter

1 package chocolate, carmel OR
butterscotch chips
½ block paraffin wax

Combine sugar, oleo and peanut butter. Mix well and shape into balls.

In a double boiler, melt the chips and paraffin together. You can use a little less than ½ of the block of paraffin. Stir until mixed.

Place candy balls on a toothpick and dip into chocolate/paraffin mixture to coat. Place dipped pieces on wax paper or foil to cool.

Jane DuBois

POTATO CANDY

1 small boiled potato
small piece of butter
dash of salt
vanilla

1 pound confectioners sugar
1 pound flaked coconut
2 squares bitter chocolate, melted

Boil potato and mash well; add butter, salt and vanilla; cool. Add confectioners sugar and coconut and mix well. Pack mixture into 13" x 9" greased pan and cool well. Cut into squares and dip into melted chocolate.

Lois Jardine

QUICK CHOCOLATE FUDGE CANDY

2 cups sugar
1 stick margarine
½ cup milk
4 tablespoons cocoa

3 cups quick oats
1 teaspoon vanilla
1 cup nuts, optional OR ½ cup
   crunchy peanut butter

Add cocoa to sugar. Stir well, then add milk and margarine. Cook mixture over medium heat and bring to a boil for 2 minutes. Remove from heat and add oats and vanilla. If using nuts or peanut butter, add and mix well.

Drop by spoonfuls on waxed paper. Cool and eat.

These can be made and eaten in ½ hour. The oats give a nutty taste.

Gladys Grammer

SEA FOAM CANDY

1½ cups dark brown sugar
½ cup cold water
1 teaspoon vinegar

1 egg white
½ cup chopped nuts
½ teaspoon vanilla

Beat egg white until stiff, not dry. Boil sugar, water and vinegar to 240°, or until mixture forms a firm ball when tried in cold water. Pour mixture slowly on egg white; beat until creamy. Add nuts and vanilla. Drop by teaspoonfuls on wax paper or spread in buttered pan and cut into squares. Refrigerate.

The Committee

SHOESTRING CANDY DROPS

1 pound white chocolate, shaved
2 cups shoestring potatoes

10 ounces dry roasted peanuts

Melt chocolate in top of double boiler. Chocolate will not melt if water is too hot. When melted, add potatoes and peanuts. Stir after each addition. After mixing drop by teaspoonfuls on waxed paper on cookie sheet. Let sit until cold, then enjoy.

Use ready-to-eat, canned shoestring potatoes.

Helen Leedy

TOFFEE CANDY

2 cups sugar
1 pound butter, no substitute
1 cup white corn syrup

½ pound shelled almonds, blanched
   and cut up
1 pound chocolate

Melt butter in a saucepan and stir in sugar. Cook until sugar is dissolved, stirring constantly for 20 minutes. Add syrup and cook 10 minutes more, stirring constantly. Add ½ of the almonds and continue cooking mixture to the hard ball stage; that is, when a small amount of mixture hardens when dropped into cold water. Pour toffee into well greased cookie sheet. Pour melted chocolate on top and sprinkle with remaining almonds (ground up) when mixture is cool. After candy is hard and cold, pop off of cookie sheet and into pieces of desired size.

This is a great Christmas treat.

Wilda Worth

DESSERTS

DESSERTS

AMBROSIA

6 Florida oranges
1 cup fresh strawberries, sliced
2 - 3 tablespoons sugar
1 ounce Kirsch

¼ cup coconut
¼ cup nuts
maraschino cherries

Section oranges and combine sections with strawberries and Kirsch; sprinkle with sugar. Turn mixture into serving bowl and sprinkle with coconut. Garnish with maraschino cherries.

The Committee

ANGEL DELIGHT

4 eggs, separated
½ cup milk
1 cup sugar
1 envelope plain gelatin
1¼ pints whipping cream

1 small angel cake, broken into 1″ pieces
1 package black walnuts
1 small can crushed pineapple, well drained
1 small can seedless grapes, well drained

Beat egg yolks until light; gradually add ½ cup sugar. Add to milk and place in top of double boiler. Cook until thickened, stirring constantly. Cool. Beat egg whites adding all remaining sugar except 2 tablespoons. Beat until very, very stiff. Whip one pint cream and add to egg white mixture. Soak gelatin in a little cold water and dissolve over boiling water. Add dissolved gelatin to egg white mixture. Blend egg yolk mixture into egg white mixture.

Using a large angel food pan, place a layer of broken cake pieces on the bottom of pan, then a layer of custard, repeat layers until all mixture and pieces are used. Refrigerate for 12 hours. Remove from pan; ice with remaining whipped cream and 2 tablespoons reserved sugar.

This dessert may be made a few days in advance. For the holidays I tint the whipped cream icing with green food coloring and decorate with red and green cherries.

Barbara Kammeraad

When slicing bananas, use a hardboiled egg slicer. This method will ensure evenly sliced bananas.

ANGEL LEMON DELIGHT

OVEN: 375° 30-40 minutes

Top part: 3 egg whites, beaten stiff
½ cup sugar

Lower part: 1 cup sugar
½ cup flour
¼ teaspoon salt

3 egg yolks
juice of 2 large lemons
grated lemon rind to suit your taste
2 tablespoons melted butter
1 cup milk

Beat egg whites and add sugar. Set aside while you mix ingredients for lower part.

In a good sized baking dish, combine ingredients in the order listed and beat with electric mixer on medium speed. Mixture should be smooth and creamy. Fold in beaten egg whites and sugar; then set baking dish in a pan of hot water, which should not be deeper than 1" around bowl. Bake in 375° oven for 30-40 minutes. This is best served warm with a garnish of whipped cream.

This recipe is inexpensive and easy to put together. The resulting dessert is a fluffy angel-cake like top with a creamy lemon sauce beneath.

Polly Crowell

APPLE CRISP

OVEN: 350° 30 minutes

½ package oatmeal cookie mix, approximately
6 apples OR 1 can apple pie filling
cinnamon

nutmeg
sugar
butter

Spread oatmeal cookie mix on bottom of 8" pan; fill with sliced apples or pie filling and season with spices to taste. Cover with ½" cookie mix and dot with butter. Bake in 350° oven for ½ hour. Serve hot or cold with ice cream. Other fruit may be substituted for apples.

Betty Durdy

To peel a pineapple, wash and slice crosswise into one inch thick slices using a large, sharp knife. With a paring knife, peel each slice deep enough to remove eyes. Cut into desired shapes such as sticks or cubes — or slice again into thinner slices.

APPLE CRISP FOR 35

OVEN: 350° 1 hour

1 — 6 pound, 12 ounce can sliced apples (not pie filling)
2 pounds sugar
⅓ cup flour
1 tablespoon salt
2 tablespoons cinnamon
2 tablespoons allspice

2 lemons, juice only, may grate rind over apples
1 cup raisins, optional
6 cups rolled oats
1 pound brown sugar
4 sticks butter OR oleo
4 cups all-purpose flour
1 teaspoon baking powder
1 teaspoon soda

Mix first seven (7) ingredients and pour into buttered 13 x 18 pan, or 2—9 x 13 pans. If using raisins, add to mixture. Cut butter into dry ingredients and sprinkle on top of apples. Wheat germ may be substituted for part of oats. You may also add nuts and/or sesame seeds. Bake in 350° oven approximately 1 hour or until brown. Let set for 1 hour or more before serving. Eat cold or warm with ice cream or whipped cream.

Suzanne Varn

APPLE DUMPLINGS

OVEN: 350° 1 hour

6-8 apples
2 cups flour
1 teaspoon salt
⅔ cup shortening
5 tablespoons milk

2 cups water
1 cup sugar
2 pounds margarine
cinnamon

Peel and quarter apples; set aside. Sift together flour and salt; add shortening and cut in until mixture is crumbly; add milk to make a soft dough. Roll dough out and divide into 8 squares. Cover squares with 4 pieces of apple; place about ½ teaspoon of sugar and sprinkle of cinnamon in center. Completely cover apple pieces with dough and place in a deep baking pan. Bring water, sugar and margarine to a boil and pour over apple dumplings. Bake at 350° for 1 hour. Serve plain or with cream or nutmeg.

Estelle King

Cut fruits for desserts ahead of time and toss lightly with lemon juice to prevent them from darkening. One or two quarts of cut fruit can be tossed with the juice from one-half of a lemon.

APPLE DUMPLINGS WITH SAUCE

OVEN: 375° until brown

YIELD: 8 servings

Apple dumplings:
2 medium-size apples, peeled and
  cored
1 box pie crust mix
3 tablespoons sugar
Sauce:
¼ cup butter

⅞ cup sugar
2 slices apple, peeled
2 egg yolks
2 egg whites, beaten stiff
½ cup milk
vanilla OR rum extract to taste

Prepare one box (2 sticks) of pie crust as package directs, or make dough for 2 pie crusts from your own recipe. Roll out crust and cut into 3″ squares. Place 2 thin apple slices, ½ teaspoon sugar, and sprinkle of cinnamon on each square; dot each with butter. Fold crust over and seal into triangles. Bake in 375° oven until brown.

For sauce, cream butter; add sugar gradually; then egg yolks and milk. Cook in double boiler over water until thick as custard with apple slices. Stir while cooking. Add beaten egg whites to mixture and cook a minute longer. Add extract to taste. Pour sauce over dumplings and let set for a few hours.

Mrs. Raymond E. Ford

APRICOT D' APHRODITE

YIELD: 6 servings

½ pound dried apricots
¾ cup sugar
⅔ cup Madeira
2 egg whites

1 cup heavy cream
¼ cup blanched, sliced, toasted almonds

Soak apricots overnight in water to cover. In the morning, place them in a saucepan; add half of the sugar, and additional water, if necessary. Water should just about cover fruit. Bring ingredients to a boil and simmer until apricots are tender. Drain apricots and cool. Puree fruit in blender with ½ cup Madeira.

Beat egg whites until stiff. Gradually beat in remaining sugar, a little at a time. Continue to beat egg whites until sugar is dissolved.

Beat cream until stiff. Fold stiff egg whites and half of cream into apricot puree. Pour into serving dish; sprinkle with almonds. Chill well before serving. Beat remaining Madeira into remaining whipped cream for topping.

Christa Lewis

BAKED ALASKA CONE

OVEN: 500° 2-3 minutes

large scoop ice cream
egg whites

cream of tartar
sugar

Place large scoop of ice cream in center of dessert shell. Freeze until ready to use. Just before serving, cover ice cream with prepared meringue. Place in pre-heated oven at 500° for 2-3 minutes, or until browned.

Wanda L. Collins

BAKED SHIRRED GRAPEFRUIT

grapefruit
brown sugar
powdered cloves

butter
cooking sherry

Cut grapefruit in half. Separate sections, but do not cut completely through. Drain juice.
Sprinkle edges with brown sugar, powdered cloves and butter. Fill center with cooking sherry. Bake under broiler or in hot oven until edges are brown. Serve hot.

Mrs. Leroy E. Oakes

BANANA DELIGHT DESSERT

1 box vanilla wafer cookies
2 eggs
1¾ cups powdered sugar
1 large can crushed pineapple
½ cup oleo, softened
1 teaspoon vanilla
4 large bananas

9 ounces prepared whipped topping
1 small package walnuts, chopped
12 cherries
4 tablespoons melted butter OR oleo

Crush 60 wafers. Place 30 in plastic bag, seal, and roll with rolling pin; repeat with remaining 30. Place crumbs in bowl and add 4 tablespoons melted butter or oleo; mix. Pour crumb mixture into 9 x 12 pyrex dish and tap all the way around.
Blend eggs, powdered sugar, soft oleo, and vanilla in a bowl for 10 minutes. Spread mixture over crumbs. Slice bananas and sprinkle lemon juice over slices. Place slices over pudding in rows; sprinkle with well drained pineapple. Spread whipped topping over pineapple and top with chopped nuts and sliced cherries. Refrigerate overnight. Serve in squares.

Mrs. Frank Stawara

BANANA JELLO PUDDING

1 — 3 ounce package strawberry banana Jello
1 small can crushed pineapple
2 ripe bananas, sliced
1 cup small marshmallows

Topping:
2 tablespoons butter

2 tablespoons flour
½ cup sugar
1 egg
reserved pineapple juice
3 ounces cream cheese, softened
1 small container whipped topping
chopped nuts

Prepare Jello as package directs; partially jell mixture. Add crushed pineapple that has been drained; reserve juice. Mix in sliced bananas and marshmallows. Place in pan and finish jelling. Use a 9″ square pan.
Combine butter, flour, sugar, egg and reserved pineapple juice and cook over low heat. Stir until mixture thickens into a sauce. Cool mixture and add softened cream cheese. Blend well and place over Jello mixture. Top with whipped topping and chopped nuts.
Double recipe if you use a large, oblong pan.

Onnie Jean Walker

BASIC FRENCH VANILLA ICE CREAM

YIELD: 2 quarts

1½ cups milk
3 eggs
¾ cup sugar

½ teaspoon salt
1 tablespoon vanilla extract
3 cups light cream

Scald milk. Beat eggs; add sugar and salt. Gradually add milk to egg mixture. Cook over hot, not boiling, water until mixture thickens and coats spoon, stirring constantly. Cool. Add vanilla extract and cream. Place custard mixture in freezer can, packing ice and ice cream salt around it per manufacturer's directions. Freeze to mush. Remove dasher; cover ice cream, drain off brine. Pack well 4 parts ice to 1 part salt. Cover with newspaper and let stand about 4 hours.

Variations:

Avocado-Walnut Ice Cream: After the custard mixture is thoroughly cooled, with cream and vanilla added, then add ¾ cup sieved or well mashed avocado pulp and ¼ cup finely chopped walnuts. Pour into freezer and freeze.

Tutti-Frutti Tropical Ice Cream: Omit vanilla from French Vanilla recipe and add 3 tablespoons sherry wine, ½ cup chopped preserved orange peel, ¾ cup finely chopped pecans, and ½ cup well-drained crushed pineapple. Freeze.

The Committee

BASIC PLAIN VANILLA ICE CREAM

YIELD: 1½ to 2 quarts

1 quart light cream OR 1 pint
  heavy cream and 1 pint milk;
  scalded and cooled

¾ cup sugar
2 teaspoons vanilla

Combine all ingredients; stir until sugar is dissolved. Freeze according to your ice cream freezer's instructions.

Variations:

For strawberry ice cream: before freezing, add 1 pint crushed strawberries, sweetened with ½ cup sugar or more to taste.

For banana ice cream: before freezing, add 5 large, very ripe mashed bananas, 2 tablespoons sugar, or more; ¼ teaspoon yellow food coloring, and ½ teaspoon lime juice.

The Committee

BOBBIE'S CHOCOLATE PUDDING

¾ cup sugar
2 tablespoons cocoa
3 tablespoons flour

pinch of salt
2 cups milk

Mix ingredients thoroughly. Gradually add milk; cook in saucepan, stirring until thickened. Chill and serve with whipped cream.

Mrs. E. J. Minton

BOILED CUSTARD

1 quart milk, scalded
4 eggs
½ cup sugar

pinch of salt
1 teaspoon vanilla

Cream together eggs, sugar and salt. Add scalded milk gradually to creamed mixture. Cook in double boiler or over pan of water only until mixture coats the spoon. Mixture should be stirred constantly. Remove pan from heat; add vanilla and chill.

I serve it over a spoon of vanilla ice cream sprinkled with fresh coconut. You might like it with a bit of whipped cream and nutmeg.

This is my favorite dessert recipe. It has been printed in the Vero Beach Press Journal several times. I'm sure you will find it very delicious. This is the perfect dessert for any meal, but it is especially good during the Thanksgiving and Christmas holidays.

Betty Roddenberry

BREAD PUDDING I

OVEN: 350° 20 minutes

2 eggs
2 cups milk
½ cup sugar
nutmeg OR cinnamon

4 cups dry bread OR cake crumbs
¼ cup raisins
sliced almonds

Beat eggs, milk, sugar and spice together. Pour over crumbs and let stand until thoroughly soaked. Add raisins and almonds. Bake for 20 minutes in 350° oven. Serve with milk or sauce.

Tabithia Purvis

BREAD PUDDING II

OVEN: 325° 1 hour

3 cups milk
3 eggs
3 big cups crumbled bread cubes
1 teaspoon vanilla
⅓ cup sugar

½ teaspoon cinnamon
½ cup tapioca
½ teaspoon salt
½ cup raisins

Preheat oven to 325°. Thoroughly mix milk, eggs, sugar, vanilla, cinnamon and salt. Add bread cubes, raisins and tapioca. Pour mixture into a buttered 2 quart baking dish, and bake for about 1 hour, or until mixture is firm in middle, or until knife inserted in center, comes out clean.

Serve warm or cold; plain or with milk or whipped cream. Add a little more sugar than the ⅓ cup, but less than ½ cup. Soak raisins in warm water and completely drain before using.

J. A. Roddenberry

CHOCOLATE CHIP ICE CREAM

YIELD: 4 quarts

4 eggs, beaten
2¼ cups sugar
5 cups milk
4 cups heavy cream

4½ teaspoons vanilla
½ teaspoon salt
1⅔ cups grated OR chopped semi-
sweet chocolate

Add sugar gradually to beaten eggs. Continue to beat until mixture is very stiff. Add milk, cream, vanilla and salt and mix throughly. Pour into gallon freezer and churn for about 15 minutes or until the ice cream has frozen to a mushy consistency. Add chocolate and continue freezing.

The Committee

CHOCOLATE ICE CREAM

YIELD: 4 quarts

5 squares unsweetened chocolate,
melted
5 cups milk
2½ cups sugar
5 tablespoons flour

¾ teaspoon salt
4 eggs, slightly beaten
5 cups cream
2 teaspoons vanilla

Scald milk over low heat. Stir in melted chocolate. Combine sugar, flour and salt in a bowl; add eggs and mix well. Pour hot milk over egg mixture carefully. Stir constantly. Cook over low heat until mixture coats a spoon. Chill in refrigerator. Stir in cream and vanilla. Freeze.

The Committee

CHOCOLATE PUDDING

8 cups milk
2 cups sugar
½ cup cocoa
½ cup flour

pinch of salt
2 eggs, well beaten with a little bit
of milk
2 tablespoons vanilla

Mix all ingredients together in milk over medium heat. Stir ingredients in before milk gets too hot. Add vanilla last. Stir constantly while cooking. Remove from heat; cool; refrigerate until ready to serve. May be placed in individual dishes before refrigerating.

This recipe has been in the family for 4 generations.

Lisa Harrison

With dessert, coffee, or after dinner, serve guests a cream sherry, port or sweet wine.

COLD COFFEE SOUFFLÉ

YIELD: 6-8 servings

1 envelope unflavored gelatin
¼ cup cold water
2 teaspoons instant coffee
1 cup sugar
4 eggs

½ teaspoon salt
1 teaspoon vanilla
1 cup heavy cream
½ cup water

Sprinkle gelatin over cold water to soften; dissolve instant coffee in ½ cup water; separate egg yolks and mix yolks with coffee, ½ cup sugar and salt in top part of double boiler. Cook over boiling water; stir constantly, until mixture is thick and custardy looking. Remove from heat; stir in gelatin and vanilla; cool. Beat egg whites until they hold shape; add ½ cup sugar gradually; beat until shiny and definite peaks form. Beat heavy cream until it holds shape. Pile cream on top of egg whites; pour coffee mixture through strainer onto cream and egg whites. Fold in gently. Pour into 2 quart bowl or souffle dish and chill for 2-3 hours, until firm but spongy. Garnish with slightly sweetened whipped cream and chocolate curls.

Ty Fender

CURRIED FRUIT

OVEN: 350° 45 minutes

¼ cup butter
1 cup light brown sugar
4 teaspoons curry powder
½ lemon, juiced
2 tablespoons cornstarch
¼ cup water

12 dried prunes
12 dried peaches
12 dried apricots
1 cup white raisins
½ cup maraschino cherries
1 small can pineapple tidbits

Place butter, sugar and curry powder in a shallow casserole dish. Place dried fruits over this mixture. Blend together lemon juice, water and cornstarch and pour over all fruit.
Bake for 45 minutes in 350° oven.

Mrs. B. Q. Waddell

CUSTARD ICE CREAM

YIELD: 4 quarts

5 eggs, slightly beaten
1¼ cups sugar
½ teaspoon salt

6 cups milk, scalded
4 cups heavy cream
2 tablespoons vanilla

Combine eggs, sugar and salt in a saucepan. Pour hot milk over egg mixture carefully, stirring constantly. Cook over low heat until mixture coats spoon. Chill in refrigerator. Stir in cream and vanilla.

The Committee

DATE NUT MERINGUE TORTE

OVEN: 325° 30 minutes

1 cup graham crackers, crushed
¼ teaspoon baking powder
3 egg whites
1 cup sugar
½ cup dates, chopped

½ cup nuts, chopped
½ teaspoon vanilla
1 cup cream, whipped
3 tablespoons brown sugar

Mix crushed graham crackers with baking powder. Beat egg whites until stiff, but not dry, and slowly add 1 cup sugar, beating all the time. Fold cracker mixture into egg whites and add dates, nuts and vanilla. Bake in a buttered 9″ pie plate for 30 minutes in 325° oven. Serve with whipped cream which has brown sugar dissolved in it before beating cream. Whipped mixture may be made the day before and kept in refrigerator. Ice cream may be used in place of whipped cream.

Mrs. D. G. Perry

DEEP SOUTH CHOCOLATE ICE CREAM

2 tablespoons instant coffee
½ cup boiling water
6 ounces semisweet chocolate
5 egg yolks
¼ cup cold water

½ cup sugar
¼ teaspoon cream of tartar
⅓ cup Grand Marnier OR creme de
cacao
3 cups heavy cream

Dissolve coffee in boiling water. Combine coffee with chocolate in top of double boiler over hot water. Stir occasionally until chocolate melts. Set aside to cool. Beat egg yolks in small bowl at high speed in electric mixer until thick and they form a ribbon. In a small saucepan, mix cold water, sugar, and cream of tartar. Bring to a boil stirring, then allow to boil without stirring for 3 minutes. It should reach the light-thread stage or 230° on a candy thermometer. When mixture is in a thin stream, add the hot syrup to egg yolks, still beating at high speed. Beat for 5 minutes longer, or until mixture cools. Stir in liqueur and chocolate mixture. Mix well. Beat the cream in a chilled bowl until it holds a soft shape, do not beat longer. Fold one cup of the cream into the chocolate mixture, then fold the chocolate/cream mixture into the remaining whipped cream.

Pour batter into a shallow pan and freeze. In about 1½ hours, when firm around the edges, beat again until smooth, then return to freezer until firm.

The Committee

Strawberries, fresh or frozen, are one of the best sources of Vitamin C. In selecting the berries look for full red color; use within one or two days. Washing and stemming before refrigeration results in loss of food value and increases spoilage.

EASY CHOCOLATE ICE CREAM

YIELD: 4 quarts

4 eggs, beaten
⅓ cup sugar
3 cups milk
4 cups heavy cream

4½ teaspoons vanilla
½ teaspoon salt
3 cups chocolate syrup

Add sugar gradually to beaten eggs. Continue to beat mixture until it is very stiff. Add remaining ingredients and mix thoroughly. Pour mixture into gallon freezer and freeze.

The Committee

EASY FLAN
(FACIL)

OVEN: 375° 45-60 minutes

1 three-inch stick cinnamon
2 cups sugar
1 cup water
1 can evaporated milk

8 slightly beaten egg yolks PLUS 1
   egg white
½ cup sugar

Combine first three ingredients and cook until mixture forms a light syrup — just a little sticky, not so it threads. For right consistency, mixture should be boiled for about 2 minutes. Let syrup cool to room temperature.

Meanwhile, blend evaporated milk with combined yolks and white. Slowly carmelize ½ cup sugar in heavy skillet, stirring constantly. Line a 1½ quart casserole with carmelized sugar and pour in evaporated milk and egg mixture. Set casserole in a pan and fill the pan to 1" with boiling water. Bake in moderate 375° oven for 45 minutes to 1 hour or until knife inserted halfway down between center and outside edge comes out clean.

The Committee

EGG KISSES

OVEN: 275° 40 minutes

2 cups sugar
6 egg whites

1½ tablespoons lemon juice

Beat egg whites until stiff. Then gradually add 1 cup of the sugar to mixture. Add remaining cup of sugar to egg whites alternately with lemon juice.

Cover a cookie sheet with brown paper and place kisses on paper in desired shape and size. Bake on low rack in 275° oven for 40 minutes or longer. The secret of success is adding the sugar slowly!

Ivy H. Haynes

ENGLISH TRIFLE

2 — 9" x 2-½" sponge cakes
¼ cup raspberry jam
1 cup blanched almonds OR walnuts, halved
1 cup medium dry sherry
2 tablespoons sugar
1 package frozen raspberries
   thawed, reserve few for top

Custard Sauce:
3 cups milk
4 teaspoons cornstarch
2 tablespoons sugar
2 egg yolks
1 teaspoon vanilla
whipped cream

Cut cake into 1" slices. Coat slices with raspberry jam and place in the bottom of a glass serving bowl. Cut remainder of cake that does not fit into bottom of bowl into 1" squares. Sprinkle squares over slices in bowl. Sprinkle cake pieces with nuts, then pour in sherry. Let stand for at least 15 minutes. Scatter thawed raspberries over cake.

Prepare custard sauce by mixing ½ cup of milk with the cornstarch. Bring remainder of milk to a boil in a saucepan and add sugar. Thicken with the cornstarch mixture. When heated mixture begins to thicken, take a small bowl and place egg yolks in the bowl. Lightly break up yolks and add a little of the sauce to the yolks; blend together. Add egg yolk and sauce mixture back to the saucepan and heat mixture to boiling.

Pour custard over cake and raspberries. Allow cake and custard to cool. Spread whipped cream over the top and place whole raspberries on top to decorate.

Robert Watson
Wayside Inn

FOOD FOR THE GODS

OVEN: 325° 35 minutes

4 egg whites, beaten very stiff
½ pound dates, cut
½ pound English walnuts

6 tablespoons rolled soda crackers
1 cup white sugar
2 teaspoons baking powder

Place cracker crumbs, nuts, dates, sugar and baking powder together and mix. Add this to stiffly beaten egg whites and bake in ungreased muffin pans for about 35 minutes in a slow oven, 325°. Cool slightly and remove from pan. Serve with whipped cream.

This recipe came from my aunt 50 years ago. I do not know where she got it.

Mrs. Parker Henry

Add an egg white to limp whipped cream, chill the mixture briefly and then whip until still.

FRESH FRUIT DESSERT

grapefruit
oranges
tangerines
bananas

2 ounces rum OR brandy OR a dry
  wine
½ teaspoon cinnamon
¼ teaspoon ginger
¼ teaspoon nutmeg
¼ teaspoon dry powdered cloves

Section fruit and cut into bite-size pieces. Slice bananas. Combine all fruit and add all spices and rum, brandy or wine. Mix well. Refrigerate. Serve cold.

Mrs. Leroy E. Oakes

FRIED BANANAS

bananas, firm, but slightly green
eggs, beaten

brown sugar
butter

Slice bananas diagonally at 45° angles. Keep slices about ½" thick. Dip slices in beaten eggs then sprinkle with sugar. Fry in butter until egg batter starts to brown. Serve in place of potatoes.

This is a quick and easy recipe for creating a new taste from something very familiar. Ask your guests if they recognize the flavor. Great for breakfast accompanied by scrambled eggs.

Mrs. David S. Keen

FROZEN DESSERT

OVEN: 350° 20 minutes

YIELD: 15 servings

1 cup flour
¼ cup brown sugar
½ cup chopped pecans
1 stick oleo

½ gallon vanilla ice cream
1 quart lime sherbet
1 quart frozen whipped topping
⅓ cup creme de menthe

Melt oleo; add flour, brown sugar and chopped pecans. Bake for 20 minutes in 350° oven. Stir until crumbly. Cool.

Stir together ice cream, sherbet, whipped topping and creme de menthe until mixture is soft and smooth. Place ⅔ of crumb mixture in a 9 x 13 pan. Add soft mixture and top with remaining crumb mixture. Freeze.

This will keep several days in refrigerator. Excellent to serve with nuts and coffee.

Beatrice Dittmar Coffman

If whipping cream will not stiffen, add 3 or 4 drops of lemon juice gradually and continue whipping.

FRUIT COMPOTE

OVEN: 350° 1 hour

YIELD: 8 servings

1 large can cling peaches
1 large can apricot halves
1 large can pears
1 large can pineapple chunks
1 medium jar maraschino cherries

1 cup walnuts
⅓ cup melted butter
¾ cup brown sugar
2¾ teaspoons curry powder

Open cans of fruit and drain overnight. This is important. Mix butter, sugar and curry powder together. Place fruit in greased casserole and pour butter and sugar sauce over fruit. Bake for 1 hour at 350°. Turn fruit up and place cherries in centers of fruits and walnut halves scattered over top.

C. F. Fawsett, Jr.

GRAPE SHERBET

2 quarts whole milk
1 large carton cream
2½ cups sugar

juice of 4 lemons
2½ cups grape juice

Chill milk and cream in freezer, then add sugar, lemon juice and grape juice. Blend well. Freeze in trays.

Elizabeth McAlister

GRAPENUT PUDDING

OVEN: moderate heat 45 minutes

½ cup butter
1 cup sugar
3 eggs, separated
1 tablespoon flour

3 tablespoons Grapenuts
2 cups milk
1 teaspoon vanilla

Cream butter, sugar and egg yolks; combine flour, Grapenuts, milk and vanilla; blend well. Beat egg whites stiff and fold into other ingredients. Put ingredients in casserole dish and place dish in pan of water. Bake in moderate oven for 45 minutes.

Mrs. Earl Sumner

Lemons will yield more juice if they are stored in a tightly sealed jar of water and refrigerated until needed.

HIMMEL TORTE

OVEN: 325°

½ cup butter OR margarine
4 egg yolks, well beaten
4 tablespoons milk
½ cup sugar
¾ cup cake flour
1 teaspoon baking powder
1 cup sugar
1 teaspoon vanilla

chopped nuts
4 egg whites

Whipped cream filling:
2½ pints whipping cream
sugar
vanilla
crushed pineapple, well drained
OR fresh OR frozen strawberries

Cream together butter and sugar, add beaten egg yolks, flour, baking powder and milk. Beat until mixture is glossy. Pour batter into 2 layer cake pans that have been greased and floured well, especially around the edges. Beat 4 egg whites and add 1 cup granulated sugar very slowly. Beat until very stiff; add vanilla. Spread meringue mixture over batter in pans and sprinkle nuts over meringue. Bake in 325° oven until meringue feels crusty. When cool, cut around edges of meringue and cake. Gently lift from pan and place cake side down on platter. Cover with whipped cream filling. Top with second layer, cake side down and ice top and sides with whipped cream. Blend whipping cream with sugar and vanilla. Gently fold in fruit of your choice.

Frances B. Guthrie

HOT PINEAPPLE CASSEROLE

OVEN: 350° 35 minutes

5 slices white bread, cubed
¼ pound butter (no substitute)
1 — #2½ can crushed pineapple

3 tablespoons flour
1 cup sugar
2 eggs, well beaten

Sauté bread cubes in butter over low heat until cubes are golden brown. This step may be done ahead of time. Mix other ingredients and place in a buttered casserole. Add bread cubes just before placing casserole in oven. Mix cubes in slightly. Bake for 35 minutes, or until set, in 350° oven.

May be used as a dessert or as a side dish with ham.

Mrs. Burnett Bartlett

For a low calorie, vitamin rich dessert, watermelon is perfect. Watermelon is rich in Vitamin C and contains thiamine and riboflavin as well. When selecting the melon, look for a well shaped one with full ends. The skin should appear fairly smooth having a dull luster in various shades of green depending on the variety. The underside should be creamy in color. Avoid choosing one that is bright yellow as it will be sunburned.

KRUMMAL TARTE

OVEN: 300° 25 minutes

3 egg yolks
¾ cup sugar
1 box dates, cut into small pieces
½ cup nuts, pecans OR walnuts
1 cup bread crumbs

dash of salt
1 teaspoon baking soda
1 teaspoon vanilla
3 egg whites

Beat egg yolks with sugar, add cut up dates, and nuts. Mix baking powder with bread crumbs. Add salt and vanilla. Combine dry ingredients with egg yolk mixture. Beat egg whites and fold into batter last. Spread batter in a buttered cake pan and bake in 300° oven for 25 minutes.

To serve, crumble into small pieces and top with whipped cream.

Vera M. Gordon

LEMON BUTTER SAUCE

YIELDS: 1 pint

6 eggs
2 cups sugar
rind of 1 lemon

juice of 2 or 3 lemons (enough for
  ½ cup)
3 tablespoons butter

Combine all ingredients and bring to a boil, stirring continuously until mixture is smooth and thickened.

Dorris Armstrong

LEMON DESSERT

vanilla wafers
4 egg yolks
¾ cup sugar

1 lemon, grated rind and juice
4 egg whites
½ pint whipping cream

Crush wafers and press in pie pan, square pan, or 2 ice trays. Beat egg yolks and add sugar slowly. Beat until creamy. Add juice and rind of lemon and place mixture in double boiler. Cook until smooth and coats the spoon; stirring constantly. Cool mixture. Beat egg whites and then add to custard mixture. Pour blended mixtures over wafers and freeze covered. Keeps for several days if pans remain covered.

Mrs. John McCarty

Oranges and grapefruit can be peeled quite easily if dropped in boiling water for a few minutes before removing the skins.

LEMON ICE CREAM

6 lemons
1 cup heavy cream

1 cup milk
1 cup sugar

Scald cream and milk, then stir in sugar and lemon juice. Mix well then place in a flat pan and freeze.

When frozen solid around the edge and mushy in the middle, stir well and return to freezer. Cover and continue to freeze until firm.

Thaw for 10-15 minutes before serving.

If using fresh lemons for juice you can use the lemons themselves for serving cups. Slice off the flower end about ¼ of the way from the top, and barely slice the stem end enough to make a flat base. Scoop out lemon pulp carefully into a bowl and set hollowed lemons aside. Strain juice and discard pulp. Otherwise, just juice the 6 lemons or enough lemons to yield ¾ cup of juice.

The Committee

LEMON SAUCE

YIELD: 1½ cups

1 tablespoon cornstarch
½ cup sugar
2 tablespoons lemon juice
1 tablespoon grated lemon rind

few grains salt
1 cup water
2 tablespoons butter OR margarine

Mix cornstarch, sugar, lemon rind and salt together. Gradually add water to mixture. Cook over low heat, stirring constantly until thickened. Cook over hot water, stirring occasionally, for 5 minutes more. Add lemon juice and melted butter or margarine.

This is very easy to make and it keeps well. You do not need to use all of it at once. It is excellent over Brown Betty or Bread Pudding.

Polly Crowell

LIME PUDDING

OVEN: 325° 1 hour

YIELD: 6 servings

1 cup sugar
3 tablespoons butter, softened
3 tablespoons flour, all-purpose
2 eggs, separated

3 tablespoons grated lime rind
1 cup milk
3 tablespoons lime juice
whipped cream, optional

Combine sugar, flour and butter in a mixing bowl. Add unbeaten egg yolks, lime juice, grated lime rind and milk. Beat egg whites until stiff, then fold into yolk mixture. Pour batter into greased 1 quart mold or 6 custard cups. Place in a pan of hot water and bake in 325° oven for 1 hour.

This pudding has a cake like top with a smooth, delicious lime sauce beneath. Serve warm or cold, with or without whipped cream.

Doris Schuster

MAMIE'S EGGNOG WHIP

1 pint sweet milk
2 envelopes gelatin
½ cup cold water
8 eggs

1¼ cups sugar
1 teaspoon salt
1 teaspoon nutmeg
½ cup rum OR bourbon

Soak gelatin in cold water. Make a custard of egg yolks, milk 1 cup sugar, salt and nutmeg. Heat mixture over stove until thick. When thick, remove from heat and add gelatin and rum. Cool thoroughly. Beat egg whites with ¼ cup sugar and add to custard. Place mixture in refrigerator to congeal. Serve with whipped cream flavored with sherry; a cherry adds a touch of color. This is a delightful dessert for Christmas time.

Elouise Padrick

MANGO MOUSSE

YIELD: 6-8 servings

1 envelope unflavored gelatin
½ cup cold water
2½ cups peeled, sliced and mashed
    mangoes
1 tablespoon lime juice

½ to ¾ cup sugar to taste
1 egg yolk
1 egg
1 cup whipping cream, whipped
spring of fresh mint

In a saucepan, soften gelatin in cold water. Stir over low heat until gelatin is dissolved. Combine mangoes, sugar, and lime juice together and mix well. Then blend into gelatin mixture. Beat egg yolk and egg together until frothy; add to mixture in pan; cool. Gently fold in whipped cream; spoon into individual compotes; and garnish with sprig of fresh mint.

Lucinda Lauser

MELON-BLUEBERRY COOLER

YIELD: 6 servings

1 large, firm cantaloupe, peeled,
    seeded, and diced
2 cups fresh blueberries, rinsed
    and drained

⅓ to ½ cup sugar, to taste
1½ cups orange juice
2 egg whites, unbeaten

Place diced cantaloupe, sugar, and orange juice in blender and whirl at top speed until smooth. When smooth, put mixture into ice cube tray and place in freezer. When mixture is half frozen, remove from freezer, put into mixing bowl and beat with electric beater until fluffy. Add egg whites and beat until again fluffy. Then gently fold in fresh blueberries. Return mixture to freezer and freeze until firm. When mixture is frozen spoon into prepared cantaloupe halves and serve immediately.

This makes a delightful and refreshing dessert or can be served as a luncheon meal.

Lucinda Lauser

MINCEMEAT TARTLETS

OVEN: 350° 30 minutes

YIELD: 8 servings

1¾ cups all-purpose flour
⅓ cup granulated sugar
⅓ cup dark brown sugar
⅔ cup ground blanched almonds
½ teaspoon cinnamon
¼ teaspoon baking powder

⅓ cup butter
2 eggs
1 cup mincemeat
2 tablespoons melted butter
½ cup chopped walnuts

In a large bowl, combine flour, sugars, almonds, cinnamon and baking powder. Cut ⅓ cup butter into mixture with a pastry blender or two knives until dough is crumbly. Blend in 1 egg and work dough until smooth. Let dough rest for about 1 hour. Meanwhile, combine mincemeat, walnuts, and 2 tablespoons melted butter.

Preheat oven to 350°. Roll out dough to ⅛" thickness. Cut out eight 5" circles. Line eight 3" greased tartlet pans with dough and fill with mincemeat. Roll out leftover dough and cut eight 3" circles. Cover top of each tartlet with dough circles. Fold rim of dough over tartlet and pinch together with fork. Brush with remaining beaten egg and prick top with fork. Bake in 350° oven for 30 minutes.

The Committee

NANA'S BREAD PUDDING

OVEN: 325° 40 minutes

2 eggs
1 pint milk
2 tablespoons sugar

nutmeg
2 slices bread, buttered well
handful of raisins

Beat eggs well in a pint measuring cup. Eggs should be frothy. Pour beaten eggs into a small baking dish. Measure milk in pint cup used to beat eggs; stir milk into eggs until liquids blend well. Stir in a few dashes of nutmeg.

Place buttered bread in the dish with liquid. Use as much of the second slice as will allow the milk to show through several cracks. Push bread under liquid several times.

Scatter raisins over all and into milk mixture. Generously sprinkle nutmeg over the top. Bake in 325° oven for 40 minutes. Do not overcook.

The result should be a custard topped with a spongy, browned crust, and have an altogether delightful flavor.

My grandmother used to vary it for us children via a teaspoon of her own jelly, made from homegrown grapes.

Caroline Bassett Haman

A variety of nuts can be served with cheese, fruit, or wine for a delicious dessert.

NANNIE'S APPLE FRITTERS

1 cup flour
1½ teaspoons baking powder
¼ teaspoon salt
4 tablespoons sugar
1 egg

⅔ cup milk
3 pounds apples, pared, cored, and
    sliced thin
powdered sugar

Sift flour, baking powder, salt and sugar together into a bowl. Add beaten egg and the milk. Beat until smooth. Fold in thinly sliced and pared apples.
Drop by spoonfuls into deep fat heated to 375°. Fry to a light brown; drain on paper towels and dust lightly with powdered sugar. Serve hot.

Carol Ann Gollnick

ORANGE CHARLOTTE ORIGINAL

4½ packages plain gelatin
3 cups sugar
4 cups boiling water
rind of 3 oranges, grated

4 cups orange juice
4 egg whites
½ pint whipping cream
Lady Finger type cookies

Add sugar to boiling water. Add gelatin and mix well. Gel until in slush state. In the meantime, beat egg whites; then beat cream separately. Fold both beaten mixtures into gel mixture. Add orange juice. Fold all mixtures together well. Place cookies across bottom of a large flat, deep casserole. Then put in partly congealed mixture to about 1". Place more cookies on sides of dish and fill in more mixture. Continue until top of dish is reached. Cover with aluminum foil and chill for 24 hours. Turn out on a large plate to serve.
This recipe has won many prizes in North Carolina and here in Florida.

Mrs. Walter Buckingham

ORANGE VELVET ICE CREAM

YIELD: about 2 quarts

2 egg yolks
1 cup light cream
¼ teaspoon salt
2 cups sugar
1 cup water

2 cups orange juice
1 cup heavy cream, whipped
¼ cup finely diced OR shredded
    candied orange peel

Place egg yolks, light cream and salt in top of double boiler and beat with egg beater until smoothly blended. Put over simmering water and cook, stirring constantly, until mixture is slightly thickened and coats metal spoon.
Cool mixture. Boil sugar, water and juice for 5 minutes. Cool. Combine mixtures and fold in cream. Partially freeze in crank-type freezer. Then add orange peel and finish freezing.

The Committee

Tropical Florida home of
Mr. and Mrs. J. Cortland Jackson
Martin County, Florida

"MARVISTA" — Spanish mission-style home of
Mr. and Mrs. Dennis S. Hudson
Martin County, Florida

OVER JOYFUL

2 quarts milk
12 eggs
2 cups sugar
vanilla

1 pint heavy cream
sugar to sweeten
nutmeg
Grand Marnier

In a heavy pot, warm milk. Beat eggs and add 2 cups of sugar to eggs. Stir beaten mixture into milk. Cook over low heat, stirring constantly, until mixture coats spoon. (I prefer to use a wooden spoon.) Remove mixture from heat and let it cool a little; then add vanilla. Refrigerate when cool. Whip heavy cream, sweeten to taste and refrigerate.

To serve, pour chilled custard in punch bowl, top with whipped cream and sprinkle with nutmeg. Add Grand Marnier to taste.

This is my grandmother's festive holiday dessert recipe which I serve with fruit cake or Christmas cookies. It is delicious with or without the liqueur.

Mrs. Charles R. P. Brown

PEACH ICE CREAM
(In Hand Churn)

3 quarts milk
3 cups sugar
6 level tablespoons flour
6 eggs, beaten

vanilla
2-3 cups sweetened fresh peaches
OR 2 packages frozen peaches

Warm milk in large heavy pot. Mix sugar and flour well; stir into beaten eggs; then into lukewarm milk. Cook over low heat, stirring constantly, until mixture coats spoon. Cool, then add vanilla. Stir peaches into cooled custard and place in a 6 quart hand churn. Freeze, using ice, ice cream salt and elbow grease.

Mangos, raspberries or any fruit in season may be substituted for peaches. This is great fun for a hot, sunny, summer afternoon.

Mrs. C. D. Mustaine

PEPPERMINT CANDY ICE CREAM

YIELD: 4 quarts

4 eggs, beaten
2¼ cups sugar
5 cups milk
4 cups heavy cream

4½ teaspoons vanilla
½ teaspoon salt
1½ cups crushed peppermint stick
candy

Add sugar gradually to beaten eggs. Continue to beat until mixture is very stiff. Add milk, cream, vanilla, and salt; mix thoroughly. Pour into gallon freezer and churn for about 15 minutes or until the ice cream has frozen to a mushy consistency. Add the crushed candy and continue freezing.

The Committee

PHILADELPHIA ICE CREAM

YIELD: 4 quarts

10 cups light cream
2 cups sugar

2 tablespoons vanilla
¼ teaspoon salt

Pour cream into a gallon freezer. Gradually add sugar, stirring constantly until sugar is dissolved. Stir in vanilla and salt. Freeze.

The Committee

PINEAPPLE-ALMOND PUDDING WITH SAUCE

OVEN: 325° 1 hour

1 package pineapple flavored cake
    mix
2 cups milk
2 eggs
½ cup sugar

¼ teaspoon salt
½ teaspoon lemon extract
½ cup chopped almonds, reserve a
    few for topping
¼ cup drained, crushed pineapple

Bake cake mix according to package directions. Cool. Cube un-iced cake to yield 4 cups.

Spread cubes in casserole; 2 quart size is best.

For pineapple sauce, beat eggs slightly, add sugar, nuts, salt, lemon extract and milk. Pour over cake cubes. Do not stir. Scatter pineapple over top and garnish with sliced nuts. Bake in slow 325° oven for 1 hour.

Filberts or Brazil nuts may be used instead of almonds. Serve warm or cold with pineapple sauce.

A yellow cake mix may be substituted for the pineapple cake mix, but add pineapple extract to the plain mix for flavor.

This is my own original recipe.

Loretta W. Scott

PINEAPPLE BISQUE

½ pound butter OR margarine
4 eggs, separated
1 — #2 can crushed pineapple
1 cup chopped nuts
1 teaspoon vanilla

¾ pound confectioners sugar
1 pint whole cream
4 ounces maraschino cherries,
    halved
crushed vanilla wafers

Blend butter, sugar and egg yolks well. Add vanilla, then add stiffly beaten egg whites. Line a well greased (with butter) baking pan with crushed vanilla wafers. Pour blended mixture into pan. Spread crushed, drained pineapple evenly over batter. Then spread nuts in a thin layer over pineapple. Whip cream until stiff. Add split cherries, and spread evenly on layers in pan. Sprinkle crushed wafers liberally on top. Refrigerate for at least 12 hours at 38° to 40°. When ready to serve, slice as pie.

Eleanor Zych

PISTACHIO DESSERT

1 small box pistachio pudding mix
1 cup milk
1 — #2 can crushed pineapple
1 - 9 ounce carton whipped topping

1 cup nuts, pecans OR walnuts
1 package miniature marshmallows

Mix pudding and milk together. Add remaining ingredients and place in refrigerator for 2-3 hours to set.

This recipe was served at a family reunion and originally came from Jean Williams. No other dish served held a light to this one.

Lucy Gant

PUDDING DELIGHT

14 whole graham crackers
1 package, 6 serving size, vanilla flavor instant pudding and pie filling

2 cups cold milk
1 cup thawed whipped topping
1 — 21 ounce can cherry pie filling

Line a 9" square pan with whole graham crackers, breaking crackers if necessary to fit. Prepare pudding mix with milk as directed on package for pudding. Let stand for 5 minutes then blend in whipped topping. Spread half of pudding mixture over the crackers. Add another layer of crackers; top with remaining pudding mixture. Add another layer of crackers. Spread cherry pie filling over the top layer of crackers. Chill for 3 hours.

Eva Mae Williams

RHUBARB CRISP

OVEN: 350° 1 hour

Topping:
1 cup sifted flour
¾ cup oatmeal
1 cup brown sugar
½ cup melted butter
1 teaspoon cinnamon

Batter:
1 cup sugar
2 tablespoons cornstarch
1 cup water
1 teaspoon vanilla
2 cups rhubarb, cut into 1" pieces

Combine sugar and cornstarch in a bowl. Blend water and vanilla together then add to sugar mixture. Add rhubarb and blend well.

Place rhubarb mixture on the bottom of a baking dish.

Combine all ingredients for topping and crumble mixture over rhubarb. Bake for 1 hour in 350° oven and serve at room temperature with whipped cream or ice cream.

Beau Pavin

RUM RAISIN ICE CREAM

YIELD: 1 gallon

2 tablespoons cornstarch
2 quarts milk
4 eggs, separated
2 cups sugar
½ teaspoon salt

2 tablespoons vanilla
¾ pound dark raisins
½ pint dark rum
1 pint heavy cream

Marinate raisins overnight in rum. Dissolve cornstarch in a few spoons of milk. Heat remaining milk and add cornstarch mixture, stirring constantly. Beat egg yolks; pour a little of the hot milk into yolks while stirring. Add sugar to yolk mixture, blend well. Mix yolk mixture with milk mixture. Stir constantly and cook over low heat until mixture coats metal spoon. Cool several hours, preferable overnight, in the refrigerator. When ready to freeze, beat egg whites with salt and vanilla until frothy.

Add beaten egg white mixture to chilled milk mixture. Add raisins and rum. Stir in cream and pour into 5 quart freezer container. Follow manufacturer's directions for freezing.

The Committee

SPANISH CUSTARD I
(Flan De Leche)

OVEN: 350° 30 minutes

YIELD: 6 servings

3 cups sugar
½ cup water
6 eggs
1 teaspoon vanilla

¼ teaspoon anisette, scant
pinch of salt
1 pint scalded milk

Boil one cup sugar and ½ cup water until sugar is brown, then pour this caramel into 6 buttered custard cups. Beat eggs and add 2 cups sugar, vanilla, anisette, and salt. Beat mixture again. Add scalded milk little by little then strain through a cloth. Pour mixture into the custard cups. Place cups in a water filled pan and bake for 30 minutes in 350° oven. Do not let water boil or custard will be filled with holes. Cool in refrigerator. When ready to serve, run around edges of custard with knife to break away from cups. Then turn upside down. Caramel tops the custard.

The Committee

SPANISH CUSTARD II

OVEN: 300° — 350°

1 quart milk
7 slices bread
9 eggs

1 can pineapple
vanilla
2 cups sugar

Soak bread in hot water. Drain bread, then mash with potato masher. Mix all ingredients together. Bake in a 300° — 350° oven until set, in a pan with hot water.

Lola Kimball

STRAWBERRIES KIRSCH

1 quart strawberries
½ cup powdered sugar

1 cup whipped cream
¼ cup Kirsch

Clean berries and remove hulls. Reserve some berries for topping. Cut berries into halves or quarter slices. Sprinkle with powdered sugar and let stand for 10 minutes. Whip cream and flavor with Kirsch; fold strawberies into cream. Garnish with reserved strawberry halves.

Mrs. Noah Lybrand, Jr.

STRAWBERRY PRETZEL

OVEN: 350° 10 minutes

¾ cup oleo
3 tablespoons brown sugar
2½ cups crushed pretzels, do not
crush too fine
1 large package strawberry flavored gelatin

2 cups boiling water
3 cups chilled OR very cold strawberries, measured after hulling
1 — 8 ounce package cream cheese
1 cup sugar, scant
1 small carton whipped topping

Cream oleo and brown sugar; blend with coarsely crushed pretzels. Pat mixture into lightly buttered 9 x 13 pan. Bake in 350° oven for 10 minutes.

Dissolve gelatin in boiling water. Add strawberries while liquid is hot. Frozen berries may be used if desired. Cool, until mixture begins to set.

Cream 1 cup sugar and cream cheese together. Fold in whipped topping to creamed mixture. Spread the cream cheese mixture over the cooled crust. When gelatin mixture begins to set, pour it over the top of cheese mixture. Refrigerate until firm.

This may be used as a dessert or a salad.

Gail Filbert Bermudez

SUGAR COATED WALNUTS

1½ cups granulated sugar
¼ cup honey, scant
½ cup water

3 cups walnuts
½ teaspoon vanilla

Place ingredients in medium size kettle and boil until soft ball stage is reached; that is when mixture dropped in cold water forms a ball. Add vanilla and blend. Stir in nuts and mix until mixture becomes thick and creamy. This takes quite a while. Turn out onto wax paper and separate.

Janiece Sumner

Give gelatins a firmer set by adding 2 tablespoons of vinegar for each package of gelatin used. The vinegar will not spoil the taste.

TEA SAUCE

YIELD: 8 dessert servings

¼ cup sugar
½ teaspoon cornstarch
dash of salt
2 egg yolks

1 cup heavy cream
¼ cup milk
⅓ cup Tea Liqueur (see recipe)
½ teaspoon vanilla

In a small, heavy saucepan, stir together sugar, cornstarch and salt; add the egg yolks and stir to blend. Scald ½ cup of the cream with milk; whisking constantly and vigorously; gradually add scalded mixture to egg yolk mixture. Cook over low heat, stirring constantly and without boiling, until thickened; 7-8 minutes. At once, stir in the tea liqueur and vanilla; continue cooking over low heat. Stir constantly and without boiling, until sauce thickens again; 1-2 minutes. If the heat is too high and the sauce curdles, it may be restored by whirling briefly with an electric blender. Cover the surface, without pressing down, with clear plastic wrap. Chill.

Up to 4 hours before serving, whip the remaining ½ cup cream and fold in.

This is marvelous with lemon snow; with a clear gelled lemon dessert; with poached or coddled pears or apples; with fresh strawberries, raspberries or blueberries.

The Committee

EGGS, CHEESE, RICE, PASTA

EGGS

CHEESE

RICE

PASTA

COMPANY EGGS

YIELD: 6-8 servings

10 eggs
6 ounces cream cheese
2 tablespoons chives

salt to taste
2 tablespoons butter

Melt butter, add beaten eggs and cook, stirring until they start to set. Add cubed cream cheese and chives and salt. Stir until cheese is melted and eggs are still soft. Don't overcook. Serve on buttered toast.

Kay Wild

EGG CASSEROLE

6 eggs
1½ tablespoons butter
1½ tablespoons flour
1 cup milk

¼ pound or more New York cheese
salt
paprika
round snack crackers, crushed

Hard boil 6 eggs. Make a cream sauce using the butter, flour and milk, Season sauce with salt and paprika. Grate cheese. In a buttered casserole, make a layer of crushed cracker crumbs. Top crumbs with a layer of sliced eggs, then a layer of sauce, followed by a layer of grated cheese. Repeat these layers 2 or 3 times. Top with more crackers and dot with butter. Sprinkle with paprika and parsley. Heat until bubbly.
This is delicious with a buffet featuring ham or turkey.

Brenda Counts Bedell

EGG SOUFFLE

OVEN: 350° 45 minutes

YIELD: 12 servings

1½ pounds sausage meat
9 eggs
12 slices bread, crusts removed and cubed
1½ teaspoons dry mustard

1½ teaspoons salt
1½ cups grated New York sharp cheddar cheese
3 cups milk

Brown sausage, drain and cool. Beat eggs into milk. Add salt, pepper, mustard and bread cubes. Fold in chesse and sausage. Pour into 9 x 13 baking dish and refrigerate overnight. Remove from refrigerator 1 hour before baking. Bake at 350° for 45 minutes. Cool 10 minutes before cutting.
Very good served with fresh fruit salad and sweet rolls.

Claudia McNulty

Add a dash of cream or milk when scrambling eggs to produce smoother and richer scrambled eggs.

EGGS BENEDICT

Canadian bacon
English muffins
6 large eggs
dash of cayenne pepper

¼ teaspoon salt
1 tablespoon lemon juice
¼ pound real butter

Simultaneously toast the muffins, fry the bacon, and poach two of the eggs in a covered egg poacher. Place butter in a metal measuring cup and heat on the stove, melting butter. Separate the yolks from 4 eggs and place yolks in a blender. Add salt, lemon juice, cayenne pepper to the egg yolks and blend at low speed. Bring butter to a boil, just short of scorching. Turn blender on high and remove center of lid. Pour hot butter into mixture in a steady stream. Stack muffin, bacon, and egg and cover with sauce.

The night before, fill two Pilsner glasses with varied size melon balls. Use watermelon and cantaloupe. Don't make balls all the same size. Fill glasses with a good dry white champagne and place in refrigerator to chill. This allows time for balls to absorb the champagne. Serve with Eggs Benedict and forget the coffee.

Ron Forsyth

FLUFFY SOUFFLÉ

OVEN: 375°

butter
6 slices thin, white bread, crusts re-
    moved*
3 eggs
3 cups milk
grated cheese, as much as you like,
    any kind

salt
pepper
1 teaspoon Worcestershire sauce
1 teaspoon prepared mustard
paprika
*use for topping

Place liquids in a bowl. Beat in egg and add mustard, Worcestershire sauce, salt and pepper. In an ovenproof bread pan, place 2 slices of bread, heavily buttered. Add a thick layer of cheese. Continue alternating layers for a total of 3 layers of bread and cheese. Pour liquid over layers until it is soaked up. Sprinkle heavily with paprika. Crush bread crusts and sprinkle on top. Cook slowly at 375°.

Please do not tell what you put in this.

Dorothy Binney Palmer

ITALIAN EGG OMELETTE

YIELD: 1 serving

¼ teaspoon oregano
2 fresh eggs
1 tablespoon grated Romano
    cheese

1 teaspoon basil leaf
¼ teaspoon pepper
¼ teaspoon salt
½ small onion, chopped

Beat eggs thoroughly and add oregano, cheese, basil, salt and pepper. Mix well. Sauté onions to tenderness, but not brown, and add egg mixture to pan. Cook over low heat until done.

Ann Callino

KENTUCKY CHEESE SOUFFLÉ

OVEN: 350° 55 minutes

2 cups milk	3 well beaten eggs
3 tablespoons minute tapioca	1 pound grated longhorn, mild
1 teaspoon salt	cheese

Cook milk, tapioca and salt in the top of a double boiler until it thickens into a soft custard; stirring most of the time. Remove from heat and gradually add cheese. Mix until well dissolved. Cool slightly and fold in eggs and mix well. Pour into casserole and set casserole in a pan of warm water. Bake casserole in pan of water, uncovered, in 350° oven for about 55 minutes; until a knife inserted comes out clean. Soufflé can be browned more under broiler.

This is a very reliable recipe. It will not fall. It can also be heated over the next day, and is very good as a sandwich filler. It is very popular, though old.

Mrs. Walter S. Buckingham

SAN FRANCISCO EGGS

OVEN: 350° 15-20 minutes

1 package frozen spinach, (10 ounces), cooked and drained	2 tablesppons milk
dash of nutmeg	4 eggs
dash of pepper	Parmesan cheese
1 can cream of shrimp soup	2 English muffins

Blend ¼ cup of the soup with the milk and set aside. Mix remaining soup with spinach. Place spinach mix in 4 individual baking cups, and break one egg into each cup. Spoon reserved milk and soup mixture over eggs. Sprinkle with cheese. Bake at 350° for 15-20 minutes, until set. Serve over toasted English muffin halves.

This may also be baked in an 8 x 8 inch baking dish if desired.

Gloria Bleck

SAUSAGE AND EGG SOUFFLE

OVEN: 350° 35-40 minutes   YIELD: 6-8 servings

1 pound hot sausage	½ teaspoon dry mustard
½ pound sharp cheese	1 onion, chopped
6 eggs	1 green pepper, chopped
6 slices bread	2 cups milk

Cook and drain sausage. Grate cheese; beat eggs lightly; cube bread. Sauté onion and pepper in mustard. Add milk. Mix all ingredients together and place in a 9 x 13 pan overnight in the refrigerator. Bake the next day at 350° for 35-40 minutes.

Bobbylee Wilson

SAUSAGE SOUFFLÉ

OVEN: 350° 45 minutes

YIELD: 8-10 servings

8 eggs
2 cups milk
1 teaspoon salt
1 teaspoon dry mustard

2 slices bread, cubed
1 pound sausage
1 cup grated cheddar cheese

Brown sausage and drain. Add milk, salt and dry mustard, beat well. Fold in bread cubes, cheese and sausage. Pour into glass baking dish and refrigerate overnight. Bake at 350° for 45 minutes. Let stand for 10 minutes before cutting.

Terrific for a large group, as the cook can prepare it the night before.

Kim Lewis

SOUFFLÉ EXCELSIOR

OVEN: 350° 30 minutes; 375° 15 minutes; 400° 5 minutes   YIELD: 6 servings

½ pound Tagliatelle
¼ pound grated Gruyere cheese
¼ pound grated Parmesan cheese
3½ tablespoons butter
¼ pound prosciutto ham
1 quart milk

2 tablespoons flour
4 egg yolks
6 egg whites, beaten stiff
salt
pepper
nutmeg

Cook the Tagliatelle for a minute or two in heavily salted, boiling water. Drain well and turn into a well buttered soufflé dish. Dress them with a white sauce. Add bits of butter, chopped ham, salt, pepper, and nutmeg so they are well flavored. When the Tagliatelle have cooled, add the egg yolks, stirring constantly and finally, fold in the stiffly beaten egg whites. Place mixture in soufflé dish. Do not fill dish more than ¾ full. Place dish in preheated oven, 350°-375°, and bake for 30 minutes at 350°, 15 minutes at 375°, and at 400° for the last 5 minutes. When a high, golden, crisp crust has formed, the souffle is ready. Let it cool a little and then serve immediately.

Annamaria Dini

Eggs should be cooked below the high boiling point to prevent toughness. To hard-cook eggs, bring the eggs to a boil, cover, remove from heat, and allow the eggs to stand for ten to fifteen minutes.

ASPARAGUS QUICHÉ I

OVEN: 375° 35 minutes

14 whole fresh asparagus spears
  cooked
1 unbaked 9″ pie shell
3 eggs, slightly beaten
¾ teaspoon salt
pinch of white pepper

1 cup half & half cream
pinch of nutmeg
¼ pound bacon, diced, cooked and
  crumbled
1 cup (4 ounces) shredded Swiss
  cheese

Reserve 8 asparagus spears for garnish. Chop remaining spears. Place pie shell in freezer for at least 15 minutes. Preheat oven to 425°. Bake pie shell for 7-10 minutes. Remove from oven. In a small bowl, mix eggs, salt, white pepper, half & half, and nutmeg. Add chopped asparagus to mixture. Sprinkle bacon and cheese over bottom of partially baked pie shell. Pour egg mixture into pie shell and arrange reserved asparagus spears on top. Bake for 35 minutes at 375°.
I use frozen asparagus.

Teresa Eidson

ASPARAGUS QUICHÉ II

OVEN: 425° 40 minutes

YIELD: 6-8 servings

pastry for 9″ pie pan
12-15 asparagus spears, cooked,
  trimed, and drained
1½ cups grated Swiss cheese
4 eggs

2 cups light cream
⅛ teaspoon ground nutmeg
½ teaspoon ground pepper
¼ teapoon salt

Preheat oven to 425°. Line a 9″ pie pan with pastry. Spread cheese in pastry crust. Place asparagus in pan like the spokes of a wheel; tips at the perimeter. Beat eggs, light cream, salt, nutmeg and pepper together. Pour over cheese and asparagus. Bake for about 40 minutes, until puffed and golden. Cool 5 minutes before cutting into wedges.

Sarah Mundy

Shells from hard boiled eggs can be removed rapidly and easily if immediately after cooking the eggs are dipped in cold water.

CHEESE CASSEROLE

OVEN: 325° 1 hour

6 slices buttered bread, cut into ½″
   cubes
¾ cup cheddar cheese OR ⅔ cup
   Cracker Barrel shredded cheese
4 eggs, well beaten
½ teaspoon dry mustard

2 cups milk
½ teaspoon salt
½ cup mushrooms
1 cup diced ham
bacon bits OR crumbled bacon

Grease a casserole dish or a 9″ x 13″ pan. Alternate layers of bread, cheese, mushrooms, and ham in pan. Combine milk and eggs and pour over layers in pan; push down into layers. Cover pan and let stand overnight. Bake for 1 hour at 325°. Sprinkle bacon bits on top 10 minutes before removing from oven.

This is good for brunch with juice and hot rolls.

Irene Baker

CHEESE SOUFFLÉ I

OVEN: 300° 1¼ hours

¼ cup butter
¼ cup flour
1 cup milk
½ teaspoon salt

few drops tabasco sauce
½ pound shredded sharp cheddar
   cheese
4 eggs, separated

Melt butter in saucepan and add flour. Slowly add milk to saucepan, stirring constantly. Cook and stir until thick. Cool. Beat egg yolks and add cheese. Blend yolk/cheese mixture with flour/milk mixture. Grently fold in stiffly beaten egg whites. Pour mixture into 1½ quart soufflé dish. Set dish in a pan containing 1″ of water. Bake at 300° for 1¼ hours.

This is also good with Swiss cheese.

Pat Brooks

CHEESE SOUFFLÉ II

OVEN: 350° 45 minutes   YIELD: 6-8 servings

½ pound processed cheese, diced
6 slices white bread, crusts removed, buttered and cubed
½ cup oleo, melted
1 pint half & half
3 eggs, well beaten

½ teaspoon salt
½ teaspoon dry mustard
½ teaspoon minced onion
1 teaspoon Worcestershire sauce
dash of tabasco

Put bread cubes in bottom of buttered casserole dish. Add cheese and pour melted oleo over this. Mix eggs, half & half, and seasonings. Pour egg mixture over ingredients in casserole. Let stand overnight in refrigerator. Before cooking, remove casserole from refrigerator and allow to reach room temperature. Bake for 45 minutes at 350°.

For variations, you can add 1½ pounds of cooked shrimp, crabmeat, chicken or ham. You can also add mushrooms if desired.

This is an excellent brunch dish and everyone loves it.

Mabel Fawsett

NEVER-FAIL CHEDDAR CHEESE SOUFFLÉ

OVEN: 350° 45 minutes

YIELD: 4-6 servings

**6 ounces sharp natural cheddar
cheese, diced
6 large eggs, separated
6 tablespoons all-purpose flour
6 tablespoons oleo OR butter
1 teaspoon salt**

**½ teaspoon paprika
1½ cups milk
½ teaspoon Worcestershire sauce
¼ teaspoon dry mustard
Parmesan cheese**

Soufflé may be baked in a 2 quart 3½" soufflé dish or a straight sided casserole dish. Butter dish and sprinkle with Parmesan cheese. Set aside.

In top of double boiler, melt butter and blend flour and seasonings using a wooden spoon. Add milk, stirring constantly until mixture is smooth and thick. Stir in cheese until melted. Remove from water and set aside.

Beat egg yolks until thick and then stir into cheese mixture. Beat egg whites to form soft peaks. Gradually stir cheese mixture into egg whites, folding with a rubber spatula until blended. Bake uncovered in preheated oven at 350° for 45 minutes. Do not open oven door.

This soufflé may be made 18 hours ahead and refrigerated — bake in a cold oven at 350° for 50 minutes. It may also be frozen for 7-10 days. Bake as for refrigerated soufflé, increasing time to 1½ hours. You may add ¼ teaspoon cream of tartar for egg whites.

We have found that an aluminum foil collar around the soufflé dish extending at least one inch above the dish gives a higher, "capped" souffle.

Mrs. Leroy E. Oakes

QUICHÉ

OVEN: 350° 40-50 minutes

YIELD: 6 servings

**1 package dried beef, chopped
2 tablespoons oleo
1 cup sliced mushrooms OR 1 — 4
ounce can mushrooms
½ cup chopped onions
1 unbaked pie shell, 10"**

**1½ cups Swiss cheese, shredded
2 tablespoons flour
4 eggs, slightly beaten
1½ cups milk
dash cayenne**

Cook onions, beef, and mushrooms in oleo until onion is tender. Spread mixture evenly on bottom of pie curst. Toss cheese with flour and place on beef mixture. Combine eggs, milk, cayenne and pour over all. Bake at 350° for 40-50 minutes. Cut into pieshaped pieces to serve.

Serve with fruit for brunch or lunch. Add green vegetable for a main meal.

Jan Archer

Cheese and cheese dishes should be cooked very slowly. Cheese will be tough and rubbery when cooked fast or at a high temperature.

QUICHÉ/CREAM CHEESE

OVEN: 350° 40 minutes

4 ounces whipped cream cheese
2 ounces sour cream
3 ounces milk
3 eggs, slightly beaten
3 tablespoons ready to use bacon
  bits
2 tablespoons grated cheese

few drops Worcestershire sauce
salt
pepper
sprinkle of chopped chives
sprinkle of chpped parsley
1 — 9" pre-cooked pastry shell

Pre-cook pie shell for 6 minutes at 400°. Blend together sour cream, creamed cheese and milk. Beat eggs slightly and add to blended ingredients. Add bacon bits, grated cheese and seasonings. Bake at 350° approximately 40 minutes or until filling is set. Serve hot or cold.

Rosaila Maggiacomo

QUICHÉ LORRAINE I

OVEN: 450° 10 minutes; 350° 20 minutes

¼ pound bacon
½ cup onions, chopped
3 eggs, lightly beaten
2 cups half & half
½ teaspoon salt

dash of cayenne
dash of nutmeg
½ pound Swiss cheese, grated
1 — 9" pie crust, pricked

Pre-bake pie crust for 5 minutes at 425°. Fry bacon until it begins to crisp. Drain bacon and break into small pieces. Mix with onions that have been sauteed in bacon fat until yellow. Combine, after draining, with bacon and place in pie shell along with grated cheese.

Mix remaining ingredients together and pour over bacon, onions, and cheese.

Bake at 450° for 10 minutes. Reduce heat to 350° for about 20 minutes or until spatula inserted in center comes out clean.

Let stand for a few minutes before serving. For a tasty brunch serve with fresh fruits or a salad.

Rose Rumsey

QUICHÉ LORRAINE II

OVEN: 325° 45 minutes   YIELD: 6 servings

½ pound Swiss cheese, grated
1 tablespoon flour
1 cup light cream
3 eggs, beaten well

salt
cayenne pepper
baked 9" pie shell

Mix grated cheese with flour. Distribute cheese evenly in pre-baked 9" pie shell. Mix eggs and cream and pour over cheese mixture. Bake for 45 minutes, in slow oven, 325°, until knife inserted in center of pie comes out clean. Do not overbake. Serve warm.

This makes a wonderful luncheon or supper dish, with green salad and simple dessert.

Peggy Hoskins

QUICHÉ LORRAINE III

OVEN: 375° 40-45 minutes

1 prepared pie crust OR make ½
  packaged pie crust mix
½ pound bacon, fried and drained
⅓ pound Swiss cheese, cut into
  strips
3-4 eggs, beaten

½ teaspoon salt
1 tablespoon flour
1½ tablespoons margarine
dash of cayenne pepper
dash of nutmeg
1 can (2 cups) evaporated milk

Line pie crust with cheese and bacon in alternating layers; beginning with cheese and ending with bacon. Pour blended egg, salt, flour, margarine, pepper, nutmeg and milk mixture over layers.

Bake in 375° oven for 40-45 minutes or until crust on pie shell is brown and custard is set. Cool for 3 minutes and serve.

This is very good served for a luncheon with a green salad. Quiche can be made ahead and frozen. Thaw and bake in 300° oven for 30 minutes.

Dorothy Klosterman

QUICHÉ LORRAINE IV

OVEN: 400° 15 minutes; 350° 35 minutes

2 commercial pie shells
12 strips lean cooked bacon OR
  equal amount of ham
1 tablespoon onion, finely chopped
½ pound Swiss cheese, shredded
3 eggs, well beaten
2 cups light cream

1 tablespoon melted butter
½ teaspoon nutmeg
dash of tabasco
dash of cayenne pepper
salt
pepper

Arrange meat in pie crusts; sprinkle onion over meat; then sprinkle cheese over onion. Combine eggs, cream, butter and seasonings and add to pie crusts. Bake in 400° oven for 15 minutes; reduce hear to 350° and bake for 35 minutes.

Set pie crusts aside for 10 minutes before serving. This allows the custard to congeal.

This recipe dates from the time of Joan of Arc.

Mrs. Jack G. Rose, Jr.

ARMENIAN RICE

OVEN: 350° 1 hour

1 cup washed rice
1 can consomme soup
1 can beef bouillon soup
1 cup water

1 diced onion
1 small can diced mushrooms
½ stick butter
parsley flakes

Combine all ingredients and bake in a casserole dish in 350° oven for 1 hour.

Leila Fries Darress

BROWN RICE

OVEN: 350° 1 hour

1 cup rice, uncooked, either quick
  cooking rice OR long grain rice
1 stick margarine
1 can onion soup

1 small can mushroom slices
2 beef bouillon cubes
2½ cups water

Brown rice in margarine over medium heat until golden. Place rice in 2 quart baking dish and add all remaining ingredients. Cook covered in 350° oven for 1 hour.

Sandi Fodi

GREEN RICE

OVEN: 350° 45 minutes   YIELD: 8-10 servings

2 cups cooked rice
⅓ cup oil
5 tablespoons chopped onion
1 tablespoon chopped green pepper
1 cup chopped parsley

2 cups grated cheese, sharp cheese
  OR mild cheese
3 eggs beaten
½ cup milk
2 teaspoons salt

Blend beaten eggs with milk. Mix all ingredients together and bake 45 minutes in 350° oven.

Sharp cheese is better than mild cheese. I usually put some grated cheese on top as I take the dish from the oven.

Joanne W. Bolton

GREEN RICE CASSEROLE I

OVEN: 350°

1 — 8 ounce jar processed cheese
1 package frozen chopped broccoli
1 cup dry rice, long grain

1 can mushroom soup
2 cups water

Mix all ingredients together well. Pour into a lightly buttered casserole dish. Bake at 350° until thoroughly heated and bubbly.

Aerline R. Shippey

With spaghetti or pasta, serve a Chianti, Zinfandel, Grignolino, Burgundy, or one of the many other red wines.

GREEN RICE CASSEROLE II

OVEN: 350° 30 minutes

2 cups uncooked rice
3 medium bell peppers
1 bunch parsley
1 pound medium cheddar cheese

1 small bunch green onions,
  chopped
garlic salt OR plain salt
black pepper
oil

Cook rice as package directs. Cut peppers and green onions into small pieces and fry in oil. Cut parsley into very small pieces. Grate cheese. Mix rice, peppers, onions, parsley and ½ of the cheese and place in a shallow baking dish. Put remaining cheese on top of casserole. Bake in 350° oven for 30 minutes or until heated thoroughly.

Regina Bishop

MEXICAN STYLE RICE

YIELD: 6-8 servings

2 cups rice
1 medium size onion, chopped
2 cloves garlic, chopped
1½ cups canned tomatoes
4 cups chicken stock OR 6 cubes
  chicken bouillon

1 teaspoon salt, or to taste
½ cup cooking oil
½ cup canned peas
6 hard boiled eggs, cut into rings
1 large avocado, peeled and sliced
6-8 fresh parsley sprigs

Cover rice with warm water and allow to stand for 5 minutes. Drain and dry rice.

Place onion, garlic, salt and tomatoes in blender with ½ cup stock and blend to a smooth puree.

Heat oil in a large skillet and sauté rice until golden; add blended ingredients and the remaining stock. Bring rice to a boil; lower heat, cover skillet and cook rice until amost all liquid is absorbed. Gently mix in peas and continue to cook rice until all liquid all liquid is absorbed.

If desired, add two whole bay leaves to the rice when heat has been lowered. Serve the rice garnished with sliced eggs, sprigs of parsley and slices of avocado. This is an economical, quick and easy recipe to prepare; total time for preparation and cooking — 25-30 minutes.

Frances H. Hughes

Rice increases three times or more in cooking. Brown rice is cooked in the same manner as white rice but requires almost twice as much time. To shorten the cooking time of brown rice, soak an hour before cooking.

MINTED RICE CASSEROLE

OVEN: 325° 55 minutes   YIELD: 6 servings

2 teaspoons salt
2 cups water
1 cup long grain rice
4 tablespoons butter
1 teaspoon dried mint leaves,
  crushed

dash of garlic salt
dash of Accent
1¾ cups chicken broth (equal to
1 — 14 ounce can)
¼ cup slivered almonds, toasted

Bring the salt and water to a boil and pour over the rice. Let stand for 30 minutes, covered. After the 30 minutes, rinse rice and drain well. Melt butter in a skillet. Add rice and cook over medium heat until butter is almost absorbed; about 5 minutes. Turn rice into a 1 quart casserole and sprinkle with garlic salt and Accent. Pour chicken broth over rice. Bake covered in a slow oven, 325°, about 45 minutes, or until all of the broth is absorbed. Add mint and fluff with a fork. Sprinkle almonds over the top. Bake uncovered about 10 minutes more.
Serve with leg of lamb.

Helen George

RED RICE

OVEN: 350° 1 hour

¼ pound bacon
2 cups red tomatoes
½ teaspoon salt
⅛ teaspoon tabasco sauce

2 cups raw rice
½ cup chopped onion
¼ teaspoon pepper

Fry bacon and dry. Remove bacon from pan and cook onions until tender. Add washed rice, tomatoes, seasonings, and crumbled bacon to pan and cook on top of stove about 10 minutes. Pour into a casserole dish. Cover dish tightly and bake in 350° oven for 1 hour. Stir with fork a couple of times while baking.

Janice G. Louks

RICE CASSEROLE I

OVEN: 350° 45 minutes   YIELD: 4-6 servings

1 cup uncooked rice
1 can beef broth

1 can onion soup
1 small can mushrooms

Place rice in a casserole dish and pour soup and broth over rice. Mix ingredients with a spoon. Pour mushrooms on top and bake in 350° oven for 45 minutes.

Mrs. Jessie Horne

RICE CASSEROLE II

OVEN: 350° 1 hour

YIELD: 8-10 servings

1 large onion
1 cup raw rice
1 can consomme
1 can water

1 teaspoon salt
1 can mushrooms
approximately 1 stick margarine

Sauté large sliced onion in not quite 1 stick margarine. Add fresh or canned mushrooms plus liquid to rice, consomme, water and salt in a 1½ quart casserole. Cover and bake at 350° about 1 hour.

Joline Frederick

RICE CASSEROLE III

2 cups cooked rice
2 cups shredded lettuce
1 cup chopped onions
1 cup diced bacon
1 cup sliced, fresh mushrooms
1½ cups diced, fresh tomatoes

2 tablespoons soy sauce
2 tablespoons Worcestershire
   sauce
salt
pepper

Heat skillet to smoking hot. Add bacon and stir-fry until one-half done. Add onions, rice, mushrooms, tomatoes and lettuce in this order. Stir well. Add soy sauce and Worcestershire sauce, salt and pepper. Stir and serve immediately.

Teresa Eidson

RICE CASSEROLE IV

OVEN: 350° 30 minutes

YIELD: 6 servings

¼ cup butter OR margarine
3 cups hot cooked rice
1 cup cooked cubed ham
1 cup cooked cubed chicken
1 cup pineapple tidbits
1 cup finely sliced green pepper

½ cup sliced water chestnuts
1 teaspoon salt
½ teaspoon pepper
2 tablespoons soy sauce
½ teaspoon garlic powder
1 teaspoon onion power

Stir butter into hot rice. Add ham, chicken, pineapple and green pepper. Stir in water chestnuts and seasonings. Mix well and spoon into buttered 1½ quart casserole. Cover and bake in 350° oven for 30 minutes.

This is good for luncheons. I increase the ham and chicken and pineapple and get 8 good servings.

Ruth Davis

Should rice or cereals stick when cooking, simply drop a small lump of butter or margarine in the boiling water before putting in the cereals.

RICE FIESTA

OVEN: 350° 45 minutes

3 cups cooked OR partially cooked
  rice
1 cup onion, chopped
½ cup green pepper, chopped

red pepper, for color
1 cup parsley, chopped fine
1 cup grated cheese
¼ teaspoon salt

Sauté onion and pepper for a few minutes in a little oleo or bacon drippings. Mix all ingredients well and pour into baking dish and bake in 350° oven for about 45 minutes. Spread grated cheese on top when it comes out of the oven; it is more easily served if cheese is not baked on top.

Carra Adams

SPANISH RICE

YIELD: 6 servings

¼ cup butter, melted
1 pound ground beef
1 large onion, sliced in rings
½ green pepper, sliced in strips
2 cups cooked long grain rice

1 — 8 ounce can tomato sauce
1 can stewed tomatoes
1 teaspoon salt
½ teaspoon mustard

Add ground beef to melted butter with sliced onion and strips of pepper. Cook ingredients until lightly brown. Add rice and tomato sauce, stewed tomatoes, salt and mustard. Blend well. Bring ingredients to a boil, cover and reduce heat and simmer 20 minutes. Then serve.

Sgt. James E. Parsley

WILD RICE

OVEN: 350° 1½ hours

2 cups rice
1⅓ sticks oleo
⅓ cup parsley

2 large onions
4 cans beef consomme

Brown rice in melted butter. Add remaining ingredients and bake in 350° oven for 1½ hours. Stir occasionally.

Margie Knott

BACKPACKER'S BREAKFAST

1 package instant grits
water as package directs
1 beef bouillon cube

salt
pepper

Boil water and dissolve bouillon cube. Add grits, stirring constantly. When grits are done, serve with salt and pepper.

A cheese snack stick may be added to make Cheese-Beef Grits.

Jerome Gilmore

BAKED GRITS

OVEN: 350° 15-20 minutes

YIELD: 8-10 servings

1 cup quick grits
4 cups water
1 tablespoon salt
1 roll garlic cheese
½ pound sharp cheese

3 tablespoons Worcestershire
sauce
1 stick butter OR oleo
paprika

Cook grits until smooth, but not thick. Add cheeses and stir until melted. Pour mixture into greased casserole and sprinkle top with paprika. Bake in 350° oven for 15-20 minutes.

Dot Gortner

BAKED MACARONI AND CHEESE

OVEN: 325° 45 minutes

YIELD: 5 servings

7-8 ounces macaroni
3 teaspoons salt
3 quarts boiling water
salt to taste

3 tablespoons butter
½ pound sharp cheese, grated
1¾ cups milk, approximately

Break macaroni into 1½″ to 2″ lengths. Add salt to rapidly boiling water, using a large saucepan. Drop macaroni into boiling water and boil for 8 to 20 minutes, or until macaroni is just tender. Stir occasionally to prevent sticking. Drain in a colander. Run hot water through macaroni and rinse well. Arrange half of the macaroni in a 6 cup, buttered casserole and sprinkle with salt and dot with half of the butter. Cover with half of the cheese, another layer of macaroni, and repeat with remaining ingredients. Add milk until it comes up to the top layer of macaroni. Set casserole in a shallow pan of water and bake in 325° oven for about 45 minutes or until surface is golden brown.

Ethel Rosier

BAKED MACARONI LOAF DELUXE

OVEN: 325° 1 hour 10 minutes

1½ cups elbow macaroni
3 quarts boiling water
5 teaspoons salt
3 cups milk
⅓ cup butter OR margarine
2 cups soft bread crumbs

⅓ cup chopped pimentos
3 cups grated cheddar cheese
⅓ cup minced parsley
¼ cup minced onion
¼ cup minced pepper
6 eggs, beaten

Cook macaroni in boiling water with the salt for about 9 minutes. Rinse with boiling water. Combine milk and butter. Scald mixture and pour over bread crumbs. Add all remaining ingredients except eggs and macaroni. Blend. Next add eggs and macaroni, stirring until blended. Place mixture in baking dish and bake at 325° for 1 hour 10 minutes. Cool for 10 minutes then unmold and serve.

June Carlton Vest

BAKED MANICOTTI WITH CHEESE FILLING

OVEN: 350° 1 hour — frozen; 30 minutes — fresh

Crepés:
6 eggs
1 cup flour
1 cup water
dash of salt

Filling:
4 pounds ricotta cheese

1 — 8 ounce package mozzarella
cheese, diced
½ cup Parmesan cheese, grated
3-4 eggs
1 teaspoon salt, or to taste
¼ teaspoon pepper, or to taste
chopped parsley

Crepés: Beat eggs, flour, water and salt until smooth. Let stand for ½ hour or longer. Slowly heat a 6"-7" skillet or crepe pan. Oil pan lightly from time to time if it is not a non-stick skillet. Pour in 2 tablespoons of batter, rotating skillet quickly to spread batter evenly over bottom. Cook over medium heat until top is dry but bottom is not brown. Do not turn over. Turn crepe out onto a wire rack to cool. Continue cooking until all of batter is used. As the crepes cool, stack them with waxed paper between them. This will make about 35 crepes.

Crepés can be frozen and used when needed. To freeze filled crepes, do so before baking. Let stand for 1 hour to thaw before baking, then cover and bake for about 1 hour in 350° oven.

Filling: Mix all ingredients together in a big bowl. Place a good spoonful of filling in center of each crepe. Fold ends over. Place your favorite tomato sauce in the bottom of a 13" x 9" x 2" or any other shallow pan. Place each filled crepe in a single layer. Top with more tomato sauce and bake in 350° oven for 30 minutes or until bubbly.

Connie Montuoro

Cheese should be kept in the refrigerator, but not in a tightly covered container. Preferably the cheese should be wrapped in cheese cloth wrung out of vinegar or cold water.

BAKED STUFFED TUFOLI

OVEN: 350° 30 minutes

Meat Balls:
1½ pounds ground beef chuck
½ pound ground lean pork
½ cup chopped onion
¼ cup minced parsley
¼ cup grated Parmesan cheese
2 tablespoons bread crumbs
2 tablespoons olive oil
2 eggs, well beaten
1 clove garlic, minced
2 teaspoons salt
¼ teaspoon pepper
olive oil

Tomato Sauce:
¼ cup olive oil
¼ cup chopped onion
¼ cup chopped green pepper

1 clove garlic, minced
1 — 6 ounce can broiled mushrooms, drained and halved
4 — 6 ounce cans tomato paste
1 — #2½ can Italian plum tomatoes
1 teaspoon sugar
2 teaspoons salt
¼ teaspoon pepper

Casserole:
1 pound tufoli, large tubed macaroni
1 — #2 can spinach, drained and
   finely chopped
1 teaspoon salt
½ cup grated Parmesan cheese
1 egg, well beaten

Combine ingredients for meat balls and form into balls about 1½" in diameter. Brown balls in hot oil. Do not overbrown meat balls. Then cook balls in tomato sauce.

To make tomato sauce, heat oil and add onion, green pepper, garlic, and
mushrooms. Sauté until golden. Stir in tomato paste and cook for 4 minutes.
Press plum tomatoes through a strainer, and add an equal amount of water.
Combine tomato mixture in an electric mixer and mix until smooth, adding
tomato paste mixture, salt, sugar and pepper. Bring ingredients to a boil, add
meat balls and cook over low heat for 1½ hours, or until sauce thickens
slightly. Remove meat balls and set aside.

The meat balls and tomato sauce may be comined for delicious spaghetti.

To build the casserole, cook tufoli in 6 quarts, boiling, salted water for 12-15
minutes, or until almost tender. Mash meat balls in a bowl and add spinach,
salt, 2 tablespoons cheese and egg. Mix well. Stuff mixture into tufoli. Cover
bottom of large casserole with ½" of sauce. Sprinkle each layer with cheese
and finish with sauce. Cover dish and bake in moderate oven at 350° for 30
minutes. Serve with extra sauce an extra cheese.

Manicotti may be used instead of tufoli.

John Klotz

Cheese flavor is greatly improved if the cheese is allowed to reach
room temperature before serving.

CHEESE GRITS

OVEN: 350° 45 minutes

YIELD: 6 servings

1 cup quick grits
1 roll garlic cheese
½ cup butter OR margarine

2 eggs
milk

Cook grits according to package directions. Break garlic cheese roll into the hot grits and add butter or margarine. Stir until blended. Break eggs into a one-cup measure and beat lightly with a fork. Fill the measure with milk. Blend mixture into grits. Pour blended ingredients into a greased casserole dish and bake in 350° oven for 45 minutes.

If you like, top with cereal crumbs before baking.

Beatrice Dittmar Coffman

EASY LASAGNE

OVEN: 350° 30-35 minutes

YIELD: 8 servings

2 tablespoons olive oil
1 clove garlic
1 onion, chopped
1 can mushroom stems and pieces
1½ pounds sweet Italian sausage

3 cups marinara sauce
1 pound lasagne noodles
1 pound ricotta OR cottage cheese
1 pound mozzarella cheese
½ cup Parmesan cheese, grated

Preheat oven to 350°. In a saucepan, heat oil and sauté garlic, onion and mushrooms for 5 minutes. Add meat and cook over medium heat until sausage is brown and crumbly. Drain fat and stir sauce into meat mixture. Cook noodles according to package directions. Drain noodles and rinse with cold water. Separate noodles to prevent sticking. Spoon a thin layer of sauce into a 9 x 13 x 2 baking pan. Add noodles, sauce, ricotta, and mozzarella. Continue layering ingredients in order listed until pan is filled. End with sauce and sprinkle top with cheese. Bake for 30-35 minutes.

This can be prepared ahead of time and reheated.

Ground beef may be substituted for sausage. This is delicious with fresh tossed salad and Italian dressing, fresh garlic bread and a mellow red wine. A rich coffee and a spumoni ice cream is suggested for dessert.

Marie and Liz Phillips

GRITS CASSEROLE

OVEN: 350° 30 minutes

YIELD: 8 servings

1 cup uncooked grits
1 small can evaporated milk
1 stick butter OR margarine

1 — 8 ounce package Gouda
cheese, grated

Cook grits as package directs until they reach a soupy consistency. Add grated cheese, reserving about 4 tablespoons of cheese for later use, and butter. Beat mixture thoroughly and add milk. Beat again until well blended. Pour into a lightly buttered 2 quart casserole and sprinkle reserved cheese on top. Bake in 350° oven for 30 minutes or until firm.

Carol I. Browder

LASAGNE

OVEN: 350° 30 minutes

1 pound ground sausage	oil
1 — 1 pound, 12 ounce can Italian tomatoes	6 ounces cream cheese
	12 ounces mozzarella cheese
1 small can tomato paste	Parmesan cheese, grated
2 garlic cloves	1 pound lasagne noodles

Heat about 2 tablespoons cooking oil or olive oil in a pot and brown garlic cloves which have been split in half. Remove garlic and add tomatoes and tomato paste. Mix well, breaking up tomatoes. Cover and cook for about 1 hour. Then add salt and pepper to taste.

Make 6 sausage patties and brown them on both sides under the broiler. Leave in oven until cooked.

Boil noodles, retaining some firmness in the center. Drain and rise with cold water.

Assemble lasagne in a 13 x 9 x 2 pan. Place a thin layer of sauce in the botton. Next add noodles followed with crumbled sausage, cream cheese, and mozzarella. Repeat these layers two more times beginning with the sauce, and sprinkle top of final layer with Parmesan cheese. Cover pan with foil and bake for 30 minutes in 350° oven.

The Italian tomatoes are a must. This is very good reheated.

Shirley O'Haire

To properly cook cheese, place in double boiler over low heat until the cheese is melted.

MANICOTTI

OVEN: 350° 30-35 minutes

Sauce:
1 can tomatoes
1 teaspoon Italian seasoning
½ teaspoon crushed red pepper
12 ounces tomato paste
2 cups water
2 tablespoons chopped parsley
1 tablespoon dried basil, crushed
1½ teaspoons salt
¼ teaspoon ground nutmeg
dash of pepper
2 pounds ground chuck

1 very large onion, slivered
1 clove garlic, minced

Filling:
2 pounds ricotta cheese
⅔ cup grated Parmesan and Romano cheese
8 ounces shredded mozzarella cheese
2 slightly beaten eggs
¼ cup snipped parsley
½ teaspoon salt
dash of pepper

Brown ground chuck together with onion and garlic. Drain off excess fat and add remaining ingredients. Simmer uncovered for about 30 minutes, stirring occasionally.

Meanwhile, combine ingredients for pasta filling and cook manicotti shells according to package directions.

Mix together all ingredients for filling and set aside. Stuff cooked shells or cut them lengthwise with knife and fill. Be sure to rinse cooked manicotti shells in cold water after preparing. This removes traces of starch.

Pour half of tomato-meat mixture into a large baking pan. Arrange stuffed manicotti shells in a row and top with remaining sauce. Sprinkle ½ cup shredded Romano and Parmesan cheeses across sauce. Bake at 350° for 30-35 minutes.

Dicksie Dudeney

NOODLE CASSEROLE

OVEN: 350° 50-60 minutes   YIELD: 6-8 servings

1 — 6 to 6½ ounce package noodles
3 tablespoons flour
¼ teaspoon pepper
½ cup Parmesan cheese, grated
1 cup dairy sour cream
1 cup large curd cottage cheese

¼ cup butter
1 teaspoon salt
2 cups milk
¼ cup sliced onions
½ cup grated sharp cheese
flaked corn cereal, crumbled

Cook noodles and drain. Melt 3 tablespoons butter in a saucepan and stir in flour, salt and pepper. Slowly add milk. Cook and stir until mixture is thick. Blend in Parmesan cheese and sharp cheese. In a casserole dish, add noodles, sour cream, cottage cheese, onions and sauce. Melt remaining butter and stir in crumbs and ½ cup Parmesan cheese. Spoon this crust mixture over the noodles. Bake in a moderate oven, 350°, for 50-60 minutes.

Mrs. Howard Burpo

NOODLES ROMANO

YIELD: 6 servings

¼ cup soft butter OR margarine
2 tablespoons parsley flakes
1 teaspoon crushed basil
1 — 8 ounce package cream cheese, softened
¼ teaspoon salt
½ teaspoon pepper

⅔ cup boiling water
1 — 8 ounce package fettucini, thin noodles, OR spaghetti
1 clove minced garlic
½ cup butter OR margarine
1 cup shredded OR grated Romano OR Parmesan cheese

Combine softened butter, parlsey flakes, and basil; blend in cream cheese, salt and pepper; stir in boiling water; blend well. Keep mixture warm.

Cook noodles in large amount of boiling salted water until just tender; drain. Cook garlic in ½ cup butter for 1-2 minutes. Pour butter mixture over noodles; toss lightly and quickly to coat. Sprinkle noodles with ½ cup of the cheese; toss again. Pile noodles on a warm serving platter and spoon warm cream chese sauce over noodles. Sprinkle with remaining ½ cup cheese. Garnish with additional parsley, if desired.

Connie Wagers

SPAGHETTI I

YIELD: 6-8 servings

2 pounds ground beef
½ pound lean pork
¾ cup onion, chopped
¾ cup green pepper, chopped
¾ cup celery, chopped
1 clove garlic
2 cans tomato sauce
1 can whole tomatoes

2 — 6 ounce cans tomato paste
1 cup water
1½ teaspoons salt
1½ teaspoons oregano
½ teaspoon pepper
1½ bay leaves
½ teaspoon basil
spaghetti

Sauté onion, celery, green peppers and garlic. Add meat and seasonings. Add tomato sauce and remaining ingredients; simmer for 20 minutes. Boil spaghetti in salted water with oil, in a large pot. Rinse and serve.

Deborah VonJoshua

When slicing hard-cooked eggs, dip the slicing knife into water before cutting each slice. This will keep the yolks from crumbling.

SPAGHETTI II

2 cans stewed tomatoes
2 — 6 ounce cans tomato paste
1 can tomato sauce
1 pound ground beef
1 pound hot Italian sausage
1 can cream of mushroom soup
1 bay leaf
1 clove garlic, chopped

1 medium onion, chopped
1 green pepper, chopped
1 teaspoon Worcestershire sauce
½ cup wine
1 tablespoon salt
½ teaspoon pepper
spaghetti

Brown beef and sausage in oil. Remove meat and brown onion, garlic and green pepper in oil. Drain grease. Combine all remaining ingredients and bring to a boil. Reduce heat and simmer for at least 4 hours.

Prepare spaghetti as package directs and serve with sauce.

The sauce's flavor is much better if it is made a day ahead.

Cathy Diaz

SPAGHETTI AND CRAB

2 tablespoons minced celery
2 tablespoons fresh parsley
1 large clove garlic, minced
2 small yellow onions, chopped
⅓ cup olive oil
1½ cups solid packed tomatoes
6 ounces tomato paste
1¼ cups water
½ teaspoon paprika
2 teaspoons salt

½ teaspoon pepper
½ teaspoon dried basil
¼ teaspoon organo
pinch of sugar
1 pound crabmeat, shelled and
    washed
1 pound spaghetti
1 cup Parmesan cheese
½ cup dry sherry

In a large skillet, using low to medium heat, sauté celery, parsley, garlic and onion in oil until light brown; about 10 minutes. Add tomatoes, paste, water, paprika, salt, pepper, basil, oregano, and sugar. Turn heat to low and simmer uncovered for 1 hour. Add well-drained crabmeat and sherry. Simmer until mixture bubbles; 5-10 minutes. Cook spaghetti and drain. Place pasta on a heated platter and cover with sauce and garnish with cheese. Serve at once.

Clorene Knowles

A stale egg rises in water; fresh eggs are heavy and sink to the bottom.

SPAGHETTI AND SARDINES

YIELD: 6 servings

1 — 15 ounce OR 4 — 3¾ ounce
cans sardines
1 onion
1 bell pepper
1 cup tomato sauce OR paste
1 tablespoon white cooking sherry,
Vino Seco

1 teaspoon salt
¼ teaspoon black pepper
¼ teaspoon cumin
¼ teaspoon oregano
1 laurel leaf
½ pound spaghetti

If sardines are packed in olive oil, pour oil into skillet and sauté onion and green pepper. If packed in soy oil or water, a bit of olive oil is suggested for the sautéeing; discared soy oil or water. Add tomato paste or sauce, salt, pepper, spices and sardines to skillet. Simmer slowly while cooking spaghetti in boiling water. Then stir cooked, drained spaghetti into sardine sauce. Allow mixture to simmer for a few minutes. Or place in oven to brown slightly.

Jalapeno or chili pepper may be substituted for bell pepper with excellent results. A dash of tabasco is also good.

This recipe was translated from the Spanish, after being found in 1972 in the nation's only tri-lingual weekly newspaper *la Gaceta,* published in Tampa, Florida. *La Gaceta* was founded in 1922 by Victoriano Mantiega, who still, at age 83, edits the Italian language section, although his son and successor, Roland, is now editor and publisher.

Tom Dunkin

SPAGHETTI AND SAUCE

2 pounds ground chuck
1-2 green peppers, chopped
2-3 onions, chopped
2 cups celery, chopped
4 large cans tomato sauce

2 bay leaves
salt, if needed
2 pounds thin spaghetti
salad oil
Parmesan cheese

Brown meat, onions, pepper and celery. Pour off any grease. Add tomato sauce and season to taste with salt if needed. Add bay leaves. Simmer for 40 minutes or longer. Remove bay leaves.

When sauce is ready, prepare spaghetti by directions on package. Add salad oil while spaghetti is cooking. Drain spaghetti and mix in a little of the sauce. Save the rest of the sauce to put on top. Sprinkle grated Parmesan cheese over each serving.

Serve with tossed salad and French bread.

Olive Peterson

Can't tell a hard-boiled egg from a raw egg? Spin them; a hard-boiled egg will spin around several times, a raw egg will only wobble briefly before stopping.

NOTES

FISH AND SHELLFISH

FISH AND SHELLFISH

ANGLER'S IMPERIAL CRAB

OVEN: 350° 30 minutes

1 cup mayonnaise	1 cup cracker crumbs
1 egg, beaten	1 stick melted butter
1 pound crabmeat	1 teaspoon dry mustard

Combine mayonnaise, egg, dry mustard and crabmeat and place in a well-greased casserole. Top with cracker crumbs mixed with melted butter. Bake in 350° oven until bubbly and brown, about 30 minutes.

Mrs. Robert P. Fletcher

ARTHUR'S NEW ENGLAND CLAM FRITTERS

YIELD: 12

1½ cups sifted flour	⅓ cup milk
2 teaspoons baking powder	¼ cup clam juice
½ teaspoon salt	1 cup OR 1 — 6½ ounce can minced
2 eggs	clams

Beat eggs well. Stir in milk and clam juice. Sift dry ingredients together. Beat egg mixture into dry ingredients. Add clams and more juice to moisten, if necessary. Drop in hot deep fat, one tablespoon at a time; fry until golden brown. Serve hot.

Carol I. Browder

BAHAMA CONCH FRITTERS

1½ pound can conch	1 bell pepper, chopped
¼ pound flour	1 stalk celery
1 teaspoon baking powder	½ teaspoon salt
1 egg	1 small hot (Mexican) pepper, op-
1 small onion, chopped	tional

Grind conch with juice in a grinder or blender; add onion, bell pepper, salt, egg, baking powder and flour. Mix together, making a stiff batter; more flour may be needed. If using hot pepper, add to blended ingredients; if a mild flavor is desired, omit. Fry in deep oil until golden brown.

Mary Colson

When purchasing live crabs, allow three hard-shell crabs per person. One pound of lump, special or claw meat is sufficient to feed six persons.

BAKED CLAMS OREGANATA

OVEN: 375°

6 clams	pepper
1 tablespoon chopped onion	1 teaspoon chopped parsley
salt	½ teaspoon dried oregano leaves
	2 tablespoons salad oil

Preheat oven to 375°. Open clams and sprinkle with onion, salt and pepper. Mix together parsley, oregano, and salad oil. Pour oil mixture over clams and bake until the clams curl a bit at the edges.

The Committee

BAKED STUFFED CLAMS ITALIANO

2 tablespoons vegetable oil	2 cans minced clams, reserve liquid
2 tablespoons butter	¾ cup Italian bread crumbs
1 large green pepper, diced	28 sprigs fresh parsley
4 cloves garlic, minced	1 large tomato
1 teaspoon oregano	1 teaspoon sage, or to taste

In a large skillet, sauté green pepper and garlic in oil and butter until pepper is soft but not browned. Add oregano. Mix clams with bread crumbs and add to skillet, stirring constantly so mixture will not burn. Add liquid from clams and continue stirring. Add parsley. Slice tomatoes and cut each slice into quarters. Add quartered tomato slices to skillet mixture along with sage and cook for 5 minutes. Stuff clam shells or whatever you are using with mixture when ready to serve. Heat in oven for about 15 minutes.

These can be made ahead and kept in refrigerator, or can be frozen for future use. If frozen, it is best to thaw them before placing in oven.

Mae Stubbs

BEST BAKED CLAMS

OVEN: 400° 20 minutes   YIELD: 2-4 servings

1 tablespoon freeze-dried chives	⅛ teaspoon tarragon
2 tablespoons margarine	1 tablespoon dry sherry
2 tablespoons flour	3 tablespoons dry bread crumbs
1½ cups minced clams with their	2 tablespoons imitation bacon bits
liquor (2 — 7 ounce cans)	1 tablespoon margarine
1 teaspoon dry parsley flakes	

In a small saucepan, sauté chives in 2 tablespoons margarine for 2—3 minutes. Blend in flour. Add 1 cup liquid drained from clams; use some water if necessary to make 1 cup. Bring mixture to a boil over moderate heat, stirring constantly. Stir in parsley and tarragon. Simmer for 2 minutes. Remove from heat. Stir in clams and sherry. Pour into greased shallow 1 quart baking dish. Sprinkle crumbs on top, spreading evenly. Top with bacon and dot with 1 tablespoon margarine. Bake in 400° oven until golden brown; about 20 minutes.

Barbara Matuszewski

BOMBAY CRAB CURRY

1 pound king OR snow OR lump
  crabmeat
1 tablespoon butter OR margarine
1 cup chopped, peeled apple
1 cup chopped onion
1 clove garlic, chopped
1 teaspoon curry powder
1 tablespoon flour
¼ teaspoon salt

1¼ cups water
1 chicken bouillon cube, crumbled
¼ cup seedless raisins
1 cup quartered cherry tomatoes
⅓ cup chopped pistachio nuts OR
  almonds
1 teaspoon grated orange rind
4 servings hot fluffy, pilaf-rice
condiments (see directions)

Melt butter or margarine, add apples, onion and garlic, then add curry powder. After about 5 minutes of cooking, add crabmeat; fold in tomatoes, and nuts and orange rind. When mixture is heated, serve on rice with condiments such as toasted coconut, orange wedges, chutney, and dried raisins.

An especially attractive table can be set. The crab curry takes center stage, with the rice just off to the side a little bit, along with the condiments.

Le Pavillon

BOUILLABAISSÉ A LA PARISIENNE

YIELD: 6 servings

3 pounds sea bass
3 pounds red snapper
4 pounds lobster
24 little neck clams
2 sliced onions
2 sliced white leeks
4 garlic cloves
2 teaspoons chopped parsley

2 teaspoons powdered saffron
¾ teaspoon chopped fennel
1 pound tomatoes in stew
2 tablespoons olive oil
¾ bay leaf
2 ounces pernod, optional
4 cups dry white wine
24 mussels

Cut fish and lobster into large pieces; crack claws of lobsters. Place together with remaining ingredients in a large bowl, add a little salt and pepper and refrigerate for 2 hours. Thirty minutes before serving, place mixture in a flat pan, add enough fish stock or boiling water to cover fish very well. Bring liquid to a boil over high heat; cover and cook for 30 minutes. Adjust seasoning of broth with salt and pepper. Before serving, remove bone and skin of fish and shell of lobster, claws and mussels. Serve hot in a large soup tureen. Make French toast with garlic butter.

Mimi Clerke

The claw portion of stone crabs makes an attractive hors d'oeuvre or appetizer.

BROILED BLUEFISH PIQUANT

YIELD: 4-6 servings

2 pounds bluefish filets
2 tablespoons lemon juice
¼ cup flour
3 tablespoons margarine

2 teaspoons dry mustard
1 tablespoon Worcestershire sauce
2 tablespoons salad oil
¼ cup dry bread crumbs

Line broiling pan with foil. Grease foil lightly. Spread fish on foil in one layer. Sprinkle with lemon juice. Allow to stand for at least 10 minutes. Sprinkle flour over fish. Dot with margarine. Broil at 500° for 6 minutes, having pan about 3 inches away from heat. Meantime, in a small jar, shake together mustard, Worcestershire, and salad oil. When fish has broiled 6 minutes, remove pan from oven and brush oil mixture on fish. Sprinkle with bread crumbs. Broil for another 3 minutes and serve immediately.

Barbara Matuszewski

BROILED SPANISH MACKEREL — FLORIDA STYLE

4 Spanish mackerel fillets, small
fresh lemon juice
1 tablespoon Accent
¼ teaspoon salt

⅛ teaspoon celery salt
dash of red pepper
1 large onion, sliced paper thin
paprika

Line baking pan with foil. Dip each fillet into fresh lemon juice and place skin side down in pan. Slice large onion and place over fillets. Mix Accent, salt, celery salt and paprika — sprinkle over fillets and onion. Broil until fish flakes with a fork; do not overcook.

This broiled Spanish mackerel has a delicious flavor and can be eaten and enjoyed by most everyone on a diet. Serve with tossed green salad and toasted bread sticks; no butter.

Mildred Brown Garrett

CAPTAIN SAM'S BATTER FRIED SNOOK

1 — 3 to 5 pound snook fillet,
  boned and skinned
1 cup cornmeal
1 cup flour
2 teaspoons salt
juice from one lime

1 teaspoon Worcestershire sauce
1 egg
1 cup milk
1 — 1 pound box saltine crackers,
  crushed medium
oil

Mix meal, flour, salt, lime juice, Worcestershire, egg and milk until well blended. Cut boned and skinned snook into 1" cubes. Dip cubes into batter; roll each piece in cracker crumbs. Fry in deep oil at 375° until just golden brown. Drain well on paper towels. Excellent served with fresh slaw and iced cold beer.

Captain Sam Crutchfield

CHEESE SHRIMP CASSEROLE

OVEN: 325° 1 hour

2½ cups cooked shrimp
½ pound cheddar cheese
7 slices bread
3 well-beaten eggs

½ teaspoon salt
½ teaspoon paprika
¼ teaspoon dry mustard
2½ cups milk

Remove crusts from bread, cut in cubes. Grate the cheese. Alternate layers of bread, shrimp, and cheese in a greased 2 quart casserole. Combine eggs, seasonings and milk. Pour over the casserole. Let stand for a few hours or overnight in the refrigerator. Before baking, fluff with a fork. Bake at 325° for 1 hour.

This makes a lavish casserole for a luncheon. Serve with cold asparagus or a green salad.

Aggie Counts

CLAM PIE

OVEN: 450° 15 minutes

3 cups minced clams
½ cup clam liquor
½ cup milk
1 well-beaten egg

½ cup cracker crumbs
¼ teaspoon salt
⅛ teaspoon pepper
1 — 9″ pie crust

Combine clams with other ingredients and place mixture in pie crust. Bake in 450° oven for 15 minutes.

Gladys M. Smith

CONCH FRITTERS

3 pounds frozen conch meat,
   thawed and cleaned
3 large green peppers
3 large onions
1 stick celery
3 teaspoons salt
¼ teaspoon oregano
2 teaspoons garlic salt

1 teaspoon Italian seasoning
1 teaspoon paprika
¼ teaspoon tabasco
3 cups flour, sifted
6 teaspoons baking powder
3 cups cold milk
oil for frying

Grind conch fine. Grind onions, green peppers and celery. Add seasonings and mix well. Set in refrigerator for about ½ hour. Add 3 cups sifted flour mixed with baking powder and cold milk. Mix thoroughly.

Heat one quart cooking oil in a 9″ frying pan. Substitute ½ cup olive oil if desired. When hot, dip a teaspoon in hot fat, then drop one teaspoon of batter into oil. Stir gently until brown; about 2 minutes. Make a dozen at a time. Remove and drop on brown paper. Serve hot with cocktail sauce or mustard sauce.

John Margetis

COQUILLE SAINT-JACQUÉS

OVEN: 350°

Sauce:
2 tablespoons flour
¼ cup cream
½ teaspoon salt
¼ teaspoon paprika
2 tablespoons butter
1 cup milk

¼ teaspoon pepper
¼ cup good, dry sherry
¾ cup cooked crabmeat
¾ cup cooked lobster, in large
  flakes
¾ cup cooked whole shrimp

This recipe is from the famous Cordon Bleu Cooking School in Paris, France. My cousin paid $3.00 for the privilege of writing this recipe down as a French Chef dictated, gestured and cooked at the same time.

Combine sauce ingredients in top of a double boiler. Cook over hot water until thick, stirring constantly. When thick, add sherry, crabmeat, lobster, and shrimp. Stir slowly; do not break shrimp if possible. Place each serving on a large white dried seashell; the Chef insisted on that; but any individual ramekin will do. Sprinkle with cheese and top with buttered bread crumbs. Bake at 350° until the top is light brown.

Annie Raulerson

CRAB AND SHRIMP AU GRATIN

OVEN: 350° 20 minutes   YIELD: 4 servings

2 cups milk
4 tablespoons plain flour
1 cup grated cheese
⅓ teaspoon salt

⅓ cup processed, pasteurized
  cheese spread
⅓ teaspoon pepper
⅛ teaspoon tabasco sauce
8 ounces cooked shrimp
4 ounces crabmeat

Combine flour, salt and pepper with part of the milk. Beat all lumps out of mixture. Add cheese spread to remaining milk in a double boiler and cook until cheese has melted. Then add flour mixture and tabasco to melted cheese. Stir until smooth and thickened. Add shrimp and crabmeat. Pour mixture into casserole dish and top with grated cheese. Bake at 350° for 20 minutes.

Janice G. Louks

Herbs such as basil, chives, and tarragon are especially suited to most seafood dishes. Thyme ground in clam chowder is a must.

CRAB AU GRATIN

OVEN: 325° 45 minutes

2 pounds crabmeat
½ stick oleo
¾ large jar processed, pasteurized
  cheese spread

pinch of salt
¼ cup milk
⅔ cup dry sherry
¼ cup flour

Remove any pieces of shell from crabmeat. Melt oleo; add flour, milk and cheese spread; stir until smooth and thick. Add wine; fold in ⅔ of this cheese mixture into the crabmeat. Place mixture in casserole dish and pour remainder of cheese mixture over top. Sprinkle with paprika and bake for 45 minutes at 325°, or until heated through.

Vern Burcham

CRAB CASSEROLE I

OVEN: 375° 45 minutes

½ cup onion, diced small
½ cup bell pepper, diced small
½ cup celery, diced
1 tablespoon margarine
1 pound crabmeat
⅔ cup mayonnaise
1 cup milk
dash black pepper

¼ teaspoon tabasco sauce
1 tablespoon soy sauce
1 tablespoon Worcestershire sauce
¾ — 1 package saltines, plus 4 (for
  top), crushed
paprika
2 tablespoons butter, for top

Sauté onion, bell pepper and celery in margarine. Add sautéed vegetables to crabmeat which has been combined with mayonnaise, milk, pepper, tabasco, soy sauce, and Worcestershire sauce. Add enough saltines, crushed, to make mixture thick; place mixture in a casserole dish and sprinkle with 4 crushed saltines on the top. Sprinkle with paprika and dot with margarine and place, covered, into 375° oven for about 45 minutes.

Tom McAlister

CRAB CASSEROLE II

OVEN: 400° 8-10 minutes

YIELD: 4 servings

1 package snow crab, thawed and
  drained
¼ cup Parmesan cheese

½ cup melted margarine
1 cup croutons
minced garlic to taste

Place crabmeat in a 1 quart casserole, cover with cheese and garlic. Cover mixture with croutons and pour melted margarine over all. Bake in 400° oven for 8-10 minutes.

Melody Streeter

CRAB CASSEROLE III

OVEN: 375° 45 minutes

1 pound crabmeat
5 boiled eggs, chopped
1½ cups soft bread crumbs
1⅓ cups milk
1 teaspoon salt

⅓ teaspoon pepper
½ teaspoon dry mustard
¼ cup butter
additional bread crumbs OR flaked
corn cereal

Mix all ingredients together. Melt butter and mix in additional bread crumbs or flaked corn cereal and sprinkle over casserole. Bake in 375° oven for 45 minutes.

Linda E. Boudet

CRABMEAT AU GRATIN

OVEN: 350°   YIELD: 4-6 servings

2 pounds crabmeat
3 tablespoons butter
2 teaspoons sherry
3 ounces American cheese
salt
pepper
½ cup Romano cheese
paprika

White cream sauce:
2 tablespoons butter
1 tablespoon cornstarch
1 egg yolk
1 cup half & half
salt
pepper

Sauté crabmeat in butter; add sherry, cheese and hot white sauce.
To make white sauce, combine all ingredients in a saucepan and blend together; use seasonings to taste. Heat ingredients until thick.
Season crabmeat and sauce mixture with salt and pepper to taste; cook thoroughly. Pour into a casserole and sprinkle with Romano cheese and paprika. Bake at about 350° until good and warm.
Ingredients for cream sauce can be varied to suit individual taste or you may substitute your own cream sauce.

Grace Barrie
The Patio

CRABMEAT STUFFING FOR SNAPPER

2½ pounds chopped onions and celery
1 loaf white bread, crusts removed, diced
1 teaspoon mustard
1 teaspoon mayonnaise

2 pounds crabmeat
4 eggs, beaten
1 teaspoon salt
1 teaspoon white pepper
enough sour cream to hold ingredients together

Cook onions and celery. Combine remaining ingredients except sour cream. Add onions and celery to blended mixture; fold in; add enough sour cream to hold mixture together.

Alvin Jackson
Driftwood Inn

CURRIED FLOUNDER

OVEN: 350° 45 minutes

1 medium fillet of flounder, white
   side only
1½ cups milk OR half & half
1 teaspoon curry powder

1 teaspoon fine herbs
2 teaspoons fresh chopped parsley
2 tablespoons butter
sliced black olives

Preheat oven to 350°. Place fish in an oblong pan, 2-½" high. Pour milk over fish; it should almost cover fish. Add more milk if necessary. Sprinkle with seasonings, and dot with butter. Bake for 45 minutes or until bubbly. Garnish with sliced olives and serve at once.

The milk sauce may be thickened and served over boiled potatoes.

Lyn Jackson

DELICIOUS CRAB CAKES

1 pound regular crabmeat
½ cup bread crumbs
1 egg, beaten
5 tablespoons mayonnaise

2 tablespoons parsley, finely
   chopped
2 teaspoons Worcestershire sauce
1 teaspoon prepared mustard
1 teaspoon salt
¼ teaspoon pepper

Mix all ingredients together well except crabmeat. Mix well and pour over crabmeat; fold in lightly but thoroughly. Form mixture into 6 cakes. Deep fry at 350° until golden brown; about 3 minutes.

Gladys Grammer

DEVILED CRAB I

OVEN: 350° 30 minutes   YIELD: 8 servings

¼ cup chopped onion
½ cup chopped celery
½ cup chopped green pepper
1 cup salad dressing

1 pound crabmeat OR half-cooked
   shrimp
½ teaspoon tabasco sauce
1 teaspoon Worcestershire sauce
1 cup milk
1½ — 2 cups crumbled saltines

Check seafood carefully for shells.

Grease a 2 quart casserole and mix all ingredients together. Cook at 350° for about 30 minutes. Serve with cheese sauce or sprinkle top with grated cheese about 5 minutes before casserole is done.

Jean Finger

Use pungent dried spices such as cayenne, mace, mustard, paprika, and saffron to add a flavorful touch to fish and seafood.

DEVILED CRAB II

OVEN: 450° 15 minutes

2 cans crabmeat
1 small box soda crackers
4 eggs
1 onion
2 cloves garlic

1 stick butter
2 cups white sauce
juice of 1 lemon
salt
pepper

Mix crabmeat, crushed crackers and eggs together. Saute onion and garlic in butter. Add to other ingredients with salt to taste. Add lemon juice. Layer ingredients in casserole beginning with onion mixture, then crabmeat-cracker mixture and then white sauce. Continue layers until all ingredients are used. Top casserole with white sauce. Bake at 450° for 15 minutes or until brown.

Annie Raulerson

EASY CONCH FRITTERS

¼ cup biscuit mix, ready mix OR
  your own recipe
1½ cups ground conch
¼ cup chopped onion

2 eggs, beaten
½ teaspoon salt
dash tabasco OR other hot pepper

Have conch ground at fish market. Mix conch, eggs, salt, tabasco and onion together. Add biscuit mix. Fry in hot fat, 375°, until golden brown. Drop by heaping teaspoons or tablespoons. May also be pan fried in ¼ cup butter and oil mixture.

A. E. "Beanie" Backus

ELEGANT FISH CAKES

YIELD: 4 servings

1 pound poached OR steamed fish;
  use any white-fleshed fish; flounder, snapper, weakfish; boned
  and skinned
2 teaspoons instant dry onion
3 tablespoons melted margarine
¼ cup dry bread crumbs

1 beaten egg
1 teaspoon Worcestershire sauce
flour, for dredging, about ½ cup
2-4 tablespoons margarine, for
  sauteing
sliced fresh lemon

Combine fish, dry onion, 3 tablespoons margarine, Worcestershire, bread crumbs and egg. Mix well and shape into 6-8 cakes. Refrigerate, if possible, for several hours. Roll cakes in flour; sauté in ⅛" margarine on both sides until brown; about 5-8 minutes. Serve immediately with lemon slices for garnish.

Barbara Matuszewski

EVE'S CRAB CAKES

3 tablespoons butter
6 tablespoons flour
1½ cups milk
salt
pepper
½ teaspoon dry mustard
1 beaten egg

1 teaspoon grated onion
dash nutmeg
dash Worcestershire sauce
1 tablespoon fresh OR dried parsley
2 cups fresh crabmeat

Cook butter, flour, mustard, onion, nutmeg, Worcestershire and milk until thick. Add parsley and crabmeat. Chill.

This base, white sauce, must be made early in the morning so that it becomes cold enough to handle and shape into cakes by evening.

When completely chilled, form cakes and roll in bread crumbs. Fry in medium hot oil until brown. Serve with soy sauce, optional.

Eve Conlon

FISH FILLETS — TARPON SPRINGS STYLE

OVEN: 325° 20-25 minutes

fish fillets
tomatoes, thinly sliced
onions, thinly sliced

olive oil
Parmesan cheese
lemon juice

Place fillets in a lightly oiled baking dish. Sprinkle a little salt over fillets. Squeeze a little lemon juice over fillets. Pour a little olive oil over length of fillets. Alternate tomato and onion slices, sprinkling Parmesan cheese between each slice. Pour a little more oil on top. Add water ¾ of the way to the top of fillets. Cover tightly with foil and a lid, if possible, and bake at 325° for 20-25 minutes.

Kenneth Philbrick

FRIED CATFISH

catfish fillets
salt
pepper

meal
fat for frying; 1 part bacon and 2 parts peanut oil

Cut fillets across grain into 1½″ strips. Salt, pepper, and roll strips in meal. Deep fry in fat. Drain well on paper towels.

Carra Adams

For a delicious topping for broiled fish, combine three-fourth pound of shredded Gruyere cheese, one one-half cup of sour cream, and one tablespoon of milk. Heat until cheese melts and pour over fish.

FRIED SHRIMP

⅔ cup pancake flour
1⅓ cups cracker meal
salt
pepper
3 eggs, well-beaten

½ cup evaporated milk
oil for frying
3 pounds raw, peeled and deveined
shrimp

Butterfly shrimp, leaving tip of tails. Mix pancake flour, cracker meal and salt and pepper together in a bowl.

Beat eggs and milk in a separate shallow bowl. Dip shrimp in dry mixture, then egg mixture, then back into dry mixture. Place in single layers on waxed paper. Cover and chill in refrigerator at least one hour, to set egg. Fry in hot, 375°, oil until golden brown, and drain on paper towels. Do not overcook as shrimp will be tough.

This is excellent with oysters too.

Jeanne Crutchfield

GRILLED SHRIMP

16 large shrimp, shelled and deveined
½ cup cognac
16 thin slices prosciutto OR ham
16 fresh bay leaves

2 tablespoons bread crumbs
½ teaspoon salt
½ teaspoon pepper
2 teaspoons lemon juice

Marinate shrimp in cognac for 1 hour. Drain and wrap each shrimp in slice of prosciutto or ham. Place shrimp on skewers, alternately with bay leaves. Place in broiler and cook until ham fat begins to sizzle. Roll skewers in bread crumbs, sprinkle with salt and pepper and return to broiler until golden brown. Sprinkle with lemon juice and serve very hot.

Mary Ann Loguidice

GROUPER PARMESAN

OVEN: 350° 25-30 minutes

2 pounds grouper fillets, fresh OR
frozen, OR kingfish, snapper or
other fish
1 cup sour cream
¼ cup grated Parmesan cheese

1 tablespoon lemon juice
1 tablespoon grated onion
½ teaspoon salt
dash of tabasco
chopped parsley

Thaw frozen fillets before using. Skin fillets and place in a single layer in a greased baking dish, approximately 12 x 8 x 2, after cutting into serving size pieces. Combine remaining ingredients and spread mixture over fish. Sprinkle with paprika and bake in moderate, 350°, oven for 25-30 minutes or until fish flakes with fork. Garnish with parsley.

Very delicious taste and different.

Mabel Fawsett

HOT TUNA SALAD

OVEN: 350° 20 minutes

YIELD: 4 servings

1 — 6½ to 7 ounce can tuna,
drained and flaked
1 cup finely diced celery
½ cup mayonnaise
¼ cup slivered, toasted almonds
2 tablespoons chopped ripe olives
2 teaspoons lemon juice

1 teaspoon finely minced onion
½ cup finely crushed corn flaked
cereal
2 tablespoons packaged, shaker
container, grated American
cheese
2 tablespoons melted butter

Combine tuna, celery, mayonnaise, almonds, olives, lemon juice and onion; toss lightly. Pile into 4 shells or baking dishes. Bake in moderate oven, 350°, for 10 minutes.

Combine crushed cereal, cheese, and melted butter and sprinkle over hot salad. Bake an additional 10 minutes or until brown.

A delicious entree in a hurry. Do use the all white tuna for this as it does make a difference.

Connie Wagers

LOBSTER THERMIDOR I

OVEN: 375°

YIELD: 8 servings

6 small lobsters, broiled and halved
4 tablespoons butter
1 teaspoon grated onion
1 cup sliced mushrooms
4 tablespoons flour
1 cup milk
1 cup cream
1 teaspoon dry mustard

1 teaspoon celery salt
dash cayenne pepper
2 egg yolks, slightly beaten
1½ cups grated cheese
3-4 tablespoons sherry, optional
1 tablespoon lemon juice
½ cup buttered crumbs

Remove meat and cut into small pieces; reserve shells. Sauté onion and mushrooms in butter; blend in flour. Slowly add milk and cook, stirring constantly, over low heat until thickened. Add cream and seasonings. Stir a little of the hot sauce into slightly beaten egg yolks; blend, then stir in remaining sauce. Add 1 cup of grated cheese and stir over low heat until cheese melts. Add sherry (optional) and lemon juice and lobster meat. Pile into halved shells, top with buttered crumbs and remaining grated cheese and a dash of paprika. Brown in moderate, 375°, oven or under broiler. Garnish with lemon slices.

Can also be baked in a casserole dish instead of lobster shells.

Hazel N. Crews

When frying fish or seafood, add one-half to one teaspoon of baking powder to the batter for a delicious and delicate crust.

LOBSTER THERMIDOR II

1½ pounds boiled lobster
4 tablespoons butter
2 tablespoons flour
1 cup heavy cream
2 egg yolks
1 cup fresh mushrooms

3-4 pimentos
2 tablespoons sherry
salt
white pepper
¼ cup Parmesan cheese

Remove lobster meat and save two shell sections. Cut meat into chunks and set aside. Sauté fresh mushrooms in 2 tablespoons butter over low heat, covering pan and stirring occasionally. Cook for about 10 minutes. Set mushrooms aside. In a double boiler top, melt 2 tablespoons butter; stir in flour, lobster, salt, pepper, and sherry. In another pan, beat egg yolks slightly; add cream and mix well. Slowly stir in lobster mixture; cook over hot water, stirring just until thickened. Stuff lobster with mixture, dividing evenly into 2 shell halves. Sprinkle lightly with Parmesan cheese and brown lightly under broiler.

Nick Midelis
Hilltop House

LOUISA'S CONCH SUPREME

1 pound ground conch
3 key limes
1 large onion, chopped
1 cup celery, chopped
¼ cup parsley, chopped
½ stick oleo
1 egg

6 ounces cheddar cheese
½ cup white wine
pinch of mace
¼ teaspoon crushed rosemary
⅛ teaspoon thyme
2 tablespoons cornstarch

Marinate conch in juice of 3 limes for 30 minutes. Sauté onion, celery, and parsley in ¼ stick oleo. Place sautéed mixture in blender and blend until smooth; add 1 egg and blend again. Sauté conch in ¼ stick oleo and juice from the key limes, for about 3 minutes. Add blended mixture to conch; add cheese and cook until cheese is melted, over low heat. Mix wine and cornstarch together until smooth; add to pan to thicken sauce.

Serve over rice or noodles.

Louisa Christen

With fish and shellfish dishes serve a chilled dry, or semi-sweet white wine, or a rose.

MAINE BAKED-STUFFED LOBSTER

OVEN: 375° 25-30 minutes

4 large lobsters, 1½ to 1¾ pounds each, split, cleaned and rinsed under running water
2 cups rolled round snack crackers
2 cups dry bread crumbs, rolled

¼ pound melted butter
tamale, optional
2 teaspoons Worcestershire sauce
2 tablespoons cooking sherry

Split, clean and rinse lobsters under running water; dry with paper towels. Boil lobster claws for 20 minutes, then cut up meat. Blend cut meat with cracker crumbs, bread crumbs, melted butter, tamale, if desired, and Worchestershire and sherry. Blend well. Preheat oven to 375°. Place mixture in oven and bake for 25-30 minutes; if large, bake for 40 minutes. Place under broiler for a few minutes. Watch carefully, brown, but do not burn.

This recipe was concocted by my mother and father and is absolutely delicious.

Dawn C. Lord

MEETING STREET CRABMEAT

YIELD: 4 servings

1 pound white crabmeat
4 tablespoons butter
4 tablespoons flour
½ pint cream

4 tablespoons sherry
¾ cup grated sharp cheese
salt
pepper

Make cream sauce using butter, flour and cream. Add salt and pepper to taste and sherry. Remove from heat and add crabmeat. Pour mixture into buttered casserole or individual baking dishes. Sprinkle with grated cheese and cook in hot oven until cheese melts. Do not overcook.

One and one-half pound shrimp may be substituted for crabmeat.

Mary Jo McDermid

MULLET MAGNIFICO

OVEN: 350° 20-25 minutes

YIELD: 6 servings

2 pounds mullet fillets, fresh OR frozen
⅔ cup dry bread crumbs
⅓ cup butter OR margarine, melted
¼ cup grated onion

1 teaspoon chili powder
1 teaspoon salt
¼ teaspoon ground thyme
dash of cayenne pepper
paprika
lemon wedges

Thaw fillets if frozen. Place fillets in a single layer, skin side down, on a well-greased bake and serve platter, about 16 x 10 inches. Combine bread crumbs, butter, onion, chili powder, salt, ground thyme, and cayenne pepper. Spread mixture over fillets and sprinkle with paprika. Bake in a moderate oven, 350°, for 20-25 minutes or until fillets flake easily when tested with a fork. Serve with lemon wedges.

Forget the canard widely circulated that Florida East Coast mullett is not as good as Gulf Coast mullet. Try both and compare.

Tom Dunkin

OYSTER CASSEROLE

1 pint oysters
1 cup bread crumbs
1 cup cracker crumbs

½ cup butter
1 cup milk
dash Worcestershire sauce

Melt butter and mix crumbs with butter. Place ⅓ of buttered crumbs in a buttered casserole dish. Next place a layer of oysters over crumbs. Add another layer of crumbs and another layer of oysters. Add last of crumb mixture over the top. Combine Worcestershire with milk and blend together. Pour mixture over layers and bake in moderate oven until hot and browned.

This recipe won $100 and was published in a magazine out West.

Mrs. L. Segerstrom

OYSTERS FIUMANO

YIELD: 3-6 servings

4 pints shucked oysters
½ pound butter
4-6 cloves garlic
1 teaspoon salt

½ teaspoon black pepper
few dashes tabasco
sprinkle of chopped parsley

Prepare sauce first by melting butter in a skillet. Sauté crushed garlic cloves over low heat; add salt, pepper and tabasco. When garlic is golden, pour mixture into chafing dish; sprinkle parsley in sauce, and keep sauce warm.

Pour oysters and their liquid in a saucepan or skillet; add just enough water to cover. Bring to a quick boil; reduce heat or remove oysters from heat. Do not allow mixture to be at boiling temperature for more than 1 minute. Drain oysters, pour in chafing dish with sauce and serve.

This recipe was demonstrated by retired Army Major Alfred Fiumano, Jr. of Orange Park, FL, with the results that three persons ate four pints of oysters.

Tom Dunkin

OYSTERS ROCKEFELLER

OVEN: 450°-475° 4 minutes

¼ cup shallots OR green onion
¼ cup celery
1 teaspoon chervil
⅓ cup fennel
⅓ cup parsley
½ pound butter
2 cups watercress

⅓ cup bread crumbs
⅓ cup anisette
salt
pepper
cayenne
2 dozen oysters, on the half shell
rock salt

Chop shallots, celery, chervil, fennel and parsley. Sauté onion, celery, and herbs in 3 tablespoons butter for 3 minutes. Add watercress and let it wilt. Add this mixture with remaining butter, bread crumbs, and anisette to blender container and season to taste; blend for 1 minute. Place about 1 tablespoon of blended mixture in each oyster; place oysters on bed of rock salt and dampen salt lightly. Bake at 450°-475° for about 4 minutes.

A tin cookie sheet is excellent for baking this dish.

Louisa Christen

PAELLA VALENCIANA

4 ounces olive oil
2 quartered tomatoes
2 sliced green peppers
2 sliced onions
1 teaspoon saffron
1 teaspoon oregano
1 teaspoon rosemary
1 teaspoon garlic
1 teaspoon white pepper
1 chicken, partly fried
4 shrimp, peeled

4 clams, whole
2 lobster tails, out of shell
2 crab legs, split
10 scallops
1 fresh fish, diced
10 ounces rice, cooked
4 ounces sherry
4 ounces stale beer
green peas
pimentos

Put oil in a large pot; add tomatoes, peppers, onions and spices. Cook until vegetables are tender. Add chicken, shrimp, clams, lobster, scallops and fish. Cook for 5 minutes, stirring continuously; add rice, sherry and beer; cover and place in oven for 15 minutes. Serve on a large platter or large casserole dish; garnish top with pimentos and green peas.

Peter A. White
Brass Sandpiper

POMPANO ALMONDINE

2½ pounds pompano fillets
2 tablespoons butter

2 tablespoons slivered, blanched
    almonds
paprika

Place fillets in a greased, flat pan. Dot with butter and sprinkle with paprika. Broil 2″ away from heat until fish is easily flaked with a fork, but moist. Sauté almonds in butter until golden brown. Spread over pompano and serve very hot with Menuiere Sauce (see recipe).

Nick Midelis
Hilltop House

RAW SHRIMP FRITTERS

Batter:
egg
milk
flour

salt
pepper
raw shrimp
oil for frying

Combine ingredients for batter and mix until fairly thick. Dip shrimp into batter and cook in boiling fat until brown.

Dorothy Binney Palmer

There is about a fifty per cent savings of the cost of ready-to-cook fish when filleting fish oneself.

RED SNAPPER WITH SAVORY SAUCE

3½ — 4 pounds red snapper
¼ cup olive oil
flour

Savory Sauce:
1 clove minced garlic

4 tablespoons tomato paste
½ teaspoon rosemary
salt
pepper
½ cup cider vinegar
1½ cups water

Scale and clean snapper thoroughly; cut into 4 steaks. Salt steaks and dust with flour. Heat olive oil in a skillet, but do not let it smoke. Place fish in skillet and quickly fry over medium heat until underside has a crisp golden crust, about 2-3 minutes. Turn carefully with a broad spatula and sauté fish only until golden brown on underside and easily flaked with a fork, but still moist, about 2-3 minutes.

Remove and set in earthenware bowl to cool.

Prepare sauce by sautéing garlic in the skillet used to fry the snapper. Add tomato paste, and stir until mixture is dissolved into a smooth paste. Blend in seasonings; add vinegar and water and simmer for 10 minutes. Pour sauce over snapper in the bowl; set aside for 2 hours and reheat in a slow, 300°, oven before serving.

Nick Midelis
Hilltop House

SALMON LOAF I

OVEN: 350° 30-40 minutes

1 pound can red OR pink salmon
1 teaspoon lemon juice
dash of pepper
1 teaspoon salt
2 eggs, beaten
⅔ cup chopped celery

½ cup chopped onions
1½ cups coarse dry bread crumbs
½ teaspoon baking powder
½ cup evaporated milk
½ cup fish liquid and water
paprika

Drain salmon and save liquid; discard skin and crush bones when flaking fish. Add lemon juice, pepper, eggs, celery, onions, salt, bread crumbs, baking powder, evaporated milk and fish liquid with water to equal ½ cup. Mix well and pack firmly into 9 x 4½ x 2½" buttered glass loaf pan. Sprinkle top with paprika and bake in moderate, 350°, oven until brown and firm, about 30-40 minutes. Unmold onto hot serving platter and serve with cheese sauce.

Ida C. Morgan

Baked oysters are delicious because the liquor is retained in the recipe when baked. To retain the natural plumpness and tenderness, cook only long enough to heat thoroughly.

SALMON LOAF II

1 heaping cup salmon
1 cup dry bread crumbs
1 cup scalded milk
1 teaspoon salt
1 tablespoon melted butter

½ teaspoon onion juice
2 egg yolks, beaten
1 teaspoon lemon juice
2 egg whites, stiffly beaten

Soak bread crumbs in scalded milk. Grease well a baking pan and place part of crumbs in pan. Combine salmon, remaining crumbs, salt, melted butter, onion juice, beaten egg yolks and lemon juice. Fold in stiffly beaten egg whites last. Place mixture in crumb lined pan and bake in moderate oven. Serve with white sauce.

Elizabeth Leonard

SALMON SOUFFLÉ

OVEN: 350° 1 hour

2 tablespoons margarine, melted
½ cup milk
4 slices bread, torn into pieces
2 — 16 ounce cans red salmon,
    drained and flaked
2 eggs, separated

3 tablespoons lemon juice
2 teaspoons minced onion
1 teaspoon salt
½ teaspoon pepper
dash of paprika

Mix butter, milk and bread together and stir in salmon, egg yolks, lemon juice, onion, salt and pepper. Beat egg whites until stiff and fold into salmon mixture.

Pour mixture into a greased 1½ quart casserole. Sprinkle top with paprika. Bake uncovered, in a pan of hot water, in 350° oven for 1 hour.

Peggy Hoskins

SCALLOPED OYSTERS

OVEN: 350° 15-20 minutes

1 pint oysters
2 cups soft bread crumbs
½ pint heavy cream
2 tablespoons butter

½ teaspoon salt
⅛ teaspoon pepper
butter to grease casserole

Preheat oven to 350°. Drain oysters and cut into small pieces. Season with salt and pepper. Melt butter in skillet, stir in bread crumbs until well coated; remove from heat. Place a layer of oysters in buttered casserole, then a layer of bread crumbs. Continue alternating layers, ending with bread crumbs. Pour cream over entire dish. Bake in 350° oven for 15-20 minutes.

Jeanne Crutchfield

SCALLOPS LA AVOCADO

YIELD: 4 servings

12 ounces fresh OR frozen scallops
2 medium avocados
2 tablespoons butter OR margarine
2 tablespoons flour
1 cup light cream OR milk
2 tablespoons parsley

¼ teaspoon salt
¼ cup onion
dash garlic powder
dash white pepper
1 egg, slightly beaten
2-3 cups hot cooked rice
lemon juice

Brush avocado with lemon; poach scallops in enough water to cover. Cook until tender, about 5 minutes then drain. In a 1 quart saucepan, cook onion in butter until tender, about 5 minutes; blend flour and cream together then add to onions; stir until mixture thickens; add scallops, parsley, salt, pepper and garlic. Gradually stir egg into mixture. Cook and stir for 1-2 minutes more. Spoon rice onto serving platter; place avocado on top of rice, spoon scallops and sauce over avocado.

Anna Baron

SEAFOOD CASSEROLE I

OVEN: 300° 20 minutes

YIELD: 6-8 servings

1 large can evaporated milk
1 cup sweet milk
1 medium onion, sliced
2 pieces celery with tops, sliced
5 whole cloves
1 bay leaf
½ stick butter
2 tablespoons flour
½ pound scallops

½ pint oysters
½ pound crabmeat
½ pound raw shelled shrimp
½ cup bread crumbs
salt
pepper
tabasco
Worcestershire sauce

Combine milk, onion, celery and spices; simmer together for 30 minutes; strain. Melt butter and add 2 tablespoons flour in saucepan; stir until smooth; add strained milk and season with salt, pepper, tabasco, and Worcestershire sauce to taste. Cook until thick. Pour into flat casserole; add scallops, oysters, crabmeat, and shrimp. Sprinkle bread crumbs over mixture and bake for 20 minutes in 300° oven. Sprinkle paprika on top of casserole for added color.

Laura Pinder

Serve a relish with fish meals such as celery, pickled onions, cabbage, cucumber, or sweet and sour beets.

SEAFOOD CASSEROLE II

OVEN: 350° 30 minutes

YIELD: 8 servings

1 pound cooked shrimp
½ pound cooked crabmeat
1 cup chopped celery
1 small chopped onion
1 large chopped green pepper

1 cup mayonnaise
1 tablespoon Worcestershire sauce
salt
pepper
round snack crackers, crushed

Combine all ingredients and mix well. Place in baking dish and cover with crushed crackers. Bake in 350° oven for 30 minutes.

Lane McCollum

SEAFOOD CREPES

OVEN: 350° 30 minutes

YIELD: 6 servings

Crepés:
2 eggs plus 2 yolks
⅛ teaspoon salt
1 tablespoon sugar
1 cup flour
1 cup milk

Sauce:
¼ pound butter
4 tablespoons flour
2 cups milk

1 pound cooked bay shrimp OR
    cooked crabmeat OR cooked
    scallops
½ cup dry sherry
1 teaspoon salt
¼ teaspoon coarsely ground pepper
1 package frozen peas and carrots, cooked
1 tablespoon chopped parsley
½ cup grated brick cheese
1 cup cooked celery

In blender container, combine crepe ingredients; eggs plus yolks, salt, sugar, flour and milk. Whirl one minute; scrape down sides with rubber spatula and whirl 15 seconds more. Refrigerate for one hour.

To make crepes, lightly butter pan and pour 2-3 tablespoons of batter into pan, rotating pan quickly to coat bottom evenly. Cook until brown, about 1 minute. With spatula, flip crepe over. Cook until light brown. Remove and cool on rack.

Prepare basic white sauce by melting butter in a 3 quart saucepan. Stir in flour and then blend in milk. Add seafood, or combination of seafoods. Stir in sherry, salt, pepper, cooked peas and carrots, chopped parsley, and cooked celery.

Place cooled crepes in an oblong decorative baking dish and fill crepes with approximately ¾ cup seafood mixture and roll up. Sprinkle grated cheese over rolled crepes. Place remaining seafood mixture over filled crepes and bake in preheated oven at 350° for 30 minutes. Garnish with parsley sprigs before serving.

Elizabeth E. Mayer

When poaching fresh fish, flavor the liquid with fresh dill leaves. Dill leaves can also be used with smoked or pickled fish.

SEAFOOD NEWBERG

1 pound lobster
3 tablespoons butter
1 tablespoon flour
½ cup mushrooms
½ teaspoon salt
dash paprika

⅛ tablespoon chopped onion
¼ cup cognac OR brandy
¼ cup sherry
3 egg yolks
1 cup heavy cream

Cut lobster into chunks. Melt butter in pan and blend in flour. Add salt, pepper, onion and mushrooms. Separately add cream to egg yolks and beat well; in blender if possible. Add lobster, brandy and sherry to onion-mushroom-butter mixture. Stir well then add cream and egg mixture. Stir until thick and hot.

Eloise Tedder

SEAFOOD THERMIDOR

YIELD: 4 servings

1 pound fresh OR frozen cod fillets
  OR other white fish
1 onion, quartered
lemon juice
1 can cream of shrimp soup
3 tablespoons flour
¼ cup dry white wine

¼ cup shredded mozzarella cheese,
  about 1 ounce
2 tablespoons snipped parsley
2 tablespoons grated Parmesan
  cheese
2 teaspoons butter
½ teaspoon paprika
¼ cup milk
½ cup bread crumbs

Cut fish into bite-sized pieces. Boil fish, onion, and lemon for 5-6 minutes in small amount of water.

Blend soup and flour in a small saucepan. Add milk and wine gradually. Cook and stir until mixture is thick and bubbly. Stir in cheese and parsley. Drain fish and add fish pieces to sauce. Spoon into 4 individual serving dishes or 1 shallow casserole.

Combine bread crumbs, cheese, butter and paprika. Sprinkle over top and broil for 1-2 minutes.

You may want to substitute some scallops or crabmeat for some of the fish.

Gloria Bleck

As a general rule, the species of fish which contain higher percentages of oil have more flavor.

SHRIMP AND CRAB QUICHE

OVEN: 350° 35-40 minutes

2 — 9" pie shells
1 — 6 ounce package frozen crab-
    meat OR fresh
1½ cups chopped cooked shrimp
1 — 8 ounce package shredded nat-
    ural Swiss cheese

½ cup finely chopped celery
½ cup finely chopped scallions
1 cup mayonnaise
2 tablespoons flour
1 cup dry white wine
4 slightly beaten eggs

Preheat oven to 350°. Ahead of time combine crab, shrimp, cheese, celery, and scallions. Divide mixture evenly into pie shells. In a bowl, combine mayonnaise, flour, wine and eggs. Pour mixture evenly over seafood in pie shells. Bake for 35-40 minutes, or until knife inserted comes out clean. Cool. Cover with plastic wrap and refrigerate. When ready to serve, reheat for 15 minutes.

To freeze, do not bake. Place on cookie sheet in freezer. When frozen, wrap in foil. To use, bake frozen in 350° oven for 50 minutes.

Carol Javert

SHRIMP AND NOODLE DELIGHT

OVEN: 350°

1 — 6 ounce package uncooked
    noodles
1 cup milk
1 can shrimp soup
1 can mushroom soup, undiluted

2 tablespoons dry sherry
2 cans shrimp
bread crumbs
1 cup grated Parmesan cheese

Cook noodles according to package directions; drain and place in a buttered casserole dish. Stir in 1 cup milk which has been added to 1 can of shrimp soup and warmed over low heat. Add mushroom soup, undiluted. Pour in dry sherry for flavor. Toss in shrimp and mix together. Top with bread crumbs and cheese. Bake in 350° oven until cheese melts.

Serve hot with tossed salad and hot rolls.

Linda Gagnon

When boiling shrimp use fresh celery leaves as it will enhance their flavor and counter-act odor.

SHRIMP CALCUTTA

2½ pounds medium size shrimp
4 cups water
3 bay leaves
pinch of Spanish saffron
¼ pound butter
1 teaspoon curry powder

¼ teaspoon celery salt
1 tablespoon Accent
3 chicken bouillon cubes
1 tall can evaporated milk
cornstarch

Peel, remove black vein of shrimp, and wash shrimp. Boil shrimp in 4 cups water with bay leaves and saffron until light pink in color. Do not overcook, as shrimp will be tough.

Remove bay leaves. Add butter, curry powder, celery salt, Accent, bouillon cubes and evaporated milk to shrimp and liquid. Bring mixture to boiling point and thicken with enough cornstarch to make a heavy sauce; color should be deep yellow. Add a few drops of yellow food coloring if yellow is not deep enough.

Shrimp Calcutta is delicious served over a bed of hot, steamed white rice. Garnish with pimento strips and fresh parsley.

Mildred Brown Garrett

SHRIMP CASSEROLE

OVEN: 375° 30 minutes

YIELD: 5-6 servings

6½ tablespoons butter, no substitute
4½ tablespoons flour
¾ cup milk
¾ cup heavy cream
1 pound medium-large shrimp, peeled and deveined, raw, fresh if possible

¼-½ pound fresh mushrooms, sliced
¼-½ cup dry white wine
1 tablespoon Worcestershire sauce
1 package frozen artichoke hearts
¼ cup freshly grated Parmesan OR Romano cheese

Combine flour and butter over low heat to make sauce. Add milk and cream, Worcestershire sauce, salt and pepper to taste. Line casserole with artichokes, cooked according to package directions. Scatter shrimp on top. Add mushrooms and add white sauce and wine. Cover liberally with cheese. Bake uncovered for 30 minutes at 375°; serve immediately.

Can be made ahead and frozen.

Elaine Matthews

Fish, stuffed or unstuffed, should be baked in a pre-heated 400° oven. If taken cold from the refrigerator and placed in a cold oven the fish will steam as the temperatures of the fish and oven rise; it will not bake.

SHRIMP CASSEROLE HARPIN

OVEN: 350° 55 minutes   YIELD: 6-8 servings

2½ pounds large raw shrimp, shelled and deveined
1 tablespoon lemon juice
3 tablespoons salad oil
¾ cup raw, regular OR processed rice
2 tablespoons butter OR oleo
¼ cup minced green pepper
¼ cup minced onion

1 teaspoon salt
⅛ teaspoon pepper
⅛ teaspoon mace, optional
dash cayenne pepper
1 — 10½ ounce can condensed tomato soup, undiluted
1 cup heavy cream
½ cup sherry
¾ cup slivered, blanched almonds

Early in the day, cook shrimp in boiling, salted water for 5 minutes. Drain. Place in a 2 quart casserole and sprinkle with lemon juice and salad oil. Meanwhile, cook rice as label directs; drain. Refrigerate all.

About 1 hour and 10 minutes before serving, heat oven to 350°. Set aside about 8 shapely shrimp for garnish. Place butter in a skillet and saute green pepper and onion for 5 minutes. Add, along with rice, salt, pepper, mace, cayenne pepper, soup, cream, sherry and ½ cup almonds, to the shrimp in the casserole. Toss well. Bake uncovered for 35 minutes; then top with reserved shrimp and ¼ cup almonds. Bake for 20 minutes more or until mixture is bubbly and shrimp are slightly browned.

Marion K. Hornung

SHRIMP MARINEE

1 pound boiled, shelled and deveined shrimp
½ cup olive oil
2 tablespoons lemon juice

½ teaspoon oregano
½ teaspoon chopped garlic
salt
pepper

Place all ingredients in an earthenware bowl and stir to blend. Marinate overnight and served chilled.

Nick Midelis
Hilltop House

Two pounds of raw unpeeled shrimp will yield one pound of cooked, peeled, and deveined shrimp which is enough protein for six persons.

SHRIMP NOODLE DINNER CASSEROLE

OVEN: 350° 30-45 minutes   YIELD: 6 servings

¾ pound peeled, cleaned and deveined shrimp, fresh OR frozen
OR 3 — 4½ ounce cans shrimp
1 — 8 ounce package medium size
noodles

2 cans condensed cream of mushroom soup
1 cup sour cream
⅓ cup sliced green onion
½ teaspoon dried dill weed
½ cup shredded cheddar cheese
1 medium tomato, sliced

Cook noodles as directed on package; drain well. Combine soup, sour cream,
onion and dill weed; mix well. Stir mixture into noodles.
Cook shrimp and cut one-fourth of shrimp into thirds. Fold cut shrimp and
cheese into noodle mixture. Spoon noodle-shrimp mixture into a shallow 2
quart baking dish. Cover dish with aluminum; crimping foil to edges of dish.
Bake in 350° oven for 20 minutes; remove from oven and remove foil. Arrange remaining shrimp in rows on top of casserole. Return csserole to oven
and bake uncovered for 10-15 minutes or until hot and bubbly.
Garnish with tomato slices.
If preferred, all shrimp may be cut and added to noodle mixture. Then entire casserole should be baked for 30 minutes or until bubbly.

Pearl M. Wyse

SHRIMP SCAMPI

36 medium shrimp, unshelled
6 garlic cloves
2 teaspoons salt
¾ cup butter, melted

¾ cup olive oil
¼ cup minced parsley
2 tablespoons lemon juice
freshly ground pepper

Split shrimp lengthwise to the tail, leaving feet and shell intact. Devein and
pat shrimp dry. Crush garlic, mix with salt and butter, olive oil, parsley,
lemon juice and pepper in a saucepan. Hold shrimp by tails; dip in butter
sauce and place, flesh side up, in a single layer in 1 or 2 baking dishes. Top
with remainder of sauce. Broil for 15 minutes with dishes 6″ away from heat.
Serve with sauce and garnish with parsley.

Mrs. Noah Lybrand, Jr.

Poaching is a low-calorie way to prepare seafood. Cook the food in a
small amount of hot liquid taking care to retain the shape of the
food. Poaching gives prominence to the flavor of the fish.

SHRIMP WITH SAUCE

1 pound ground fresh pork
1 medium onion, chopped
2 carrots, chopped
¼ cup celery, chopped
2 pounds raw shrimp
1 cup chicken stock
1 beaten egg

2 tablespoons cornstarch
2 tablespoons soy sauce
2 tablespoons cold water
salt
pepper
Accent
2 tablespoons oil

Combine pork, chopped vegetables and seasonings in hot oil and cook for 5 minutes. Add shrimp and stir fry until shrimp turn pink. Add stock and cook covered for 5 minutes. Add egg and stir for 2 minutes. Blend together cornstarch, soy sauce, water, salt, pepper, and Accent. Add blended cornstarch mixture to shrimp and stir until thick.
Serve over rice.

Mrs. B. Q. Waddell

SNAPPY HARD-SHELLED CRABS

2 dozen live blue crabs
1 — 9½ ounce box cracker meal
2 teaspoons salt

tabasco sauce
oil to deep fry
melted butter

Clean crabs by removing all inedible parts; reserving claws. Claws can be steamed in salted water later. Snip or cut off legs with a knife to avoid tearing out meat. With a soft-bristled brush, scrub body clean under running water. If not used immediately, refrigerate.
Mix cracker meal with salt. Break crab body in half. Sprinkle each half with 2-3 drops of tabasco sauce then coat with cracker meal. Deep fry in hot oil, 375°, until lightly golden. Do not overcook. Drain well on paper towels. Pick meat from shell, dip in melted butter and enjoy.

Jeanne Crutchfield

SNOOK PARMESAN

OVEN: 350° 30 minutes

YIELD: 6 servings

2 pounds snook OR snapper
1 large lemon
¼ cup grated Parmesan cheese

¼ teaspoon basil
paprika
3 tablespoons butter

Skin snook and place in a greased baking dish; squeeze lemon juice over fillets and let rest for ½ hour. Salt and pepper fillets and sprinkle with paprika, basil, and cheese. Bake in 350° oven for about 30 minutes. If not browned, turn on broiler for a few seconds. Garnish with parsley.

Louisa Christen

SOUTHERN FRANCE KINGFISH

6 slices kingfish, 1½" thick
4 tablespoons cooking oil, preferably peanut oil
4 tablespoons chopped onion

½ pound sliced mushrooms
½ cup dry white wine
1 cup tomato sauce
chopped parsley

Fry kingfish briskly in oil; remove from pan. In same oil, brown onions. When onions are brown, add mushrooms, Return fish to pan and add white wine and tomato sauce; cover and simmer for 25 minutes. Sprinkle with parsley when ready to serve.

Replace onions with shallots when available.

Louise Hayes

STUFFED BAKED SNAPPER

OVEN: 350° 40 minutes

3 pounds red snapper

Gravy:
3 tablespoons flour
3 tablespoons oil OR butter
3-4 green onions, chopped
½ green pepper, chopped
juice of ½ lemon
2 cans tomato sauce
water, as needed to thin mixture to
  gravy consistency

½ lemon, thinly sliced
Dressing:
½ pound shrimp, raw, cleaned, and
  cut
3-4 green onions, chopped
½ green pepper, chopped
2 celery stalks, chopped
½ teaspoon salt
½ teaspoon pepper
4 slices wet bread
dash of garlic powder

For gravy, brown flour and add chopped onion and green pepper; sauté until wilted. Add lemon juice and tomato sauce; simmer; add water as needed.

For fish, remove eyes, or cut heads from cleaned fish; remove backbone.

For dressing, sauté onions, pepper, and celery in butter until wilted. Add cut shrimp and moist bread. Fry all until mixture is fairly dry. Add one beaten egg if needed to bind mixture.

Arrange half of fish in large baking dish or pan. Squeeze lemon juice over fish; salt to taste. Place dressing over fish and cover with other half of fish; pour gravy over all and arrange lemon slices on top. Bake in 350° oven for 40 minutes or until fish flakes with fork. Serve with egg noodles and cole slaw.

B. J. Nelson

Fresh shucked oysters are quite plump and have a creamy natural coloring and clear liquid. The oysters will maintain quality for about a week in the refrigerator if packed in ice properly.

STUFFED FLOUNDER

OVEN: 325°-350° 15 minutes

4 ounces jumbo crabmeat
4 ounces deluxe crabmeat
6 ounces bread crumbs
1 teaspoon garlic powder
1 teaspoon white pepper
2 ounces diced pimentos

3 ounces mayonnaise
1 teaspoon Worcestershire sauce
24 — 4 ounce pieces of flounder
8 ounces lemon butter
paprika

Bone crabmeat and flake; add bread crumbs, spices, mayonnaise and pimentos. Mix very well. Spread mixture over one piece of flounder and top with a second piece of flounder. Top with lemon butter and paprika and bake for 15 minutes in moderate, 325°-350°, oven.

Peter A. White
Brass Sandpiper

TUNA OR SALMON CASSEROLE

OVEN: 425° 25 minutes

2 cups sliced, boiled potatoes
1 — 7 ounce can flaked tuna, drain
and reserve oil
2 tablespoons diced onion

1 cup condensed celery OR mushroom soup
6 tablespoons water

Grease a baking dish and fill with alternating layers of potatoes, tuna and onion. Dilute soup with 6 tablespoons water. Add soup to baking dish. Season mixture lightly with salt and pepper and paprika. Pour oil, reserved from tuna, over ingredients and bake for 25 minutes in 425° oven.

Gladys Grammer

When selecting a whole fish, check for these signs of freshness: bright, clear eyes; bright red gills; firm and elastic flesh; skin irridescent and unfaded characteristic markings and coloring of that species; and an odor that is not disagreeable, but fresh and mild.

TURTLE (SOFT SHELL) CHOWDER

1 — 1½ pounds turtle meat, scraps
  and bones
5 cups water
¼ pound salt pork, diced
1 cup diced potatoes
1 cup diced celery
1 cup chopped onion
1 cup chopped green pepper
¾ cup ketchup
1 — #2 can tomatoes
6 tablespoons tomato paste
pinch of thyme

pinch of mace
pinch of cinnamon
pinch of allspice
pinch of rosemary
dash of tabasco
½ teaspoon Worcestershire sauce
¼ cup sliced pimento stuffed olives
½ lemon
1 bay leaf
salt
pepper

Place turtle meat and bones in a large pot with water, salt, pepper and bay leaf. Simmer until meat is very tender; about 1-½ hours. Fry salt pork in a large skillet; add potatoes, celery, onion, and green pepper; cook very slowly in skillet until potatoes are soft, almost mushy. Remove turtle and bones from broth; pick meat off bones and chop meat fine. Return meat to broth and add ketchup, tomatoes, and tomato paste. Mash tomatoes with spoon. Simmer about 30 minutes. Mix potatoes and other vegetables with broth. Add tomato juice if mixture is too thick. Season with salt and freshly ground pepper; then add spices and tabasco and Worcestershire. Add olives and simmer 2-3 minutes. Add thinly sliced lemons and serve hot.
Fantastic.

Tom Dunkin

WALKER'S OKEECHOBEE FRIED CATFISH

3-4 channel catfish, cleaned and
  dressed
salt

pepper
cracker meal
oil

Dip catfish in cracker meal or place catfish in a paper bag filled with cracker meal and shake. Place oil into a heavy skillet to a depth of ½". When oil is very hot, place fish in skillet and fry until brown; turn twice. Cooking time is from 5-7 minutes. Serve with swamp cabbage and corn doggers.

Use "sharpies" as these catfish are best. They are small and have a forked tail. The regular catfish, called "pollywogs," have a square tail, and are not as tender as the "sharpies."

Wade Walker

To scale fish, pour scalding water over the fish and it will scale twice as easily. Dash the water on and do not let the fish stand in it.

GAME

DOVE AND DRESSING

OVEN: 375° 45 minutes

6 doves
1 package cornbread dressing mix
2 eggs, boiled and chopped
1 onion, chopped

celery, chopped
bell pepper, chopped
milk

Clean doves and split down the breast. Salt and pepper to taste. Mix other ingredients, adding milk until very moist. Place mixture in baking dish and lay doves on top, pressing slightly down into mixture. Bake at 375° for 45 minutes. Strips of bacon may be placed across doves if desired.

Pearl Raulerson

DUCKLING AU GRANDE MARNIER

OVEN: 350° 2½ hours   YIELD: 6 servings

4 — 4½ pounds dressed duckling
2 oranges, halved
salt
pepper
thyme

1 cup claret wine
½ teaspoon grated orange rind
3 brandied orange slices
½ cup Grande Marnier cordial
2 cups water

Place duckling in a roasting pan. Squeeze juice of oranges over duckling and insert peels into cavity. Season with salt, pepper and thyme. Place in shallow, open pan, breast side up, on rack. Roast in 325° oven about 2 hours, until brown on both sides. Drain fat and add 2 cups water and the wine to pan. Continue roasting until done; about 30 minutes. Strain juices from pan; keeping duckling warm. Place pan juices over direct heat in blazer of chafing dish; add grated orange rinds, brandied orange slices and Grande Marnier. Flambe (set fire to) the sauce and pour over duckling. Serve at once.

Nick Midelis
Hilltop House

To tenderize wild game or chicken, parboil with a teaspoonful of lemon juice or vinegar before frying or baking.

FRIED WILD TURKEY WITH MILK GRAVY

small wild turkey, skinned and
  boned
evaporated milk*
4-5 cups flour*
salt

pepper
oil

*leftover milk and flour will be
  used in milk gravy

Cut boned raw turkey into 1½" x 3" pieces. Place in large deep bowl. Pour evaporated milk over pieces to cover. Chill at least 2 hours or overnight if possible.

Mix flour with ample salt and pepper. Dredge soaked turkey in flour and fry in 375° oil until golden brown. Be very careful not to overcook. Overcooking will dry out meat. Drain well on paper towels.

Milk gravy: pour all but 4 tablespoons of oil out of pan, retaining browned bits. Add 4 generous tablespoons of reserved flour. Simmer for 5 minutes. Add ½ of reserved milk and ½ water to make 2½ cups liquid. Pour into flour mixture. Bring to a boil and simmer until thick. Use less flour or more milk if thinner gravy is desired.

Serve over hot steamed rice. Round out the meal with sliced tomatoes, fresh collard greens with white bacon, and home-made cornbread.

Quail or dove may be substituted for wild turkey, but do not debone.

Jeanne Crutchfield

GAMEBIRD SPECIAL

doves, one dozen if you are lucky
  OR 6 quail OR 1 small duck, cut
  up
2 cans celery soup
2 cans water
clove of garlic
salt to taste

pepper to taste
1 cup rice
2 cups cold water
½ teaspoon salt
1 teaspoon butter
¼ cup oil

Brown birds in oil. Drain pan and mix in soup, water and chopped garlic. Add birds again. Simmer until tender.

Serve over rice cooked in water with salt and butter.

I add 1 teaspoon Italian seasoning to soup.

Jerome Gilmore

Game should be marinated for three days; then roasted in a hot oven.

PEPPY VENISON

1½ — 2 pounds venison steak OR
stew meat, sliced thin
¼ cup olive oil
4 cloves garlic, sliced and peeled
½ cup water
½ cup port wine
salt
pepper

1 seeded hot cherry pepper
4 medium potatoes, peeled and
chopped
6 medium onions, peeled and julienne sliced
6 medium green peppers, seeded
and sliced in julienne pieces

Heat olive oil in deep iron or heavy pot. Sauté venison in oil about 10 minutes. Add garlic, water, wine, salt, pepper, seeded cherry pepper and potatoes. Simmer covered, stirring often, for about 1 hour. Add onions and green peppers. Cover and stir often until vegetables are tender crisp. More water may be added during cooking if needed. Serve with bib lettuce and fresh mushroom salad with a garlic, olive oil and vinegar dressing, lots of hot bread, and chilled port wine.

Boned duck breast from wild duck may be substituted for venison.

Jeanne Crutchfield

PHEASANT A LA ROMA
(Italian)

OVEN: 350° 1 hour

1 pheasant
1 cup light red wine
¼ cup olive oil

flour
garlic
1 can cream of mushroom soup

Cut pheasant into serving pieces and marinate in wine and olive oil for 2 hours. Pheasant can be dredged in flour (save wine and olive oil) and browned in heavy cast iron pot in olive oil and garlic. Add a small amount of hot water plus reserved wine and olive oil to pan; stir into gravy. Pour liquid over pheasant. Bake for 1 hour in 350° oven. Add soup last and heat in oven.

Kristin P. Wagers

QUAIL AND OYSTERS

OVEN: moderate oven 30 minutes

quail
3 oysters per quail
melted butter
cornmeal
flour

butter
salt to taste
pepper to taste
bacon strips
toast

Wipe birds inside and out with damp cloth. Dip oysters in melted butter, then in cornmeal and place inside bird. Make flour and butter into paste and rub breasts well. Place birds in baking dish with strip of bacon across each bird. Bake for 30 minutes, basting well with butter.

Serve on toast.

Mary Jo McDermid

STUFFED CORNISH HENS

OVEN: 425° 20 minutes; 325° 35 minutes

3 pepperoni sausages
2 cloves garlic, quartered
1 small can mushrooms
½ teaspoon salt
6 tablespoons olive oil OR other oil
1 — 8 ounce can tomato sauce

6 green onions, sliced thin
¼ cup butter
1 small can pitted, ripe olives (36 sliced)
3 Cornish hens

Simmer sausages for about 15 minutes in skillet with ½ inch water. Drain and cut sausage into thin slices. Cook onions and garlic in butter in skillet until limp. Add to this mushrooms, olives, salt and ½ of the oil. Stir together and stuff hens. Close openings with skewers.

Arrange hens in baking dish and brush with remaining oil. Bake in preheated oven at 425° for 20 minutes. Reduce heat to 325°, baste hens with ½ of tomato sauce and bake 20 minutes more. Baste with remaining tomato sauce and bake 15 minutes, or until legs move easily.

Kitty Brown

VENISON AND NOODLES

YIELD: 4 servings

2 pounds venison
¼ cup flour
1 teaspoon salt
ground pepper to taste
3 tablespoons bacon fat

1 stalk celery, cut up
3 medium onions, sliced
1 tablespoon Worcestershire sauce
2 cups tomatoes
noodles

Cut venison into serving size pieces. Mix flour with salt and pepper to taste. Coat venison with flour mixture. Heat bacon fat in skillet and brown venison on both sides. Add celery and onions and brown. Add Worcestershire and tomatoes and cook until tender, covered for about 1-2 hours. Cook noodles and drain.

Serve venison with noodles.

Pearl Raulerson

A savory marinade for deer is made with one part of sour red wine to two parts of water, with onion, celery, garlic, bay leaves, cloves, peppercorns, salt, carrots, caraway seeds, and a dash of sugar.

JAMS, JELLIES,
PICKLES, RELISHES

JAMS, JELLIES

PICKLES

RELISHES

BAKED APPLE BUTTER

10 pounds (approximately 24) apples
6 cups apple cider
brown sugar

4 teaspoons cinnamon
2 teaspoons allspice
1 teaspoon cloves
1 teaspoon nutmeg

Peel and quarter apples. Add cider, cover and cook until apples are soft. When soft, mash apples and place in roaster. Add ½ cup brown sugar for each cup of fruit. Add spices and cover with a brown paper bag and cook at 275° for 4-5 hours, stirring frequently until thick. Place in jars.
Very good. This recipe was given to me by Kitty Waddell.

Betty Dezzutti

CALAMONDIN MARMALADE

ripe calamondins
sugar

water

Wash fruit. Cut fruit in half and extract seeds. Do not peel fruit. Grind fruit or use liquidizer. For each cup of fruit pulp, add 3 cups water and boil for 15 minutes. Then (or next day after refrigeration) use 1 cup sugar to 1 cup of stock. Boil mixture to 225° or "jell" on candy thermometer. Pour into glasses and seal. About 3 cups of stock and 3 cups of sugar makes a good "batch." More is too much. This recipe came from the Agricultural Department of the State of Florida.

Vivian H. Davis

CHRISTMAS MARMALADE

YIELD: 15 six-ounce glasses

2 pint-size packages frozen strawberries (4 cups thawed)
6 cups sugar
3 oranges

1 cup white, seedless raisins
1 — 4 ounce can crushed pineapple
¼ cup lemon juice

Combine 4 cups sugar to 4 cups defrosted strawberries. Wash and slice oranges, remove seeds, and put fruit through a coarse grinder. Ground oranges should equal 2½ cups. Combine oranges, raisins, pineapple and lemon juice in a saucepan. Add remaining 2 cups of sugar. Boil mixture for about 20 minutes, stirring constantly. Add sweetened strawberries. Cook gently, stirring often, for about 45 minutes. Pour mixture into sterilized glasses and seal with paraffin.

Peggy Hoskins

When preparing fruit for jam, cook no more than three to four quarts of the fruit at one time.

GUAVA JELLY

sour guavas
water

sugar
lemon juice

Wash, stem and quarter sour guavas. Cover completely with water. Boil covered about 30 minutes. Strain through cloth. Boil 3 cups guava juice for 10 minutes, uncovered. Add 2 cups sugar and ½ teaspoon lemon juice. Boil uncovered until a table fork dipped in the hot liquid will hold the liquid between the tines. Pour into sterilized jelly glasses and cover with melted paraffin.

Annie Raulerson

HOT PEPPER JELLY

¾ cup hot pepper
1 cup bell pepper
1½ cups cider vinegar

6½ cups sugar
1½ bottles Certo
food coloring

Chop peppers in blender and measure after chopping. Boil sugar and vinegar 3-4 minutes. Add peppers, simmer 5 minutes until transparent. Remove from heat, add Certo and food coloring. Pour into sterilized jars.

Serve over block of cream cheese with melba rounds.

Ty Fender

KUMQUAT MARMALADE

4 cups kumquats
3 cups sugar

3 cups water

Wash and seed kumquats. Place in blender with equal amount of water. Blend. Then measure 3 cups water and 1 cup fruit. Combine in saucepan and boil. Reduce heat and cook for 15 minutes. Let stand to cool. When ready to make jelly, measure equal amount of sugar and fruit — 3 cups each — and cook rapidly to 230°. Cool and seal in hot jars.

Small amounts are easier to handle.

Barbara Gallup

KUMQUAT PRESERVES

6 cups kumquats
½ cup lime juice

water
sugar

Wash six cups of kumquats. Slice them into 2 or 4 slices each and remove seeds. Place sliced fruit into preserving kettle and add lime juice. Cover with water and boil for 15 minutes. Pour off all water, thus removing the bitter oil of the fruit. Add the same amount of water; just enough to cover the fruit; and for every cup of fruit, add one cup sugar. Cook mixture slowly until the preserves are the right consistency.

Eva Mae Williams

LIME JELLY

YIELD: 8 medium glasses

1 cup lime juice (about 6 limes)
2½ cups water
5 cups sugar

1 box powdered fruit pectin
green food coloring

First, prepare the juice. Squeeze and strain the juice from about 6 medium limes. Measure 1 cup into a large saucepan. Add water, mix well. Then, to make jelly, measure sugar and set aside. Add pectin to juice, mix well. Bring mixture to a hard boil over high heat stirring constantly. Add food coloring to desired shade. At once, stir in sugar. Bring to a full rolling boil and boil hard for one minute. Stir constantly. Remove from heat; skim off foam with a metal spoon, and pour into glasses. Cover with ⅛″ of hot paraffin

Marguerite R. Brock

PEPPER JELLY

5 bell peppers, ground
2 tablespoons tabasco
6½ cups sugar

1½ cups cider vinegar
1 bottle Certo
green food coloring

Combine all ingredients except Certo in saucepan and bring to a hard boil. Strain mixture through cheesecloth and return to stove. Bring to a hard boil again. Remove from heat. Add Certo, stir and pour into canning jars. Cover with paraffin.

Joan Henderson

RUBY CONSERVE

3 — 8 ounce cans tomato sauce
1 orange, thinly sliced
2 lemons, thinly sliced
2 cups sugar
1 cup orange marmalade

½ cup chopped walnuts
½ cup cut up Brazil nuts
1 cup seeded raisins
½ cup cut up almonds

Combine tomato sauce, orange and lemon slices, and sugar in saucepan. Simmer slowly for 1½ to 2 hours. Stir often. Add other ingredients and cook 20-30 minutes longer. Pour into jars.

Dot Gortner

Be certain to properly seal jam or jelly because an imperfect seal will allow air to get into the container thus forming a mold.

SEA GRAPE JELLY

3 cups juice from boiled grapes   ¼ cup sour orange OR lemon juice
2 cups sugar

Wash ripe grapes and place in a large pot and cover with water. Boil until water is purple, crushing grapes with potato masher. Strain mixture through jelly bag. Combine juice with sugar and lemon or orange juice and boil rapidly until jelly flakes off of spoon. Pour into sterile jars and cover with wax and seal.

Dot Gortner

SURINAM CHERRY JELLY

1 quart Surinam cherries   5 cups sugar
3 tablespoons lemon OR lime juice   1 package powdered pectin

Wash and measure cherries. Place in pot with half as much water (1 cup water for 2 cups cherries). Bring to a boil, mashing often until fruit is a soft pulp; about 25-30 minutes. Drain in a jelly bag. Do not squeeze. Place 1 quart juice in a wide pan on high heat and add juice, sugar and pectin. Boil until jelly sheets from spoon. Pour into glasses and seal with paraffin.

Dot Gortner

AUNT MAGGIE'S GREEN TOMATO PICKLES

7 pounds sliced green tomatoes   1 teaspoon cloves
2 gallons water   1 teaspoon allspice
3 cups lime   1 teaspoon celery seed
3 pints vinegar   1 teaspoon mace
5 pounds sugar   1 teaspoon ginger
pinch of salt   1 teaspoon cinnamon

Soak sliced tomatoes for 24 hours in 2 gallons of water to which lime has been added. Drain and soak tomatoes in fresh water for 4 hours, changing water every hour.

Combine all spices together and tie in a bag. In a saucepan, place vinegar, sugar, salt, and bag of spices. Bring to a boil and pour over drained tomatoes. Let this stand overnight and the next morning, boil for 1 hour. Pour into jars and seal.

Elouise Padrick

Crystals throughout jelly may be caused by too much sugar in the jelly mixture, or cooking the mixture too little, too slowly, or too long. Crystals that form at the top of jelly that has been opened and allowed to stand are caused by evaporation of liquid.

BAKED KUMQUAT PICKLES

OVEN: 350° 20-25 minutes

1½ pounds kumquats
2 cups sugar
½ cup light corn syrup
1 cup vinegar

1 cup water
1½ teaspoons whole cloves
2 sticks cinnamon

Wash kumquats and slice in half lengthwise. Boil kumquats in a small amount of water until tender, about 8-10 minutes. Drain. Mix remaining ingredients in a saucepan. Bring to a boil and add kumquats. Boil for 3-4 minutes. Pour into baking dish and bake in 350° oven until syrup is thick and kumquats are transparent; 20-25 minutes.

Dot Gortner

BETTY'S SWEDISH CUCUMBER PICKLES

6-8 medium cucumbers
2 tablespoons salt
2 medium onions, sliced thin

¼ cup parsley, chopped OR dry
⅞ cup sugar
½ cup vinegar

Slice cucumbers very thin and add 2 tablespoons salt and cover with water and let stand for 2 minutes. Drain. Add onions, parsley, sugar and vinegar. Put in bowl and cover with small plate and weight plate down. Refrigerate overnight. Place in jars.
This will keep in the refrigerator for 3-4 weeks.

Mrs. John McCarty

BREAD AND BUTTER PICKLES

8-10 quarts cucumbers, sliced
6-8 onions, sliced
4 cups vinegar
8 cups sugar
1 small box mustard seed

1 tablespoon celery seed
1½ tablespoons turmeric
1 cup salt
water

Pour salt over cucumbers and onions; cover with water and let set for 3 hours. Drain.
Bring to a boil the vinegar, sugar, and spices. Add drained cucumbers and onions; stir until they are heated through. Do not boil. Remove from stove; pour into jars and seal.
Yellow crookneck squash may be substituted for the cucumbers.

Dorothy A. Bishop

Overcooking makes jelly gummy; too little pectin, acid, or sugar makes jelly sirupy.

CRISP PICKLES

YIELD: 7 pints

4 quarts cucumbers, sliced thin
6 medium white onions, coarsely
  chopped
2 green peppers, chopped (optional)
3 cloves garlic
⅓ cup salt

5 cups sugar OR 2 cups light syrup
  and 3 cups sugar
1½ teaspoons turmeric
1½ teaspoons celery seed
2 tablespoons mustard seed
3 cups vinegar

Do not peel cucumbers. Slice cucumbers thin, add onions, pepper, whole garlic and cloves. Add salt and cover with ice cubes; mix thoroughly. Let stand 3 hours.

Drain and combine remaining ingredients and pour over cucumber mixture. Heat just to boiling. Seal in hot jars. Refrigerate before serving.

Dorothy White

CRISP SWEET-DILL PICKLES

½ cup cider vinegar
¼ cup mixed pickling spice

1 quart dill pickles, sliced and
  drained
3 cups sugar

Place vinegar and spices in a glass jar that can be sealed. Drop in pickles and pour in sugar but do not mix. Fasten lid and refrigerate for 10 days.

To make a second batch, you may use the same liquid, but add one cup sugar only.

This makes wonderful, crisp, sweet dill pickles. Makes expensive pickles at a cheap price.

Eileen Schiavone

GUARANTEED CRISPY BREAD AND BUTTER PICKLES

5 quarts cucumbers, sliced
1 quart onions, sliced
½ cup salt
5 cups sugar
1 quart vinegar

½ teaspoon pepper
2 tablespoons mustard seeds
1 tablespoon celery seeds
1 teaspoon turmeric
1 tablespoon ginger

Mix cucumbers and onions with three trays of ice cubes and salt. Let this mixture stand for 2-3 hours and then drain well.

Combine remaining ingredients in saucepan and simmer. Add cucumber and onion mixture to simmering ingredients. Pack and seal while warm.

The flavor improves if the pickles are allowed to set for 2 weeks after canning.

Dicksie Dudeney

MUSHROOMS AND PEPPERS

3 pounds mushrooms
1 pint jar hot cherry peppers
1 cup wine vinegar
½ teaspoon salt

3 cloves garlic
1 tablespoon oregano
olive oil

Slice mushrooms about ¼" thick and wash thoroughly. Boil mushrooms for 3 minutes in vinegar and salt. Remove stems and seeds from peppers, and slice thin. Drain mushrooms and add to peppers. Mix in oregano and finely chopped garlic. Put in glass jars and cover with olive oil. Serve with French or Italian bread. Keeps well for several weeks in refrigerator.

Mrs. G. Catenaci

QUICK PICKLES

1 quart kosher dill pickles

1 cup sugar

Drain and wash pickles several times. Slice ¼" thick and add sugar. Refrigerate for 2-3 days stirring several times.

Dot Gortner

SPICED MANGO PICKLES

YIELD: 3 pints

1½ cups white vinegar
1½ cups water
3 cups sugar
5 sticks cinnamon OR ½ teaspoon
  ground cinnamon

1 tablespoon whole cloves
¼ teaspoon mace
1 teaspoon nutmeg
3 pounds peeled, sliced, green mangos

Combine all ingredients except mangos in saucepan and boil syrup for 5 minutes. Add mango slices and cook until mangos are tender and clear; about 30-45 minutes. Pack mangos into hot sterilized jars. Add syrup and seal. For really tart mangos, use ¼ to ½ cup less sugar in the syrup.

The Committee

Tough shriveled pickles are the result of too much salt or sugar, or too strong a vinegar; soft pickles are the result of too weak a brine or too strong a vinegar.

WATERMELON RIND PICKLES

YIELD: 7 pints

1 tablespoon Lillip Lime
5 pounds rind
1 gallon water

Syrup:
2 quarts vinegar
1 pint water

5 pounds sugar
1 lemon, sliced
2 tablespoons stick cinnamon
2 tablespoons whole allspice
3-4 pieces whole ginger
2 tablespoons whole cloves

Soak peeled and cut up rind in lime water overnight. Next morning wash and boil in clear water for 1 hour.

Tie dry ingredients in cheese cloth bag. Boil rind in syrup and spices until rind is clear; about 45 minutes. Pour into sterilized jars. Seal while hot.

Dot Gortner

YESTERDAY'S BREAD AND BUTTER PICKLES

1 gallon firm, unpeeled cucumbers,
    thinly sliced
1 quart crushed ice
4 large white onions, thinly sliced
½ cup salt

Syrup:
5 cups white vinegar
5 cups white sugar
½ teaspoon ground cloves
2 teaspoons mustard seed
1 teaspoon celery seed
1 to 1½ teaspoons turmeric

This is a delightfully tart pickle, crisp and perfect for family enjoyment and gift giving.

If you use waxed cucumbers, scrub well. Layer the cucumbers, ice, onions, and salt in a large mixing bowl. Cover with a weighted lid and refrigerate for at least 3 hours.

Combine all ingredients for syrup. Drain cucumbers and onions and add to syrup in large kettle. Heat slowly to scald, but do not boil. Stir as little as possible. When small bubbles appear, remove from heat. Carefully place pickles in sterilized jars and seal at once.

Dell Lockwood

HEALTH RELISH

4 large carrots, chopped fine
2 heads cabbage, chopped fine
9 peppers, red and green, chopped
8 medium onions, chopped fine
½ cup salt

2 tablespoons celery seed
2 tablespoons mustard seed
2 pints vinegar
3 pints sugar

Mix vegetables well and add salt, let stand 2-3 hours. Drain.

Add spices and vinegar and sugar. Mix well and place into jars without cooking.

Keep refrigerated.

Wonderful and refreshing — great with meats!

Barbara Gallup

KUMQUATS IN SYRUP

1½ cups sugar
2 cups water

1 pint kumquats
¼ teaspoon baking soda

Boil water and sugar. Wash kumquats and cut ¼″ slit on bottom of fruit. Cover fruit with tap water in a saucepan, bring to a boil, and simmer for 10 minutes. Add baking soda just before removing pan from heat. This prevents bitterness in the skin. Pour off water and soda, drain well before adding to boiling sugar and water syrup. Boil or simmer fruit in syrup at least ½ hour. Remove from heat and seal tight in jars, or pour in bowl to use as dessert or on ice cream.

Ruth Hallstrom

MAMIE'S PEPPER RELISH

12 large sweet red peppers
12 large green peppers
15 onions
4 cups water
2 cups vinegar

2 cups vinegar
2 cups sugar
3 tablespoons salt
2 tablespoons mixed spice

Remove seed from peppers and chop fine with onions. Pour boiling water over peppers and onions to cover, and let stand for 5 minutes. Drain. Add mixture to 2 cups vinegar and water and bring to a boil. Let stand for 10 minutes. Drain, and discard liquid.

Then add 2 cups vinegar, 2 cups sugar, salt and mixed spices which have been tied in a bag to mixture and boil for 5 minutes or more. Seal in jars.

Elouise Padrick

MANGO CHUTNEY I

5 pounds mature green mangos
2 large onions
4 ounces preserved ginger
2 green peppers
1 cup near ripe papaya
2 cloves garlic
1 lime
1 tablespoon cinnamon

1 teaspoon allspice
1 cup seeded raisins
3 cups brown sugar
1 teaspoon cloves
2 teaspoons salt
¼ teaspoon cayenne
1 quart vinegar

Chop first seven ingredients into small pieces. Mix pieces well with spices, raisins, sugar, and vinegar. Bring mixture to a boil and cook until tender, but not soft; stirring frequently. Pour chutney into sterile jars and seal.

Ada Hancock

MANGO CHUTNEY II

YIELD: 3 pints

1 lemon, chopped
1 clove garlic, chopped
5 cups mangos, chopped
2½ cups brown sugar
1½ cups seedless raisins

3 ounces OR ¾ cup ginger,
  chopped
1½ teaspoons salt
2 cups cider vinegar
¼ teaspoon cayenne pepper

Combine all ingredients and mix. Cook until tender.

Marge Wambley

MARINATED PINEAPPLE CHUNKS

2½ cups canned pineapple chunks
¾ cup vinegar
1½ cups granulated sugar

dash of salt
6-8 whole cloves
1 — 4" piece cinnamon stick

Two to three days ahead of serving, drain pineapple, reserving ¾ cup of the syrup. To this syrup add all remaining ingredients except pineapple chunks. Simmer the liquid for 10 minutes then add the pineapple chunks and bring mixture to a boil. Cool and refrigerate until ready for serving.

Mrs. E. E. Jones

PEAR CHUTNEY

1½ pounds peeled, cored pears
1 pound raisins
½ cup chopped onion
¾ cup chopped celery
1 red bell pepper, chopped
1 green bell pepper, chopped
3 tablespoons whole mustard seed

1½ cups sugar
2½ cups vinegar
1 cup water
3 teaspoons salt
1-2 cloves garlic
½ teaspoon ginger
pinch of mace

Place all ingredients in a large saucepan. Bring mixture to a boil then simmer until pears are tender but not mushy. Remove saucepan from heat and let set overnight. Reheat the next morning and pack in sterilized jars. Cover tightly.

Apples may be added if desired.

Carolyn Davis

When making homemade pickles spices should be bought fresh.

SPICED KUMQUATS

1 pint kumquats   2 cups water
1 whole clove for each kumquat   2 cups sugar

Wash and cover kumquats with boiling water. Let steep for 2 minutes, then pour off water. Stick clove in each kumquat. Poach kumquats in water/sugar syrup for 20 minutes or until tender.

The Committee

WHOLE PRESERVED KUMQUATS

1 quart kumquats   1½ cups water
1½ cups sugar

Wash kumquats thoroughly. Cut two slight gashes at right angles across blossom end. Make a syrup of the sugar and water. Cool.

Add kumquats to syrup mixture and cook very slowly, from 1-2 hours until clear. Do not remove fruit. Cover mixture until cold. Then place in jars and cover with syrup and seal.

This is good served with fowl or meat.

Faith Meserve

Since the mango is a short-seasoned fruit, can mangoes for a year-round flavorful tropical fruit — a fruit that rivals any fruit in the world for flavor. Select firm-ripe mangoes that are not fibrous. Peel and slice. Prepare a medium syrup by bringing to a boil one cup of sugar to one cup of water. Add mango slices and heat through. Pack in hot, sterilized jars and cover with boiling syrup to within one-half inch of top. Seal and process for ten minutes in boiling water bath. Mangoes may also be packed cold in containers, sealed and processed.

NOTES

MEATS

APPLE SAUERKRAUT WITH SAUSAGES

OVEN: 400° YIELD: 3-4 servings

1 — 1 pound can sauerkraut, undrained
¼ cup water
3 tart apples, cored and quartered,
but not peeled
1 medium onion, peeled and sliced

2 bay leaves
dash of caraway seeds
2 slices bacon (optional)
6-8 hot dogs, knockwurst, etc.
dash of pepper

In an ovenproof casserole, mix the sauerkraut with its juice and the water,
apple quarters, onion, bay leaves, pepper and caraway seeds. Top with bacon
slices and cover. Bake at 400° for 30 minutes.

Remove cover and lay sausages on top of the sauerkraut. Return the casserole, uncovered, to the oven for 15 minutes or until the sausages are heated
through. Serve with mashed potatoes.

Ann VanDyke Grace Kennedy

BAKED BEEF STEW

OVEN: 300° 5 hours

2 pounds raw stew meat
1 large onion, sliced
1 cup celery, chopped
2 cups carrots, chopped

2 cups potatoes, chopped
1 tablespoon sugar
4 tablespoons tapioca
1 — #2 ½ can tomatoes

Place all ingredients in a large pan, cover and bake for 5 hours in 300° oven.

Edie Stretch

BAKED HAM SLICE

OVEN: 375° 40 minutes

1 center cut ham slice, 1½" thick
2 tablespoons mustard

½ cup brown sugar
milk to cover

Place ham in pan and cover with water and boil for 2 minutes. Drain and
place ham in baking pan and spread with mustard and sugar. Pour in enough
milk to cover ham. Let this stand for 30 minutes. Bake in 375° oven for 40
minutes or until tender. Thicken milk for gravy.

Margaret Lockard

BAKED STEW

OVEN: 300° 3½ to 4 hours

2 pounds stew beef
1 can tomato soup
3 large potatoes, cut up
2 onions, cut up

1 cup carrots, cut up
mushrooms
1 cup water OR mushroom juice
1 green pepper, cut up

Place all ingredients in a casserole and bake in 300° oven for 3½ to 4 hours.
Elizabeth Leonard

BARBECUE MEAT LOAF

OVEN: 350° 1 hour   YIELD: 6-8 patties

1½ pounds ground beef
¾ cup oatmeal
3 tablespoons chopped onion
1 cup milk
1½ teaspoons salt
¼ teaspoon pepper

Sauce:
2 tablespoons Worchestershire
  sauce
2 tablespoons sugar
6 tablespoons chopped onion
½ cup ketchup
½ cup water
3 tablespoons vinegar

Mix together loaf ingredients and shape into patties. Fry slowly. Combine ingredients for sauce. Place patties in a baking dish and pour sauce over patties. Bake for 1 hour at 350°.

Olive Smith

BARBECUE POT ROAST

OVEN: 325°-350° 1 hour

4 pound beef roast
salt
pepper
2 tablespoons shortening
½ cup water
1 — 8 ounce can tomato sauce
3 medium onions

2 cloves garlic
2 tablespoons brown sugar
½ teaspoons dry mustard
¼ cup lemon juice OR vinegar
¼ cup ketchup
1 tablespoon Worchestershire
  sauce

Salt and pepper roast to taste and brown in the shortening. Mix together water, tomato sauce, onions and garlic. Add this mixture to the roast and simmer for 1 hour at 325° to 350°.
Mix remaining ingredients together and add to roast. Simmer until done.

Rita Sowinski

BARBECUED RIBS

OVEN: 350° 1 hour

1 onion, grated
2 tablespoons butter
2 tablespoons vinegar
4 tablespoons lemon juice
2 tablespoons brown sugar
½ cup celery, chopped fine
⅛ teaspoon pepper

1 cup ketchup
3 tablespoons Worcestershire
  sauce
½ tablespoon dry mustard
1 cup water

ribs, 1 pound per person

Slowly parboil ribs if desired, to tenderize them. Place ribs in baking pan lined with foil. Salt ribs and add the sauce from combining all ingredients listed. Bake for 1 hour at 350°.

Mrs. John Hostetter

BARBECUED STEAK SUPREME

OVEN: 350° 1-½ hours   YIELD: 6 servings

2 pounds round steak
2 tablespoons seasoned flour
2 tablespoons shortening
⅓ cup minced onion
⅓ cup minced celery
½ clove garlic, minced
1 — 10¾ ounce can tomato soup

2 tablespoons brown sugar
2 tablespoons Worcestershire
   sauce
2 tablespoons lemon juice
2 teaspoons prepared mustard
dash of tabasco sauce

Pound flour into steak. Brown steak in shortening in a heavy saucepan or skillet, along with onion, celery, and garlic. Add remaining ingredients, stir well, and cover. Cook in a 350° oven, or on top of range if desired, for about 1-½ hours or until tender.

Double all sauce ingredients for additional barbecue sauce to serve over fluffy rice or mashed potatoes.

Nancy Gollnick

BEAN CHAULOPA

1 pound dry pinto beans (can use
   the 1¼ pound bag)
3 pounds pork roast
7 cups water
½ cup chopped onions
2 cloves garlic OR ½ teaspoon dry

1 tablespoon salt
2 tablespoons chili powder
1 tablespoon cumin
1 teaspoon oregano
1 — 4 ounce can chopped chili peppers

Combine all ingredients and place in crock pot. Cook until meat is done (can be cooked overnight).

Serve over rice; sprinkled with raw chopped onion, chopped fresh tomatoes, and grated cheddar cheese and shredded fresh lettuce.

This makes a big meal. For extra spice, add one chopped jalapeno pepper.

Eileen Schiavone

Always cut meats across the grain instead of with the grain for better eating and appearance.

BEEF AND PORK PASTIES

OVEN: 375° 25-30 minutes

YIELD: 18 pasties

1 pound ground beef
1 pound ground pork OR sausage
1 large onion, chopped fine
1 cup celery, chopped fine
salt to taste
½ teaspoon savory
½ teaspoon sage
½ teaspoon dry mustard
½ teaspoon white pepper

2 tablespoons minced parsley
2 cups beef bouillon OR stock
1 cup unseasoned mashed potatoes
1 cup fine dry bread crumbs
3 eggs, beaten
3 packages frozen puff pastry
  shells, defrosted OR homemade
  puff pastry
1 egg, beaten

Cook beef and pork in large skillet until mixture begins to brown. Add onion and celery; cook until meat is thoroughly browned. Pour off excess fat. Add seasonings and beef stock. Heat until stock begins to simmer. Remove from heat, stir in potatoes and bread crumbs. Add 3 beaten eggs; mix thoroughly. Allow mixture to cool. Roll out each puff pastry shell in to a 6"x3-¾"x½" thick rectangle. Place a heaping ¼ cup of filling in center and brush edges of pastry with beaten egg. Fold dough in half, sealing edges and shape into crescent. Roll over sealed edges, brush top with egg. Place on cookie sheets and bake in 375° oven for 25-30 minutes; until tops are golden brown. Serve lukewarm or at room temperature, but not hot. They can be baked and frozen, then reheated at 350°.

The Committee

BEEF BAKE

OVEN: 350° 30 minutes

YIELD: 6-8 servings

1½ pounds ground round steak
½ cup chopped onion
½ teaspoon sugar
2 — 8 ounce cans tomato sauce
¾ teaspoon salt
¼ teaspoon garlic salt
¼ teaspoon pepper
1 pound uncooked spaghetti OR
  vermicelli

1 cup cream style cottage cheese
1 — 8 ounce package cream cheese,
  softened
¼ cup dairy sour cream
½ cup sliced green onion
¼ cup chopped green pepper
¼ cup freshly grated Parmesan
  cheese

In large skillet, sauté meat and onion until all pink is gone from meat and onions are tender. Stir in tomato sauce, sugar, salt, garlic salt and pepper. Remove from heat. Cook spaghetti according to package directions. Combine cottage cheese, cream cheese, sour cream, green onion and green pepper.

Spread ½ of the noodles in a 7 × 11 casserole and top with ½ of the meat sauce. Cover with the cheese mixture. Add remaining noodles and meat sauce. Sprinkle with Parmesan cheese. Bake at 350° for 30 minutes.

Small or medium noodles may also be used.

Connie Wagers

BEEF-NOODLE CASSEROLE

OVEN: 350° 45-60 minutes

1½ pounds ground beef
8 ounces fine noodles
1 medium onion, chopped
1 green pepper, chopped
¾ pound New York State cheese

1 can creamed corn
1 can tomato soup
2 small cans mushrooms, drained
butter

Sauté onion and green pepper in butter. Brown ground beef. Cook noodles according to package directions. Grate cheese.

Stir all ingredients together and place in a casserole. Bake at 350° for 45-60 minutes.

Marilyn Link

BEEF ROULADEN

8 pieces round roast
3 medium onions, sliced
3 dill pickles, sliced
4 strips bacon, chopped

salt
pepper
European style mustard

Slice beef into thin strips.

Baste each strip on one side with mustard. Sprinkle with salt, pepper, and nutmeg. Add onion slices, pickle slices and bacon. Roll together and secure with toothpicks. Brown in a heavy Dutch oven.

After rolls are browned, cut up 1 onion and brown in Dutch oven. Return rouladen and cover with water and simmer until done.

When meat is done, take out rolls and stir 4 tablespoons flour into remaining boiling liquid. Simmer for 5 minutes. Add 3 tablespoons sour cream and 1 tablespoon white wine and 1 tablespoon mustard, if desired.

Christa Lewis

BEEF ROULADES

OVEN: 350° 2 hours   YIELD: 8 servings

2½ pounds round steak
¾ pound ground beef
1 teaspoon poultry seasoning
¾ teaspoon salt
½ clove garlic, crushed
2 tablespoons onion, finely
chopped
1 tablespoon parsley, chopped
¼ cup cracker crumbs
3 tablespoons vegetable oil

1½ pounds small white onions
1 bay leaf
⅓ cup all purpose flour
1 tablespoon brown gravy flavoring
1 — 10½ ounce can condensed beef
bouillon
2½ cups burgundy wine
1½ pounds fresh mushrooms

Pound steak ⅛" thick; cut into 8 pieces. Combine ground beef, poultry seasoning, salt, garlic, onion, and cracker crumbs; toss to mix. Place about 2 tablespoons of the meat mixture on each beef slice and roll up from the short side. Tie rolls with heavy string. Brown rolled meat in oil in a Dutch oven. Remove meat. Add onions and brown. Stir in flour and gravy flavoring. Add bouillon and wine. Bring mixture to a boil, stirring constantly. Return roulades to Dutch oven with mushrooms and bay leaf. Cover and bake in 350° oven for 2 hours or until tender. Sprinkle with parsley before serving.

Serve with parslied noodles, green salad, and fruit.

Betty Morse Hendershott

BEEF STROGANOFF I

2 pounds lean meat
1 can beef broth
1 large onion, minced
1 small garlic clove, crushed
1 can mushrooms
½ cup red wine, dry if desired

½ teaspoon dry mustard
salt
pepper
1 pound cottage cheese OR 1 cup
  sour cream

Cut beef cross-grain in small, thin strips, then salt, pepper and flour strips. Saute meat in hot oil and drain.

Place meat in pot and add all other ingredients except mushrooms. Cook slowly until very tender. Add mushrooms and cook for 10-15 minutes. Just before serving add cottage cheese (or sour cream) and stir until melted. Thicken with cornstarch if needed, and serve over hot noodles or rice.

Carra Adams

BEEF STROGANOFF II

2 pounds beef tenderloin, cut into
  ¼" thick strips
¼ cup flour
1½ teaspoons salt
¼ teaspoon pepper
½ cup butter
1 clove garlic

1 cup onion, chopped
1½ pounds fresh, sliced mushrooms
4 tablespoons butter
3 tablespoons flour
1 can undiluted beef broth
3 tablespoons tomato paste
1 pint sour cream

Combine flour, salt and pepper; coat meat. Melt ½ cup butter in frying pan; brown meat on both sides. Add garlic, onion and mushrooms; fry until onion is golden. Move meat and vegetables to one side of pan. To other side of pan add 4 tablespoons butter and 3 tablespoons flour. Blend. Add tomato paste and beef broth; mix well with meat and vegetables. Cook until thickened. Add sour cream and heat through; do not boil. Sprinkle with parsley.

The more mushrooms you use, the better. You can also put the sour cream in and simmer for a couple of hours. This makes it real yummy.

Serve with buttered noodles or white rice.

Josephine Zaeh

Serve a dry, full-bodied red or rose wine with steaks, chops, and roasts.

BEEF WELLINGTON

OVEN: slow oven 20 minutes

YIELD: 8 individual servings

5 pounds beef tenderloin OR sirloin
1½ cups dry red wine
juice of one fresh lemon
1 tablespoon Worcestershire sauce
2 teaspoons black pepper
1 teaspoon salt

Stuffing:
2 tablespoons butter
1½ pounds fresh mushrooms, finely
diced
8 green onions, minced
2 — 5 ounce cans paté de foie gras
salt and pepper to taste
pastry dough, enough for two 2-
crust pies

Cut beef into bite size pieces and marinate for 24 hours in wine, lemon juice, Worcestershire sauce, salt and pepper mixture, refrigerated.

Heat butter in skillet. Saute mushrooms and green onions for 8-10 minutes. Season with salt and pepper. Stir in paté and remove from heat. Mix well, allow mixture to cool, then refrigerate.

Three or four hours before serving, bring meat and stuffing to room temperature. Drain meat well. Combine meat with stuffing and mix thoroughly. Make pastry rounds from your favorite pie dough, approximately 9" in diameter; as you would roll out crusts for individual small pizzas. Spread generous portions of beef/stuffing mixture over pastry, but not completely out to the ends. Fold pastry up and over meat mixture and seal ends. Place, seamed sides down, on greased cookie sheet and brush with a mixture of one egg, lightly beaten with one teaspoon of water (an "egg-wash"). Prick pastry rounds with fork. If desired, top with decorative pastry cut outs. There will be enough pastry dough left for this. Cut outs may be made with cookie cutters. Place cookie sheet in very slow oven for 20 minutes or until pastry turns light brown.

This version of traditional Beef Wellington has several advantages, over the whole, pastry-wrapped tenderloin, in that it may be prepared in three easy steps, days ahead of serving time (if you prefer), and that the recipe may be modified to serve as few as two. Also, it does not require the inconvenience of carving a whole tenderloin at the table, and, in addition, it provides for more even distribution of the paté mixture throughout the beef, and more thorough absorption of the marinade.

This recipe also took a Rosette at the 1978 St. Lucie County Fair.

Linda Price

Some chuck roasts contain what is called a "chuck eye." Remove this eye from the meat and serve as a rib eye steak.

BIG BEAN CHILI CON CARNE

YIELD: 4 servings

1 pound ground beef
1 tablespoon fat
1 cup diced onion
1 clove garlic, chopped fine
½ cup diced green pepper
2 cups canned tomatoes

2 teaspoons chili powder
1 teaspoon salt
1 teaspoon sugar
1 teaspoon Worcestershire sauce
1 — 15½ ounce can kidney beans

Brown beef in fat. Add diced onion, garlic, and green pepper and cook until onions are transparent. Add canned tomatoes, chili powder, salt, sugar, and Worcestershire sauce. Cover and simmer for 1 hour. Add kidney beans and cook for one hour, uncovered. Do not drain.

The Committee

BITTERSWEET SPRING LAMB

OVEN: 350° 2 hours

1 boned leg of lamb
1 cup water
1 cup dry white wine
juice of 2 oranges

Stuffing:
1 onion, finely chopped
1 tablespoon butter
2 cups fresh breadcrumbs
2 tablespoons grated orange rind
3 tablespoons chopped mint
1 beaten egg

salt
pepper

Glaze:
2 tablespoons honey
1 tablespoon orange juice
1 tablespoon chopped mint

Garnish:
1 whole orange
sugar
1 tablespoon butter

Prepare stuffing by sautéing onion in butter until onion is soft. Mix with breadcrumbs, orange rind, mint and bind with beaten egg and season to taste. Place stuffing in the cavity in the leg of lamb and sew up. Place lamb in a roasting dish with water and sprinkle with salt and pepper. Bake at 350° for ½ hour then add orange juice and wine and baste meat frequently for one hour. Remove meat from oven and make light criss-cross incisions in the surface fat and spread surface with warmed glaze ingredients. Return lamb to oven and cook for ½ hour. Make gravy from pan juices.

For the garnish, slice the complete orange into rounds, sprinkle rounds with superfine sugar and saute lightly in the butter. Place meat either whole or carved on dish surrounded by orange rounds. Serve gravy separately.

Nyra Harriman

For variety, thread cubed liver on skewers alternately with bacon and cooked or canned small whole onions; then broil.

BRANDIED BEEF CREPES

12 — 5-½" to 6" crepes
3 tablespoons butter
1 pound beef tenderloin, cut into
½" chunks
½ pound fresh mushrooms, sliced
3 tablespoons brandy

1 — 8 ounce carton plain yogurt
½ teaspoon salt
dash of pepper
cherry tomatoes
scallions

Melt butter in a skillet and add beef. Stir until beef is browned. Remove meat from skillet and add mushrooms and onions, cook for 2 minutes. Remove onions and mushrooms from skillet. Pour brandy into skillet and simmer for 1 minute. Blend yogurt into simmered brandy, mixing well. Add meat, mushrooms and onions. Mix well. Spoon about 3 tablespoons of mixture into each crepe and roll.
Garnish with cherry tomatoes and scallions.

Mrs. Noah Lybrand, Jr.

BUFFET GLAZED CORNED BEEF

6 pounds corned-beef brisket
10 peppercorns

1 bay leaf
¼ cup firmly packed brown sugar

Simmer corned beef with peppercorns and bay leaf in water to cover brisket in a kettle for 3½ to 4 hours, or until tender. Let stand in broth until ready to glaze.
Place meat, fat side up, on broiler rack or broiler-proof platter. Sprinkle brown sugar evenly over the top, and broil just until the sugar bubbles up.
Place meat on carving board. Slice very thin across the grain, then slice into serving size pieces. Serve with tangy mustard sauce and rye party bread.
This is always popular. It's a breeze to prepare and a different choice for a party.

Mrs. Ralph Wilson

CALICO BEAN BAKE

OVEN: 350° 1¼ hours

1 pound hamburger
1 medium onion, chopped
3 strips bacon, more if you like,
chopped fine
1 — 15 or 16 ounce can pork and
beans
1 — 15 or 16 ounce can baked
beans in molasses sauce

1 — 15 or 16 ounce can red kidney
beans, drained
1 — 15 or 16 ounce can butter
beans, drained
¾ cup brown sugar
½ cup ketchup
1 tablespoon prepared mustard
salt and pepper to taste

Fry hamburger and onion with bacon that has been chopped fine. Open cans of beans, draining kidney and butter beans, and put ingredients in a large 2½ or 3 quart casserole. Add brown sugar, ketchup, salt, pepper and mustard. Mix ingredients together and bake for 1¼ hours at 350°.

Jo Stapleton

Palmetto Hammock Pasture Lands
Okeechobee County, Florida

Okeechobee County Court House
Historical Landmark
Okeechobee County, Florida

CALVES LIVER

1½ pounds calves liver, ¾" thick	pepper
2 sliced onions	6 tablespoons olive oil
½ cup wine vinegar	½ cup flour
salt	

Sprinkle liver with salt and pepper and roll in flour. Cook onions in oil on medium heat until soft. Remove onions. Increase heat and fry liver quickly, about 3 minutes on each side. Replace onion in pan and add vinegar. Cook for about 1 minute. To serve, pour sauce over each serving.

Ditty Jeffers

CAMPFIRE STEW

1 pound ground beef	celery, optional
1 can condensed vegetable soup	peppers, optional
raw onions, optional	garlic, optional

Sauté beef and other raw vegetables if used. Add condensed soup and stir. Heat well. Serve.

After a late day at work, you can fix this lickety-split.

Charlotte Sparling

CHILI

5 pounds lean beef, cut in ½" to ¾" cubes	1 lemon, juiced
1½ ounces olive oil	dash of red OR cayenne pepper
2 medium onions, chopped	½ teaspoon black pepper
2 cloves garlic, minced	1 teaspoon paprika
2 cups beef stock OR 6 bouillon cubes dissolved in hot water	4 ounces prepared mustard
1 — #2 can tomatoes	½ cup steak sauce
1 — #2 can tomato sauce	1 teaspoon ground cominos
	salt
	flour

Cook meat slowly in the oil for about 5 minutes. Stir in chili powder, onions, garlic, red and black pepper, paprika and ground cominos. Cover and cook slowly for about 5 minutes. Add beef stock, tomatoes, tomato sauce, lemon juice, mustard, steak sauce, and salt to taste. If chili gets dry while cooking add a little water. Chili can be made thicker just before serving by stirring in a thin flour and water paste.

Cook 1½ to 2 hours or until meat is tender. Keep lid on the chili pot as much as possible while cooking. Cook in a cast iron pot with lid, if possible. Serve tabasco and hot sauce on the side for folks who like it a little hotter.

Claude C. Davis

CHILI CON CARNE

YIELD: 10 cups

2 tablespoons salad oil
2-3 medium onions, chopped, about 2½ cups
2 garlic cloves, crushed
2 pounds ground beef
1 — 28 ounce can tomatoes, undrained
1 — 6 ounce can tomato paste

1 — 4 ounce can chopped green chilies (optional)
2-3 tablespoons chili powder
1 tablespoon ground cumin
1 bay leaf
2½ teaspoons salt
6 whole cloves
¼ teaspoon cayenne pepper
2 — 15 ounce cans red kidney beans, drained

In Dutch oven, heat salad oil. Add onions and garlic, sauté until tender; about 5 minutes, stirring occasionally. Add ground beef and cook until browned, breaking up the pieces with spoon. Spoon off fat. Add tomatoes, tomato paste, chilies (if desired) and seasonings. Simmer covered, over low heat, stirring occasionally, for about 2 hours. Add drained beans to chili. Cook just until heated through.

This recipe can be prepared in advance. Cover and refrigerate up to 24 hours. Or, to freeze, spoon into freezer-proof containers; freeze up to 2 months. If frozen, thaw in refrigerator overnight. Cook over low heat about 30 minutes, stirring occasionally until heated through.

The Committee

CHILI MAC

½ pound hot Italian sausage
½ pound ground beef
1 medium onion, chopped
1 cup tomato sauce
1 — 8 ounce can chili beans

½ cup Dilalini OR small elbow macaroni
tabasco sauce
Worcestershire sauce
salt
pepper

Remove sausage meat from casing. Sauté first three ingredients. Cook macaroni and drain well. Add drained macaroni, tomato sauce and chili beans to the sautéd meat mixture. Season to taste, heat thoroughly and serve with French bread.

A great Sunday supper for a chilly night in Indian River County.

Rosaila Maggiacomo

Burgundy goes well with roast beef; so does any other good, stout red wine.

CHINESE BARBECUE

OVEN: 350° 1 hour

YIELD: 4 servings

1 — 10 ounce jar plum jelly
⅓ cup dark corn syrup
⅓ cup soy sauce
¼ cup chopped green onion

2 cloves garlic, minced
2 teaspoons ground ginger
2 pounds spareribs OR beef ribs,
 cut into serving pieces

Heat first six ingredients and pour over ribs. Cover and marinate. Place ribs and marinade in foil lined pan on rack in oven. Bake at 350° for 1 hour, turning and basting with marinade.

Beef ribs taste better than spareribs.

Theresa Haisley

CHINESE CASSEROLE

OVEN: 325° 55 minutes

YIELD: 6 servings

1 pound hamburger
onion, thinly sliced
celery, thinly sliced
1 package frozen pea pods, do not
 thaw

1 can cream of mushroom soup
3 tablespoons milk
1 tablespoon soy sauce
1 can french fried onion rings

Brown and drain hamburger. Layer ingredients in a 2 quart casserole in the order they are listed. Dilute soup with milk and soy sauce. Bake in 325° oven for 40 minutes. Place onion rings on top and bake another 15 minutes.

Melody Streeter

CHINESE RICE CASSEROLE

OVEN: 325° 1½ hours

1 pound beef stew, cubed
2 teaspoons soy sauce
½ cup rice
1 can cream of mushroom soup
1 cup water

1 can English peas, drained
1 cup celery, chopped
1 cup green pepper, chopped
1 cup onion, chopped
1 can chow mein noodles

Brown beef; add celery, onions, and peppers. Cook until well browned. Add rice, soup, water, peas and soy sauce. Cook until bubbly. Place in a casserole dish and bake in 325° oven for 1½ hours. Add chow mein noodles on top then heat through.

Mary Culbreth

Hot dogs will retain their flavor and not burst open if cooked as follows: bring water to a boil, add hot dogs, remove from heat, cover pan, and allow to stand for ten minutes.

CHINESE SPARERIBS

4 pounds spareribs
1 cup soy sauce
½ cup water
3 tablespoons red wine

1 tablespoon sugar
1 teaspoon salt
1 clove garlic, minced

Score meat between ribs, but not all the way through. Combine ingredients and pour over meat. Let stand for one hour or so, turning once. Place ribs on grill over medium coals. Cook and baste for 1½ hours or bake in oven for 1½ hours.

Ty Fender

CHIP BEEF AND GRAVY

YIELD: 4-6 servings

2 packages dried beef
4 onions, chopped
1 package fresh mushrooms
1 pint oysters

2 tablespoons flour OR cornstarch
2 cups milk
¼ stick butter

Pre-cook onions. Break beef into small pieces in melted butter; add oysters and mushrooms. Simmer for about 30 minutes. Combine flour or cornstarch with milk and make gravy. Pour mixture slowly into pan and bring to a soft boil. Add additional milk slowly for desired thickness. Serve on hot biscuits or toast.

We use a lot of garlic and spices. Also, a can of cold green peas as a side dish is tasty.

Larry Ramsey

CHOP-CHOP CASSEROLE

OVEN: 375° 1 hour

1 pound ground beef
1 tablespoon butter
1 package frozen peas
1 can mushroom soup
1 small onion, chopped

2 cups celery, cut up
1 teaspoon salt
½ teaspoon pepper
1 cup potato chips, crushed OR
  buttered bread crumbs

Brown beef in butter and place beef in casserole. Put peas on top of meat. In a bowl, mix together the soup, onion, celery, salt and pepper. Pour mixture on top of peas. Spread chips or crumbs over top.
Bake for 1 hour at 375°.

Elizabeth Leonard

Boiling sausage for about seven minutes before frying greatly improves the flavor and prevents links from breaking.

CITY CHICKEN

OVEN: 325° or 350° 2½ hours

1 pound veal, sirloin, OR round
  steak
1 pound pork
1 egg
1 cup or more bread crumbs
1 medium onion, chopped

wooden skewers
milk
fat OR oil for frying
2 tablespoons butter OR oleo
salt
pepper

Cut meat into squares, keeping pork separate. Beat egg well into a little milk. Alternate pork and beef on skewers and dip in beaten egg/milk mixture. Roll in bread crumbs. Lay filled skewers on waxed paper until all are breaded.

In a frying pan, heat about 1″ or so of fat or oil and brown City Chickens on all sides. Place in a roasting pan with the chopped onion, and salt and pepper to taste. Add butter and enough water to almost cover ingredients. More water may be added during roasting if needed. Roast at 325° or 350° for 2½ hours or until fork tender.

Enjoy!

Sara R. Whitacre

CLOSE-TO-COUNTRY HAM

¼ cup cider vinegar
6 tablespoons dark brown sugar
6 tablespoons lemon juice
1 teaspoon dry mustard
1 teaspoon salt

½ teaspoon pepper
½ cup water
2 pounds precooked boneless ham,
  cut in 1/16″ slices

In a 12″ skillet mix all ingredients except ham. Stir over moderately high heat until sugar and mustard are dissolved. Add ham slices in an even layer. Cook about 10 minutes, turning ham slices 2 or 3 times, until most of the liquid has evaporated and only a small amount of thick syrup remains in the pan. Turn ham in syrup to coat.

Close-to-country ham is very good served between biscuits. It can be used as hors d'oeuvres or as a main course.

This may be prepared a day ahead, covered and refrigerated. Heat for 10 minutes in uncovered pan in oven while biscuits are baking.

Drusilla Powell

Enjoy a dry, crisp white wine, a rose, or a dry, fruity red wine with veal, pork, or ham.

COMPANY BEEF CASSEROLE

OVEN: 350° 30 minutes

1 pound ground beef
2 tablespoons shortening
1 medium onion, chopped
1 tablespoon ketchup
1 tablespoon steak sauce
2 cups canned tomatoes

¼ cup green pepper, chopped
2 tablespoons parsley, chopped
1 — 8 ounce box elbow macaroni
1 can cream of mushroom soup
1 cup grated cheese

Brown beef in shortening until all red color disappears. Add onion, tomatoes, ketchup, steak sauce, green pepper and parsley. Simmer for 30 minutes. Cook macaroni and drain. Mix macaroni with beef mixture in a baking dish. Season to taste. Gently spoon soup into mixture. Mix lightly, lifting from the bottom. Sprinkle grated cheese over the top. Bake in 350° oven for 30 minutes until top is bubbly and brown.

Marian Pearce

COMPANY MEAT LOAF — DELUXE

OVEN: 350° 1 hour

1½ pounds lean ground beef
1 pound bulk pork sausage
2 cups white bread crumbs
1 cup mushrooms, chopped
¼ cup parsley, chopped
½ cup sour cream
1 egg, slightly beaten
⅓ cup white dry wine

Sauce:
1½ to 2 cups fresh mushrooms, sliced
2 tablespoons butter
1 can condensed cream of mushroom soup, undiluted
⅓ cup white wine

In large bowl, combine beef, sausage, crumbs, chopped mushrooms, parsley, sour cream, egg and wine. Mix lightly but thoroughly.

Place ½ cup of the sliced mushrooms in the bottom of a greased 8 cup ring mold. Spoon meat mixture over mushrooms. Bake in 350° oven for 1 hour. About 10 minutes before loaf is done, saute remaining mushrooms. Blend in soup and remaining wine smoothly and heat. Pour small amount over meat loaf when ready to serve and pass rest of sauce.

Parsley potatoes are good to put in center of the ring mold, or bake in a bundt pan with water-cress center. Be sure to use 1 full pound of fresh mushrooms.

Connie Wagers

Four tablespoons of milk mixed with a pound of ground chuck will make a delicious juicy ground chuck steak.

CORN CHEESEBURGER CASSEROLE

OVEN: 350° 30 minutes

1 pound ground beef
1 large onion, chopped
1 cup cheddar cheese, grated
1 can whole kernel corn, drained
1 tablespoon Worcestershire sauce

¾ cup ketchup
1 teaspoon salt
32 round snack crackers, crushed
1 stick margarine, melted

Brown ground beef and onion, drain. Add cheese, corn, ketchup, Worcestershire and salt. Pour into a 1½ quart casserole and top with cracker crumbs. Drizzle melted margarine over the top. Bake in 350° oven for 30 minutes.

Marie Mann

CREAMED HAM AND ARTICHOKES

OVEN: 400° 25-30 minutes   YIELD: 8 servings

2 — 9 ounce packages frozen artichoke hearts
2 cans cream of mushroom soup
1 tablespoon chopped onion
¼ cup sherry
½ teaspoon salt

dash of pepper
¼ teaspoon garlic salt
2 cups diced, cooked ham
8 hard-boiled eges, quartered
4 slices American cheese
1 bay leaf

Cook artichoke hearts with bay leaf according to package directions. Drain, remove bay leaf. Combine soup, onion, salt, sherry, garlic salt and pepper and mix well. Arrange artichokes, ham and eggs in a 3 quart casserole; add soup mixture and top with cheese. Bake in a hot oven, 400°, for 25-30 minutes.

Sara F. Haughton

CREOLE WIENERS

YIELD: 5-6 servings

8 slices bacon, diced
3 cups minced onion
1 — 16 ounce can tomatoes

¾ teaspoon salt
⅛ teaspoon pepper
1 pound frankfurters

In a large skillet, fry bacon and onion until bacon is crisp and onion is tender. Drain all but 2 tablespoons bacon drippings from skillet. Stir in tomatoes, salt and pepper. Heat mixture to boiling; reduce heat and simmer for 15 minutes, stirring occasionally. Add frankfurters, cover and simmer for 15 minutes.

Annie Parker
Villa Capri

CUBE STEAK STROGANOFF

1 small onion	1 cup water
1 small can mushrooms	beef bouillon cube
1 pound cube steak, cut into small	2 tablespoons lemon juice
pieces	margarine
flour	8 ounces sour cream

Slice onion into thin slivers and sauté in margarine in a skillet; add mushrooms and cook about 5 minutes. Remove from pan and set aside.

Brown cube steak pieces in margarine on both sides. Add bouillon cube which has been dissolved in water with lemon juice and simmer about 20 minutes. Skillet should be covered. Add sour cream, heat through and serve immediately over rice or noodles.

Dorothy A. Bishop

CUCUMBER-NUT BURGERS

1 pound ground round	¼ teaspoon ground pepper
½ cup walnuts, finely chopped	1 tablespoon vegetable oil
2 tablespoons green onion,	4 hamburger buns, split
chopped fine	cucumber
1 egg	sour cream
2 tablespoons soy sauce	chopped green onion for garnish
½ teaspoon salt	chopped walnuts for garnish

Lightly mix meat with ½ cup chopped nuts. Combine 2 tablespoons of onion, egg, soy sauce, salt and pepper and shape into four equal size patties.

Heat oil in a skillet and pan fry burgers over medium heat, four minutes on each side. Toast and butter hamburger buns. Place burgers on bottom halves of buns and top each with thin slice of cucumber, thin spreading of sour cream, sprinkling of green onion and walnuts. Cover with top of buns.

Sandy Little

Add one-fourth cup of cold water for every two pounds of ground chuck for flavorful, juicy grilled hamburgers.

EASTER HAM SUPREME

OVEN: 300° 4¼ hours   YIELD: 25 servings

1 — 10 pound ham
1 cup honey
1 cup light brown sugar
1 — 1 pound, 8 ounce jar spiced
  peaches
½ cup cider vinegar

8 whole cloves
1 large, unpeeled orange, quartered
1 medium size can chunk pineapple, drained
1 medium size can seedless grapes

Drain juice from spiced peaches and save juice for later use. Wash ham and remove rind. Score no deeper than half of the thickness of the fat. Stick in cloves, evenly distributed. Place ham, fat side up in roaster. Pour vinegar and 2 cups of reserved peach juice over ham. If there is not enough peach juice, add pineapple juice to make 2 cups. Spread ham with honey, then with brown sugar.
Bake uncovered in 300° preheated oven for 1 hour. Cover and bake for 2¼ hours, basting every half hour. Place fruit around ham in roaster and bake uncovered 1 more hour, or until ham is tender (test with fork). Garnish with spiced peaches and a little of the fruit sauce. Serve sauce hot from roaster, in a bowl.
A favorite of our family.

Peggy Hoskins

EASY BURGUNDY BEEF STEW

OVEN: 300° 3 hours

1 pound beef chuck OR stewing
  beef, cut into 2″ pieces
½ cup burgundy wine
1 — 10½ ounce can condensed consommé, undiluted

¾ teaspoon salt
⅛ teaspoon pepper
1 medium onion, sliced
¼ cup fine, dry bread crumbs
¼ cup sifted all-purpose flour

Combine beef, wine, consommé, salt, pepper and onion in casserole. Mix flour with crumbs and stir into casserole mixture.
Cover and bake in slow, 300°, oven about 3 hours or until beef is tender.
This is an easy recipe since the beef is not browned ahead of time.

Marge Dunklee

A serving is from two and one-half to three and one-half ounces of cooked, lean, edible meat from one pound of fresh meat.

EASY ROAST BEEF

OVEN: 325° 3 hours

3½ to 4 pound chuck roast
1 can mushroom soup
salt
pepper

celery, cut in chunks, optional
carrots, cut in chunks, optional
potatoes, cut in chunks, optional
onions, cut in chunks, optional

Place meat on enough aluminum foil to cover and seal it in a baking pan. Salt and pepper meat to taste. Pour mushroom soup over meat and fold foil to seal meat. Bake for 3 hours at 325°.
Make gravy with meat drippings in foil (optional).
This recipe is for well-done, tender beef. If desired, you may substitute onion soup, wet or dry, for mushroom soup. If you use a dry onion soup, add some water.

Jan Archer

EMERGENCY STEAK

OVEN: Broil
YIELD: 2-4 servings

1 pound lean ground beef
1 tablespoon finely chopped onion
½ cup milk
1 teaspoon salt

¼ teaspoon pepper
¼ cup dry bread crumbs
1 — 4 ounce can mushroom stems
and pieces

Thoroughly mix all ingredients except mushrooms. Shape meat mixture into one large, flat patty about 1″ thick. Drain mushrooms, and reserve juice. Place meat on broiler pan. Broil 3-5 minutes, according to taste. Turn meat over. Arrange drained mushrooms on top of patty. Broil for 3-5 minutes. Remove meat to warm platter. Pour mushroom juice in broiler pan. Scrape up brown bits into liquid. Return pan to broiler and bring mixture to a boil. Pour over meat and serve immediately. Will serve 2-4 persons, depending on appetites.

Barbara Matuszewski

ENGLISH ROAST A LA MARINE

1 — 6 pound English cut roast
1 clove garlic, pressed
1 cup soy sauce
1½ teaspoons vinegar

¼ cup bourbon
1 cup water
1 tablespoon meat tenderizer

Combine pressed garlic, soy sauce, vinegar, bourbon, water and meat tenderizer. Pour over roast and marinate, covered, for 24 hours. Charcoal for 45 minutes on an open grill or for 30-35 minutes on a covered grill.

K. Prindible

FAMILY MEAT LOAF

OVEN: 375° 1¼ hours   YIELD: 8-10 servings

4 cups corn flake cereal OR 3 cups flaked nut cereal OR 3 cups oatmeal
2 pounds ground meat
1 egg
1 cup applesauce

¾ cup chopped celery
1 tablespoon minced onion
½ teaspoon sage
¼ teaspoon pepper
¼ cup ketchup
1 cup milk

Crush cereal flakes slightly if you are using cereal. Combine remaining ingredients in order given and mix well. Add cereal and pack into a greased 9" x 5" x 3" loaf pan. Bake in 375° oven for 1¼ hours.

Mary Thornton

FLANK STEAK

OVEN: Broil

1½ pounds flank steak   ¼ cup red OR white wine
¼ cup soy sauce

Combine soy sauce and wine in a shallow dish. Marinate steak for 1 hour or longer in mixture, turning occasionally. For medium-rare, broil steak 5 minutes on each side. Baste once with marinade. Let steak rest for a couple of minutes before slicing in thin slices, across the grain. Always salt steak after it is cooked to avoid toughening.

Rosalynn Carter
The White House

FOOL-PROOF CHILI

YIELD: 6 large servings

2 pounds ground chuck steak
4 onions
2 teaspoons salt
4 tablespoons chili powder

2 — 28 ounce cans tomatoes
2 — 15 ounce cans kidney beans
1-4 tablespoons sugar
2 large sliced potatoes, optional

Buy a crock pot. In a skillet, brown beef and chopped onions. Throw everything into crock pot and stir well to mix ingredients. Cook on low setting for 6-8 hours or 2-4 hours on high setting.

This is a hearty, but mild chili. Put chili powder on table so each person can adjust taste. Tastes good the first day, better the second day, and better yet on the third day. The cooking of this recipe allows a 5 hour time spread to plan other activities around. Makes 6 big servings so you can count on lunch later in the week.

Ron Forsyth

GINGERED HAM SLICES

OVEN: Broil

1 fully cooked OR semi-cooked ham slice, 1" thick	1 tablespoon salad oil
½ cup gingerale	1½ teaspoons wine vinegar
½ cup orange juice	1 teaspoon dry mustard
¼ cup brown sugar	¼ teaspoon ground ginger
	⅛ teaspoon ground cloves

Slash fat edges of ham. Combine remaining ingredients and pour over ham in a shallow dish. Refrigerate overnight, or let stand at room temperature for several hours, spooning marinade over ham several times. Broil ham slice over low coals for 15 minutes on each side, brushing frequently with marinade. Ham may be broiled inside on oven broiler. To serve, spoon marinade over ham.

Mrs. Craig Johnson

GLAZED SAUSAGE

YIELD: 6-8 servings

6 pieces mild sausage	½ cup or more brown sugar
6 pieces hot sausage	1 teaspoon cinnamon
1 can peaches, fuzzy variety	½ teaspoon nutmeg

Cut sausage into 6 pieces no longer than 2 inches in length. Fry sausages until light brown. Drain excess fat. Add peaches, if halved, slice in half again; and seasoning. When sugar thickens cook slowly and baste until peaches are glazed. A tiny bit of sherry may be added with spices.

I use a large pan and serve directly out of the pan.

Serve with scrambled eggs. I put 2 tablespoons of parsley in egg mixture before cooking. This is my company Sunday Brunch specialty.

Lyn Jackson

GOLABKI

OVEN: 350° 2 hours   YIELD: approximately 24 rolls

1 large head cabbage	2 teaspoons salt
3 pounds ground chuck	2 medium onions, chopped
2 cups cooked rice	1 — 4 ounce can sliced mushrooms
½ cup water	3 medium size cans tomatoes
1 teaspoon pepper	¼ pound bacon

Wash and trim cabbage. Separate leaves by placing into boiling water. Add ½ cup water to cooked rice. Pour rice over meat. Add salt, pepper, onions and mushrooms, including liquid. Mix well. Place about ¼ cup or more of the mixture on each cabbage leaf. Roll up leaves and place in a large roasting pan. Top rolled leaves with tomatoes, slightly crushed, including the juice. Arrange bacon strips over top and bake covered in 350° oven for about 2 hours.

Remove cover and bake 15 minutes longer for slight browning. Wooden toothpicks may be used to secure rolls. Mushrooms are optional. This is a Polish recipe passed down from my mother, Mrs. Stephanie Udziela.

Jean Rusnak

GRAB-BAG CASSEROLE

OVEN: 350° 45 minutes   YIELD: 6-8 servings

1 pound ground beef
2 tablespoons fat
¼ cup chopped onion
1 — 10½ ounce can condensed tomato soup
1½ cups water

½ of an 8 ounce package noodles
salt
pepper
1 — #2 can (2½ cups) cream style
corn
1 cup grated processed cheese

Brown the meat in the heated fat. Add onion and cook until tender. Add undiluted tomato soup, water, and noodles. Cook mixture until noodles are
tender, stirring frequently. Season to taste. Add corn and ½ cup of the cheese.
Pour mixture into a greased 2 quart casserole. Sprinkle with the remaining
cheese. Bake in moderate oven at 350° for 45 minutes. Serve very hot.

Emily Johnson

GREEN BEAN MOUSSAKA
(Greek)

OVEN: 350° 30 minutes   YIELD: 6 servings

1 — 16 ounce can cut green beans,
well drained
1½ pounds ground beef
1 — 8 ounce can tomato sauce
½ teaspoon garlic salt
⅛ teaspoon ground cinnamon

2 slightly beaten eggs
1½ cups cream style cottage cheese
with chives OR plain
¼ cup grated Parmesan cheese
2 tablespoons sliced pitted ripe olives (optional)

Place beans in 1½ quart casserole. In medium skillet, brown beef and drain
off excess fat. Stir tomato sauce, garlic salt and cinnamon in to beef. Spread
mixture over green beans. Combine eggs and cottage cheese; spread over
meat mixture, and sprinkle with Parmesan cheese. Bake in 350° oven for
about 30 minutes. Casserole may have to be baked longer as it should be firm
enough to cut into serving pieces. Let it cool a little and garnish with olive
slices.
Serve with salad or anything else you like.

Carol R. Lyons

Wait until roast beef is three-quarters done before salting as the salt
draws out the juices and flavor.

GROUND ROUND CASSEROLE

OVEN: 350° 40 minutes

1½ pounds ground round
⅔ cup chopped onion
⅓ cup chopped green pepper
2 tablespoons butter
1 can cream of mushroom soup

1 can tomato soup
⅔ soup can water
1 cup shredded sharp cheese
½ pound thin spaghetti, cooked
  and drained

In a large skillet, cook beef, onion, and green pepper in butter until meat is lightly browned and vegetables are tender. Stir often to separate meat particles. Add soups with water. Blend with spaghetti and some of the cheese. Place mixture in a 3 quart casserole and top with remaining cheese. Bake at 350° about 40 minutes until cheese is bubbly and hot.

Mary Lolene Stokes

HAM HAWAII

OVEN: 375° 20-25 minutes

YIELD: 4-5 servings

1 thick slice ham
1 banana
1 can cling peach halves
1 small can pineapple chunks
⅓ cup brown sugar

¼ cup shredded coconut
1 tablespoon butter
½ cup sherry
2 tablespoons wine vinegar
nutmeg

Slash fat and brown ham. Drain peaches. Peel and quarter banana. Add all fruit on top of ham. Sprinkle brown sugar over ham and fruit, then sprinkle coconut over the sugar. Pour sherry and wine vinegar over all and dot with butter. Sprinkle with nutmeg. Bake at 375° for 20-25 minutes.

Walt Wisnicky

HAM LOAF

OVEN: 350° 1 hour

YIELD: 6-8 servings

1 pound smoked ham
1½ pounds pork
1 cup bread crumbs
2 eggs
1 cup milk

Basting sauce:
1 tablespoon mustard
½ cup brown sugar
½ cup vinegar
½ cup water

Have meats ground together. Mix meats with remaining ingredients and shape mixture into a loaf in baking pan. Cover with additional bread crumbs. Baste with sauce a couple of times while baking in 350° oven for 1 hour.

Karen Egan

HAM LOAF OR HAM BALLS

OVEN: 350° 1½ hours   YIELD: 6-8 servings

1 pound ground ham
1 pound ground pork
2 eggs
⅔ cup oatmeal
⅓ cup tapioca

dash of nutmeg
dash of pepper (no salt)
1 can pickled peaches, reserve
 juice

Mix together first seven ingredients as for meat loaf and form into loaf or balls. Balls are ideal for hors d'oeuvres or buffet.

Pour ½ cup of juice over meat and bake in 350° oven for 1½ hours. Heat pickled peaches in remaining juice and place around loaf when served, or add to meat balls.

Ham loaf is a favorite dish in the midwest, and this is a variation of John Glenn's mother's recipe blended with several other recipes I have collected.

Hilda N. Perkins

HELEN'S CASSEROLE

OVEN: 375° 45 minutes

1 large onion
1 pound hamburger
½ pound soft cheese, cubed
8 ounces fine noodles, cooked
1 — 4 ounce can mushrooms
½ teaspoon salt
½ teaspoon pepper
1 can mushroom soup

½ cup milk
½ cup olives, chopped

Topping:
½ cup chopped almonds
½ cup chow mein noodles

butter or oil

Sauté onions in butter or oil. Add hamburger and brown. Add all remaining ingredients with noodles in a buttered 1½ quart casserole. Bake uncovered for 30 minutes at 375°. Add topping, sprinkling over entire casserole and continue to bake 15 minutes longer.

K. Prindible

Raw meat is easier to cut when cold. Meat that has been heated to room temperature is hard to manage. Chill meat in the freezer for about ten minutes before cutting.

HODGE PODGE

YIELD: 12-14 servings

1½ to 2 pounds ground beef
¾ cup chopped onion
1 clove garlic, minced
3 cans condensed minestrone soup

1 — 31 ounce can pork and beans
1½ cups chopped celery
1 tablespoon Worcestershire sauce
½ teaspoon crushed oregano

Cook beef, onion and garlic in a saucepan until beef is browned and onion is tender. Stir in soup, beans and 1 or 3 cups water; depending on the consistency you want. Add the celery, Worcestershire sauce and oregano. Simmer covered for 15-20 minutes.

Hodge Podge is an easy way to serve a large number of people in a very casual manner. You can even use disposable cups and plastic spoons if you wish to simplify even more. Hodge Podge, together with garlic bread makes for a complete meal. Often for dessert I serve chocolate chip ice cream mixed with chocolate covered Graham crackers. All of this should be prepared a day in advance. It's so very simple and delicious.

Adele Graham
The Governor's Mansion
Tallahassee, Florida

HOMEMADE CANNED CHILI

YIELD: 4 servings

3 medium onions, sliced thin
¼ cup butter OR margarine
½ pound ground beef
2 — 1 pound cans chili with beans
½ cup chili sauce

2 cloves garlic, crushed
½ teaspoon salt
dash of pepper
few drops hot pepper sauce

Sauté onions in butter until soft. Remove onions from pan. Cook beef until brown. Add cooked onions and remaining ingredients to beef. Heat, stirring until well blended. Cover and cook over medium heat, stirring occasionally, for 10 minutes.

Shirley W. Myers

To enhance the flavor of beef and veal, choose seasonings such as celery, basil, bay leaves, marjoram, thyme, peppercorns, onion, parsley, and green pepper.

INDIAN BEEF CURRY

YIELD: 4-6 servings

3 medium onions, chopped
1 clove garlic, chopped
1-2 tablespoons curry powder
1 teaspoon cinnamon
¼ teaspoon cloves
2 tablespoons sugar
3 pounds beef, cut in 1″ cubes

1 can tomato sauce
½ can water
1 can beansprouts OR Chinese vegetables

cooked rice
oil

Brown onions and garlic in oil in a skillet. Add spices and sugar. Set aside. Brown meat separately then add water and tomato sauce. Stir in onion mixture and simmer until meat is tender. This slow cooks well for up to 12 hours depending on the toughness of the meat used. It is very good prepared ahead of time and reheated. This freezes well.

Just before serving, rinse beansprouts in water and stir into sauce. Do not cook longer than 15 minutes after the beansprouts have been added. Do not freeze mixture with beansprouts in it.

Serve over cooked rice with the following condiments: sliced bananas, pineapple cubes, raisins, shredded coconut, and unsalted peanuts. It can also be served with Chinese egg noodles for crunch and hot peppers for spice.

Curry can be very spicy and drinking only makes your mouth hotter, so curry is served with fruit and nuts and these are mixed into the sauce and rice to each individual taste on each person's plate or eaten on the side.

Curry needs no side vegetables or salad served with it. Hot rolls or crackers make a nice addition. I serve iced water or milk and sangria. Most people do not need dessert afterwards, however, I put out more fruits and crackers to help cool off mouths.

This recipe is easily and cheaply stretched by adding extra tomato sauce and Chinese vegetables.

Brands of curry powder differ immensely in spiciness and the cook should season to taste — season lightly in the beginning and taste about ½ hour before serving. Extended cooking periods strengthens curry flavor.

Rosellen Wall

JACK SCOTT'S FAMILY BRUNSWICK STEW

1½ pounds ground pork
4 cups tomatoes, not stewed tomatoes
2 cups cream style corn
2 onions, chopped
salt and pepper to taste
⅛ to ¼ cup white vinegar

½ cup ketchup, approximately
1 to 1½ lemons
½ chicken, cooked and cut up
1 — 2 cups chicken broth
4 double soda crackers, crushed fine

Cook first seven ingredients for 1 hour. Add whole lemon(s) cut in quarters and cook for 1 hour more. Next, add cut up, cooked chicken and chicken broth and cook for 30 minutes more. Add soda crackers, crushed fine. (Use more or less crackers to thicken stew.)

Dorothy Peterson

HUNGARIAN GOULASH

YIELD: 8 servings

2 pounds beef cubes
¼ cup flour
½ teaspoon salt
¼ teaspoon pepper
6 tablespoons butter
3 cups V-8 Juice
1 large container sour cream

3 tablespoons grated onion
3 tablespoons minced parsley
additional salt, if needed
2 tablespoons paprika
cooked rice
1 pound mushrooms, if desired

Cut meat into 1″ cubes. Roll cubes in flour, salt and pepper. Brown meat in fat in a kettle. Add V-8 Juice and cover tightly. Simmer 1½ hours or until meat is tender. Remove cover and cook to reduce liquid. Add remaining ingredients and heat to boiling; simmer for 10 minutes. Serve with cooked buttered rice or noodles.

I cook my meat in a pressure cooker half of the time and it keeps the flavor in the meat. Veal or pork may be substituted for the beef. My family likes the beef best. You do not have to use the mushrooms.

Josephine Zaeh

JAILHOUSE CHILI

YIELD: 12 cups

1 pound dry red kidney beans OR
  pinto beans, washed and drained
8 cups water
1 teaspoon salt
2 tablespoons salad oil
3 cups chopped onions
2 pounds ground beef
2 — 28 ounce cans tomatoes, undrained
1 — 4 ounce can chopped green
  chilies
1 — 6 ounce can tomato paste

3 tablespoons chili powder
1 tablespoon salt
1 teaspoon sugar
2 teaspoons ground cumin
¼ teaspoon cayenne pepper

Fixings:
chopped onions
shredded cheddar cheese
red pepper flakes
fresh chopped green chilies
vinegar
corn chips

Wash beans, drain and place in large saucepan. For quick soak method, combine beans and water; bring to a boil. Boil for 2 minutes. Remove from heat; cover and let stand for 1 hour. Or, cover with water and soak overnight. Then add 1 teaspoon salt and simmer for 1 hour in soaking liquid or until beans are almost tender. Drain and set aside.

Meanwhile, in Dutch oven, heat oil. Add onions and sauté until tender. Add ground beef and cook until browned, breaking up pieces with a spoon. Spoon off fat. Add remaining ingredients and beans. Heat to boiling. Reduce heat and simmer, uncovered, for 2 hours, stirring occasionally.

Chili can be prepared in advance. Cover and refrigerate up to 24 hours. Or, to freeze, spoon into freezer-proof containers; freeze up to 2 months. If frozen, thaw in refrigerator overnight. Cook over low heat, stirring occasionally, about 30-40 minutes until heated through.

Serve with fixings.

The Committee

IT — MEAT DISH

OVEN: 325° 45 minutes

YIELD: 6-8 servings

1 pound ground beef
3 tablespoons oil
2 onions, sliced
1 clove garlic, minced
1 medium can mushrooms
1 can tomato paste
1 — #2½ can tomatoes
½-¾ cup red wine
⅛ teaspoon marjoram

⅛ teaspoon thyme
2 cups water
1 tablespoon Worcestershire sauce
1 tablespoon salt plus 1 teaspoon
  salt
½ package wide, uncooked noodles
1 bay leaf
1 teaspoon tabasco sauce

Brown beef in oil and add onions, garlic, mushrooms, tomato paste, tomatoes, wine, spices, bay leaf, water, Worcestershire sauce, and tabasco sauce. Mix well. Add salt to flavor.

Bring all ingredients to a boil. Place uncooked noodles in a fairly large baking dish. Pour sauce over this and bake at 325° for 45 minutes.

C. F. Fawsett, Jr.

ITALIAN MEAT LOAF

OVEN: 350° 1 hour

YIELD: 6-8 servings

½ cup cracker crumbs
1½ pounds ground beef
1 — 6 ounce can tomato paste
2 eggs
½ cup chopped onion
¼ cup chopped green pepper

½ cup cracker crumbs
1 — 12 ounce carton small curd
  cottage cheese
1 — 3 ounce can mushrooms
1 tablespoon parsley flakes
¼ teaspoon oregano

Combine ½ cup cracker crumbs with ground beef, tomato paste, eggs, onion and pepper. Mix well. Pat half of mixture into loaf pan. Combine ½ cup crumbs with cottage cheese, drained and chopped mushrooms, parsley and oregano. Spread mixture evenly over meat in pan. Top with remaining meat mixture. Bake at 350° for 1 hour. Let meat loaf stand for 10 minutes before serving.

This meat loaf is delicious and fit for "company-fare."

Jeanette R. White

Because cooking time varies with intensity of heat produced, a roast cooked on an outdoor rotisserie may require a longer time to cook on a breezy day than on a calm day.

JEANIE'S STUFFED PORK CHOPS

OVEN: 300° 2 hours

4 pork chops, 1½" thick, split
2 cups corn
2 cups herbal dressing (bread)
1 small onion
1 teaspoon parsley
1 tablespoon butter, melted
½ apple, grated
1 egg

1 teaspoon sage
¼ cup cream
salt and pepper
¼ cup sausage
1 teaspoon cornstarch
milk
water

Sauté sausage and onion. Reserve fat. Mix corn, bread, apple, egg, sage, salt and pepper with sausage mixture. Stir in cream.

Lightly flour chops and brown in skillet. Stuff chops and place in baking dish. Left-over stuffing mix should be placed in baking dish around chops. Bake, covered, for 1½ hours at 300°. Mix milk and water with cornstarch until mixture is smooth. Pour over chops and cook uncovered for 30 minutes more.

Jeanie Fowler

LAZY MAN'S STEW

OVEN: 250° 3-4 hours

1-2 pounds stew meat
1 package onion soup mix
1 can tomato soup
1½ cans water
2-3 celery stems
3-4 carrots

1 package frozen peas OR 1 can
  peas, drained
1 can sliced potatoes
½-1 cup red wine
flour

Coat meat with flour, salt and pepper. Brown in a skillet. In a Dutch oven, place meat, onion soup mix, tomato soup, water, celery, and carrots. Celery and carrots should be cut into 1" chunks.

Place Dutch oven in 250° oven and cook, covered, 3-4 hours, until meat is tender.

Before serving, place Dutch oven on top burner and add peas, potatoes, and wine; simmer for about 15 minutes.

Canned potatoes do not cook apart and are particularly suited in this dish.

Edith K. Balint

Cook tougher cuts of meat in strong tea. The tannin in the tea acts as a tenderizer.

LEFT-OVER MEAT PIE

OVEN: 450° 30 minutes

left-over cooked beef OR steak
2 cups cubed, boiled potatoes
1 large OR 2 small onions

baking powder biscuit dough
flour OR gravy
butter OR oil

Cut left-over meat into cubes. Cover with boiling water and cook over low heat for 45 minutes. Then thicken with flour or left-over gravy. Fry onions in butter or oil until transparent. Place meat in greased baking dish and add potatoes. Place fried onions over top. Cover with baking powder biscuit dough and bake in 450° oven for 30 minutes. Cut a large cross in the biscuit dough to let steam escape.

The fried onions add a distinctive taste. Any other cooked vegetables can be added. I suggest thoroughly thawed mixed vegetables.

Rex Coulson

LEG OF LAMB WITH PLUM SAUCE

OVEN: 325° 2½ to 3 hours   YIELD: 8-10 servings

4-5 pound leg of lamb
salt and pepper
1 — 1 pound can purple plums
2 tablespoons lemon juice

1 tablespoon soy sauce
1 teaspoon Worcestershire sauce
½ teaspoon basil, crushed
½ clove garlic, crushed

Place lamb, fat side up on a rack in a shallow roasting pan. Season with salt and pepper. Roast in slow oven, 325°, for 2½ to 3 hours, or until meat thermometer reads 175-180. Meanwhile, drain plums and reserve ½ cup of the syrup. Pit and sieve plums. Combine syrup with remaining ingredients. Baste lamb with syrup 4 times during last hour of roasting. Simmer remaining sauce for 5 minutes. Pass with lamb.

I serve this with a minted rice casserole and a citrus salad.

Helen George

Flouring or breading meat before frying gives the meat a crisp brown exterior.

LOBSTER-STUFFED TENDERLOIN OF BEEF

OVEN: 425° 45-50 minutes   YIELD: 8 servings

3-4 pound whole beef tenderloin
2 — 4 ounce frozen lobster tails
1 tablespoon butter OR oleo,
  melted
1½ teaspoons lemon juice

6 slices bacon, partially cooked
½ cup green onion, sliced
½ cup butter OR margarine
½ cup dry white wine
⅛ teaspoon garlic salt

Butterfly tenderloin lengthwise to within ½" of the bottom. Place frozen lobster tails in boiling, salted water to cover. Return to boiling; reduce heat and simmer 5-6 minutes. Remove lobster from shells and cut in half lengthwise. Place lobster end to end inside beef. Combine 1 tablespoon butter with lemon juice and drizzle on lobster. Close meat around lobster and tie roast together with string every 1". Place on rack in shallow pan and roast in 425° oven for 45-50 minutes. Tenderloin will be rare. Lay bacon atop beef and roast for 5 minutes more. Meanwhile in saucepan cook green onion in remaining butter over low heat, stirring occasionally. Cook until tender. Add wine and garlic salt and heat through. Slice roast and spoon on wine sauce. Garnish with fluted whole mushrooms and watercress.

Drusilla Powell

McDEW — DEVILED HAM

YIELD: approximately 1 pint

1 — 12 ounce can Spam
2 large green peppers

1 medium onion
mayonnaise to taste

Put first three ingredients through fine food grinder. Add mayonnaise to taste. This will keep at least two weeks in the refrigerator.

This economical form of deviled ham is a great favorite with family and friends.

I took the first letters from my children's names to get McDew: Margaret, Clare, David, Elizabeth, William.

McDew can be served as is on crackers or topped with cheese and broiled. It can also be used in a cream sauce for pasta.

Virginia Q. Hack

MEAT LOAF I

OVEN: 350° 1 hour

2 pounds meat loaf mixture OR all
  beef
⅓ cup canned beef broth
⅓ cup ketchup
2 eggs

1 cup Italian seasoned bread
  crumbs
1 tablespoon instant minced onion
3 tablespoons parsley
1½ teaspoons salt
½ teaspoon pepper

Combine all ingredients together and mix well. Press mixture into a greased 9" x 5" x 3" bread pan. Bake in 350° oven for 1 hour or until loaf shrinks from sides of pan.

Dorothy Riesbeck

MEAT LOAF II

OVEN: 350° 1¼ hours

2 pounds ground chuck
1 cup oatmeal
3 eggs
4 teaspoons salt
2 teaspoons pepper

1 teaspoon garlic powder
2 teaspoons Worcestershire sauce
½ cup onion, chopped
½ cup green pepper, chopped
½ cup sauce tomatoes

Combine all ingredients and mix well. Pack lightly into a greased loaf pan. Dilute ½ cup of sauce tomatoes with ½ cup water and pour over meat loaf. Bake for about 1¼ hours at 350°.

Mrs. Kerr's Boarding House

MEATBALLS IN SOUR CREAM

4 slices bread
⅔ cup milk
1 large onion, minced
1 stick butter
2 pounds ground beef
2 eggs, separated

1 tablespoon dill, snipped
½ teaspoon tarragon
salt and pepper to taste
½ pound mushrooms, sliced
1½ cups sour cream
flour

Trim crusts from bread. In a small bowl, soak bread in milk. In large skillet, sauté onion in ½ stick of butter. In a large bowl, combine meat with egg yolks that have been slightly beaten. Then add the bread mixture, onions and seasonings. Beat egg whites until they hold a soft peak and fold them into beef mixture. Form mixture into balls about 1½" in diameter and dust with flour. In a skillet, brown meatballs in remaining ½ stick butter, over moderate heat. In another skillet, saute mushrooms in 3 tablespoons butter until browned. Add mushrooms to meatballs and stir in sour cream. Turn balls in sour cream to coat; simmer, partially covered for approximately 30 minutes; stir occasionally.

These may also be made into cocktail size meatballs and served as hot chafing dish hors d'oeuvres.

Rosaila Maggiacomo

MEXICAN MADNESS

1 green pepper
2 onions
¼ cup oil
1 cup stewed tomatoes
1 cup macaroni

1 cup sour cream
1 pound sausage meat
¼ teaspoon chili powder
salt and pepper to taste

Cut pepper in thin strips. Dice onions and sauté in oil until light brown. Add remaining raw ingredients. If sausage is fatty, lightly saute to drain off fat. Cover and cook over low heat until macaroni is tender.

Use enough chili powder to taste.

Barbara Gallup

MOM'S GONE TO COLLEGE DINNER

OVEN: 325° 1½ hours

1½ pounds ground chuck
4 medium potatoes
2 small carrots
celery (optional)
2 eggs

1 cup bread crumbs, dampened OR
  2 slices bread
½ package barbecued flavor poultry or meat coating mix

Mix meat, bread, and coating mix with eggs. Make a mound. Place on electric fry pan, surrounding with potatoes, halved onions, and pieces of carrots. For variety, use green peppers. Top with bacon bits if desired. Bake at 325° for 1½ hours.

The coating mix gives a delicious flavor to the vegetables. If you prefer to make a large meat loaf, increase ingredients and cook. Slice and use for lunch.

Aurelia Shaw

NORMA'S CASSEROLE

2 pounds chuck, roast OR steak,
  boneless
1 cup sliced onions
1 cup sliced celery
1 cup sliced carrots
other vegetables if desired
¼ cup soy sauce

1 tablespoon brown gravy flavoring
2 cups water
3 tablespoons bacon fat
4 tablespoons cornstarch
½ cup water

Cut meat into thin 1″ strips and brown in bacon fat in a deep skillet. Remove meat and add onions. Cook until clear. Return meat to skillet and add soy sauce. Cook for 5 minutes and add celery, carrots, water, and gravy flavoring. Cook over low heat, simmering, until vegetables are tender. Thicken by adding the cornstarch which has been dissolved in ½ cup water. Serve over rice or noodles.

Norma Isenhour

ONION BEEF MACARONI CASSEROLE

OVEN: 400° 15 minutes

YIELD: 6 servings

1½ pounds ground beef
1 envelope onion soup mix
1 tablespoon flour
1 — 8 ounce can tomato sauce

2 cups water
1 cup macaroni, uncooked
¼ cup grated cheddar cheese

Cook macaroni according to directions; then set aside. In a large skillet, brown meat and drain off excess fat. Stir in soup mix, flour, tomato sauce and water. Simmer covered for 5 minutes. Stir in cooked macaroni and turn mixture into 1½ quart casserole dish. Sprinkle with cheese and bake for 15 minutes in preheated 400° oven.

Elizabeth Leonard

ORIENTAL BEEF

1 pound boneless round steak, ¾"
thick
1 cup carrots, diagonally sliced
1 cup celery, diagonally sliced
½ cup green onions, diagonally
sliced
½ teaspoon ground ginger

2 tablespoons butter OR margarine
1 can beefy mushroom soup
1 — 16 ounce can Chinese vegetables, drained
1 tablespoon cornstarch
1 tablespoon soy sauce
1 teaspoon brown sugar
½ teaspoon salt, OR salt to taste

Slice meat into thin strips. If meat is partially frozen it will slice easier.
In a skillet, cook carrots, celery, and onions with ginger in butter until just
tender. Remove from pan. Add meat to pan and cook until color just changes;
3-4 minutes. Add remaining ingredients and cooked vegetables. Cook, stirring
until thickened. Add some water as it thickens.
Serve on cooked rice.
This recipe has gone over well with guests.

Ruth Davis

OUR FAVORITE MEATBALLS

OVEN: 350° 1 hour

2 pounds ground beef
1 can chicken-rice soup
2 tablespoons grated onion
1 cup dry bread crumbs
1 egg

1 teaspoon salt
pepper to taste
3 cups crushed flaked corn cereal
1 can cream of mushroom soup

Combine beef with chicken-rice soup, onion, bread crumbs, egg, salt and
pepper. Form meat mixture into meatballs. Brown in oil in a fry pan. Drain
on paper towels. Roll meatballs in cereal crumbs and place in a casserole dish.
Pour mushroom soup, diluted, over meatballs. Bake in 350° oven for 40 minutes, covered. Then bake for 20 minutes, uncovered.
This is delicious served with brown rice.

Pat Brooks

OVEN STEW WITH RICE OR NOODLES

OVEN: 325° 3 hours

2 pounds stewing beef
1 package dry onion soup mix

1 can mushrooms
2 cans golden mushroom soup

Cover bottom of pan with beef, then add soup mix, mushrooms, and mushroom soup (canned). Cover and bake in 325° oven for 3 hours. Serve with rice
or noodles.

Rex Coulson

PARTY HAM LOAF

OVEN: 375° 45 minutes   YIELD: 8 servings

5 cups ground ham, cooked
⅔ cup minced onion
1 cup rolled oats
½ teaspoon pepper
1 teaspoon Worcestershire sauce

¼ teaspoon ground cloves
2 eggs, slightly beaten
⅓ cup milk
¼ cup currant jelly
1 tablespoon horseradish

Combine ham, onion, oats, seasonings, eggs and milk together, mixing thoroughly. Shape in form of a ham and place in a shallow baking dish. Score the top to make diamonds. Bake at 375° for 45 minutes. Remove and brush top with melted currant jelly mixed with horseradish. Use red cherries and pineapple slices to garnish.

This is delicious either hot or cold when served with cornbread and Waldorf salad.

Mrs. C. L. Elias

PASTICCIO
(Greek Dish)

OVEN: 350° 1 hour

2 pounds lean hamburger
¼ cup butter
½ can tomato, whole OR sauce
2 large onions, chopped fine
1 teaspoon cinnamon
½ cup boiling water
salt and pepper

1 pound macaroni, medium elbow

½ cup butter, melted
3-4 eggs, well beaten
1 cup Romano cheese, grated

3 cups milk
½ stick butter
2 heaping tablespoons flour OR
    cornstarch
3 eggs, well beaten

Sauté hamburger for 5 minutes; add butter and onion and brown 10 minutes. Add tomato, cinnamon, water, salt and pepper to taste. Cover and cook for 15 minutes over medium flame. Remove and cook for 10 minutes or until thickened, stirring occasionally. Remove from heat and cool.

Cook macaroni in rapidly boiling water which has been salted, for no longer than 10 minutes. Drain well. Place macaroni in bowl; add melted butter, eggs, cheese, meat sauce and 1 cup milk, mixing thoroughly. Pour mixture into 11″ x 13″ or 10″ x 12″ baking pan. Do not pour mixture into pan in separate layers, but mix the sauce and macaroni together. This will prevent crumbling when served.

Heat ½ of the milk in a large saucepan over medium heat for 7 minutes. Into remaining milk gradually sift flour or cornstarch and stir until mixture is smooth. Add eggs and stir vigorously until all is well blended and smooth. Slowly add this to the hot milk; salt to taste and continue cooking until mixture thickens. Remove immediately and stir. Pour over macaroni/meat mixture in pan and bake for 1 hour in 350° oven.

Leila J. Komara

PEGGY'S AMERICAN CHILIES RELLEÑOS

OVEN: 350° 45-50 minutes

1 pound ground beef	4 beaten eggs
½ cup chopped onion	¼ cup flour
3 — 4 ounce cans green chilies	½ teaspoon salt
6 ounces sharp cheddar OR Monterey Jack cheese, grated	dash of pepper
	several dashes tabasco
1½ cups milk	

Brown beef and onions; drain and season with ½ teaspoon salt and dash of pepper. Split chilies and remove seeds. Arrange one half of chilies in 10 x 6 casserole dish and sprinkle with cheese. Top with meat mixture. Arrange remaining chilies over meat. Combine all remaining ingredients and beat until smooth. Pour over all ingredients in casserole. Bake in 350° oven for 45-50 minutes until knife inserted comes out clean.

If desired, dish may be lined with slightly fried tortillas.

B. J. Nelson

PELOPONNESIAN POT ROAST

1 — 2½ to 3 pound beef pot roast	2 tablespoons vinegar
8 cloves garlic	1 teaspoon ground nutmeg
salt	6-8 whole cloves
pepper	½ teaspoon ground cinnamon
2 tablespoons cooking oil	½ teaspoon ground allspice
3 cups (1 — 30 ounce can) tomato sauce	hot cooked spaghetti

Make slits in top of roast with tip of knife and insert garlic cloves in slits. Sprinkle roast with salt and pepper to taste. In a large skillet, brown meat on both sides in hot oil. Combine tomato sauce, vinegar, nutmeg, cloves, cinnamon and allspice; pour mixture over roast in skillet, cover and simmer for 1½ hours, or until meat is tender. Remove meat to cutting board, keeping warm. Bring juices in skillet to boiling, uncovered, until juices are reduced to thick saucelike consistency. Slice meat, add back to sauce and serve over hot cooked spaghetti.

Mae Zuver

PEPPER STEAK

YIELD: 4 servings

2 tablespoons seasoned flour	½ cup ketchup
1½ pounds round steak, ¾" thick	1 medium green pepper, cut in strips
2 tablespoons shortening	
1 can onion soup	1 — 4 ounce can mushrooms

Pound flour into meat. Brown meat in shortening and add soup, ketchup and mushrooms. Cover and simmer for 1 hour. Stir, and add green pepper. Cook until tender.

Pearl M. Wyse

PEPPERY SWISS STEAK

YIELD: 4 servings

1½ pounds 1" thick steak	2 large bell peppers, cut in strips
1 — 10 ounce bottle Worcester-	2 cups quick cooking rice
shire sauce	2 cups water
2 large onions	3 tablespoons oil

Fry steak strips in oil, browning lightly. Cut up onions and add to steak. Cook until onions are brown. Salt and pepper to taste. Pour Worcestershire sauce on meat and onions, then cover with water. Simmer for 1 hour. Twenty minutes before serving add green peppers to meat and onions. Serve over cooked rice.

This recipe could serve 6. The whole bottle of Worcestershire sauce gives the good flavor.

Anna Mintkenbaugh

PICADILLO

2 onions, diced	2 tablespoons Worcestershire
2 green peppers, diced	sauce
1 medium jar stuffed olives	½ juice from olive jar
1 small jar capers	½ teaspoon Accent
½ box seedless raisins	¼ teaspoon oregano
1½ pounds ground beef	½ teaspoon salt
large can tomato sauce (12 ounce)	¼ teaspoon pepper
4 tablespoons olive oil	½ teaspoon garlic powder
	½ teaspoon celery salt
	¼ teaspoon paprika

Sauté peppers and onions in 2 tablespoons of the olive oil and set aside. Sauté beef in the remaining olive oil. Combine peppers, onions and beef in a large pan, adding olives, capers, raisins, tomato sauce and remaining seasonings, and mix well. Cook covered for 40 minutes over low heat.

Serve with black beans with fresh diced onions and rice, either white or yellow.

Mrs. David H. Willard

Many cuts of beef can be braised without added liquid. Steam from their own juices provides moisture.

PLANTATION CASSEROLE

OVEN: 400° 30 minutes

2 cups cooked, chopped ham,
chicken, OR beef
1½ cups cooked peas, drained
1 — 1 pound can cream style corn
¼ pound processed cheese, cubed
1 cup evaporated milk
¼ cup chopped onion

1 tablespoon Worcestershire sauce
1 cup biscuit mix
½ cup cornmeal
2 tablespoons sugar
½ teaspoon salt
1 egg, beaten

Mix meat, peas, corn, cheese and ⅓ cup milk with onion and Worcestershire sauce. Pour into greased 12 x 8 baking dish and bake at 400° for 10 minutes, or until mixture bubbles around edges. Combine biscuit mix, cornmeal, sugar, salt and beaten egg. Add remaining evaporated milk and mix well. Pour mixture around edges of hot meat mixture, leaving center uncovered. Bake for 20 minutes longer.

I use ham and chicken together.

Ruth Davis

PORCUPINES

OVEN: 350° 1 hour   YIELD: 6 servings

Sauce:
1 can tomatoes
1 can tomato paste
1 teaspoon sugar
1 teaspoon salt

Porcupines:
1 pound ground beef

½ cup uncooked rice
½ cup onion, chopped
½ cup celery, finely chopped
1 egg, beaten
1 teaspoon prepared mustard
1½ teaspoons salt
¼ teaspoon pepper

Combine ingredients for sauce and bring to a boil. Cover and simmer for 10 minutes. Meanwhile, combine ingredients for porcupines and mix well. Form mixture into 1½" balls. Place balls in a baking dish and pour sauce over balls. Cover and bake at 350° for 1 hour.

Nancy Maxwell

PORK CHOP ONION-RICE BAKE

OVEN: 350° 1 hour

6 pork chops, 1½" thick
2 tablespoons fat
1 cup uncooked rice
1 envelope onion soup mix

1 — 4 ounce can sliced mushrooms
and juice
2 tablespoons diced pimento
3 cups hot water

Brown chops in fat and set aside. Combine all other ingredients and mix well. Place in a large baking dish and arrange chops on top. Bake for 1 hour at 350°.

Nadine Cherry

PORK ROAST

OVEN: 325° 1½ hours   YIELD: 7 servings

3 pound boned loin of pork
1 clove garlic, minced
1 teaspoon salt
¼ teaspoon ground pepper

2 tablespoons honey
¼ cup soy sauce
1 cup beef broth
2 tablespoons dry sherry

Rub pork with garlic, salt and pepper. In a deep skillet, brown pork on all sides. Pour off all fat but 2 tablespoons. Mix together honey, soy sauce, broth and sherry.

Bring mixture to a boil and pour over pork. Cover and cook over low heat in oven at 325° for 1½ hours or until tender. Baste and turn frequently.

Carmen I. Carroll

REG'S PEPPER STEAK

½ pound flank steak, cut into ⅛" x
  2" x 1" pieces (partially freeze
  steak to make cutting easier)
½ cup slivered almonds
1 green pepper
1 red pepper
12 water chestnuts, thinly sliced
1 — 4 ounce can mushrooms

½ cup chicken OR beef broth
2 tablespoons soy sauce
½ cup sherry
1 tablespoon cornstarch
1 tablespoon fresh ginger root,
  chopped
oil

Marinate cut steak for 1 hour in soy sauce, sherry, cornstarch and ginger root. Blanch peppers in boiling water for 3 minutes. Refresh peppers in ice water and cut into 1" x 2" pieces. Sauté almonds in ½ tablespoon oil and set aside. Stir fry steak in 1 tablespoon oil just until meat loses its red color. Add all other ingredients to steak. Toss together with spatula until sauce thickens, about 2 minutes. Serve over rice or noodles.

Substitute boned chicken breast, pork, or veal for steak. Substitute celery and onions or zucchini squash for peppers.

Reg Peterson

A shallow pan is better than a deep one for roasting because it allows heat to circulate around the roast.

RIB ROAST

OVEN: 375°

standing rib roast

Preheat oven to 375° and place meat in a shallow pan with fat side up. Place pan in center of oven. Do not season meat.
Roast meat to required doneness: rare — medium — well.
3 ribs — 1 hour (rare)
4 ribs — 1 hour (rare)
     — 1½ hours (medium or well)
After required cooking time, turn oven off, but DO NOT open oven door. Forty-five minutes before serving turn oven on to 375°. Now, open door for the first time since placing meat in oven.
If center pieces are not done well enough, place roast back in oven for a few minutes.
This recipe was received about 25 years ago from a cousin in Wisconsin. This recipe was used in Sturgeon Bay, Wisconsin, by a very popular tavern.

Marion Maenpaa

RIPPCHEN AND KRAUT
(German)

2 tablespoons fat, margarine, OR
  bacon grease
4 pounds pork loin, smoked
1 large onion, chopped
3 pounds sauerkraut

1 small apple, cored, peeled, and
  chopped
1 tablespoon caraway seed
2 tablespoons bacon bits OR crumbled bacon
1 cup water

When buying pork loin, have butcher saw through and across to bottom bone. This will facilitate carving later.
Drain and rinse kraut with cold water. Melt fat in a Dutch oven and brown pork quickly on all sides. Remove pork to plate and add drained kraut; browning very quickly. Remove pan from heat; add cup of water, onion, apple and all spices to kraut. Return pan to stove and simmer. Make a well in kraut and return meat to pan. Cover Dutch oven and simmer for 1½ hours.

Kristin P. Wagers

To increase the juiciness of veal roasts that have little outside fat, lay strips of bacon or salt pork across the top.

ROAST PORK DIVINE

OVEN: 350° 1½ hours

5 - 6 pound rolled, boneless, pork roast	parsley
French wine-Dijon mustard	tomatoes
brown sugar	potatoes
12 prunes	asparagus
2 cups beef bouillon	thyme
½ cup Kentucky bourbon	bread crumbs
	salt and pepper

Spread entire roast with mustard and roll in brown sugar. Place roast in Dutch oven and brown, being careful not to burn sugar. Turn frequently. Steep prunes in bouillon and set aside. Pour half of the bourbon over the roast and ignite. When the alcohol has burned off, place roast in 350° oven for 1-½ hours or until done. Turn roast every 20 minutes. Halfway through roasting time add prune broth to roast. When done, remove from oven and de-glaze pan with ¼ cup bourbon. Serve roast on a platter with prunes and parsley. Ignite for effect, and serve with de-glazed and de-greased pan juices.

Delicious with fresh asparagus, oven roast potatoes, and thyme tomatoes (3 slices tomato, sprinkled with thyme, parsley, salt and pepper and bread crumbs, sautéd in heated butter).

Lorraine Helms

ROULADEN

8 thin slices beef, ⅛" to ¼" thick	salt and pepper
8 slices onion	water
4 slices bacon, cut in half	½ cup cognac
prepared mustard	

Salt and pepper one side of each slice of beef and spread beef with mustard. Cover each slice with a large slice of onion and a half strip of raw bacon. Roll and tie with cotton sewing thread (nylon thread will melt). Large toothpicks may be used. Brown meat on all sides and cover with water. Add ½ cup cognac. Simmer for 2 hours if using slices of bottom round. When finished, thicken broth to make gravy.

This can be prepared the day before and refrigerated overnight. Peel off fat and then make gravy with the broth. Adding fresh, sautéed mushrooms adds to the taste.

Elva Heise

Canned luncheon meats can be sliced easier if chilled in the refrigerator and both ends of the can are removed to push meat out in one piece.

ROULADEN BAVARIAN STYLE

YIELD: 4 servings

4 large, thinly sliced pieces of top
  round of beef (each 12 x 6" by ¼"
  thick)
salt, to taste
freshly ground pepper, to taste
6 teaspoons prepared mustard
2¼ cups finely chopped onions

4 strips bacon
4 dill pickles (sliced lengthwise
  into spears)
2 cups beef bouillon
¼ cup butter
1 tablespoon paprika

Sprinkle meat with salt and pepper; spread each piece with mustard; sprinkle each piece with three tablespoons chopped onions. Cut bacon slices in half, and cut again lengthwise. Then place four pieces of bacon, ladder-style, on beef slice, top to bottom. Place two dill spears between bacon slices. Roll up beef and filling, tying securely with string. Heat butter in heavy skillet; add remaining onion, stirring constantly until golden brown, and then add paprika. Cook and stir for approximately 5 seconds, no longer — otherwise paprika will burn. (While cooking onions with paprika, aroma should smell like mushrooms.) Add rolled beef to paprika and onion mixture and coat beef on all sides. Add one cup of beef bouillon, cover and cook over medium heat for 30 minutes. Turn meat and add remaining cup of bouillon. Turn meat again and continue cooking for 15 to 30 minutes until meat is tender.

As prepared by Anneliese for Craig Claiborne, noted food gourmet for *The New York Times* and author of several cookbooks. This recipe appeared in *The New York Times* and *The New York Times International Cookbook,* authored by Craig Claiborne.

Anneliese von der Cron

ST. PAUL'S RICE

OVEN: 350° 1 hour

YIELD: 6 servings

1 pound ground beef
2 envelopes chicken noodle soup
  mix
½ cup rice, uncooked

1 green pepper, diced
1 cup finely diced celery
1 medium onion, finely chopped
paprika

Brown beef and drain fat. Bring 4½ cups water to a boil and add soup mix and rice. Boil for 7 minutes. In a large mixing bowl, combine all ingredients except paprika. Grease a 3 quart casserole or baking dish of equal capacity. Spoon mixture into dish and top with paprika. Bake at 350° for 1 hour.
This is delicious served with a salad and French rolls.

Carol I. Browder

Bacon slices will not curl if cooked on low heat and the grease removed as it melts.

SASSY SAUSAGES

YIELD: 5-6 servings

1 cup water
⅓ cup red cinnamon candies
red food coloring

3 red tart apples, cored and cut
   into ½" rings
1 pound pork sausage links
3 tablespoons water

In a skillet, heat 1 cup water, cinnamon candies and a few drops red food coloring until candies are melted. Place apple rings in candy syrup mixture; cook slowly, turning occasionally, for about 20 minutes, or until apples are tender. In another skillet, place sausage links and add 3 tablespoons water. Cover tightly and cook slowly for 8 minutes. Uncover, and cook sausages until well browned.

To serve, insert hot sausage link in center of each apple slice.

Annie Parker
Villa Capri

SAUERBRATEN

2 pounds chuck roast
2 cups white vinegar
1 medium size onion, sliced
1 slice lemon
1 bay leaf

2 tablespoons salt
1 tablespoon fat
1 tablespoon flour
½ cup sour cream
1 cup water

Make brine by combining water, vinegar, lemon slice, salt, onion slices, and bay leaf to a boil. Cool mixture. When cool, pour it over meat and let meat stand in a cool place (refrigerated) for 3-4 days; turn daily.

Take meat out of brine, dry with a cloth and sprinkle with flour. Brown meat in hot fat. Add ½ of brine and simmer meat for 1-2 hours. Remove meat from gravy and mix flour with a little water to make the cup full and add this to gravy. Stir, simmering gravy for about 5 minutes. Stir in sour cream and bring mixture to a boil. Strain gravy and serve over sliced meat.

Louise Beerhalter

Prevent link sausage from bursting open when frying by piercing with a fork.

SAUERBRATEN BAVARIAN STYLE

OVEN: 400° 60 minutes, 300° 70 minutes   YIELD: 6 servings

3 pounds bottom round of beef
3 large onions, peeled, and sliced
3 tablespoons whole peppercorns
25 whole cloves
25 bay leaves
1 tablespoon mustard seeds
¼ cup butter

2 cups wine vinegar
6 slices bacon
2 tablespoons all-purpose flour
4 cups beef bouillon
¼ cup cold water
2 to 3 tablespoons heavy cream

In advance, marinate the meat for three days. Prepare meat by trimming fat and cutting into six large pieces. Place meat in a large mixing bowl; combine onions, peppercorns, cloves, bay leaves, mustard seeds, and vinegar, and pour over beef. Cover and place in refrigerator for three days. After marination period, preheat oven to 400 degrees; melt butter in casserole; place meat with marinade and seasonings in casserole; cook uncovered for 1 hour after which time reduce heat to 300 degrees. Turn, meat in the liquid and place a slice of bacon on each piece of meat. Continue cooking another hour, or until meat is tender. Remove bacon and cook meat 10 minutes longer; strain liquid and place meat on platter. To cooking liquid, add four cups of beef bouillon. Return meat to casserole and add liquid bringing to a boil. Blend flour with ¼ cup cold water; add to liquid, stirring constantly. Simmer for five minutes; stir in cream.

Delicious served piping hot with dumplings.

As prepared by Anneliese for Craig Claiborne, noted food gourmet for *The New York Times* and author of several cookbooks. This recipe appeared in *The New York Times* and *The New York Times International Cookbook*, authored by Craig Claiborne.

Anneliese von der Cron

SCRAMBLED-DEVILED DRIED BEEF

YIELD: 2-4 servings

1 tablespoon margarine
1 cup shredded, dried beef
4 eggs

1 teaspoon prepared mustard
1 tablespoon vinegar
⅛ teaspoon pepper

In a skillet, heat margarine. Gently sauté dried beef for about 5 minutes. Beat eggs, mustard, vinegar and pepper together. Pour over dried beef and cook slowly, stirring occasionally, until eggs are set. Serve immediately.

Barbara Matuszewski

For easier slicing, allow roast to stand fifteen or twenty minutes after removing from oven before carving.

SHISH KEBAB

1 pound boneless lamb shoulder
  OR beef round, cut into 1" cubes
½ cup vegetable oil
¼ cup lemon juice
1 clove garlic, minced
½ pound small white onions

2 small zucchini, cut into ¼" slices
¾ teaspoon salt
½ teaspoon rosemary
¼ teaspoon pepper
½ basket cherry tomatoes

Trim excess fat from meat; place meat in a glass bowl. Mix oil, lemon juice, garlic, salt, rosemary, and pepper together in a measuring cup for marinade. Pour marinade over meat; cover bowl tightly with plastic wrap; marinate at room temperature for at least 2 hours, or overnight in refrigerator. Pre-cook onions in boiling water for 10-15 minutes, or until tender. Drain and cool slightly. Cut off ends of onions and remove skins. Preheat broiler and thread marinated meat, onions, tomatoes and zucchini slices on eight wood or metal skewers. Place side by side on broiling pan. Brush meat and vegetables with marinade and broil about 4" from heat for 15 minutes. Turn skewers several times during broiling, and occasionally brush with marinade. Arrange on a bed of rice and serve.

Shrimp, scallops or fish may be substituted for the meat. Do not marinate seafood, just baste occasionally with marinade as it broils. It will also cook in less time.

Other vegetables may be used; potatoes, mushrooms, green pepper. Potatoes must be precooked. If using tomatoes, put on a separate skewer and broil for just a few minutes.

Debbie Jameson

SMALL RIBS — BAKED

OVEN: 350° 45-60 minutes

1½ to 2 pounds small ribs
soy sauce
brown sugar

ginger
garlic

Trim fat from ribs. Marinate ribs in enough soy sauce, brown sugar, ginger and garlic to cover. Turn ribs now and then. Marinate, refrigerated for 24 hours. Cook on racks in 350° oven for 45-60 minutes.

If you desire to serve them as an appetizer, cut ribs into bite size pieces to handle. If you serve them as the main course, leave them in larger pieces. It is very different and delicious for a change from barbecued ribs.

Mabel Fawsett

Pepper looses its biting quality during cooking; season cuts of meat after cooking.

SOMERVILLE MEAT LOAF

OVEN: 400° 30 or 45 minutes

YIELD: 6 servings

2 pounds lean ground beef
2 small onions, finely chopped
2 cups soft bread crumbs
1 tablespoon salt
¼ cup Worcestershire sauce
2 eggs, beaten

2-4 tablespoons horseradish
1 teaspoon dry mustard
¼ cup green pepper, finely
  chopped
¾ cup ketchup

Using hands, thoroughly mix all ingredients except ketchup. Pack tightly into one 9″ x 5″ loaf pan, or two 4″ x 6″ pans. Spread ketchup on top. Wrap and freeze for later use, or bake at 400°, 45 minutes for larger loaf, 30 minutes for smaller loaves. Delicious hot or cold.

My mother always served Somerville Meat Loaf with baked potatoes and fresh spinach. This recipe was adapted from a recipe originally published about 1927 in *Good Housekeeping's Book of Good Meals* and is still our family's favorite meat loaf.

Barbara Matuszewski

STEAK DIANNE

2½ pounds boneless sirloin
salt
2 tablespoons coarsely ground
  black pepper
2 tablespoons peanut oil
3 tablespoons butter

2 tablespoons finely chopped shallots
¾ cup dry red wine
2 tablespoons cognac
1 cup brown sauce (see recipe) OR
  canned beef gravy
1 tablespoon lemon juice

Sprinkle steak with salt to taste. Make shallow slices in meat and rub in pepper. Brown meat on all sides in peanut oil. Cook for 30-40 minutes to desired doneness. Transfer steak to warm serving platter and pour off fat and oil from skillet. Add 1 tablespoon butter and shallots to skillet and stir fry for 1½ minutes. Add wine and stir to dissolve brown particles on bottom of pan. Cook until wine is reduced to ¼ cup. Add cognac, cook for 1 minute, and stir in brown sauce. Remove sauce from heat and add remaining butter. Swirl butter in pan until it melts. Add lemon juice and serve over sliced steak.

Mrs. David S. Keen

Scoring steaks by cutting slashes across surfaces or pounding steaks with a mallet before braising helps make the steaks more tender.

STEFAN BEEF STEW WITH DUMPLINGS

2 pounds stew meat
4 medium onions
1 cup celery, chopped
3 medium carrots
4 medium potatoes
1 cup red OR burgundy wine
1 tablespoon parsley
1 teaspoon Worcestershire sauce
1 bay leaf

½ teaspoon minced garlic
½ teaspoon basil leaves, crushed
salt and pepper
1 cup flour
1 egg
½ cup milk
1 teaspoon salt
cooking oil
2 tablespoons paprika

Cut beef into 1″ squares. Sauté onions in oil and add paprika. When onions are soft, add beef and all vegetables and seasonings. Cover with water and add wine. Cook on top of stove, uncovered, on medium heat for 1 hour.

For dumplings, beat egg and mix with milk and salt and flour. Drop dumplings in stew and cook for 10 minutes.

Dumpling mixture may be mixed ahead of time and refrigerated. To use, let stand to room temperature before dropping into stew.

Jeanie Fowler

STIFATHO WITH BEEF
(ONION STEW)

YIELD: 6-8 servings

4 pounds beef stew OR round
  steak, cut into cubes
4 pounds small whole onions
¼ cup vinegar
¼ cup burgundy wine
1 — #2½ can tomatoes
salt and pepper to taste
¼ cup olive oil

¼ cup salad oil
6 cloves garlic
5-6 bay leaves
12 cloves
½ red pepper
handful of spices
butter

Place spices, cloves and red pepper into cheesecloth and tie. Brown meat in half butter and oil. Place browned meat in a pot. Brown onions and add to pot. Strain tomatoes; discarding juice; and add to pot with baged spices and remaining ingredients. Cook until meat is tender. Just before serving, remove spice bag.

Serve with rice or creamed potatoes, or spaghetti.

Sophie Reeves

Save the drippings from meat as they are great to use for cooking.

STUFFED FRANKS

1 pound frankfurters	1 can tomato sauce
bacon slices	½ stick butter OR margarine
1 green pepper, sliced lengthwise	toothpicks
mustard	diced onions

Slice franks lengthwise to form a pocket. Smear with mustard and sprinkle liberally with diced onions and pepper strips. Wrap franks in bacon slices, securing with toothpicks.

Melt butter in a heavy skillet and cover franks with tomato sauce. Cook for 15 minutes or until bacon is crisp.

Serve these unusual and delicious franks on garlic toasted hot dog buns or, if you prefer, with German potato salad or baked beans.

John E. Graye

STUFFED GRAPE LEAVES

1 pound ground lamb	½ teaspoon cinnamon
1 small can tomatoes	salt and pepper
⅔ cup uncooked rice	grape leaves

Mix together all ingredients except grape leaves. Line Dutch oven with grape leaves. Put about 1 teaspoon of lamb mixture into a grape leaf, and roll as you would for stuffed cabbage. Stack stuffed leaves in leaf-lined pot. Cover with water and simmer for 2 hours. Add more water if necessary. Serve in or with Paella bread, dotted with butter.

This is an inexpensive meal that goes very far. It is very good for buffets.

Beau Pavin

SWEDISH CASSEROLE

OVEN: 350° 1 hour 45 minutes

¾ pound hamburger	1 package frozen string beans
4-5 wieners	¼ head cabbage, shredded
1 large onion, sliced	1 cup ketchup
2 medium potatoes, sliced	½ cup water

Brown hamburger in dutch oven and add wieners that have been cut into bite size pieces. Remove from heat and lightly salt. Add a layer of onions, layer of potatoes, and lightly salt again. Add a layer of frozen string beans that have been broken up, and a layer of shredded cabbage. Pour ketchup over cabbage, then pour water over ketchup. Cover and bake in 350° oven for 1 hour and 45 minutes.

Mushrooms and water chestnuts may be added if desired. I strongly suggest using only the basic recipe.

Jean C. Dean

SWEDISH MEATBALLS

¾ pound beef, ground
¼ pound pork, ground
⅓ cup bread crumbs OR 2 slices
white bread
1 cup whole milk
1 tablespoon onion, finely chopped
1 tablespoon butter

1½ teaspoons salt
¼ teaspoon white pepper
⅛ teaspoon allspice
½ teaspoon sugar
2-3 tablespoons butter OR margarine

Sauté onions in 1 tablespoon butter until they are a pale golden color. Soak bread crumbs in milk, then add beef, pork, onion, and seasonings. Mix thoroughly until very smooth. Shape into small balls, walnut size, using 2 tablespoons that have been dipped in cold water. Fry in 2-3 tablespoons butter or margarine until evenly brown, shaking pan continuously to make balls round. Serve hot or cold as a smorgasbord dish.

In Sweden, meatballs are served with pickled cucumbers and lingon berries, similar to our cranberries.

Ruth Hallstrom

SWEET AND SOUR PORK

YIELD: 6-8 servings

3 pounds boneless pork, cubed
flour
salt
pepper
1 cup barbecue sauce
½ cup vinegar

1 cup water
1 large green pepper
24 ounce jar pineapple preserves
garlic salt to taste
3 tablespoons oil

Coat meat with seasoned flour. Brown meat in oil. Add barbecue sauce, vinegar and water. Cover and simmer for 1 hour. Add chopped green pepper and preserves for the last 15 minutes. Serve over rice.

This recipe freezes well. It is good without rice and served with a vegetable and congealed or fruit salad.

Lucy Gant

SWEET AND SPICY PORK CHOPS

4 pork chops
2 onions, sliced thin
2 cups orange juice
2 tablespoons lemon juice
4 tablespoons brown sugar
2 teaspoons ground ginger

1 teaspoon poultry seasoning
1 teaspoon marjoram
1 cup seedless golden raisins
salt
pepper

Season and brown chops. Remove from pan and brown onions until tender. Mix remaining ingredients in a bowl. Return chops to pan, cover with onions, and pour mixture over chops. Cover and simmer for 20-30 minutes, until chops are done.

I found my electric skillet cooks this recipe nicely. Make sure chops do not burn when everything is mixed together. I have doubled the original ingredients to suit our personal taste.

Nancy Walther

SWEET-SOUR STEW

YIELD: 6-8 servings

¼ cup all-purpose flour
1 teaspoon salt
dash of pepper
2 pounds beef stew meat, cubed
½ cup shortening
1 cup water
½ cup ketchup

¼ cup brown sugar
¼ cup vinegar
1 tablespoon Worcestershire sauce
1 cup chopped onion
6 large carrots, cut into ¾" pieces
(3 cups)

Combine flour, salt and pepper in a plastic or paper bag. Add meat and shake to coat. In a large skillet, brown meat well in hot shortening. Combine water, ketchup, brown sugar, vinegar, Worcestershire sauce and 1 teaspoon salt. Stir into browned meat. Add onion. Cover and cook over low heat for 45 minutes, stirring once or twice. Add carrots and cook for 45 minutes more, or until meat and carrots are tender.

Diana E. Enck

TOASTED DEVILED HAMBURGERS

YIELD: 6 servings

1 pound very lean ground beef
1 tablespoon grated onion
2 tablespoons chili sauce
1 teaspoon Worcestershire sauce
⅛ teaspoon pepper

2 tablespoons milk
2 teaspoons prepared mustard
12 slices bread
¼ pound butter OR margarine

Mix thoroughly all ingredients except bread and butter or margarine. Melt butter or margarine and brush lightly on both sides of bread slices. Spread bread on cookie sheet in one layer. Toast in broiler about 1 minute on one side only. Remove pan from broiler. Turn each slice of bread over and spread untoasted sides with meat mixture, covering each slice completely. Return to broiler for 2-3 minutes.

Barbara Matuszewski

TREET MAIN DISH

YIELD: 4 servings

1 — 12 ounce can Armour Star
Treet
½ cup packed brown sugar
2 tablespoons cornstarch
1 — 13¼ ounce can pineapple
chunks

pineapple syrup, reserved from
canned pineapple
1 cup water
2 tablespoons vinegar
1 cup bell pepper strips
4 servings hot rice

Add brown sugar to cornstarch in a small saucepan and blend in pineapple syrup, water and vinegar. Cook, stirring constantly until mixture is clear and thick. Cut Treet into cubes and stir into thickened mixture. Add pineapple chunks and bell pepper strips. Continue cooking until hot, about 10 minutes. Serve over hot rice.

Debbie Charlton

TRICKY MEAT LOAF

OVEN: 350° 50 minutes

1 pound ground chuck
1 cup dry uncooked oatmeal
1 teaspoon soy sauce
1 teaspoon Worcestershire sauce

½ of a 1¼ ounce box raisins,
  soaked in hot water
chopped onion, optional

Mix all ingredients together loosely, by hand. Cook in loaf pan at 350° for approximately 50 minutes.
The oatmeal keeps the meat loaf moist and fluffy.

Dorothy Binney Palmer

UPSIDE-DOWN MEAT AND PEPPER CORN BREAD

OVEN: 400° 30-40 minutes

1 pound ground meat
1 small onion, chopped
1 small can tomato sauce
1 teaspoon salt

green pepper rings
1 — 7½ ounce package corn bread
  mix OR ½ regular corn bread recipe

Brown onion and ground meat in 8″ iron skillet. Add tomato sauce and salt. Simmer over low heat while mixing corn bread. Remove skillet from heat and arrange green pepper rings under meat sauce in skillet. Spread corn bread mix over the top of meat mixture and bake for 30-40 minutes at 400°, or until toothpick inserted comes out clean. Invert onto round platter and serve.
The new varieties of tomato sauce are nice to use, especially tomato with mushroom.

Mrs. James Briggs

VEAL MARSALA

1 — 12 ounce can beef stock
⅔ stick butter
1 can mushrooms
salt
pepper

parsley
¼ cup Marsala wine
1½ pounds veal cutlet, Italian style
2 eggs, beaten
flour

Combine beef stock, mushrooms, salt, pepper, parsley, and wine with melted butter and simmer until mushrooms are tender. Dip veal cutlet into mixture of flour, salt and pepper, then into beaten eggs and back into flour. Fry each cutlet in butter, 2 minutes on each side. Put veal into wine sauce and simmer for 5 minutes. Let stand for 10 minutes before serving.
Sauce may be used for other meats.

Ginny Villa

VEAL ROLL-UPS

OVEN: 350° 1 hour 10 minutes

1½ to 1¾ pounds veal round steak
  or cutlets, ¼" thick
6 slices thin boiled ham
3 slices Swiss cheese
1 egg, slightly beaten

¾ cup fine, dry bread crumbs
2 tablespoons dry white wine
1 cup cream of mushroom soup
2 tablespoons plus ½ cup milk

Pound 6 pieces of veal to ⅛" thickness. If chicken is used, have breasts boned and skinned. Top meat with a slice of ham and a strip of cheese. Roll meat around cheese and secure with a toothpick. Mix egg with 2 tablespoons milk. Dip rolls in egg mixture then into crumbs. Place seam side down in a 9" x 13" pan. Combine soup, wine, and ½ cup milk and heat to bubbling. Pour around rolls, cover pan and bake at 350° for 1 hour or until tender. Uncover and sprinkle with paprika and bake 10 minutes more.

Dee Furst

WATER CHESTNUT MEATBALLS

OVEN: 350° 20 minutes

YIELD: 5 dozen meat balls

2 cups soft bread crumbs
½ cup milk
1 tablespoon soy sauce
½ teaspoon garlic salt

1 small onion
½ pound ground beef
½ pound ground sausage
1 — 6 ounce can water chestnuts

Drain and finely chop water chestnuts. Combine bread crumbs with milk, soy sauce, garlic salt, and onion. Add ground beef and pork sausage and water chestnuts. Mix well. Form into 1" balls. Place on a 15½" x 10½" x 1" baking pan and bake in 350° oven for about 20 minutes, or until done.

Natalie Myers

When a recipe calls for meatballs, place the prepared meatballs on a cookie sheet and bake at 350 degrees for about thirty minutes.

WONDER-WHY STEAK

2 of the best broiling steaks you
  can afford, ½" to ¾" thick
1 tablespoon garlic spread
1 tablespoon real butter

2 or more cast aluminum steak
  platters
broiled meat seasoning
oregano
Italian salad dressing

Set oven on broil at maximum heat, about 500°. Melt over low heat butter and garlic spread. While oven is heating, trim excess fat from steak and make small cuts every 1" around sides. Pierce thoroughly with fork, turn over and repeat. Sprinkle meat seasonings and oregano lightly on both sides of meat. Grease steak platters with salad dressing and place meat under broiler for 3 minutes. Remove and baste both sides with melted butter and garlic spread. Turn meat over and baste again. Broil for 3 minutes more. Steak should turn out medium rare. Adjust times to cook meat to your liking.

Serve with simple tossed salad and boil-in-a-bag frozen vegetables. The best steaks are dark (aged longer) and well marbled with fat. Shop on a Saturday night. Others will buy the bright red meat — no fat beef. On Saturday night you get the best meat usually at ½ price.

Ron Forsyth

PIES AND PASTRIES

PIES AND PASTRIES

AMBROSIA PIE

1 cup granulated sugar
¼ cup all-purpose flour
¼ teaspoon salt
1 tablespoon butter
1⅓ cups fresh orange juice
grated rind of 1 orange
3 egg yolks, beaten
2 drops red food coloring

2 ounces grated sweetened coconut
1 cup chopped pecans
2 ripe, firm bananas
½ pint whipping cream
⅓ cup sugar
½ teaspoon vanilla
graham cracker pie crust

Filling — Combine sugar, flour, salt, butter, orange juice, and rind in a saucepan and add food coloring. Cook mixture over medium heat, stirring constantly, until all lumps dissolve and disappear. Slowly add beaten egg yolks and continue stirring until mixture becomes thick. Remove from heat and cool. Stir in coconut and nuts.

Slice bananas and spread evenly in graham cracker crust. Spoon cooked orange-coconut filling over bananas. Chill thoroughly, but do not freeze.

Whip cream, sugar and vanilla to a firm consistency. Spread over chilled pie and return to refrigerator. Before serving, garnish with fresh orange slices.

This recipe won a prize about 15 years ago in the cooking contest sponsored annually by the Florida Citrus Commission and Florida Power and Light.

Betty Gene Hensick

ANGEL FOOD PIE

1 — 9" pie crust, baked
4½ tablespoons cornstarch
¾ cup sugar
1½ cups boiling water
⅜ teaspoon salt
3 egg whites

3 tablespoons sugar
1½ teaspoons vanilla
½ cup cream, whipped
½ to 1 square unsweetened chocolate, grated

Mix cornstarch and sugar in a saucepan or double boiler. Add boiling water; cook, stirring constantly for 10-12 minutes or until thick and clear. Add salt to egg whites; beat until stiff. Add sugar and vanilla; beat until well mixed. Pour hot cornstarch mixture into egg white mixture slowly, beating constantly; cool slightly. Place mixture into pastry shell. Cover with whipped cream; sprinkle or grate chocolate over top. Refrigerate for at least 2 hours before serving, or longer.

Mrs. Leslie Carlin

Chill pie dough thoroughly before rolling the pastry shell. This makes it easier to handle.

ANGEL PIE

1 cup sugar
1 cup water
1 small can crushed pineapple, do
  not drain

3 tablespoons cornstarch
2 egg whites, beaten very stiff
1 baked pie crust

Combine sugar, water, pineapple and juice and cornstarch in a saucepan and cook, stirring constantly until mixture is transparent and very thick. Cool thoroughly.

Mixture should be prepared several hours ahead or the night before.

When mixture is cold, fold it into egg whites. Pile mixture into pie shell and spread whipped topping on pie before serving.

Chopped nuts and maraschino cherries on topping make the pie very festive. Delicious.

Jean C. Dean

APPLE PIE

OVEN: 350°-400° 30-40 minutes

1 unbaked pie shell
sliced apples to fill shell
½ cup sugar
1 teaspoon cinnamon

½ cup butter
¾ cup flour
½ to ¾ cup sugar

Combine sugar and cinnamon and sprinkle over apple slices, mix to coat. Place apples into pie shell.

Mix butter, flour and ½ to ¾ cup sugar together and sprinkle over top of apples. Bake in 350° to 400° oven for 30-40 minutes. Test with a toothpick to be sure apples are done.

Flossie Rouse

AVOCADO AND LEMON PIE

¼ cup cornstarch
¼ cup sugar
½ teaspoon salt
2 tablespoons vinegar
1½ cups milk
½ cup cream cheese, softened
¼ cup lemon juice

2 cups cubed avocados
2-3 teaspoons green food coloring
1 prepared graham cracker pie
  crust

Topping:
¼ cup cubed avocados
2 lemons, sliced

In medium saucepan, mix cornstarch, sugar and salt. Gradually stir in vinegar and milk. Cook mixture on medium heat, stirring constantly. Bring mixture to a boil and boil for 1 minute or until mixture thickens. Remove from heat and let mixture cool.

Stir cream cheese, lemon juice and avocados into cooled mixture; blend well. Stir in food coloring until it is well mixed.

Pour mixture into pie crust. Decorate with cubed avocados and lemon slices. Chill for 2 hours. Pie's flavor will be even better if you chill it overnight.

Rosie Boromei

BLACKBERRY JAM PIE

4 egg yolks
1 cup sugar
2 rounded tablespoons flour
1 cup milk

¼ cup melted butter
1 cup blackberry jam, thick
½ teaspoon vanilla
unbaked pie shell

Beat egg yolks and add sugar and flour. Mix in other ingredients and place in pie shell. Bake pie shell according to packaged directions for fruit pie. When cool, cover with meringue topping.

This is a famous southern recipe from the "Purefoy Hotel" in Talladega, Alabama.

Eileen Schiavone

BLUEBERRY TOPPED CHEESE PIE

YIELD: 6-8 servings

1 — 3 ounce package cream cheese
½ cup powdered sugar
½ teaspoon vanilla
½ pint (1 cup) whipping cream

1 — 9" baked pastry shell
1 tablespoon lemon juice
1 — 1 pound, 5 ounce can prepared
blueberry pie filling

Cream together the cheese, sugar and vanilla. Whip cream until stiff, but not dry and fold cream in. Turn mixture into baked pastry shell and spread evenly. Stir lemon juice into blueberry filling and carefully spoon mixture over the cream filling. Chill.

Connie Montuoro

BRANDY ALEXANDER PIE

YIELD: 8 servings

1 envelope unflavored gelatin
½ cup cold water
⅔ cup sugar
⅛ teaspoon salt
3 eggs, separated

chocolate curls
¼ cup cognac
¼ cup cream de cocoa
2 cups heavy cream, whipped
1 prepared pie crust

Sprinkle gelatin over cold water in a saucepan. Add ⅓ cup sugar and salt and egg yolks. Stir to blend. Over low heat, stir until gelatin dissolves and mixture thickens. Do not boil. Remove from heat and stir in cognac and cream de cocoa. Chill until mixture begins to mold. This will happen quickly.

Beat egg whites until stiff. Gradually beat in remaining sugar and fold into thickened mixture. Fold in 1 cup whipped cream. Turn mixture into graham cracker crust or baked shell. Garnish with whipped cream and chocolate curls.

Mal Lowry

Custard pies can be made rich brown and attractive by adding two tablespoons of butter to the milk before scalding.

BUTTERMILK PIE

OVEN: 350° 45 minutes

½ cup butter
1½ cups sugar
2 tablespoons flour
½ cup buttermilk

3 eggs
2 teaspoons vanilla
unbaked pie shell

Melt butter then add sugar and flour; add eggs, one at a time, beating well after each addition. Add buttermilk and vanilla, blend well and pour into unbaked pie shell. Bake for 45 minutes or until knife inserted in center comes out clean at 350°.

Julia Hall

BUTTERSCOTCH PIE

1 cup brown sugar
1 tablespoon flour
1 teaspoon butter
2 egg yolks
1 cup rich milk

1 teaspoon vanilla

Meringue:
2 egg whites, beaten stiff
3 tablespoons sugar

Combine brown sugar, flour and butter; mix well. Add egg yolks and milk to mixture and cook until thick. Blend in vanilla.
Cool mixture and place in baked pie shell.
Combine egg whites and sugar to make meringue and cover filling with meringue. Brown meringue slowly in oven.
This recipe has originated about 90 years ago by Mrs. G.C. Haas-Weston, Savannah, Georgia.

Sheila Grose

CALAMONDIN CHIFFON PIE

1 baked 9" pie shell
1 envelope unflavored gelatin
¼ cup water
3 eggs, separated

1 cup sugar
¾ cup calamondin juice
⅛ teaspoon salt
½ pint whipped cream

Soften gelatin in water, set aside. Beat egg yolks until lemon colored. Add ½ cup sugar, juice and salt to egg yolks. Mix well and cook in top of double boiler, stirring constantly until mixture coats spoon, about 10 minutes. Add gelatin, stir and cook two or three minutes longer. Remove from heat, cool thoroughly. Beat egg whites stiff, gradually add remaining sugar. Fold into well cooled custard. Pour mixture into pie shell. Chill until firm; top with whopped cream, garnish with curls of calamondin peel.

The Committee·

CHERRY COBBLER

OVEN: 350° 50 minutes

3 cups cherries
1 cup sugar
2 tablespoons butter
1 egg
½ cup butter

1 cup sugar
½ cup milk
1 cup flour
1 teaspoon boiling water

Combine cherries, 1 cup sugar and 2 tablespoons butter and place into a baking dish. Cream together all remaining ingredients and pour over cherry mixture. Bake in 350° oven for 50 minutes.

Edie Stretch

CHESS PIE

OVEN: 375° 10 minutes; 325° 30 minutes

1 stick butter
3 eggs, slightly beaten
1½ cups white sugar

½ tablespoon vanilla
1 tablespoon vinegar

Melt butter and add beaten eggs, sugar, vanilla and vinegar. Blend well. Pour into pie pan and bake in 375° oven for 10 minutes. Reduce heat to 325° and bake for 30 minutes more.

Nancy Davis

CHOCOLATE PIE

YIELD: 6-8 servings

1 — 8" pie shell
2 bars German sweet chocolate
   (about ½ pound)
2 tablespoons sugar

4 eggs, separated
¼ cup water
whipped cream

Prepare and bake pie shell; cool.
In the top of a double boiler, combine sugar, chocolate, and ¼ cup water. Cook over hot, not boiling, water, stirring frequently, until chocolate is melted. Remove from hot water and let mixture cool slightly. Add egg yolks, stir until well blended.
Beat egg whites until stiff. Fold into chocolate mixture until well combined. Turn mixture into prepared pie shell. Refrigerate until well chilled, at least 6 hours.
Decorate top with whipped cream.

Mrs. Robert Harris, Jr.

CHOCOLATE SILK PIE

YIELD: 6 servings

Pie shell:
2 cups shredded coconut
⅓ cup butter, melted

Filling:
½ cup butter
½ cup sugar
1 square unsweetened chocolate
1 teaspoon vanilla
2 eggs

For shell, mix melted butter and coconut. Press mixture into 9″ pie pan. Chill in freezer while preparing the filling.

For filling, cream butter. Add sugar and cream well. Blend in melted chocolate. Add vanilla; add eggs, one at a time, and beat 5 minutes after each addition. Turn mixture into pie shell. Chill filled pie in refrigerator for 2-3 hours. Garnish with whipped cream and shaved chocolate.

Ann VanDyke Grace Kennedy

COCONUT PIE

OVEN: 350° 1 hour

¼ pound margarine
1½ cups sugar
3 eggs
1 tablespoon vinegar

1 teaspoon vanilla
1 can shredded coconut, not flaked
1 unbaked pie shell

Mix ingredients in order given. Blend well. Bake in unbaked pie shell at 350° for 1 hour.

Jackie Brice

COCONUT PIE SHELL

OVEN: 300° 20 minutes

3 tablespoons butter

2 — 3½ ounce cans flaked coconut (2½ cups)

Mix coconut and butter together and press into a 9″ pie pan. Build up sides. Bake in 300° oven for 20 minutes, until golden brown. Cool

Fill with cream filling of your choice and garnish with toasted coconut on top.

Mrs. C.L. Wharton

To make stretching and shaping of pastry dough easier, add about 1 tablespoon of lemon juice or vinegar to each 4 cups of flour used. The acid helps soften the gluten in the flour, making the dough softer and more pliable.

CREME DE MENTHE PIE

OVEN: 300° 10 minutes

1 — 15 ounce package creme filled
chocolate cookies (sandwich
type)
⅔ cup scalded milk

30 large marshmallows
2 ounces creme de menthe
1 ounce creme de cacao
½ pint whipping cream, whipped

Place cookies in blender, 4 or 5 at a time, including filling and blend into crumbs. Place crumbs in pie pan and place pat of butter on top; bake for 10 minutes in 300° oven. Remove from oven and mold crumbs into pie pan for crust.

Scald milk; place milk in double boiler and add marshmallows. Allow marshmallows to melt. Add creme de menthe and creme de cacao. Mix well. Allow mixture to cool before adding whipping cream. Blend whipped cream into mixture and fold into pie crust. Freeze.

Garnish with chocolate shavings or cookie crumbs. Remove pie from freezer 10-15 minutes before serving.

Deedie Montgomery

CRUSTLESS COCONUT PIE

OVEN: 350° 45 minutes

1½ cups sugar
½ cup flour
2 cups whole milk
1 teaspoon lemon juice

1 teaspoon vanilla
1 — 14 ounce bag coconut
4 well beaten eggs
½ cup butter

Mix sugar and flour together. Slowly add milk, lemon juice and vanilla to dry ingredients. Add coconut. Add eggs and blend well. Melt butter in pie plate. Drain butter into mixture and blend well. Pour mixture into buttered pie plate and bake in 350° oven for 45 minutes.

Theresa Haisley

DELUXE PECAN PIE

OVEN: 400° 15 minutes; 350° 30-35 minutes

1 unbaked 9″ pastry shell
3 eggs
1 cup dark corn syrup
1 cup sugar

2 tablespoons melted margarine
1 teaspoon vanilla
⅛ teaspoon salt
1 cup pecans, cut up if preferred

Beat eggs slightly; mix in syrup, sugar, margarine, vanilla, salt and pecans. Blend well. Pour into unbaked pastry shell. Bake in 400° oven for 15 minutes; reduce heat to 350° and bake for 30-35 minutes longer.

Filling should be slightly less set in center than around edge.

Mrs. James W. Mueller

DIVINE LIME PIE

OVEN: 275° 20 minutes; 300° 40 minutes

4 egg whites	⅓ cup lime juice
¼ teaspoon cream of tartar	green food coloring, optional
1 cup sugar	1 tablespoon grated lime rind
4 egg yolks	2 cups whipped cream, divided into
¼ teaspoon salt	2 — 1 cup measures
½ cup sugar	

Sprinkle cream of tartar on egg whites; beat until frothy. Gradually beat in sugar. Beat mixture until stiff and glossy. Spread into greased 9″ pie pan, making slight depression in the center. Bake for 20 minutes at 275°, increase temperature to 300° and bake for 40 minutes. Cool slowly.

Mix beaten egg yolks with salt, ½ cup sugar and lime juice. Cook over hot water for 10 minutes or until thick. Cool. Add food coloring and fold in rind and 1 cup of whipped cream. Spread over meringue shell in pan. Whip remaining cream and sugar if desired, and spread over filling. Sprinkle with more grated lime rind. Chill for at least 4 hours.

Mary Jo McDermid

EASY LIME CHIFFON PIE

YIELD: 2 — 8″ pies

1 cup evaporated milk	½ to 1 cup sugar
1 package lime gelatin	2 tablespoons lemon OR lime juice
1 cup boiling water MINUS 2 tablespoons	graham cracker pie crusts

Place evaporated milk in an ice cube tray and chill until ice starts to form at edges. Mix gelatin with boiling water; add sugar, allow mixture to cool. Whip milk with 1 tablespoon of juice until mixture is stiff. Add 1 tablespoon of juice to gelatin mixture and pour in whipped milk. Stir in slowly. Place mixture in graham cracker crust and chill at least 1 hour.

Annie Raulerson

EASY PEACH COBBLER

OVEN: 375° 30-40 minutes

1 stick margarine, melted in 10″ x 10″ pan	1 cup sugar
1 large can sweetened, sliced peaches, drained	¾ cup flour
	¾ cup milk
	2 teaspoons baking powder

Cover buttered pan with peaches. Sift dry ingredients together and add milk; stir gently to mix. Pour batter over peaches and bake in moderate oven, 375°, for 30-40 minutes.

Best when served warm.

Mrs. Harold Runte

ESKIMO PIE

2 egg yolks
½ cup white sugar
½ cup milk
pinch of salt
¾ tablespoons unflavored gelatin
½ cup cold water

½ pint whipping cream
2 egg whites, stiffly beaten
1 teaspoon vanilla
10 graham crackers
2 tablespoons melted butter
1 tablespoon brown sugar

Cook egg yolks, sugar, milk and salt into a custard. Dissolve gelatin in cold water and add to custard while custard is hot. Cool, add whipped cream and then fold in the stiffly beaten egg whites. Add vanilla; blend.

Roll graham crackers into crumbs. Add brown sugar and melted butter to crumbs and mix. Place half of crumbs in bottom of 9″ pie pan. Pour in custard and sprinkle remaining crumbs on top. Let chill for 2 hours in refrigerator before serving.

Prepare graham cracker crust while custard mixture is cooling.

Rita Sowinski

FRENCH CHOCOLATE PIE

½ cup butter
¾ cup sugar
2 squares unsweetened chocolate, melted

2 cups whipped topping
2 eggs
1 — 9″ pie shell, baked

Cream butter with sugar. Stir in melted, cooled chocolate. Add eggs, one at a time, beating at high speed for 5 minutes after each addition. Fold in whipped topping that has been thawed. Pour into cooled, baked pie shell. Cool until firm, about 2 hours.

Can be frozen ahead and thawed 2 hours before use.

Marie and Liz Phillips

FRENCH SILK PIE I

OVEN: 400° 15 minutes

½ cup brown sugar
1 cup flour
1 stick butter
½ cup toasted almonds OR pecans

Filling:
2 sticks butter

1½ cups white sugar
3½ squares bitter chocolate, melted
4 eggs
1 tablespoon vanilla
whipped cream OR whipped topping

Stir together brown sugar, flour, butter and nuts. Pat into bottom of greased 9 x 13 pan. Bake at 400° for 15 minutes. When partially cool, break apart into crumbs. Pat into greased 7½″ x 11½″ oven-proof dish.

Cream butter and sugar. Add vanilla and chocolate. Beat in eggs, one at a time; beat 5 minutes after adding each egg. This is very important. Pour over crumbs and chill overnight. Cover with whipped cream when ready to serve.

Mrs. C.L. Wharton

FRENCH SILK PIE II

OVEN: 300° 50-55 minutes

Meringue Shell:
2 egg whites
⅛ teaspoon cream of tartar
1 teaspoon vanilla
½ cup sugar
½ cup chopped nuts

Filling:
½ cup butter
¾ cup sugar
1½ squares semi-sweet chocolate,
  melted and cooled
1 teaspoon vanilla
2 eggs
whipped topping

For meringue shell, beat egg whites until foamy. Add sugar, 2 tablespoons at a time; beating well after each addition. Add cream of tartar. Beat until mixture stands in very stiff peaks. Fold in nuts and vanilla. Place mixture in lightly greased 9″ pie pan. Bake at 300° for 50-55 minutes.

For filling, cream butter and gradually add sugar, cream well. Blend melted and cooled chocolate and vanilla. Add eggs, one at a time, beating for 5 minutes after each addition. Turn mixture into cooled, baked pie shell and refrigerate for 2 hours. Top with whipped topping.

Glenda H. Shelfer

FRESH COCONUT CREAM PIE

OVEN: 350° 12 minutes

⅓ cup sifted flour
⅔ cup sugar
¼ teaspoon salt
2 cups scalded milk
1½ cups shredded fresh coconut

3 eggs, separated
2 tablespoons butter
½ teaspoon vanilla
1 baked 9″ pie shell
6 tablespoons sugar

Mix flour, sugar and salt together in a saucepan. Gradually stir in milk. Cook over moderate heat, stirring constantly, until mixture thickens and boils. Cook for 2 minutes longer. Remove from heat and add 1 cup of coconut; beat egg yolks and then stir yolks into hot mixture. Cook for 1 minute. Remove from heat and add butter and vanilla. Cool slightly and pour into pie shell.

Beat egg whites until they stand in soft mounds. Gradually beat in 6 tablespoons sugar, continuing to beat until egg whites stand in stiff peaks. Spread meringue over pie, making sure it comes to edge of crust. Sprinkle with remaining ½ cup coconut and place in 350° oven to brown slightly, about 12 minutes.

The Committee

To prevent fruit fillings from soaking into the bottom of the crust, dust the bottoms of the crust with equal amounts of flour and sugar. Then add the fruit.

FRESH STRAWBERRY PIE I

1 quart fresh strawberries
1 cup sugar
3 tablespoons cornstarch

1 baked pie shell
1 teaspoon almond flavoring

Pick over berries, selecting 1 pint of the best fruit. Wash fruit well and drain thoroughly. Place fruit in baked pie shell. Wash and slice remaining pint of fruit. Add ½ cup sugar to sliced fruit. Place in a warm part of range to extract juice. Then mix with cornstarch, and bring to a boil and cook until thick and clear. Add food coloring and almond extract. Add remaining ½ cup sugar and stir until dissolved. This mixture is then poured over raw berries in pie shell. Chill and serve with whipped cream.

Hazel N. Crews

FRESH STRAWBERRY PIE II

1 baked pie crust
1 cup sugar
1 pinch salt
1½ pints fresh strawberries

1 cup water
7 teaspoons cornstarch
4 tablespoons strawberry flavored
    gelatin powder

Boil sugar, water, salt and cornstarch until thick. Add gelatin powder. Let mixture cool. Wash berries, slice and fold into cooled filling and refrigerate. When set, cover with whipped topping or whipped cream.

Blanche Hunt

FRIED GUAVA PIES

2 — 20 ounce packages guava
    paste, sliced

Pastry:
4 cups sifted all-purpose flour
1 teaspoon salt

1 teaspoon baking powder
¼ cup sugar
¾ cup shortening
¾ to 1 cup milk
pure vegetable oil

Sift flour, salt, baking powder and sugar together in a large bowl. Add shortening and cut in with pastry blender until mixture resembles corn meal. Stir in milk gradually until mixture clings together. Press dough together gently. Roll out, a quarter at a time, on lightly floured board, to a 10" rectangle, ⅛" thick. Cut into 5" circles. Put sliced guava paste in center of each circle. Fold over dough, and moisten edges to form a semi-circle. Press edges together with fork. Seams must be tightly sealed.

Pour oil into skillet to 2" depth. Heat to 375° and fry pies until they are golden brown on both sides. Remove and drain on paper towel. Sprinkle with powdered sugar if desired.

Apple sauce may be used instead of guava paste; or any other preserves you might have on hand.

Jewell Hoyt

FROZEN STRAWBERRY PIE

YIELD: 6 servings

1 — 3 ounce package cream cheese, softened
¼ cup sugar
¼ cup milk
2 cups strawberries, hulled

1 — 8 ounce container whipped topping, thawed

Crumb crust:
1¼ cups vanilla wafer crumbs, melted butter OR margarine

Combine cream cheese, sugar, milk and strawberries in electric blender. Cover and blend at medium speed for 30 seconds. Fold into whipped topping. Spoon mixture into crust.

To make crust, combine crumbs and melted butter and press firmly into pie pan on sides and bottom. Chill for at least 1 hour before adding filling.

Pie must be frozen until firm, about 4 hours. Let stand at room temperature for 10 minutes before serving for creamier texture. Store any leftover pie in freezer.

Garnish with chocolate covered strawberries if desired.

Strawberries may be dipped in melted semi-sweet chocolate and cooled before placing on pie.

Ruth Wiggins

FUDGE SUNDAE PIE

YIELD: 10 servings

6 ounces chocolate morsels
1 cup evaporated milk
¼ teaspoon salt

1 cup miniature marshmallows
1 pint coffee OR pecan ice cream
1 — 9″ pie crust

For crust, grease and line sides and bottom of pan with vanilla cookies or make a graham cracker crust.

Place chocolate morsels, milk, and salt in a heavy pan and melt over low heat, stirring constantly until all the morsels are melted. Remove from heat and cool. Spoon half of ice cream over pie crust and add half of chocolate mixture, which has been cooled. Add another layer of ice cream and then a layer of chocolate mixture. Place pie in freezer. It stores well for a month.

Arlene Rossway

GERMAN CHEESE PIE

OVEN: Slow oven 1 hour

1 pound cream cheese
1 cup sugar
3 eggs

rind of 1 lemon
1 tablespoon flour
½ cup milk

Combine cheese, sugar, egg yolks, flour and lemon rind rogether; add milk. Beat egg whites and fold into cheese mixture.

Pour batter into baked graham cracker crust and bake for 1 hour in slow oven.

Lewis Jones

GIBSON'S COFFEE TOFFEE PIE

OVEN: 375° 15 minutes

YIELD: 8 servings

Crust:
1 cup flour
½ cup shortening
½ teaspoon salt
¼ cup brown sugar, packed
¾ cup walnuts, grated
1 tablespoon ice water

Filling:
½ cup soft butter
¾ cup granulated sugar

1 square melted unsweetened chocolate
2 teaspoons instant coffee
2 eggs

Topping:
2 cups heavy cream
2 tablespoons instant coffee
½ cup confectioners sugar
1 tablespoon dark rum

For crust, combine flour and salt in a bowl and cut in shortening. Lightly stir in brown sugar and walnuts. Sprinkle in ice water and mix quickly. Pat mixture into a 10″ pie pan and bake in preheated 375° oven for 15 minutes or until firm.

For filling, beat butter until creamy. Add sugar and beat until fluffy. Blend in chocolate and coffee. Add 1 egg and beat for 5 minutes; add second egg and beat for 5 minutes more. Pour mixture into pie shell, cover with plastic wrap and refrigerate overnight.

For topping, the next day, combine cream, rum, coffee and sugar and refrigerate, covered, for 15 minutes. Beat mixture until stiff. Swirl whipped cream on top of pie. Decorate with chocolate curls, if desired, and chill for 2 hours before serving.

Mrs. Noble Gibson

HOT FUDGE PIE

OVEN: 350° 30 minutes

⅓ cup margarine
3 squares chocolate
4 eggs, beaten

2 cups sugar
1 teaspoon vanilla

Melt chocolate and margarine. Beat well. Add eggs and other ingredients. Pour into unbaked pastry shell. Bake at 350° for 30 minutes. Serve pie warm with ice cream or whipped cream.

Jean Huck

Keep whipped cream garnishes on hand for pies by preparing several dozen and freezing. Whip cream, spoon small mounds onto a cookie sheet, and freeze. When frozen store the mounds in a tightly sealed plastic container in the freezer. Defrost fifteen minutes before use.

ICE CREAM PIE WITH VARIATIONS

2 cups crisp rice cereal
2 tablespoons soft butter, not
melted

½ jar marshmallow fluff OR creme
bitter chocolate, coarsely grated
coffee ice cream

Gently mix rice cereal and soft butter with a fork. Add ½ jar of marshmallow fluff and mix. Line 8 or 9" pie plate with mixture, pressing down well all around.

Soften coffee ice cream and place in shell. Return to freezer until meal time. Then remove and grate bitter chocolate over top and place in refrigerator awhile before serving.

Variations: Butter pecan ice cream — stir in 3 tablespoons dark rum and top with whipped cream. Pistachio ice cream — encircle with halves of maraschino cherries. Strawberry swirl ice cream — encircle with halves of fresh strawberries.

Mrs. Edmund Boots

KEY LIME PIE I

OVEN: 350°   YIELD: 2 — 8" pies or 1 — 10-12" pie

1 cup sweetened condensed milk
6 eggs, separated
½ cup lime juice
1 tablespoon cream of tartar

1 cup sugar
pinch of salt
1 baked pie shell

Whip together egg yolks and condensed milk until mixture is light and creamy. Using regular electric beater on medium high speed for about 8 minutes. Add lime juice; let beater rotate on low speed about 1 second. Fold a few times with rubber spatula to be sure juice is thoroughly blended. Pour into baked pie shell. Let stand.

Beat egg whites with cream of tartar and salt for 5 full minutes. Add sugar and beat for 5 minutes more; put meringue on pie and brown in 350° oven.

It is of the utmost importance to follow directions exactly.

Marguerite R. Brock

To glaze pie crust, brush the crust with melted butter or milk before baking. For a browner glaze, brush the crust with a combination of melted butter and egg mixture.

KEY LIME PIE II

OVEN: 350° 10 minutes

1 pastry shell OR graham cracker
   crust
3 eggs

1 — 15 or 16 ounce can sweetened
   condensed milk
½ cup key lime juice
scant ¼ teaspoon cream of tartar
4-6 tablespoons sugar

Prepare pie shell, bake and cool. Separate eggs, beat yolks until pale yellow. Thoroughly blend in condensed milk. Slowly add lime juice; blend until smooth. To prevent curdling, be sure to combine ingredients in this order. Pour filling into cooled pie shell.

Beat egg whites and cream of tartar until whites are foamy. While beating constantly, add sugar, 1 tablespoon at a time, until whites are glossy and stand in soft peaks. Spread meringue over pie, starting with small amounts at the edges and making certain meringue touches pastry at every point around pie. Allow no space to remain between meringue and crust. Cover pie with remaining meringue and spread evenly into attractive swirls. Bake in 350° oven about 10 minutes or until swirls are lightly browned. Cool at room temperature.

Nancy Maxwell

KEY LIME PIE III

OVEN: 325° 15 minutes

2 eggs, separated
½ cup key lime juice
1 can sweetened condensed milk
2 teaspoons grated lime peel

baked pie shell OR graham cracker
   crust
2 tablespoons sugar
pinch baking powder OR cream of
   tartar

Separate eggs. Stir yolks and add milk, grated lime and lime juice. Blend. Let stand a few minutes before pouring into baked pie crust.

For pie crust, use either baked 9" pie shell or make graham cracker crust according to package directions.

For meringue, beat egg whites until foamy. Add heaping tablespoons of sugar, gradually, and a pinch of baking powder or cream of tartar. Beat until meringue forms a peak. Spread meringue over filling and right up to crust to seal pie. Bake in 325° oven for about 15 minutes until slightly browned.

Mrs. Booth Chilcutt

LEMON CHESS PIE

OVEN: 350° 35-45 minutes

2 cups sugar
2 lemons, juice and rind
2 tablespoons flour
¼ cup milk

4 eggs
¼ cup melted butter
1 tablespoon corn meal

Combine all ingredients and beat together. Pour into unbaked pie shell and bake at 350° for 35-45 minutes.

Mrs. M.M. Alsobrook

LEMON CLOUD PIE

¾ cup sugar
¼ cup cornstarch
1 cup water
⅓ cup lemon juice
1 teaspoon grated lemon rind

2 slightly beaten egg yolks
1 small package cream cheese
2 egg whites
¼ cup sugar
precooked pie shell

Combine sugar (¾ cup) and cornstarch; add water, lemon juice, rind, and beaten egg yolks. Cook over medium heat until thick, stirring constantly. Cool; then add cream cheese; blend.

Beat egg whites until stiff and add ¼ cup sugar. Fold egg whites into lemon mixture and spoon into precooked pie shell. Chill.

Anne Davis Reynolds

LEMON PIE

2 cook spoons flour
2 cups sugar
4 egg yolks

lump of butter
juice of 2 lemons

Combine flour, sugar, egg yolks, butter and lemons, beat well. Then add boiling water. Cook mixture in double boiler until thick. Place in baked pie crust and put two whites of eggs, beaten, on top; brown in oven.

Sheila Grose

LEMON TARTS

3 eggs
3 lemons (9 tablespoons lemon
  juice)
2 tablespoons butter

1½ cups sugar
grated rind of 3 lemons
miniature tart shells

Melt butter, add sugar; then grated rind and juice of lemons. Add beaten eggs, stir thoroughly and cook over very low heat until thick. When cold put into miniature tart shells.

Eve Conlon

For a flakier pie crust, measure the flour and shortening into a mixing bowl and chill in the refrigerator for an hour before mixing.

LIME FLUFF PIE

YIELD: 2 — 9" pies

2½ cups applesauce
1 — 3 ounce package lime flavored
  gelatin
1 cup sugar
2 tablespoons lime juice
⅛ teaspoon grated lime rind

1 — 13 ounce can evaporated milk,
  chilled
2 — 9" ready-made graham
  cracker pie crusts
lime twists

Heat applesauce in a medium size pan; stir in gelatin; add sugar, lime juice and rind, mixing well. Whip evaporated milk until thickened. Fold milk into gelatin mixture. Spoon mixture into pie crusts. Chill until set. Serve.

Amanda Skaggs

LIME OR LEMON PIE

1 — 6 ounce can frozen lemonade
  OR limeade concentrate
1 — 14 ounce can sweetened condensed milk

1 — 13 ounce container whipped
  topping
food coloring if desired
pie shell or crust

Mix concentrate, condensed milk, whipped topping and food coloring together and pour into baked pie shell or unbaked graham cracker crust. Refrigerate.

Jean Finger

LITTLE PECAN TARTS

OVEN: 350° 15 minutes; 250° 10 minutes

1¾ sticks butter
2 cups flour
2 — 3 ounce packages cream
  cheese
¼ teaspoon salt
2 eggs, beaten

1½ cups brown sugar
2 tablespoons butter, melted
2 cups pecans
¼ teaspoon salt
1 teaspoon vanilla

Combine butter, flour, cream cheese and salt; blend well. Break off pieces about as big as a walnut and press into tiny muffin tins. Bake at 350° for 15 minutes.

Combine eggs, brown sugar, melted butter, pecans, salt and vanilla for filling. Mix ingredients thoroughly and fill baked tart shells. Bake in 250° for 10 minutes.

Mrs. M.M. Alsobrook

MACAROON PIE

OVEN: 300° 30 minutes

12 soda crackers	½ cup pecans, chopped
12 dates, cut fine	1 cup sugar
3 egg whites	½ pint whipping cream
1 teaspoon almond extract	¼ teaspoon baking powder

Roll soda crackers finely. Chop dates and pecans and add to sugar and baking powder; blend. Beat egg whites until stiff, add almond extract and blend well. Fold in egg whites to dates mixture. Pour into well-buttered pie pan. Bake at 300° for 30 minutes. Serve warm or cold with whipped cream.

Tina Markham

MANGO COBBLER

OVEN: 400° 30-40 minutes

4 cups ripe, sliced mangos	1 tablespoon lemon juice
¾ cup sugar	dash of salt
1 tablespoon flour	6 tablespoons butter
½ teaspoon cinnamon	6 tablespoons water, if needed
¼ teaspoon nutmeg	your favorite pie crust recipe

Place sliced mango in a 9″ square pan. Sprinkle other ingredients, one at a time over mango slices. Add butter on top and water, if needed. Top mixture with your favorite pie crust. Bake in 400° oven for 30-40 minutes.

Elizabeth McAlister

MERINGUE TOPPING FOR PIES

1 tablespoon cornstarch	1 teaspoon fresh lemon juice
2 tablespoons cold water	3 egg whites
½ cup boiling water	6 tablespoons sugar

Mix cornstarch and cold water, after well blended, add boiling water. Bring mixture to a boil over medium heat for 2 minutes or until thickened. Remove from heat and set pan in cold water to bring mixture to room temperature. Add lemon juice to egg whites and beat until frothy. Add sugar, gradually, to egg whites and beat until satin smooth. Add cornstarch all at once and beat until well blended.

Use with your favorite pie for topping.

Emily Gasper

Use a clean, non-porous bowl for whipping meringues. Before whipping wash the bowl with cold salted water, then rinse under cold running water. Do not dry. Hidden grease on the bowl will cut the volume of the egg whites.

MOLASSES PIE

OVEN: 300°-350° 45-60 minutes

1 cup sugar
1 cup syrup
½ to ¾ cup butter
4 eggs

1 teaspoon vanilla
2 tablespoons flour
unbaked pie shell

Combine all ingredients and blend until smooth. Pour into unbaked pie shell and bake in 300°-350° oven for 45 to 60 minutes.
Cane syrup is good to use in this recipe.

Florrie Chandler

MOTHER PETERSON'S PUMPKIN PIE

OVEN: 450° 10 minutes; 350° until done   YIELD: 2 pies

1 big can pumpkin
1½ cups brown sugar
1 teaspoon salt
1 teaspoon ginger

2 teaspoons cinnamon
4 eggs
2 cups milk
2 unbaked pie shells

Combine pumpkin, sugar, salt and spices. Add eggs, well beaten, and milk. Pour batter into unbaked pie shells. Bake in hot oven, 450°, for 10 minutes; reduce heat to 350° and bake until done.
My husband's mother, Mrs. O.A. Peterson of Prairie du Sac, Wisconsin, visits in Fort Pierce often. She is an excellent cook and has passed on to me many delicious recipes.

Olive Peterson

When making pastry, melt butter or lard and beat it to a cream before mixing with the flour — only half the usual quantity is required.

MRS. OLAF SIMONSEN'S PEANUT BUTTER PIE

OVEN: 350° 15-20 minutes

⅓ cup peanut butter
¾ cup confectioners sugar
9″ pastry shell, baked

3 egg yolks, beaten
2 tablespoons butter
1 teaspoon vanilla

Cream Filling:
⅓ cup flour
½ cup sugar
⅛ teaspoons salt
2 cups milk, scalded

Meringue:
3 egg whites
9 tablespoons sugar
¼ teaspoon cream of tartar
1 teaspoon cornstarch

Blend peanut butter and sugar together as for pastry until well mixed and mealy. Spread about ⅔ of mixture over baked pie crust. Reserve remainder for top.

Combine flour, sugar, and salt together; blend in scalded milk. Cook mixture over boiling water until thickened, stirring constantly. Blend mixture into slightly beaten egg yolks. Return to double boiler and cook about 2 minutes more. Add butter and vanilla. Turn into pie shell and top with meringue.

For meringue, beat egg whites until stiff enough to hold their shape. Add cream of tartar and beat until blended. Mix sugar and cornstarch and add to egg whites. Beat until very stiff and shiny. Spread on filled pie shell and sprinkle on remaining peanut butter crumbs. Bake in 350° oven for 15-20 minutes. Cool away from draft.

Mrs. Olaf Simonsen

MUD PIE

YIELD: 8 servings

1½ cups chocolate sandwich cookies with vanilla filling, crushed
⅓ cup melted oleo
3 pints coffee ice cream
1 tablespoon butter

1 ounce unsweetened chocolate
½ cup sugar
¼ cup water
½ teaspoon vanilla

Mix melted oleo and cookie crumbs together. Place mixture in a 9″ pie plate. Refrigerate for an hour. Spread softened ice cream in chocolate crumb crust. Freeze until ready to serve; pie should be covered. Just before serving, top with chocolate sauce: melt chocolate and oleo over low heat. Stir in sugar and water. Cook, stirring constantly until sauce is as thick as you like. Add vanilla.

Other variations include graham cracker crust with peppermint ice cream and chocolate sauce. For an even richer dessert, just before serving, cover pie with whipped cream and then top with sauce.

Joan Kite

Add a nutty flavor to your next pie crust; include 1 tablespoon of poppy seeds when adding the flour into pie pastry.

MY FAVORITE PUMPKIN PIE

OVEN: 450° 12 minutes; 320° 1 hour

1 can pumpkin
4 eggs
½ cup brown sugar
½ cup white sugar

1 heaping teaspoon pumpkin spice
1½ cups light cream
unbaked pastry shell

Beat eggs, add sugars, spice and milk and eggs to pumpkin and mix well. Pour batter into unbaked pastry shell and bake for 12 minutes at 450°. Reduce heat to 350° and bake for about 1 hour or until pie does not adhere to knife.

Harriet Walting

NEVER-FAIL PIE CRUST

OVEN: 450° 10-15 minutes

4 cups unsifted flour
1¼ tablespoons sugar
2 teaspoons salt
1¾ cups shortening

2 tablespoons white vinegar
1 large egg
¼ cup water

Have all ingredients at room temperature. Use shortening only, no substitutes. Spoon flour lightly into measuring cup.

Combine flour, sugar and salt in a bowl and mix well with a fork. Add shortening and mix until all is crumbly.

In a small bowl, beat together water, egg and vinegar, add lightly to flour until all ingredients are moistened. Discard left over liquid. Divide dough into 4 parts, flatten out dough and wrap each one in plastic or waxed paper. Chill for ½ hour before rolling. Dough can be frozen for future use if desired.

Bake at 450° for about 10-15 minutes or until brown.

Prick crust with fork all over before baking a pie.

Gladys Grammer

NEW YORK STYLE CHEESE PIE

OVEN: 350° 20-25 minutes; 450° 5 minutes

1¼ cups cream cheese (about 20 ounces)
⅞ cup sugar
½ teaspoon vanilla
3 eggs

Topping:
12 ounces soured cream
⅛ cup sugar
few drops vanilla

Preheat oven to 350°. Cream the cheese, sugar, and vanilla for about 15 minutes. Scrape sides while creaming mixture. Add eggs and beat for additional 5 minutes. Place mixture in graham cracker crust in 9" pie plate. Bake for 20-25 minutes until firm. Let cool for 15 minutes, then add topping. Blend soured cream, sugar and vanilla together. Spread on top of pie. Return to oven after increasing temperature to 450° and bake for 5 minutes. Cool.

Add your favorite topping of fruit, strawberries, cherries or blueberries.

Emily Johnson

NORWEGIAN PIE

OVEN: 350° 30-35 minutes   YIELD: 2 — 9″ pies

1½ cups sugar
1 cup flour
2 whole eggs
2 teaspoons baking powder

½ teaspoon vanilla
½ teaspoon salt
2 cups diced apples
1 cup chopped English walnuts

Combine sugar, flour and unbeaten eggs. Mix well. Add baking powder, salt and vanilla and mix. Stir in nuts and apples. Pour into greased pie plates. Bake for 30-35 minutes in 350° oven.

This recipe was given to me by Eleanor Tennant of Fort Pierce in 1969. It is very good. I usually add a little less sugar as pie is very sweet.

Marilyn Dorsette

PAPER BAG APPLE PIE

OVEN: 425° 1 hour

1 unbaked 9″ pie shell
3-4 large baking apples, about 2½
   pounds, to equal about 7 cups
½ cup sugar
2 tablespoons flour
2 tablespoons lemon juice

½ teaspoon nutmeg
½ cup sugar (for topping)
½ cup flour (for topping)
½ cup OR 1 stick butter OR margarine

Make pastry shell using packaged mix, or your own, or use unbaked pie shell.

Pare, core and quarter apples, then halve each quarter cross-wise to make chunks. You should have about 7 cups. Place pieces in bowl and combine with ½ cup sugar and 2 tablespoons flour and nutmeg. Spoon pieces into pie shell and drizzle with lemon juice.

Combine ½ cup sugar and ½ cup flour; cut in butter and sprinkle over apples. Slide pie into heavy brown paper bag, large enough to cover pie loosely. Fold open end over 2 times and fasten with paper clips. Place on large cookie sheet for easy handling. Bake in hot oven, 425° for 1 hour. Apples will be tender and top bubbling. Split bag open and remove pie. Cool on wire rack. Serve plain or with cheese or ice cream.

R.M. Croghan

PEACH COBBLER I

OVEN: 350° 35 minutes

¾ cup sugar
¾ cup flour
¾ cup milk
1 teaspoon baking powder

1 large can peaches OR 3 cups
   fresh peaches
1 stick butter OR margarine

Melt butter in a dish. Mix sugar, flour and baking powder; add milk. Pour into dish with butter. Add peaches and 1 cup of juice (if using canned peaches). Bake at 350° for 35 minutes or until brown.

Lee Anita Williams

PEACH COBBLER II

OVEN: 350° 1 hour

1 large can sliced peaches
½ cup sugar
1 stick pure butter

Topping:
1 stick butter, melted
½ cup flour
½ cup sugar
1 egg
1 tablespoon vanilla

Melt butter in pan you will use for baking cobbler. Then add peaches and sugar; stir lightly.

Mix topping ingredients together and spoon over top of peaches; be careful so topping doesn't sink in. Then sprinkle sugar over top, just enough so you can see it. Cook for 1 hour in 350° oven or until done.

Best when served warm. Other fruits may be substituted for peaches.

Stella Dicks

PEACH DUMPLINGS

OVEN: 450° 10 minutes; 350° 25 minutes

6 peaches
2 cups flour
½ teaspoon salt
3 teaspoons baking powder
4 tablespoons shortening
¾ to 1 cup milk

Syrup for dumplings:
1 cup water
1 cup sugar
4 tablespoons butter
1 teaspoon cinnamon

Sift flour with salt and baking powder; cut in shortening until mixture resembles coarse crumbs; stir in enough milk to make a moist, not wet, dough. Turn out on a floured surface, roll into ¼" thickness. Cut in squares large enough to cover peach; which has been peeled and stone removed. Fold corners of dough to center and pinch edges securely. Place dumplings 2" apart in a dripping pan and pour syrup mixture over.

To make syrup mixture, boil water, sugar and butter for 3 minutes, then add cinnamon. Bake at 450° for 10 minutes then reduce heat to 350° and bake for 25 minutes or until peaches are done.

Helen Schulz

PEACHES 'N CREAM PIE

OVEN: 400° 32-37 minutes   YIELD: 1 — 9" pie

1 unbaked 9" pie shell
⅓ cup sugar
2 tablespoons all-purpose flour
¼ teaspoon ground nutmeg

¼ teaspoon grated lemon rind
1 cup commercial sour cream
5-6 medium peaches, peeled and
    thinly sliced

Bake pie shell in 400° oven for 7 minutes, set aside. Combine remaining ingredients, mixing well. Spoon into pie shell. Bake for 25-30 additional minutes.

Pearl M. Wyse

PEANUT BUTTER PIE

¾ cup light brown sugar
4½ tablespoons flour
1½ tablespoons cornstarch
½ teaspoon salt
2 cups milk
5 egg yolks, slightly beaten
½ cup peanut butter

Meringue:
5 egg whites
¼ teaspoon cream of tartar
¼ teaspoon salt
½ teaspoon vanilla
10 tablespoons sugar

Blend sugar, flour, cornstarch and salt in the top of double boiler. Gradually add milk and stir over boiling water until mixture starts to thicken. Mix ½ cup of mixture with egg yolks and stir into remaining mixture. Continue cooking until thick. Mix ½ to ¾ cup of mixture with peanut butter. Spread this mixture on bottom of baked 9″ pie shell. Add remaining mixture and top with meringue.

For meringue, beat egg whites until quite foamy; add cream of tartar, salt and vanilla; then add sugar, one spoonful at a time, beating after each addition until stiff peaks form.

Jean Huck

PECAN PIE I

OVEN: 375° 40-50 minutes

3 eggs
1 cup sugar
½ teaspoon salt
2 tablespoons butter, melted
½ cup dark corn syrup

½ cup whipping cream
1 teaspoon vanilla
¼ cup brandy
1 cup pecan halves

Heat oven to 375°. Prepare pastry. In mixing bowl, beat eggs, sugar, salt, butter, syrup and cream. Stir in vanilla, brandy and pecans. Pour into pastry lined pan and bake 40-50 minutes or until filling is set and pastry is nicely browned. Cool, but serve warm with vanilla ice cream.

Gladys Baldwin

PECAN PIE II

OVEN: 325° 1 hour

½ cup sugar
1 cup sugar cane syrup
3 eggs
4 tablespoons melted butter

1 teaspoon vanilla extract
1 cup pecans
1 tablespoon salt

Cook sugar and syrup until sugar has hardened down. Let mixture boil up, but don't scorch. Beat eggs slightly and add hot syrup to eggs in a small stream, beating eggs to keep them from scrambling. Reverse and pour mixture into syrup; continue to beat. Add melted butter, vanilla, salt and nuts. Let mixture cool. Pour into unbaked pie shell which is lined with additional nuts, if desired.

Bake at 325° for 1 hour, or until done.

Loretta Hunter

PECAN PIE III

OVEN: 325° 1 hour

½ cup sugar
1 tablespoon self-rising flour
¼ teaspoon salt
3 eggs, slightly beaten

1 cup green label corn syrup
1½ cups chopped pecans
1 tablespoon vanilla flavoring
unbaked pie shell

Mix ingredients together in order given. Blend well. Pour into unbaked pie shell and bake for 1 hour at 325°.

Jackie Brice

PERFECT PIE CRUST

4 cups flour
1 tablespoon sugar
1 tablespoon vinegar

2 teaspoons salt
1¾ cups solid shortening
1 egg

Mix flour, sugar and salt; add shortening until crumbly. Beat together ½ cup water with vinegar and egg. Mix well. Make into 5 balls, wrap each individually and place in plastic bag. Place in refrigerator until needed.
If planning to use right away, chill for ½ hour.
When using after freezing, lay out one or 2 balls at night and they will be ready to use by morning.

Olive Smith

PIE DOUGH

OVEN: 425° 10-12 or 30-40 min. YIELD: 2 single crusts or 1 double crust

2 cups all purpose flour
1 teaspoon salt
1 cup shortening

1 egg, beaten
1 tablespoon white vinegar
3 tablespoons water

Work flour, salt and shortening by hand until shortening is well blended. Add beaten egg, vinegar and water. Blend well. Divide into two balls and roll each ball between floured wax paper.
Bake one shell at 425° for 10-12 minutes. Bake two shells at 425° for 30-40 minutes.

Ruth Lester

Use a greased knife when cutting a meringue pie to prevent pulling and sticking.

PIE SUPERB

OVEN: 350° 40-45 minutes

Crust:
2 sticks butter OR margarine
1 tablespoon sugar
1 cup chopped pecans

Filling:
1 — 8 ounce package cream cheese
3 cups confectioners sugar
2 — 9 ounce containers whipped
topping, thawed
2 cans pie cherries OR blueberries

Cream butter and sugar together in a large mixing bowl. Add flour in small amounts, mixing well after each addition. Add nuts and mix well. Press firmly into 9 x 14 baking dish or pan and bake at 350° for 40-45 minutes, until lightly browned. Allow to cool. Beat cream and gradually add confectioners sugar, beating after each addition. Fold in thawed whipped topping and spread over cooled crust. Spread pie filling evenly over topping mixture. Refrigerate until ready to serve.

This is much better if made in the morning or 4-6 hours before serving.

Mrs. Arthur Causier

PINA COLADA PIE

YIELD: 6 servings

1 — 3 ounce package cream cheese,
softened
2 tablespoons sugar
⅓ cup milk
2 tablespoons light rum

1 — 8 ounce can crushed pineapple
in juice, drained
1⅓ cups flaked coconut
1 — 8 ounce container frozen
whipped topping, thawed
1 — 8" or 9" graham cracker crust

Combine cream cheese, sugar, milk, rum, ½ of the pineapple and the coconut in electric blender. Cover and blend at medium speed for 30 seconds. Fold into whipped topping. Spoon into crust and sprinkle with additional coconut, toasted, if desired. Freeze until firm, about 4 hours. Let stand at room temperature for 5 minutes (or longer for softer texture) before cutting. Garnish with remaining pineapple and orange slices, if desired. Store any left-over pie in freezer.

Ruth Wiggins

Try beating a pinch of cornstarch into egg whites along with the sugar when preparing meringue. This will keep the meringue from falling.

PINEAPPLE CHEESE TARTS

OVEN: 375° 20 minutes   YIELD: 12

1½ cups graham cracker crumbs,
  about 18 squares
1 — 8 ounce package cream cheese
1 — 3 ounce package cream cheese
⅛ teaspoon cinnamon
1 — 1 pound, 4 ounce can crushed
  pineapple, well drained

5 tablespoons sugar
¼ cup (½ stick) butter, melted
½ cup sugar
1 egg
½ cup sour cream
1 tablespoon sugar

Line muffin cups with paper liners and set aside. In a bowl, combine crumbs, 5 tablespoons sugar, and butter; blend thoroughly. Set aside 2 tablespoons of mixture for topping. Press remaining crumbs on bottoms and sides of paper cups to form shell. In a medium mixing bowl, beat cheeses until smooth. Add ½ cup sugar, cinnamon and egg; beat until thoroughly blended. Add pineapple; beat at low speed only until blended. Spoon mixture into crumb shells. Bake for 20 minutes. Meanwhile, combine sour cream and 1 tablespoon sugar. Remove tarts from oven and top each with about 2 teaspoonfuls of sour cream mixture. Sprinkle with reserved crumbs. Allow to cool to room temperature. Chill.

Elizabeth Leonard

PRALINE PUMPKIN PIE

OVEN: 450° 10 minutes; 350° 50-60 minutes

⅓ cup chopped pecans
⅓ cup brown sugar
3 tablespoons soft butter
3 slightly beaten eggs
½ cup sugar
½ cup brown sugar
2 tablespoons flour

¾ teaspoon salt
¾ teaspoon cinnamon
½ teaspoon ginger
¼ teaspoon mace
¼ teaspoon pumpkin spice
1½ cups pumpkin
1¼ cups hot light cream

Combine chopped pecans with brown sugar and soft butter. Press into bottom of pie pan. Prick sides and bake for 10 minutes at 450°.

Combine remaining ingredients except hot cream and blend well. When blended, gradually add hot cream to mixture and blend well. Pour mixture into baked crust and bake at 350° for 50-60 minutes.

Joline Frederick

Flavor apple or pear pies with a combination of cardamon and coriander seeds.

PUMPKIN CHIFFON PIE I

1 envelope unflavored gelatin
1½ cups canned pumpkin
½ cup milk
½ teaspoon ginger
½ teaspoon nutmeg

½ teaspoon cinnamon
½ teaspoon salt
⅓ cup sugar
3 eggs, separated
baked pastry shell

Add one half cup sugar, pumpkin, milk, salt and spices to slightly beaten egg yolks. Cook mixture until thick using double boiler. Pour cold water in a small bowl and sprinkle gelatin on top of water. Add gelatin to hot pumpkin mixture and mix thoroughly, cool. When mixture begins to thicken, add remaining sugar and fold in stiffly beaten egg whites. Pour into previously baked pie shell. Chill in refrigerator. Pie may be garnished with whipped cream just before serving.

This is delicious served in a gingersnap or graham cracker crust.

Louise Gaines

PUMPKIN CHIFFON PIE II

YIELD: 2 pies

2½ envelopes unflavored gelatin
1½ cups dark brown sugar
1 teaspoon salt
2 teaspoons cinnamon
1 teaspoon nutmeg
1 cup milk
¼ cup water
6 eggs, separated

2 cans pumpkin pie filling
¼ cup granulated sugar
2 graham cracker crusts
1 pint whipping cream
¾ cup chopped walnuts, chopped
fine
2 baked pastry shells

In a saucepan, combine gelatin, brown sugar, salt, cinnamon and nutmeg; add milk and water. Beat slightly with fork the egg yolks and add to saucepan. Blend mixture; then add pie filling and place mixture over medium heat. Stir constantly with wire whip until mixture is very hot; just to boiling point. Remove from heat and add ¼ cup chopped nuts. Place saucepan in refrigerator to cool. Stir occasionally while mixture is cooling.

Meanwhile, beat egg whites and granulated sugar until stiff. When filling is very cold, being careful not to let it set, fold filling into beaten egg whites. Divide mixture between 2 pie crusts and place in refrigerator to chill and set. Top with whipped cream and sprinkle with chopped walnuts and a little nutmeg.

I submitted this recipe to the Vero Beach Press Journal in 1973 and it was used in a special Thanksgiving section.

Rosaila Maggiacomo

Superfine sugar gives better results when beating egg whites since its fineness interferes less with air bubbles in the beaten eggs.

PUMPKIN ICE CREAM PIE

baked pastry shell
1 cup pumpkin puree
¼ teaspoon nutmeg
1 cup sugar
½ teaspoon ginger

½ teaspoon salt
1 teaspoon cinnamon
1 cup whipped cream OR prepared
   whipped topping mix
vanilla ice cream

Line baked pastry shell with ½ inch of ice cream. Place shell into freezer. Blend together pumpkin, nutmeg, sugar, ginger, salt and cinnamon. Fold mixture into 1 cup of whipping cream or topping. Add to pie shell and chill until firm.

This is much lighter than traditional pumpkin pie. It is terrific for dessert after a heavy meal; very rich, but still light.

Kim Lewis

QUAKERTOWN PIE

OVEN: 350°

1 cup brown sugar
½ cup corn syrup
2 tablespoons flour
1 egg
2 cups hot milk
½ teaspoon vanilla

2 cups flour
1 cup brown sugar
1 teaspoon soda
½ cup shortening
½ teaspoon salt
2 unbaked pie crusts

Combine first five ingredients in saucepan and cook until mixture thickens like cream. Add vanilla. Pour mixture into 2 unbaked pie shells. Mix remaining ingredients and blend into crumbs, like pie dough, and sprinkle on top of filling. Bake in 350° oven until done.

If desired, add ½ cup chopped hickory nuts, walnuts, or pecans to the crumbs. This is an old Pennsylvania Dutch recipe from the area where I grew up.

Pauline Beers

QUICK APRICOT PASTRIES

OVEN: 425° 20 minutes

YIELD: 12

1 package refrigerated crescent
   rolls (8 rolls)
½ cup apricot jam
1 cup sour cream

1 egg, beaten
1 tablespoon sugar
½ teaspoon vanilla

Unroll crescent rolls and pat into bottom of buttered 13 x 9 x 2 baking dish. Spread jam on top of rolls. Bake at 425° for 15 minutes; remove from oven.

Combine remaining ingredients and blend well. Pour evenly over rolls and return dish to oven. Bake for 5-6 minutes more.

Serve warm.

Mrs. Jack G. Rose, Jr.

RITZ PIE

OVEN: 325°-350° 30 minutes

3 egg whites
1 cup sugar
14 Ritz crackers
½ teaspoon baking powder
½ teaspoon vanilla

⅔ cup chopped pecans
1 cup whipping cream
1-3 tablespoons sifted confectioners sugar
½ teaspoon vanilla

Break crackers into 4 pieces each. Beat egg whites until very stiff. Gradually add baking powder, sugar and vanilla. Fold in coarsely broken crackers and chopped pecans. Bake in greased pie pan in 325°-350° oven for 30 minutes. Cool. Whip cream until stiff. Fold in confectioners sugar and vanilla. Top pie with whipped cream mixture and chill.

A few tablespoons of coffee flavored liqueur folded into the whipped cream gives a delightful flavor to this dessert.

Mrs. Edward Jackson, Jr.

RUM CREAM PIE

1 tablespoon gelatin
¼ cup cold water
½ cup sugar
½ teaspoon salt
4 tablespoons cornstarch
2 cups milk
4 eggs, separated

6 ounces chocolate bits
1 teaspoon vanilla
¼ cup rum
¼ teaspoon cream of tartar
½ cup sugar
1 cup whipping cream
1 baked pie shell

Soften gelatin in cold water. Combine sugar, salt, cornstarch in a saucepan and gradually add milk. Cook over low heat, stirring constantly, until mixture thickens. Beat yolks and stir some of the hot mixture into them slowly. Return mixture to heat and cook for 2 minutes. Melt chocolate over hot water. Remove from heat and blend 1½ cups of custard with the chocolate. Blend well. Add vanilla to chocolate mixture and pour into baked shell. Add gelatin to remaining custard and cool mixture to lukewarn. Add rum and mix well. Beat egg whites and cream of tartar until stiff. Gradually add ½ cup sugar. Beat. Fold into custard. Pour over chocolate custard and chill. Serve topped with whipped cream and garnish with shaved chocolate.

Substitute 1 teaspoon rum flavoring for rum.

Mrs. Richard Cook

Grated orange peel added to a meringue creates a delightful zesty flavor.

SHONEY'S STRAWBERRY PIE

1 baked deep-dish pie shell
1 cup sugar
3 tablespoons cornstarch

4 tablespoons strawberry flavored
gelatin
1 cup boiling water
1 quart fresh strawberries

Dissolve sugar, cornstarch, and gelatin in boiling water. Place on stove and boil mixture until it thickens and coats spoon.
Fix strawberries and fill pie shell. Pour mixture over strawberries. Chill and top with whipped cream.
This can be made the day before.

Carol I. Browder

SKY HIGH LIME PIE

OVEN: 350° 12 minutes

1 — 9″ baked pie shell
2 cups sugar
4 tablespoons cornstarch
4 tablespoons flour
¼ teaspoon salt
2 cups water

4 eggs, separated
1 tablespoon grated lemon rind
6 tablespoons lemon juice
2 tablespoons butter OR margarine
¼ teaspoon lemon extract

Mix 1½ cups sugar with cornstarch, flour and salt in a medium bowl. Reserve remaining sugar for meringue.
Heat water to boiling in a medium-size saucepan. Lower heat to medium and slowly add sugar mixture, stirring gently but constantly for 5-7 minutes, or until mixture holds a line when cut with a spoon. Remove from heat at once; do not let mixture boil. Beat egg yolks slightly in a small bowl; stir in a generous ½ cup of hot mixture and quickly stir egg yolk mixture back into mixture in sauce pan. Cook, stirring constantly, over medium heat for 3 minutes or until mixture thickens again and mounds softly. Remove from heat and stir in lemon juice and rind and butter. Mix until completely blended.
Pour into cooled pastry shell.
Beat egg whites with lemon extract until foamy-white and double in volume, using a medium bowl. Sprinkle with remaining ½ cup sugar; adding sugar a tablespoon at a time and beating all the time until sugar is completely dissolved and meringue stands in firm peaks.
Pile meringue onto hot filling, spreading to edge of crust, this keeps meringue from shrinking, and bake in moderate oven, 350°, for 12 minutes or until peaks are golden brown.

Norma Isenhour

To increase the quantity of beaten egg whites in meringue, add 1 tablespoon of water for each egg white.

SOUTHERN CHESS PIE

OVEN: 350°

1 stick butter	4 whole eggs
1 teaspoon vanilla	1-2 cups cut up pecans
½ teaspoon salt	pie crust mix, OR your favorite
1 package light brown sugar	recipe

Mix all ingredients until the butter is completely melted; do not pre-cook. For crust, make dough according to package instructions or your favorite recipe. Use ice water and handle as little as possible. Use muffin tins for shells. Fill with mixture and bake in slow oven, 350°, until done. Stick toothpick in tart, it should come out clean and dry if pie is done. Serve individual tarts with whipped cream.

This easy dessert is always a hit at small luncheons and bridge parties.

Chess pie is the original southern pecan pie. It has been handed down through "word of mouth" in our family.

Mary-Frazier Palmore

STRAWBERRY PIE I

1 quart fresh berries, any fresh berry can be used	3½ tablespoons cornstarch
1 cup PLUS 1 tablespoon sugar	1 baked pie shell

Wash and drain 1 pint of the best berries. Place berries in pie shell; if they are large, cut in half. Wash and drain the remaining berries. Add ½ cup plus 1 tablespoon sugar to these berries and place in a warm part of the range to extract juice. Mix juiced berries with cornstarch and bring to a boil. Cook until thick and clear, stirring constantly. Add food coloring if desired. Add ½ cup sugar and stir until dissolved. This mixture is poured over the berries in the pie shell. Chill and serve with whipped cream.

Elsie Lunceford

STRAWBERRY PIE II

1 baked pie crust, cooled	2 tablespoons strawberry flavored
½ cup sugar	gelatin
1 tablespoon cornstarch	1 quart strawberries, fresh,
½ cup water	cleaned and hulled

Mix sugar, cornstarch and water together and cook until mixture is thick and clear. Add gelatin when mixture is cool. Place berries in pie shell and pour mixture over berries. Refrigerate to set. Serve with whipped cream.

Rose Rumsey

Cut soft pie meringues easily by first dipping the knife into hot water or rubbing it with butter.

SWEET POTATO PECAN PIE

OVEN: 425° 15 minutes; 375° 25-30 minutes

2 cups sweet potatoes
5 tablespoons melted butter
¾ cup firmly packed brown sugar
4 eggs
¼ teaspoon salt

1 teaspoon cinnamon
¼ teaspoon mace
⅓ cup broken pecans
2 cups milk
unbaked pie shell

Mash sweet potatoes and combine with butter, brown sugar, eggs, salt, cinnamon and mace. Add pecans. Blend in milk. Pour mixture into unbaked pie shell and bake in hot, 425°, oven for 15 minutes. Reduce heat to 375° and bake for 25-30 minutes longer or until firm.

Mary Lee Ramsey

TANGERINE CHIFFON PIE

YIELD: 6-8 servings

1 envelope unflavored gelatin
½ cup sugar
dash of salt
4 egg yolks
½ cup lemon juice
¾ cup tangerine juice

½ teaspoon grated lemon peel
½ teaspoon grated tangerine peel
4 egg whites
⅓ cup sugar
1 baked 9″ pastry shell OR crumb crust

Mix gelatin with ½ cup sugar and salt in a small saucepan. Beat egg yolks and fruit juices together; stir into gelatin mixture. Cook and stir mixture over low heat just until mixture comes to a boil. Remove from heat and add grated peels. Chill mixture, stirring now and then, until partially set. Beat egg whites until soft peaks form; gradually add ⅓ cup sugar and beat until stiff. Fold in gelatin mixture. Pile into the pie shell and chill until firm. Spread with whipped cream or whipped topping and garnish with tangerine sections.

Mrs. Charles A. Proctor

VANILLA WAFER PIE

vanilla wafers
½ cup flaked coconut
⅓ cup chopped pecans
⅓ cup brown sugar
3 tablespoons butter OR oleo

1 package instant vanilla pudding mix
1½ cups milk
1 cup whipped cream

Line bottom and sides of a pie pan with wafers. Into skillet, place coconut, pecans and sugar and butter. Cook, stirring until mixture is a nice golden brown. Do not overcook. Remove from heat and as it cools, stir occasionally so that it becomes crumbs.

After mixture is completely cooled, and very crumbly, sprinkle half over wafers in pan. In the meantime, mix pudding, milk and cream together and pour over wafers and crumbs in pie pan. Sprinkle other half of crumbs on top. Chill for at least 4 hours.

Elinor Blum

VINEGAR PIE

OVEN: 350° 45-50 minutes

4 eggs
1¼ cups sugar
¼ cup butter
1½ tablespoons vinegar
¼ cup margarine, melted

1 teaspoon vanilla extract
1 — 9″ unbaked pie crust, defrosted, OR pie crust you have made

Preheat oven to 350°. In a large bowl, combine eggs, sugar, and butter. Add vinegar and vanilla and mix well. Pour into pie shell and bake until firm, about 45-50 minutes. Cool on rack and garnish with chopped nuts or whipped topping if desired.

Allie McMillan

WHOOPIE PIES

OVEN: 350° 8-10 minutes

⅓ cup oleo
1 cup sugar
1 egg
1 cup milk
1 teaspoon vanilla
2 cups flour
½ teaspoon salt
1¼ teaspoons baking soda

5 tablespoons cocoa
2 tablespoons oleo
½ cup milk
2 tablespoons flour
½ cup solid shortening
½ cup sugar
1 teaspoon vanilla
dash of salt

Add first nine (9) ingredients in the order given and mix well. Place batter by tablespoons on a greased cookie sheet and bake in 350° oven for 8-10 minutes; until they are puffy.

Cook together 2 tablespoons oleo, ½ cup milk and 2 tablespoons flour, until mixture is smooth and creamy. Cool mixture. Then add shortening, ½ cup sugar, vanilla and salt. Place mixture in pies as filling.

Anita Smith

Try sprinkling fresh coconut over meringue before browning — simply delicious.

POULTRY

AMANDA'S COOKED AND CRUMBLED CASSEROLE

YIELD: 4 servings

2 cups cubed left-over turkey
3 slices bacon, cooked and crumbled
1 — 6¼ ounce package quick cooking rice

⅓ cup raisins
¼ cup toasted almonds
2 tablespoons margarine
¼ cup green onion salad dressing
2 cups water

Pour a little boiling water over raisins to plump them up. Pat raisins dry and set aside for later use. Fix rice in water and butter; cover tightly until water is absorbed. Add raisins, turkey, and almonds to rice. Mix well. Add dressing and mix well again. If mixture is too cool, heat in oven for a few minutes, using a pan wrapped in alumnium foil to keep from messing up another pan. Serve with crumbled bacon on top.

Amanda Skaggs

ARROZ CON POLLO
(CHICKEN WITH RICE)

YIELD: 6-8 servings

2 — 2½ pound whole chickens
1 package rice
1 — 15 ounce can tomato sauce
2 large green bell peppers
2 medium onions
½ teaspoon comino
2 teaspoons salt
½ teaspoon oregano

½ teaspoon pepper
3 garlic cloves
1 cup dry wine
½ cup olive oil
1 can asparagus
1 small jar pimentos
1 small bay leaf
1 small can peas

Filet raw chicken and cut each into 8 pieces. Season pieces with salt, pepper, oregano, garlic and comino. In a large pot with lid, heat ½ cup olive oil until it boils, then sauté chicken for 5 minutes; add chopped onions and green peppers and cook for 5 minutes more. Next, add tomato sauce and cook for 10 minutes. Then make a bouillon from the chicken bones. To make bouillon, boil 4 cups of water with onion, green pepper and salt for ½ hour. Add rice and 3 cups bouillon to the chicken. After 10 minutes, add wine, bay leaf and cook for 10 minutes on high heat. Turn temperature to medium and cook for 10 minutes.

To serve, decorate with asparagus, peas and pimento. For coloring the rice, add 1 teaspoon of bijol condiment.

Carmen Prieto

To make chicken more tender and for a delightfully different flavor, soak chicken in buttermilk and let stand for an hour before frying.

ARROZ RELLENO
(STUFFED RICE)

OVEN: 350° 30 minutes

YIELD: 8-10 servings

3 fryers
3 stalks celery, chopped
1 teaspoon oregano
½ teaspoon cumin
2 cups uncooked rice
1 jar stuffed green olives
2 onions, chopped

½ green pepper, chopped
2 bay leaves
salt
pepper
1 bottle capers
1 pint sour cream

Brown onion, celery and green pepper in a little bacon drippings or oleo; add fryers, whole or cut up. Add all seasonings and about 1 cup water. Cook chicken over low flame, covered, until very tender and almost off the bone. Add water, a little at a time, as needed. Do not let it dry out. Save the broth. Allow fryers to cool, then bone and tear meat into bite-size pieces.

Cook rice using broth and extra water, if needed. Grease a large rectangular pan, about 2" or 3" high; preferably a dish the rice can also be served in. Layer ingredients into the pan or dish beginning with rice, then chicken, capers, olives, and sour cream. Continue alternating layers in this fashion until all ingredients are used. ending with sour cream. Sprinkle some Parmesan cheese lightly over the top, dot with butter and place in 350° oven for about 30 minutes or until thoroughly heated.

This dish can be prepared the night before serving.

Cathy Birnhak

AUNT PEARL'S HAWAIIAN CHICKEN CURRY

1 large chicken (3½ pounds or
  more)
1 whole onion
1 carrot
celery tops if available
1 clove garlic
1 bay leaf
salt
pepper

Sauce:
chicken broth
1 cup hot milk
2 cans cream of chicken soup
2 teaspoons ground ginger
3 chopped green onions
1 — 4 ounce package coconut
2 cloves garlic
1-2 tablespoons curry powder
½ teaspoon salt
2 tablespoons butter
flour

Cook chicken until it is tender with onion, carrot, celery tops, garlic clove, bay leaf and salt and pepper. When tender, cover all above ingredients with water and let chicken jelly in broth overnight. Remove chicken from bones. Cut into bite-size pieces.

Combine hot milk with coconut and let mixture stand for 30 minutes. Dry coconut. Saute onions in 2 tablespoons butter. Combine all other ingredients with coconut and chicken pieces with flour and chicken broth. Blend well and serve over baked rice.

Serve with containers of chutney, any remaining coconut, sieved hardboiled eggs, chopped peanuts, chopped green onions, chopped green peppers and crumbled, crisp-fried bacon.

Annie Raulerson

BAKED CHICKEN SALAD

OVEN: 350° 30 minutes

YIELD: 6 servings

2 cups cubed cooked chicken
1 jar diced pimentos
1 can water chestnuts, drained and
sliced thin
½ cup celery
¼ cup minced onions
¾ cup mayonnaise

¼ teaspoon pepper
½ teaspoon salt
1 bag slivered almonds
1 — 8 ounce package shredded
cheddar cheese
1 can French fried onions

Combine the first nine ingredients ahead of time, if desired. Place this mixture in a casserole dish and top with cheese and onions. Bake in 350° oven for 30 minutes.

Add more chicken and mayonnaise to stretch the number of servings. Turkey may be substituted for the chicken, and potato chips for the fried onions if you like.

Sarah Mundy

BAKED CHICKEN WITH WINE

OVEN: 350° 1 hour

1 — 2½ to 3 pound broiler fryer,
cut in pieces
¼ cup butter, margarine OR oil
1 medium onion, chopped
1 can sliced mushrooms
1 can cream of mushroom soup, undiluted

¾ cup dry sherry
1 tablespoon chopped parsley
1 teaspoon salt
1 teaspoon paprika
dash of pepper
1-2 lemon slices

Brown chicken slowly in butter. Remove from skillet and place in a single layer in a baking dish or 11 x 7 shallow pan. Add mushrooms and onions to butter remaining in skillet and cook until tender, not brown. Add soup, sherry, seasonings and lemon slices to skillet mixture and blend thoroughly. Pour mixture over chicken pieces and bake in 350° oven for about 1 hour.

Saundra H. Rohn

For that extra special flavor use herbs such as dill, marjoram, savory, and thyme when preparing poultry stuffing.

BOMBAY CHICKEN
(INDONESIAN)

OVEN: 350° 45 minutes

8 pieces chicken, seasoned in salt,
pepper, paprika and flour to
taste
½ cup sherry
2 tablespoons brown sugar

1 tablespoon soy sauce
½ cup water
½ teaspoon ginger
2 tablespoons sesame seeds
1 small can mushrooms plus liquid

Brown seasoned chicken in oil. Remove chicken to baking dish. In pan used to brown chicken, add all other ingredients. Bring to a boil, then pour over chicken. Cover tightly and cook for 45 minutes in 350° oven.

This recipe can be held nicely for latecomers by cooking at 300° for 1½ hours.

Kristen P. Wagers

BUTTERMILK CHICKEN

OVEN: 400° 50-60 minutes

1 cup buttermilk
8 chicken thighs
½ cup flour
salt

pepper
½ teaspoon powdered ginger
paprika
oleo

Preheat oven to 400°. Marinate chicken with buttermilk in a shallow pan. Place flour with salt and pepper to taste in a paper bag; add ginger.

Lightly oil a baking pan. Place each thigh separately into brown bag and shake slightly; place on oiled pan. Repeat with each piece. When all are coated and on the pan, sprinkle each piece with paprika and place a dot of oleo on each. Bake in 400° oven for 50-60 minutes, or until brown. No basting, no turning.

This is an excellent dish for 4, 8 or 40 that can be made at one time; just increase ingredients accordingly. Serve with fruit salad on a soft lettuce cup with dressing for color.

Olga P. Morgan

CHICKEN AND DRESSING

OVEN: 350° 45 minutes   YIELD: 6-8 servings

1 — 7 ounce package herb seasoned
stuffing
1 — 10½ ounce can condensed
cream of mushroom soup
2 cups chicken broth

2 well-beaten eggs
2½ cups diced cooked chicken
½ cup milk
2 tablespoons pimento, optional

Toss stuffing with ½ of the can of soup, the broth and egg. Spread 11 × 7 × 1½ inch pan with stuffing mixture. Top with chicken combined with remaining soup, milk and pimento. Pour mixture over ingredients in dish. Cover with foil and bake at 350° for 45 minutes or until set.

Rex Coulson

CHICKEN AND SWISS CHEESE

OVEN: 350° 1 hour

4 large chicken breasts, split,
  boned and skinned
8 slices Swiss cheese
½ cup dry white wine

1 can cream of chicken soup
2½ cups herb seasoned stuffing
  mix
⅓ cup melted butter

Lay raw chicken breasts in shallow baking dish. Place slice of cheese on top of each piece. Mix wine and soup together and pour over top of pieces. Crush stuffing mix and sprinkle over the soup mixture. Drizzle butter over the top. Bake in 350° oven for 1 hour or until done.

Gertrude Weh

CHICKEN AND YELLOW RICE

YIELD: 6 servings

2 fryers, cut into serving pieces
garlic salt, freely
olive oil
1 large onion
1 bell pepper
1 large can whole tomatoes
1 can mushrooms

1 bay leaf and/or pinch of oregano
3 capfuls yellow food coloring
minute rice
1 can tiny English peas
1 can diced pimentos
salt
pepper

Season fryers with garlic salt and salt and pepper; sauté, not brown, in olive oil. Add cut or diced onion and bell pepper, bay leaf and/or oregano, whole tomatoes, and can of mushrooms, and bring to a boil in covered roaster or Dutch oven. Reduce heat to simmer and cook for 20-35 minutes. When chicken is tender, remove all pieces from the juices and set aside.

Add food coloring to juices; remove from heat and add rice in same proportion as liquid. Stir. Place chicken back in pot on top; pour on drained peas and add pimentos. Cover tightly and let stand away from heat at least 10-15 minutes or longer.

The Committee

With chicken serve either a white or red wine. The wine should be dry such as Claret, Burgundy, Graves, Riesling, Pinot Chardonnay, or Italian Soave — all would be delicious.

CHICKEN CASSEROLE I

OVEN: 350° 45 minutes   YIELD: 10-12 servings

4 cups cooked, diced chicken
2 cans cream of chicken soup, undiluted
2 cups celery, cut fine
4 tablespoons minced onion
1½ cups slivered almonds
½ cup mayonnaise
½ cup sour cream
½ cup chicken stock

½ cup sliced mushrooms
3 tablespoons lemon juice, fresh
½ cup sherry
6 hard-boiled eggs, chopped
1 teaspoon salt
½ teaspoon black pepper
1½ cups soft buttered bread
   crumbs

Combine all ingredients except bread crumbs. Turn into a 3-4 quart buttered casserole. Bake at 350° for 30 minutes. Remove from oven and cover
with buttered bread crumbs. Return casserole to oven and continue cooking
for 15 minutes, or until brown.

Bread crumbs may be omitted and casserole served in baked patty shells if
desired.

Ruth Huggins

CHICKEN CASSEROLE II

OVEN: 375° 30-45 minutes

1 — 2½ to 3 pound fryer
1 can cream of mushroom soup
1 small can mushrooms

½ package onion soup mix
½ pint sour cream
½ can chow mein noodles

Cook chicken; skin and debone. Cut chicken into bite-size pieces. Combine
pieces with soup, sour cream, sliced mushrooms and soup mix. Place in casserole dish and sprinkle with chow mein noodles. Bake in 375° oven for 30 minutes.

This may be made ahead and frozen. Allow another 15 minutes baking time
if frozen.

Emma A. Kasulat

CHICKEN CASSEROLE III

OVEN: 350°

4 cups cooked, diced chicken
1 can water chestnuts, drained and
   sliced
1 — 6 ounce package slivered almonds
1 small jar chopped pimentos

1 cup mayonnaise
½ cup sour cream
salt
pepper
1 can fried onion rings

Mix ingredients (except onion rings) together and place in a buttered casserole dish. Bake in 350° oven until bubbly; then sprinkle onion rings on top
and bake until brown.

Shirley Krueger

CHICKEN DELIGHT

OVEN: 350° 20 minutes, 300° 1½ hours

1 cup dry rice
4 chicken thighs OR breasts
1 can mushroom OR celery soup

½ soup can milk
1 can tiny peas, reserve juice
½ package dry onion soup mix

Grease a casserole dish with oil. Sprinkle rice over oil. Lay chicken parts on rice and sprinkle peas over top of chicken. Pour juice from peas over all. Combine milk and soup; blending well. Pour mixture over other ingredients. Sprinkle dry soup mix over all.

Place casserole in 350° oven uncovered and bake for 20 minutes. Reduce temperature to 300° and bake for 1½ hours. Or, cook for 30 minutes at 300° and then turn to low and bake for a couple of hours. This is good to do while you are at church. Turn heat up 15 minutes before serving.

An excellent Sunday dinner.

Mrs. Walter Buckingham

CHICKEN DIVAN

OVEN: 350° 25-30 minutes

6-8 chicken breasts, cooked and
    boned
1 cup shredded cheddar cheese
4 packages frozen broccoli spears
3 cans cream of chicken soup

¼ cup milk
2 cups mayonnaise
1 tablespoon lemon juice
1½ cups bread crumbs
½ cup pimento strips

Cook broccoli as package directs and drain. Arrange broccoli in a buttered baking dish. Place chicken pieces on top. Combine soup, milk, mayonnaise and lemon juice and pour over chicken. Sprinkle with cheese. Top with bread crumbs. Bake at 350° for 25 to 30 minutes or more. Garnish with pimento.

Rosemary Sowinski

CHICKEN ELITE

OVEN: 350° 50-60 minutes

4 chicken breasts, medium size
1 small bottle marinated arti-
    chokes

1 small can mushrooms, drained
¼ cup white wine

Debone and skin chicken. Place pieces in baking dish; lightly salt; spread mushrooms over chicken; add artichoke and marinade; pour wine over all. Sprinkle with paprika and bake in 350° oven for 50-60 minutes. Serve.

This is delicious served with wild rice or herbed rice.

Jean C. Dean

CHICKEN IN CHERRIES WITH WINE SAUCE

OVEN: 400° 1 hour

Sauce:
1 cup brown sugar
1 cup dry red wine
1 — #2 can black sweet cherries
1 cup terragon wine vinegar
2 cloves garlic, crushed
2 whole cloves, crushed
¼ teaspoon ground ginger
¼ teaspoon basil
¼ teaspoon oregano

2 teaspoons salt
½ teaspoon seasoning salt
1 tablespoon cornstarch

Chicken:
12-14 pieces of chicken
cut lemon
1 teaspoon seasoning salt
1 tablespoon paprika
1 cup flour

Combine ingredients for sauce; simmer for 20 minutes. Remove from heat and pour into roasting pan and cover.

Rub chicken pieces with lemon. Combine flour and seasonings. Dredge chicken in flour mixture and fry until brown. Marinate chicken in wine sauce for 2 hours or more. Bake at 400° for 1 hour, basting occasionally.

Serve with rice and pour sauce over all.

I sometimes add slivered almonds over the top before baking. Garnish with parsley.

Eleanor Sexton

CHICKEN IN ESCABECHE SAUCE
(Spanish)

Sauce:
2 cups salad oil
1 cup vinegar
12 grains whole pepper
½ teaspoon salt

2 bay leaves
1½ pounds onions, sliced

Chicken:
3 pounds chicken breasts
1 teaspoon salt

Prepare sauce by cooking ingredients just until tender, then simmer for 30 minutes. Meanwhile, boil chicken breasts and bone the meat. Cut meat into bite-size chunks. Place meat in glass pan. When sauce is cold, pour it over the chicken, covering chicken completely. Cover and refrigerate for 12-24 hours. Serve cold with crackers.

The sauce may also be used over cooked chicken gizzards, fried fish, and other foods.

Adela Waymouth

Try rubbing broiling chickens with melted butter mixed with onion juice and powdered ginger for a distinctive flavor.

CHICKEN JUBILEE

OVEN: 325° 1 hour

2 chickens, cut up
1 teaspoon salt
¼ teaspoon pepper
¼ cup butter, melted
1 — 8 ounce jar sweet-sour sauce

1 cup sliced peaches
1½ cups dark sweet pitted cherries
1 medium onion, chopped fine
½ cup chili sauce

Place chicken pieces, skin side up, in baking pan. Sprinkle with salt and pepper; drizzle with melted butter. Broil until golden brown.

Combine sweet-sour sauce, peaches, cherries, onion and chili sauce. Spoon mixture over chicken and bake for 1 hour at 325°.

This recipe may be frozen for later use.

Mrs. Roger Keilholtz

CHICKEN KIEV

YIELD: 4-6 servings

4 whole chicken breasts
salt
3 tablespoons chopped green onion
3 tablespoons chopped fresh parsley
1 stick chilled butter

flour
2 beaten eggs
1 cup fine dry bread crumbs, approximately
deep fat for frying

Carefully bone chicken breasts; discard skin and cut each piece in half. Place each half, boned side up, between two pieces of plastic wrap. Working from the center, pound with wooden mallet to form cutlets not quite ¼" thick. Peel off plastic wrap and sprinkle cutlets with salt, parsley and green onion. Cut the stick of butter into 8 sticks. Place a stick of butter at the end of each cutlet. Roll meat as for jelly roll tucking in sides. Press ends to seal well. Dust each roll completely in flour and dip in beaten eggs; then roll in bread crumbs. Chill thoroughly; at least 1 hour. Fry chicken rolls in deep fat (350°) for about 5 minutes or until golden brown.

Lemon wedges and a creamy fresh mushroom sauce complement this dish.

Joyce Emmi

For the finest roast chicken, rub the chicken with brandy, season to taste, and roast.

CHICKEN KOREAN

YIELD: 4 servings

½ cup olive oil
½ cup soy sauce
½ cup dry white wine
½ cup sliced green onions
2 cloves garlic, minced OR mashed

½ teaspoon freshly ground pepper
½ teaspoon dry mustard
2 teaspoons mashed fresh OR dried
    ginger root
6 chicken breasts

Combine oil, soy sauce, white wine, green onions, garlic, pepper, mustard and ginger together; pour over chicken. Marinate for several hours. Arrange chicken in a low roasting pan and pour on marinade. Broil 3″ from heat for 15 minutes on each side. Baste frequently.

Serve with rice.

This is an authentic recipe from Korea, and even if you don't particularly care for chicken, the excellent sauce will make you forget it.

Lyle Gustavsson

CHICKEN O-RANG A-TANG

OVEN: 350° 40 minutes, 400° 5 minutes

YIELD: 6-8 servings

18 pieces broiler-fryer chicken
½ cup orange-flavor instant break-
    fast drink powder
½ cup wheatgerm

1 cup crushed ready-to-eat rice ce-
    real
1 tablespoon Accent
½ cup margarine

Mix the four dry ingredients together in a plastic bag. Dip chicken pieces in melted margarine and shake in coating mixture. Place in one layer on a large cookie sheet. Bake at 350° for 40 minutes, then at 400° for 5 minutes.

This is an original recipe chosen by the National Chicken Cooking Contest as a semi-finalist for the 1972 Maryland Cook-Off.

Bettye Detamore

CHICKEN OR TURKEY CASSEROLE

OVEN: 450° 20 minutes

1 cup celery, chopped
2 tablespoons onion, grated
½ cup slivered almonds
1½ cups cooked rice
3 hard-cooked eggs, chopped

¼ cup water
¾ cup mayonnaise
4 cups chicken, cut in bits
2 cups crushed potato chips

Mix mayonnaise and water together first, stir lightly, but well. Combine dry ingredients together in a large casserole dish. Add liquid. Sprinkle crushed chips on top just before baking.

Bake in 450° oven, uncovered, for about 20 minutes, until mixture bubbles. Celery should be crunchy like nuts.

The ingredients may be mixed a couple of days before and refrigerated. If this is done, wait to put the chips on top until ready to bake. Then bake for 30-35 minutes at 450°.

Mrs. Winfield Brown

CHICKEN ORIENTAL

OVEN: 375° 50 minutes

1 — 3 pound chicken, cut into serving pieces

Marinade:
¼ cup salad oil
¼ cup teriyaki sauce
¼ cup pale, dry sherry
1 tablespoon dry chives, chopped

½ teaspoon red pepper seeds
1 teaspoon granulated sugar
1 teaspoon onion powder
1 teaspoon ground ginger
1 tablespoon sesame seeds
salt to taste
chopped parsley to taste

Mix ingredients for marinade thoroughly in a deep bowl. Place chicken pieces in marinade for 1 hour; turning frequently. To cook, place chicken in a shallow baking dish and pour all marinade over pieces. Cook uncovered in 375° oven for 50 minutes.

This is the perfect entree to serve with cheesed zucchini en casserole, as they both require the same oven temperatures.

Rosalila Maggiacomo

CHICKEN PILAU

1 large fat hen
1 onion
1 bay leaf
4 stalks celery

salt
pepper
water
4 cups rice

Cut chicken into serving pieces and place in a large vessel. Cover chicken with water to equal 4 cups when done. (One cup broth for 1 cup of rice.)

When chicken is tender, remove from vessel; cool and bone. Measure broth and add rice. Cook on low heat until nearly dry. Add boned chicken and stir with fork.

The Committee

CHICKEN PIQUANT

3 pounds chicken parts
¾ cup white wine OR rose wine
¼ cup salad oil
¼ cup soy sauce

1 cup canned chicken broth
2 teaspoons powdered ginger
1 tablespoon brown sugar
¼ teaspoon oregano

Arrange chicken pieces in a flat casserole. Combine all remaining ingredients and pour over chicken. Bake for 1½ hours. I bake mine uncovered.

Serve with rice, cooked in chicken broth. I bake this at the same time.

Mrs. Robert Terry

Before frying chicken, squeeze some fresh lemon juice on the bird to enhance the flavor and make the chicken more tender.

CHICKEN SAITIMBOCCA

OVEN: 350° 40-45 minutes   YIELD: 6 servings

3 large chicken breasts, skinned, boned, and halved lengthwise
6 thin slices boiled ham
3 slices mozzarella cheese OR Monterrey Jack cheese
1 medium tomato, seeded and chopped

4 tablespoons butter OR margarine, melted
½ teaspoon dried sage, chopped
⅓ cup fine dry bread crumbs
2 tablespoons grated Parmesan cheese
2 tablespoons snipped parsley

Heat oven to 350°. Place chicken, boned side up on cutting board. Place a piece of clear plastic wrap over chicken. Working from the center out, pound lightly with a meat mallet to a 5″×5″ piece. Remove plastic wrap; place a ham slice and a slice of cheese on each cutlet, cutting the edges. Top with some tomato and a dash of sage. Tuck in sides; roll up jelly roll style, pressing to seal well.

Combine bread crumbs, Parmesan and parsley. Dip chicken in melted butter or margarine, then roll in crumbs. Place in shallow baking pan. Bake in 350° oven for 40 to 45 minutes.

                                                    Carmen I. Carroll

CHICKEN SOUFFLE LOAF

OVEN: 350° 1 hour

¾ cup ground cooked chicken
2 cups soft bread crumbs
1 cup cooked rice
¼ cup chopped pimento

3 cups milk OR 2 cups milk and 1 cup broth
1 teaspoon salt
¼ teaspoon pepper
1 tablespoon minced onion
3 well-beaten eggs

Mix ingredients in order given; pack into buttered loaf pan and bake in 350° oven for 1 hour or until firm and lightly browned.

Serve with mushrooms in cream gravy.

                                                    Jessie Backus Guhse

Paprika is a natural spice to sprinkle over chicken for a tasty-looking color and flavor.

CHICKEN SUPREME

OVEN: 275° 3 hours

8 whole chicken breasts, boned,
  skinned and halved
flour
½ teaspoon pepper
¾ cup olive oil
1 stick butter
4 tablespoons flour

1 medium onion, chopped
2-3 tablespoons fresh parsley
2 medium cans chicken broth
2 envelopes chicken flavored broth
  mix
¾ cup tomato juice
½ cup dry sherry

Melt olive oil and butter in a skillet. Flour chicken and season. Brown pieces slowly. Remove and arrange in a casserole.

Reserve drippings from pan and smooth in flour. Add onion and parsley. Slowly add canned chicken broth and broth mixes, tomato juice and sherry. Cover and cook for 10 minutes. Add mixture to chicken in the casserole. Bake uncovered for 3 hours at 275°.

Serve with wild or white rice.

Betty Erni

CHICKEN SURPRISE

OVEN: 325°-350° 1½ to 2 hours

1 small chicken
1 cup regular uncooked rice
1 can mushroom soup, undiluted
1 tablespoon chopped parsley

1 tablespoon minced onion
1 cup crushed dried bread crumbs
salt
pepper

Cover chicken with salted water and cook until tender. Let cool in broth. When cool, remove chicken from bone and cut into small pieces. Wash rice and cook in chicken broth, boiling rapidly for 20 minutes. Add mushroom soup, onion, salt and pepper. Combine mixture with chicken pieces and pour into greased baking dish. Heat a few tablespoons of margarine in a skillet and saute bread crumbs in it. Mix thoroughly and spread over chicken and rice mixture. Bake in 325°-350° oven for 1½ to 2 hours. Cook in a flat pan and serve in squares.

Mary Thornton

Heat chopped pecans with chutney and serve with poultry — adds a flavorful pungent taste.

CHICKEN TERIYAKI

OVEN: 400° 50 minutes

YIELD: 6 servings

6 large chicken half breasts
1 large garlic clove, crushed, OR ¼
  teaspoon garlic powder
3 tablespoons lemon juice

2 tablespoons soy sauce
6 tablespoons butter
¼ teaspoon pepper
¼ teaspoon salt

Preheat oven to 400°. Melt butter over low heat, being careful not to brown. Add lemon juice, Soy sauce and garlic puree. Stir until well mixed. Set aside. Lightly season chicken breasts with salt and pepper. Place chicken pieces in a foil-lined aluminum baking pan that is large enough so pieces do not over-lap. Bake for 40 minutes or until light golden brown and crispy looking. Baste generously with sauce and return to oven for 10 minutes longer. Turn pieces 2-3 times during the last few minutes of cooking; basting with the sauce.

Salt may be omitted for low-sodium diets; lemon juice is an excellent substitute. Amount of soy sauce may also be reduced.

Kim Lybrand

CHILI CHICKEN

1 cup rice, uncooked
1 — 12 ounce can V-8 Vegetable
  Juice
3 medium onions, diced
1 chicken, quartered

1 large can peas OR 1 package frozen peas
1 tablespoon chili powder
salt
pepper
garlic

Brown chicken in cooking oil; add onions, cook until onions are soft. Stir in V-8 juice, salt, pepper, and garlic to taste, and chili powder.

Cook rice separately, then add to chicken mixture. Cook, covered, over low heat until chicken is soft. Add peas and cook an additional 5 minutes; serve.

Rochelle Horenstein

When roasting a bird, always place breast-side-up on a rack of an open roasting pan. The bird should be turned once on each side during the roasting process in order to obtain even browning. Baste occasionally.

"IMMOKOLEE" — tropical grounds surrounding the
home of Mrs. Dorothy Binney Palmer
St. Lucie County, Florida

Patio garden at the home of
Mrs. June Carlton Vest
St. Lucie County, Florida

CHINESE WALNUT CHICKEN

YIELD: 6-8 servings

4 whole chicken breasts
1 tablespoon cornstrach
salt
½ teaspoon pepper
½ teaspoon sugar
2 tablespoons soy sauce
5 tablespoons cooking oil

½ cup walnuts, coarsely chopped
1 cup smoked ham, diced into ½"
squares
½ cup hot chicken broth
1 — 6 ounce package frozen chinese pea pods, optional

Bone breasts, discarding skin. Press pieces with hands to make into uniform thickness. Cut pieces into 1½" squares. Mix cornstarch, ½ teaspoon salt, the pepper, sugar and 1 tablespoon of the soy sauce and 2 tablespoons of the oil together. Add chicken pieces and stir to coat evenly. Sauté walnuts in 1 table-spoon of oil until golden brown; sprinkle with salt. Heat remaining oil; add chicken mixture and stir-fry for about 2-3 minutes. Add walnuts and ham and stir-fry for about 5 minutes. Stir in remaining soy sauce and broth, scraping up browned bits from bottom of pan. Cook for 1 minute longer.

Pea pods add a nice color and extra texture. If using, thaw first and add during the last minute or two of cooking.

This is nice served from a chafing dish over rice or thin Chinese noodles; the kind of noodles you cook, not the canned crisp ones.

Joyce Emmi

CITRUS CHICKEN

OVEN: 400° 15 minutes, 350° 35 minutes

3 boned chicken breasts, halved,
skinned and slightly flattened
¼ cup butter, melted
1 tablespoon orange liqueur
6 thin slices cooked ham
flour
2 eggs, slightly beaten
⅔ cup fine seasoned bread crumbs

1 stick butter, cut into bits
2 cups orange juice
1 tablespoon tarragon
1 teaspoon grated orange peel
½ teaspoon salt
6 orange slices, ½" thick
finely grated orange peel
minced parsley for garnish

Preheat oven to 400°. Place chicken breast halves on a flat surface, smooth side down; brush with melted butter mixed with liqueur. Place one slice of ham on each breast and roll up, fasten with toothpicks. Roll in flour; shake off excess. Dip in beaten egg, then roll in bread crumbs. Place in buttered shallow baking pan. Dot with butter. Bake for 15 minutes, turning once. Mix orange juice, salt, tarragon and orange peel together, pour over chicken. Reduce heat to 350°, cover and bake for 35 minutes longer, turning and basting occasion-ally with sauce. Remove toothpicks and place each chicken roll on an orange slice. Spoon sauce over chicken. Garnish with grated orange peel and finely minced parsley.

Bette Grossman

COUNTRY CAPTAIN

OVEN: 350° 60 minutes

YIELD: 6-8 servings

2 large fryers
2 tablespoons fat
3 onions, chopped
3 green peppers, cut fine
1 cup currants
1 garlic button
1 teaspoon salt

1 teaspoon curry powder
1 teaspoon thyme
½ teaspoon black pepper
1 cup almonds, blanched
1 large can tomatoes
1 tablespoon butter
2 cups cooked rice

Brown chicken in hot fat and place in a roasting pan. Fry onions in butter; then add peppers, salt, garlic, curry powder, thyme, pepper and tomatoes. Let mixture simmer for 15 minutes, then add chicken. Simmer in 350° oven for 60 minutes.

When ready to serve, place cooked rice in center of a large platter and place chicken around on edge. Add blanched almonds to sauce and pour over the rice.

A good green salad may be served with this one-dish meal.

Country Captain is a favorite Georgia recipe. This particular version was used by Daisy Bonner, a cook for President Franklin D. Roosevelt at Warm Springs.

Mrs. Ralph Wilson

CREAMY CHICKEN-WILD RICE CASSEROLE

OVEN: 350° 25-30 minutes

YIELD: 6 servings

½ cup chopped onion
½ cup butter
¼ cup flour
1 — 6 ounce can mushrooms, drained
1½ cups chicken broth
1½ cups rich milk or evaporated milk

1 — 6 ounce package long grain and wild rice, cooked
3 cups diced cooked chicken
¼ cup diced pimento
1½ teaspoons salt
¼ teaspoon pepper
½ cup slivered almonds

Cook onion in butter until tender, but not brown. Remove from heat, stir in flour. Gradually add 1½ cups of chicken stock to flour mixture; add milk. Cook and stir until mixture thickens. Add cooked rice, mushrooms, chicken pieces, pimento, salt and pepper. Place mixture in a 2 quart casserole and sprinkle with almonds. Bake in 350° oven for 25-30 minutes.

The amount of salt needed depends on the amount used in cooking the rice and chicken; so taste and adjust. Stew two large fryers, 3 pounds or more, for 6 servings; use 4 chickens and double recipe for 12-15 servings.

Libby Miller

Roll cut-up chicken pieces in a mixture of turmeric and a little flour before oven-frying or barbecuing. The chicken will have a nice gold color and a delicious flavor.

EAST INDIAN CURRY

YIELD: 12 servings

3 large fryers OR 7 pounds green
  shrimp OR 1 leg of lamb
olive oil
6 large onions
6-7 garlic clove buds
½ tablespoon ginger
½ tablespoon nutmeg
½ tablespoon salt
½ tablespoon paprika
½ tablespoon ground clove
½ tablespoon cinnamon
6 tablespoons curry powder
bay leaves
whole cloves

2 fresh coconuts, and milk
1 lemon
2 egg yolks
milk

Condiments:
chopped hard boiled eggs
chopped onions
chopped tomatoes
hot peppers
cucumbers, sliced
raisins
peanuts
coconut
bottled chutney

Boil large fryers and save broth; debone chicken. Place 2 cups olive oil in a large pot, add 1 garlic clove and cut up onions; fry until golden brown. Add ginger, nutmeg, paprika, ground cloves, cinnamon, and salt along with curry powder and 2 cups of chicken stock, a few bay leaves and whole cloves; blend ingredients together and turn off heat. Grate fresh coconuts and mix half into a cup of hot milk; stir, and add to curry; add coconut milk.

Just before serving, mix juice of one lemon with egg yolks, bring up heat and add along with chicken, shrimp OR lamb pieces, cut up, and serve. If you use either the shrimp or lamb, substitute 2 cups of beef consumme for 2 cups of broth.

Serve with condiments. Hope you enjoy it.

George Berry

FESTIVE CHICKEN CASSEROLE

OVEN: 275° 2 hours

8 good-size chicken breasts, boned
  and skinned.
8 slices bacon

2 — 4 ounce packages chipped beef
1 can mushroom soup, undiluted
½ pint sour cream

Wrap each chicken breast with beef and a slice of bacon. Cover the bottom of a flat, greased baking dish, about 8 × 12 × 2", with wrapped chicken. Mix soup and sour cream together and pour over all. If desired, cut up can of water chestnuts and add to sauce. Refrigerate until ready to bake. Bake in 275° oven for 2 hours, uncovered.

Sunny Gates

Sesame seeds, sprinkled over chicken, makes a crunchy topping.

FLORIDA TANGERINE CHICKEN

OVEN: 350° 1 hour   YIELD: 6 servings

2 — 2½ to 3 pound frying chickens,   1 teaspoon salt
  cut up   ¼ teaspoon pepper
2 — ⅝ ounce boxes fortified rice   ¼ cup butter
  cereal   ¼ cup corn oil
1 tablespoon flour   3 tangerines
½ teaspoon rosemary

Reduce cereal and rosemary to fine crumbs and pour into a paper sack. Add flour, salt, and pepper and shake to mix. Reserve 2 tablespoons of the butter. Melt rest of butter in a small saucepan and add oil. Remove and discard, or use for another purpose wing tips and backs of chicken. Preheat oven to 350°. Brush chicken pieces with butter-oil mixture and drop into sack. Shake to coat. Brush a shallow baking pan with remaining butter-oil mixture. Place chicken in pan, skin side down, in a single layer. Bake for 30 minutes. Peel and section tangerines. With a sharp knife, remove a thin strip from inside each section and remove seeds. Melt reserved butter in a saucepan, add tangerine sections and stir to coat. Remove chicken from oven, turn, sprinkle tangerines over top. Return to oven, bake for 30 minutes longer or until fork tender.

Paul Mahan

FRIED CHICKEN

2½ pounds fryers, poached and cut   salt
  up   pepper
evaporated milk   poultry seasoning
flour   oil to fry

Poach cut up fryers. Bring to a boil and turn off heat.

When chicken has cooled, drain. Put chicken in evaporated milk, then into flour, seasoned with salt, pepper, and poultry seasoning. Shake off excess flour and fry until golden brown.

Cooking time is less because chicken has been poached.

Mrs. Kerr's Boarding House

When serving chicken or turkey, figure three-quarters to one pound per person when purchasing it.

GERMAN STYLE VINEGAR CHICKEN

1 chicken
equal parts flour and Italian bread
  crumbs

shortening
28 ounces brown vinegar
4 ounces water

Prepare chicken for frying. Coat in flour and bread crumbs mixture and deep-fat fry until chicken is golden brown. Remove chicken from shortening and drain.

Pour off all but about 3 tablespoons shortening and cracklings in the bottom of the pan. Add vinegar and water and return pan to burner. Bring this mixture to a boil and add chicken pieces. Cook for 3 minutes, covered. Vinegar mixture should appear somewhat thickened. Remove chicken and serve immediately.

If chicken is cooked too long in the vinegar solution, all of the tangy flavor will be "cooked out." This method produces extremely tender and moist chicken with a tangy taste expressly its own.

Dicksie Dudeney

HOT CHICKEN SALAD CASSEROLE

OVEN: 350° 30 minutes   YIELD: 6 servings

2 cups cooked chicken
1 can cream of chicken soup
½ soup can water
¾ cup mayonnaise
½ cup celery, diced
1 small onion, diced
1 small can water chestnuts,
  drained

1 — 4 ounce bag sliced almonds
2 ounce jar pimentos
1 — 16 ounce can English peas
½ teaspoon salt, or to taste
½ teaspoon pepper
¼ cup grated cheddar cheese
1 can chow mein noodles

Dice cooked chicken. Drain water chestnuts, peas, and pimentos. Dice celery and onion. In a 13 × 9 oven-proof pan or medium size casserole, combine all ingredients except cheese and noodles. Sprinkle grated cheese over the top. Cook at 350° for 30 minutes. Sprinkle with noodles right before serving.

Brenda Campbell

HOT CHICKEN SALAD I

OVEN: 350°   YIELD: 8 servings

3 cups cooked chicken, cut up
1 cup, approximately 20 saltine
  crackers, crumbed
½ cup chicken broth
1 cup sliced almonds
1 cup mayonnaise

2 cups celery, cut very fine
4 tablespoons onion, cut very fine
1 tablespoon lemon juice
1 teaspoon pepper
2 cans cream of chicken soup

Mix all ingredients except cracker crumbs and almonds. Pour mixture into casserole dish; add cracker crumbs and almonds just before baking; mix in. Bake in 350° oven until bubbly; serve very hot. Serve in large casserole dish or in patty shells.

Mary Klueppelberg

HOT CHICKEN SALAD II

OVEN: 350° 45 minutes

3-4 chicken breasts, boiled and
   diced
1 cup celery, chopped
1 teaspoon minced onion
3 hard boiled eggs, diced
2 cups crushed potato chips
½ cup slivered almonds

1 can cream of chicken soup
1 teaspoon lemon juice
¾ cup mayonnaise
¼ teaspoon salt
⅛ teaspoon pepper
1½ cups grated cheddar cheese

Blend all ingredients together except potato chips. Place in a casserole and sprinkle chips on top. Bake for 45 minutes in 350° oven.
Serve on a bed of lettuce. Hot rolls are a nice complement to this dish.

Lesa Kitzmiller

HOT TURKEY SALAD

OVEN: 450° 15 minutes

3 cups turkey, cooked, ground or
   cubed
1½ cups celery
½ teaspoon salt

1 tablespoon onion, chopped fine
2 tablespoons lemon juice
½ cup mayonnaise
1 cup whole cranberry sauce

Combine all ingredients except cranberry sauce; place in a flat baking dish that has been greased
Arrange cranberry sauce around the edge. Bake in 450° oven for 15 minutes.

Kim Nelson

KOTES RIGANATES (CHICKEN WITH OREGANO)

OVEN: 325° 50-60 minutes

6 chicken breasts
2 teaspoons oregano
2 teaspoons salt

¼ pound butter
1 teaspoon pepper
4 tablespoons lemon juice

Place chicken, skin side down in a shallow roasting pan. Combine all other ingredients and heat until butter melts. Spoon mixture over chicken and bake at 325° for 20 minutes. Turn chicken and spoon remaining mixture over each piece. Bake for an additional 30-40 minutes, or until chicken is done.

Sophie Reeves

Chicken fat is very rich and can be used in place of butter in making pastry.

LEMON CHICKEN

OVEN: 350° 30 minutes

washed chicken pieces
salt
lemon and pepper seasoning

½ cup lemon juice for each 4-5 chicken quarters

Broil salted and peppered chicken until brown on both sides. Pour lemon juice over all and bake for 30 minutes at 350°

Delicious with rice pilau or new potatoes. May add mushrooms and slivered onions while baking. Save drippings, chill, skim fat and use for flavoring when boiling next rice dish.

Suzanne Varn

LEMON-LIME RICKEY CHICKEN

OVEN: 350 1½ hours

1 — 7 ounce bottle lemon-lime
  rickey
2 cloves garlic, ground fine
2 teaspoons salt

2 teaspoons paprika
¾ teaspoon ginger
frying chicken, cut up

Mix all seasonings with lemon-lime drink. Arrange chicken in a large flat baking dish. Pour lemon-lime mixture over chicken and bake for about 1½ hours, basting every fifteen minutes or so.

For a party, I use chicken parts and double or triple the recipe. It's so nice not to have to brown the chicken, and it is delicious when done. I replace the lemon-lime drink, which is sometimes hard to find, with other lemon-lime carbonated drink.

Mrs. John S. Stobbelaar

LEMON-PEPPER CHICKEN

4 broiler chicken halves
salt
1 tablespoon lemon-pepper marinade
⅛ teaspoon garlic powder

1 teaspoon parsley flakes
½ cup butter OR margarine,
  melted
¼ cup lemon juice

Sprinkle chicken with salt on both sides. Combine remaining ingredients and season chicken on both sides. Broil skin side up until chicken is brown and bubbly, about 10 minutes. Turn and broil on other side, 10 minutes more.

Carol I. Browder

Insure even broiling of poultry by cutting the tendons of the poultry so pieces will lie as flat as possible.

MAE ZUVER'S SWISS CHICKEN CASSEROLE

OVEN: 350° 30 minutes   YIELD: 6-8 servings

4 cups diced cooked chicken
2 cups sliced celery
2 cups toasted bread cubes
1 cup mayonnaise
¼ cup chopped onion OR 1 small
   onion

½ cup milk
1 teaspoon salt
½ teaspoon pepper
6-8 ounces Swiss cheese cut in julienne strips
¼ cup slivered almonds

Combine all ingredients except nuts. Turn into 2 quart casserole and sprinkle with nuts. Bake in moderate oven, 350°, for 30 minutes or until heated
through.

This can be made several days ahead. Simply refrigerate until the day
needed. If you prefer, you can wait and add milk and mayonnaise the day of
use.

A great lunch or dinner casserole and really delicious. Good served with
tossed salad, some crusty bread and chilled white wine.

R. M. Croghan

OLD FASHIONED PRESSED CHICKEN

YIELD: 8 servings

3½ pound stewing chicken
3 envelopes gelatin
1 cup finely diced celery
2 chopped pimentos

4 tablespoons vinegar
salt
white pepper

Remove all fat from surface of broth after cooking chicken. Simmer to reduce broth to 2½ cups. Soften gelatin in ½ cup cold broth for 5 minutes. Add
gelatin mixture to hot broth and stir until dissolved. Chill until syrupy. Meanwhile, discard skin and bones. Add chopped chicken pieces, celery, pimentos
and vinegar to thickened broth. Season well to taste with salt and white pepper. Pour into mold and place in refrigerator until firm.

The Committee

ORIENTAL CHICKEN

OVEN: 300° 2 hours

½ cup soy sauce
¼ cup sugar
1½ teaspoons ginger
½ teaspoon Accent
6-8 drops tabasco

1½ cloves, chopped fine OR ½ teaspoon ground cloves
dash of paprika
1 fryer OR 6-8 pieces of chicken
bacon

Mix all ingredients together, stir well. Wrap each piece of chicken in bacon;
place in a baking dish. Pour sauce over chicken and let marinate overnight in
refrigerator. When ready to bake, turn pieces over. Cook uncovered for 2
hours in 300° degree oven.

Hazel N. Crews

OVEN BROWNED RICE WITH CHICKEN

OVEN: 325° 1½ hours

1 chicken, quartered or cut into
  serving pieces
4 chicken bouillon cubes
1 medium green pepper, diced
1 can sliced mushrooms, optional

1 cup long grain rice
1½ cups water
1 stick butter
1 medium onion, diced
salt

Salt and pepper chicken pieces and brown in butter. Remove chicken and using same pan, add green pepper and onion. Sauté until beginning to tender. Remove from heat, add mushrooms and pulverized bouillon cubes. Add water, rice, and 1 teaspoon salt to the mixture, making sure that all is evenly distributed over the pan. Arrange chicken on top. Cover and bake slowly for 1½ hours at 325°.

Mrs. Pete Clemons

OVEN FRIED CHICKEN

OVEN: 375° 50 minutes

1 broiler-fryer cut into serving
  pieces
¼ cup butter or margarine, melted
  OR cooking oil

1 teaspoon salt
¼ teaspoon pepper
½ cup Italian flavor bread crumbs

Heat oven to 375°. Melt butter or margarine. Mix salt and pepper. Place bread crumbs in a plastic bag with salt and pepper. Coat chicken pieces in butter or oil and then shake in bread crumbs, covering thoroughly. Place chicken pieces on lightly greased baking sheet and bake for about 50 minutes or until brown and crispy.

Nancy Carlton

PARTY TIME CHICKEN

OVEN: 350° 50-60 minutes

6 half chicken breasts
12 thin slices lean ham OR chipped
  dried beef
½ pound mushrooms

1½ tablespoons flour
½ cup mushroom juice
½ cup evaporated milk
½ pound grated mozarella cheese

Grease a casserole dish— Place double layers of cheese, ham or beef on bottom. Place chicken breasts on meat. Saute mushrooms in about 1½ tablespoons butter or oleo and make a sauce with the flour and milk and juice. Spread sauce on top of chicken pieces.
Grate and add cheese on top of the sauce. Bake in 350° oven, uncovered, for 50-60 minutes.
This can be made a day ahead and refrigerated. Top with grated cheese and garlic croutons. A 6-ounce can of mushrooms may be substituted for fresh mushrooms; use either chopped or sliced.

Mrs. Richard Keefe

PICKLED CHICKEN DRUMSTICKS

YIELD: 6-8 servings

18 broiler-fryer drumsticks
4 cups thinly sliced onion
1½ cups salad oil
¾ cup vinegar
2 teaspoons salt
1 teaspoon Accent

1 teaspoon dill weed
2 bay leaves
8 peppercorns
2 cloves garlic
3 tablespoons lemon juice.

In a saucepan, place drumsticks, onion, oil, vinegar, salt, Accent, dill weed, bay leaves, and peppercorns. Bring to a boil. Cover tightly; reduce heat and simmer for about 45 minutes or until chicken is fork-tender. Remove from heat. Stir in garlic and lemon juice. Leave chicken in marinade, uncovered. Refrigerate until thoroughly chilled. To serve, drain and discard marinade. Serve chicken cold, smothered with onion rings from the marinade.

Barbara Matuszewski

POULET AUX FROMAGE
(Chicken With Cheese)

OVEN: 300° 45 minutes

YIELD: 9-12 servings

Sauce:
3 tablespoons butter
½ cup onion, chopped
1 bell pepper, chopped
1 can cream of chicken soup
⅓ cup milk
1 — 6 ounce can sliced mushrooms
¼ cup pimento, diced
½ teaspoon basil

8 ounces wide noodles, uncooked
2½ cups cream sauce (ingredients
   above)
3 cups diced chicken
1½ cups cream style cottage cheese
½ cup Parmesan cheese
2 cups grated American cheese
bread crumbs
paprika

Sauté onion and bell pepper in butter. Add soup, milk, mushrooms, pimento and basil. Blend well to make cream sauce. Preheat oven to 300°. Prepare noodles according to package directions.

In a 3 quart casserole, combine cooked noodles, sauce, diced chicken, and cheeses. Top with bread crumbs and/or paprika. Bake for 45 minutes.

May be prepared ahead of time.

Edna M. Nobles

POULETTE PARISIENNE

2 pounds chicken parts
2 tablespoons shortening
1 can cream of mushroom soup
⅓ cup canned tomatoes, chopped

generous dash of crushed basil
1 — 9 ounce package frozen artichoke hearts, cooked and
   drained

In a skillet, brown chicken in shortening; pour off fat. Add remaining ingredients except artichokes. Cover, cook over low heat for 45 minutes or until chicken is tender. Add artichokes and heat through.

Dee Furst

PRECIOUS CHICKEN, BONED AND STUFFED

OVEN: 375° 1 hour

1 chicken
½ cup onions, chopped
½ cup celery, chopped
½ pound chopped beef
½ cup flavored bread crumbs
12 water chestnuts, chopped

1 — 2½ ounce can sliced mushrooms
1 small jar pimentos, chopped
½ cup chopped parsley
½ cup almonds, slivered and sauteed

To bone chicken, pull skin back to wing joint and cut through joint. Remove wish bone and two small bones on either side. Scrape breast meat along rib cage with sharp knife, as far as thumb and knife can reach. Turn chicken over and scrape back skin away from bones. Through bottom opening, continue scraping meat from front. Turn chicken over and scrape meat from back to thigh bones. Detach thigh bones from back at joint. Scrape meat from thigh bone to drumstick. Detach thigh bone and remove. Sew up top opening of chicken. Mix sauteed onions and celery with other ingredients in a bowl and stuff chicken through bottom opening. Sew bottom skin, rub with salt, pepper and butter. Roast to 170° in 375° oven for about 1 hour.

Reg Peterson

QUICK BARBECUED CHICKEN

OVEN: 350° 20-30 minutes   YIELD: 4 servings

½ cup butter, melted
2 tablespoons lemon juice
1 tablespoon white horseradish
1 tablespoon vinegar
1 tablespoon ketchup

¾ teaspoon Worcestershire sauce
½ teaspoon tabasco sauce
¼ teaspoon salt
2 — 6 ounce cans boned chicken

Mix ingredients for barbeque sauce and bring to a boil. Drain boned chicken and place in a shallow baking dish. Pour hot barbeque sauce over chicken. Bake at 350° until chicken absorbs most of the sauce; about 20-30 minutes.

Aline Andrews

ROLLED CHICKEN BREAST

OVEN: 300°-350° 45 minutes

6 individual breasts of chicken
6 slices baked ham
6 slices Swiss cheese

2 cups seasoned bread stuffing
2 eggs, lightly beaten
1 stick butter, melted

Debone chicken breasts. Roll the chicken, then wrap cheese around it, then ham. Secure with toothpicks. Repeat with each chicken breast. Roll the stuffing into fine bread crumbs. Dip each piece of chicken into egg, then into crumbs. Melt butter in shallow baking dish. Lay each piece in the butter and bake for 45 minutes in 300° or 350° oven. Turn once and baste while baking. Bake on a low rack in the oven so pieces won't get too brown.

Aggie Counts

SATURDAY NIGHT BARBECUE CHICKEN

2 chickens, cut in half

Sauce:
2 tablespoons white vinegar
2 tablespoons lemon juice
2 tablespoons margarine

2 tablespoons Worcestershire sauce
4 tablespoons prepared mustard
2 tablespoons garlic salt
tabasco
pepper

This recipe is for use in oven or on charcoal grill; charcoal grill is best, I prefer a grill with hood.

Make sure chickens are done before applying sauce. Turn pieces frequently to avoid burning.

I like to close the dampers all the way for the last few applications of sauce. If you are on a diet, don't eat the skin.

Sauce may be applied during last 30 minutes of cooking.

James O. Briggs, D.V.M.

SEVEN-UP BARBECUE CHICKEN

OVEN: 350° 50-60 minutes

1 — 7 ounce bottle 7-Up
¼ cup ketchup
1 teaspoon light brown sugar
1 teaspoon Worcestershire sauce
1 teaspoon salt
1 teaspoon vinegar

¼ teaspoon dry mustard
¼ teaspoon celery seed
¼ cup onion, chopped
dash of pepper
1 large fryer, 2½ to 3 pounds

Mix all ingredients. Pour over cut up fryer and bake in 350° oven for 50-60 minutes or until tender. If using a larger fryer, bake longer.

Mrs. R. E. Doyle

SKILLET FLORENTINE

2 pounds chicken parts
2 tablespoons shortening
1 can cream of chicken soup
1 tablespoon lemon juice

1 medium clove garlic, minced
½ teaspoon oregano, crushed
4 servings, cooked spinach

In a skillet, brown chicken in shortening; pour off fat. Stir in remaining ingredients except spinach. Cover and cook over low heat for 45 minutes or until tender. Stir occasionally. Serve with spinach.

Dee Furst

Larger turkeys are meatier than smaller ones and more servings per pound will be obtained by purchasing a larger bird.

SWEDISH CHICKEN

OVEN: 350° 30 minutes

YIELD: 8 servings

1 large fowl
1 package stuffing
¾ cup melted chicken fat OR butter (1½ sticks)
¼ cup chicken broth
1 onion, minced
1 teaspoon sage

salt and pepper to taste

Gravy:
4 tablespoons chicken fat OR butter
4 tablespoons flour
1 quart chicken broth

Cook fowl in boiling water; simmer until tender, but firm. Cube meat and cover the bottom of a 3 quart casserole. Make a dressing of stuffing, melted fat OR butter, chicken broth, onion and sage. Salt and pepper to taste. Cover cubed chicken with dressing. Just before placing in oven, pour gravy over dressing. Bake in 350° oven for ½ hour.

This is excellent for buffets. Mushrooms may be added to cubed chicken.

I have used this recipe since 1943. Guests have always asked for the recipe. I finally had it mimeographed.

Virginia Q. Hack

SWEET AND SOUR CHICKEN

OVEN: 350° 1 hour

1 jar apricot preserves
1 small bottle Russian salad dressing

1 package onion soup mix
1 chicken, cut up OR chicken pieces

Salt and pepper chicken and place in a baking pan. Mix other ingredients together in electric blender and pour over chicken. Bake for 1 hour, uncovered, in 350° oven.

Good served with rice.

Bettie Bertzel

TURKEY PIE

OVEN: 450°

turkey
3-4 diced potatoes
several carrots
diced celery pieces
chopped onions

flour
canned biscuits
salt
pepper

Boil turkey until tender. Remove bones and cut meat into small pieces. Place potatoes, carrots, celery and onions in the same water used to cook turkey. Boil until tender. Add cut up turkey, salt and pepper;thicken with flour. Pour mixture into a casserole dish and place canned biscuits on top; flatten biscuits until very thin. Bake at 450° until biscuits are brown.

Nadine Cherry

URUGUAYAN CHICKEN CASSEROLE

OVEN: 350° 1 hour

2 whole chickens
1 cup water, or more
1 cup sherry
1½ teaspoons salt
½ teaspoon curry powder
1 medium onion
½ cup celery, sliced

1 pound fresh mushrooms
¼ cup butter
2 — 6 ounce packages wild rice
1 cup sour cream
1 — 10½ ounce can cream of mushroom soup

Boil chicken in deep kettle with water, sherry, salt, curry powder, onion, and celery. Cover tightly and simmer 1 hour. Remove chicken, strain broth, and cool. Discard contents of strainer. Bone chicken and cut into bite-size pieces. Sauté mushrooms in butter. Use chicken broth for cooking rice as package directs for firm rice. Combine chicken, rice, mushrooms in a 3½ to 4 quart casserole. Blend sour cream and mushroom soup together. Toss together with chicken and rice. Bake at 350° for 1 hour until bubbly, covered. If casserole is still runny after 1 hour, cook uncovered for 10-15 minutes.

Carmen I. Carroll

WA SU GUI

3 chicken breasts
2-3 chicken bouillon cubes
salt
pepper
1 tablespoon peanut oil
1 head lettuce

1 heaping tablespoon cornstarch, or more
10 drops yellow cake coloring
12 soda crackers
1 cup all-purpose flour
2 eggs, beaten
green onions, diced, tops included
½ cup water

Bone chicken breasts and separate muscles or cut into thin slices, ½″ to 1″ wide. Place pieces between wax paper and flatten with a mallet. This makes about 12 slices. Place bones in saucepan with about 1 quart water; add bouillon cubes and bring to a boil and cook until meat can be easily removed from bones. Discard bones. Salt and pepper liquid to taste. Mix cornstarch with ½ cup water. Stir into broth. Repeat this until desired consistency is obtained, then add coloring until desired color is obtained. Using a rolling pin, crush crackers until crumbled. Mix an equal amount of flour with crumbs and place in a shallow pan. Dip flattened chicken into crumb mixture first, then into beaten egg, then back into crumbs.

Put about ⅛ inch of peanut oil in frying pan and cook chicken at medium heat. Do not get oil too hot. Cook in all, about 5 minutes. Shred lettuce in food processor and place on each plate along with diced onion. Place chicken slices on top and spoon chicken broth over all. May be served with rice, soy sauce, and snow peas as an accompaniment.

This is a fast and easy Chinese preparation of chicken breast that will please your most discriminating guests.

Mrs. David S. Keen

WRAPPED CHICKEN BREASTS SUPREME

OVEN: 275° 3 hours

8 chicken breasts, uncooked, de-
  boned and skinned
1 — 4 ounce jar dried beef
8 slices bacon, uncooked

½ pint sour cream
1 can cream of mushroom soup, undiluted

Grease the bottom of a 9 × 13 casserole and line the bottom with dried beef. Wrap each chicken breast with a slice of bacon and secure with a toothpick. Place chicken breasts on top of beef. Mix sour cream with soup and pour over chicken. Bake uncovered in 275° oven for 3 hours.

Juanita Geary

NOTES

SALADS AND SALAD DRESSINGS

SALADS

SALAD DRESSINGS

AMBROSIA

YIELD: About 8 servings

4 cups Florida orange and grapefruit sections
½ cup flaked OR shredded coconut
1 cup miniature marshmallows

1 cup heavy cream, whipped
strawberry slices OR maraschino
cherries

Drain citrus sections. Juice may be saved for beverages, salad dressings, gelatin salads and so on.

Combine citrus sections, coconut, marshmallows and sour cream. Fold in whipped cream. Chill thoroughly and garnish with strawberry slices or maraschino cherries.

Marguerite R. Brock

APRICOT DELIGHT

2 — 3 ounce boxes apricot flavored
gelatin
2 cups hot water
2 cups cold water
1 — #2 can crushed pinapple
2 bananas, sliced
2 cups miniature marshmallows

Topping:
½ cup pineapple juice
¾ cup sugar
1 beaten egg
2 tablespoons flour
1 — 8 ounce package cream cheese
1 carton whipped topping
1 can flaked coconut

Mix gelatin slightly using hot and cold water. Add crushed pineapple that has been drained (reserve juice), bananas, and miniature marshmallows. Congeal gelatin completely.

For topping, cook pineapple juice, sugar, egg and flour until thick. Add cream cheese and stir until smooth. Let mixture cool. Mix in whipped topping. Spread mixture on gelatin. Sprinkle coconut on top.

Pat Tenniswood

To enhance the flavor of vegetable salads of all kinds, add a small amount of lemon juice.

APRICOT JELLO SALAD I

2 — 3 ounce packages apricot flavored Jello
1 — #2 can crushed pineapple,
drained; reserve juice
1 cup miniature marshmallows
2 bananas, sliced

Topping:
1 egg, slightly beaten
½ cup pineapple juice
½ cup sugar
2 tablespoons flour
2 tablespoons butter
1 envelope dry whipped topping
mix

Mix gelatin according to package directions. Add fruit and marshmallows to slightly thickened Jello.

Cook topping ingredients until thick. Cool mixture; then fold in 1 package dry whipped topping mix. Spread over congealed Jello.

Edna M. Nobles

APRICOT JELLO SALAD II

2 small boxes apricot flavored
Jello
2 cups hot water
2 cups cold water
1 can crushed pineapple
3 bananas
2 cups miniature marshmallows

½ cup sugar
3 teaspoons cornstarch
1 egg
½ pint whipping cream
1 can flaked coconut
1 — 8 ounce package cream cheese

Dissolve Jello in hot and cold water. When almost congealed add drained pineapple. Save liquid. Also add bananas and marshmallows.

Prepare topping by mixing pineapple juice, sugar, cornstarch, and well beaten egg together. Cook until mixture is thick enough to spread. Cool; then add cream cheese and whip. Spread mixture on top of congealed Jello. Whip the cream until stiff and spread on top of cream cheese mixture. Sprinkle with coconut.

Evelyn Walker

BING CHERRY RING MOLD

2 cans Bing cherries, pitted
2 cups orange juice
1 cup sugar
4 tablespoons gelatin

1 cup finely chopped nut meats
1 small package cream cheese
1½ cups sherry

Mix 1½ cups orange juice with 1 cup cherry juice. Bring liquids to a boil. Soak gelatin in remaining ½ cup orange juice and add to hot juice mixture. Stir liquids until smooth. Mix nuts with cream cheese and roll in small balls. Place balls in each cherry. When mixture is cool, add cherries and pour in ring mold. Refrigerate. Serve on lettuce with fruit and salad dressing. Use more cherry juice instead of orange juice if you prefer.

Mrs. John McCarty

BLUEBERRY SALAD I

2 — 3 ounce packages black raspberry flavored gelatin
1 — 3 ounce package lemon flavored gelatin
1 cup boiling water
½ cup cold water

2 tablespoons lemon juice
1 can crushed pineapple with juice
(15¼ ounce)
1 can blueberry pie filling
1 pint sour cream

Dissolve gelatins together in boiling water; add cold water and lemon juice. Stir in pineapple and pie filling. Pour mixture into 12 × 8 baking dish. Chill in refrigerator until real firm. Spread with sour cream.

This also makes a good molded salad without the sour cream.

Grace Whitson

BLUEBERRY SALAD II

2 packages raspberry flavored gelatin
1 large can crushed pineapple

1 large can blueberries
1 cup chopped pecans
1 packages whipped topping mix

Dissolve gelatin in hot water. Let mixture cool. Drain pineapple and blueberries, combine juices in measuring cup. Measure 1¾ cups of juices and add to gelatin. Reserve an additional ¾ cup of juices and set aside. Add blueberries, pineapple, and nuts to gelatin. Place mixture in refrigerator.

Prepare whipped topping as packages direct. Add ¾ cup reserved juices to topping. Spread mixture on top of congealed gelatin.

This keeps in refrigerator for 10 days.

Barbara Wells Steele

CABBAGE SALAD BAVARIAN STYLE

1 medium size head of green cabbage
8 slices bacon, finely diced
1½ to 2 tablespoons wine vinegar

salt, to taste
freshly ground pepper, to taste
⅓ cup finely chopped onion

Prepare raw cabbage by cutting out core and discarding outer loose leaves; cut cabbage into quarters. Boil enough water to cover cabbage; add salted cabbage and cook uncovered for twenty minutes or until tender but crisp. Drain and run cabbage under cold water; drain again. Shred, then chop cabbage; add wine vinegar, pepper, and onions. In saute pan, cook bacon, stirring, until crisp. Remove pan from heat and pour bacon bits, including bacon fat, over drained cabbage. Toss and serve.

As prepared by Anneliese for Craig Claiborne, noted food gourmet for *The New York Times* and author of several cookbooks. This recipe appeared in *The New York Times* and *The New York Times International Cookbook,* authored by Craig Claiborne.

Anneliese von der Cron

CALICO BEAN SALAD

1 — 1 pound can green beans	¾ cup sugar
1 — 1 pound can wax beans	⅔ cup vinegar
1 — 1 pound can kidney beans	½ teaspoon pepper
1 can water chestnuts	⅓ cup oil
½ cup green pepper, chopped	1 teaspoon salt

Drain beans; place beans in a large bowl. Slice chestnuts and add to beans. Add chopped green pepper. Mix sugar, vinegar, pepper, oil and salt together. Pour liquid over vegetables. Cover and refrigerate for 24 hours. Toss and drain before serving.

If desired, you may add 1 can green lima beans or black-eyed peas. For additional flavor add ½ teaspoon dry mustard, ½ teaspoon tarragon, ½ teaspoon basil and 2 tablespoons parsley.

Mrs. Richard Cook

CARROT SALAD

3 cans sliced carrots	1 cup sugar
1 green pepper, chopped	½ cup cooking oil
1 medium onion, chopped	½ cup vinegar
1 can tomato soup	

Heat undiluted soup, sugar, oil and vinegar until boiling. Remove from heat and pour mixture over drained carrots and chopped peppers. Let stand in refrigerator for 24 hours while marinating.

This salad goes over big at parties.

Edith K. Balint

CHERRY SALAD

1 — #2 can pie cherries	1 package lemon flavored gelatin
1 orange	1 package plain gelatin
1 lemon	¼ cup cold water
1 cup sugar	1 cup chopped pecans
1 small can crushed pineapple	

Grate orange and lemon rind and squeeze out juice. Add to undrained pineapple, cherries and sugar. Bring mixture to a boil, and use to dissolve lemon flavored gelatin. Soak plain gelatin in cold water. Add combined ingredients to plain gelatin. Stir until gelatin dissolves. Add nuts and pour mixture into a mold. Chill until firm.

Mary-Frazier Palmore

Substitute a carbonated soft drink such as gingerale or cola when preparing gelatin salads for an added zest.

CHERRY-SHERRY SALAD

1 package plain gelatin
1 package cherry flavored gelatin

1 can dark, sweet cherries
sweet sherry OR cream sherry

Place plain gelatin in a quart bowl or cup. Cover with cold water. Heat juice from cherries to boiling and pour over soaked gelatin. Immediately add cherry gelatin and pitted cherries. Add enough sherry to make mixture equal 1 quart. Pour into pan or mold and refrigerate. After salad is congealed it may be frozen.

I do not use the best quality sherry or cooking sherry in this recipe. If you wish more cherries, use 2 cans and less sherry. When mixture is half congealed, I stir to distribute fruit.

Kathryn "Kitty" Scott

COCA-COLA SALAD

YIELD: 6-8 servings

2 — 3 ounce packages orange flavored gelatin
2 small packages cream cheese

2 — 10 ounce Coca-Colas
1 cup chopped pecans

Let cream cheese come to room temperature. Mix gelatin into cream cheese. Heat cola in a saucepan just to boiling point and pour over cheese mixture. Mix well. Add nuts and pour mixture into a deep mold. Leave filled mold out for 2 hours before placing in refrigerator. After 2 hours, refrigerate until firm. Salad separates into three layers.

Mrs. Conrad Hardie, Jr.

CONGEALED SALAD

1 — 15½ ounce can crushed pineapple
1 package lemon flavored gelatin
1 package lime flavored gelatin

1 cup mayonnaise
1 cup cottage cheese
dash of salt
1 package plain gelatin

Drain pineapple, using liquid from pineapple, add enough water to make 2 cups. Boil liquid. Stir in lemon and lime gelatins. Soften plain gelatin in a little cold water. Add softened gelatin to mixture. Chill until partially set. Then stir in cottage cheese, mayonnaise and pineapple.

Olive Peterson

When preparing vegetables for a salad such as carrots and beets, scrub the skin with a vegetable brush and rinse in cold water. Since many nutrients are contained in the skins, refrain from peeling.

CORNED BEEF SUPPER SALAD

YIELD: 12 servings

2 — 12 ounce cans corned beef
1 cup chopped celery
1 green pepper, chopped fine
3 hard boiled eggs
1 cup mayonnaise

1 chicken bouillon cube
1 cup hot water
2 envelopes gelatin, softened in ½
cup cold water

Dissolve softened gelatin in hot water and add bouillon cube. Partially cool. Add mayonnaise. Chop or coarsely grind corned beef, celery, green pepper and eggs. Add these ingredients to gelatin mixture. Pour mixture into standard size loaf pan or 2 quart flat casserole.

Serve with a sauce made from 1 small jar apple jelly, ⅓ cup salad mustard. Melt jelly and stir in mustard. Cool and serve with salad.

Mrs. T. N. McMullan

CRABMEAT SALAD

2 cups white crabmeat
½ cup celery, chopped
1 tablespoon onion, chopped
1 teaspoon key lime juice

1 teaspoon sweet pickle juice
½ cup salad dressing
salt and pepper to taste

Combine all ingredients and mix well. This is delicious used for sandwiches or served on crisp lettuce leaves with saltine crackers.

Peggy Hoskins

CRANBERRY SALAD I

2 — 3 ounce packages raspberry
flavored gelatin
2 cups boiling water
1 tablespoon unflavored gelatin
1 — #2 can whole cranberry sauce

1 small can crushed pineapple, undrained
1 cup celery, chopped
1 cup pecans, chopped
1 cup apple, chopped

Mix flavored gelatin with boiling water and add unflavored gelatin. When gelatin is almost set, add the other ingredients. This salad may be served plain or with a dressing made of equal parts of salad dressing and sour cream.

Mrs. Raymond E. Ford

When using fragile garnishes on salads such as slices of hard boiled eggs and avocado, toss the salad and then add the garnishes.

CRANBERRY SALAD II

1 — 13½ ounce can crushed pineapple OR 1⅔ cups
2 — 3 ounce packages OR 1 — 6 ounce package lemon flavored gelatin
1 — 7 ounce bottle gingerale, OR 1 cup

1 — 1 pound can jellied cranberry sauce, OR 2 cups
1 — 2 ounce package whipped topping mix
1 — 8 ounce package cream cheese, softened
½ cup pecans, chopped

Drain pineapple. Save syrup and add water to syrup to make one cup. Heat liquid to a boil. Dissolve gelatin in hot liquid. Cool. Gently stir in gingerale and chill until partially set. Blend drained pineapple and cranberry sauce together. Fold fruits into mixture; chill until firm. Prepare dessert topping as package directs. Fold cheese into topping. Spread on top of salad a few hours before serving.

Toast pecans in 1 tablespoon of butter at 350° for 10 minutes. Spread on top of dessert topping.

I use a 9 × 9 × 2 pan. This salad is especially nice at Christmas time.

Eleanor Colean

CRANBERRY-SOUR CREAM SALAD

YIELD: 10 servings

2 — 3 ounce packages cherry flavored gelatin
2 cups boiling water

1 — 16 ounce can whole berry cranberry sauce
1 pint commercial sour cream

Dissolve gelatin in boiling water; stir in cranberry sauce. Cool mixture, then fold in sour cream. Pour mixture into a 6 cup mold; chill until firm.

Margie Knott

CREAMY NUT CARROT SALAD

1 — 3 ounce package orange flavored gelatin
1 cup boiling water
1 cup sour cream
1 tablespoon mayonnaise

1 small can crushed pineapple, undrained
¼ cup golden raisins
¼ cup nuts
1 cup shredded carrots

Pour boiling water over gelatin until gelatin is dissolved. Spoon mayonnaise into a bowl with sour cream. Mix thoroughly, then add gelatin. Stir until blended. Chill until slightly thick. Stir in pineapple, raisins, carrots and nuts. Chill until serving time.

Mary M. Hardee

Parsley will stay fresh if stored in water in a tightly covered container in the refrigerator.

CUCUMBER SALAD
"FUR DEN FEINSCHMECKER"

2 large cucumbers
¼ cup fresh cut dill
salt, to taste

freshly ground pepper, to taste
2 tablespoons wine vinegar
¾ cup sour cream

Peel and thinly slice cucumbers. Sprinkle with salt, pepper, and fresh dill; mix thoroughly. Then add wine vinegar and sour cream. Blend together carefully with cucumbers; chill for one hour and serve.

As prepared by Anneliese for Craig Caliborne, noted food gourmet for *The New York Times* and author of several cookbooks. This recipe appeared in *The New York Times* and *The New York Times International Cookbook,* authored by Craig Claiborne.

Anneliese von der Cron

CURRIED FRUIT

OVEN: 350° 1 hour

1 large can cling peach halves
1 large can pineapple slices
1 large can pear halves
⅓ cup butter

¾ cup light brown sugar, packed
2 teaspoons curry powder
maraschino cherries, if desired

Drain fruit and arrange in a large pan. Make liquid of of butter, sugar and curry powder. Pour over fruit. Bake for 1 hour uncovered at 350°.

Can be refrigerated after baking. Then reheat at 350° for 30 minutes when ready to serve.

I use this in place of salad with ham, chicken, or casseroles. It goes over well.

Ruth Davis

DLR SALAD

½ cup raw converted rice
1¼ cups water
1 chicken bouillon cube
1½ tablespoons mild vinegar
½ teaspoon salt
dash of pepper

2 tablespoons salad oil
1 tablespoon chopped pimento
1 — 8 ounce can tiny peas, drained
1 — 4 ounce can mushroom stems
  and pieces, drained
1 teaspoon lemon juice

Cook rice in covered pan with water and bouillon cube, at low heat for about 25 minutes, until done and all liquid is absorbed. Remove from heat, uncover, and allow to cool slightly. While still warm, with a fork, stir in vinegar, salt and pepper. Then stir in oil, one tablespoon at a time. Mix in pimento, peas, mushrooms and lemon juice. Serve at room temperature.

Barbara Matuszewski

DELUXE CRANBERRY SALAD

2 — 3 ounce packages raspberry
    flavored gelatin OR 1 family size
    package
2 cups boiling water
1 — #2 can crushed pineapple

1 cup celery, chopped fine
1 cup walnuts, chopped
1 can whole cranberry sauce
½ pint sour cream
1 — 3 ounce package cream cheese

Dissolve gelatin in boiling water. Stir in pineapple, celery, nuts and cranberry sauce. Pour all into 2½ quart mold or individual dishes. Chill until firm. While this is chilling, combine sour cream and softened cream cheese. Blend until smooth. Spread over chilled mixture; sprinkle top with chopped nuts and serve.

Alice Dibo

FINEST TOMATO ASPIC

YIELD: 8 servings

3½ cups tomato juice
½ teaspoon salt
5-6 onion slices
few drops tabasco
1 bay leaf

2 tablespoons plain gelatin dis-
    solved in ⅔ cup cold water
2 tablespoons tarragon vinegar OR
    plain vinegar

Combine first five ingredients and simmer for 10 minutes. After softening gelatin in cold water add to hot tomato mixture. Add vinegar; stir, then strain. Pour mixture into mold and chill until firm. Serve on lettuce with mayonnaise.

This is such a tasty aspic that I sometimes add other chopped or minced vegetables such celery and cucumber after the aspic is cool and beginning to set. In this case, I don't strain it and it is a good vegetable salad that can be cut into squares and looks pretty on a lettuce leaf.

Tarragon vinegar gives a special flavor.

Isabelle Dorland McClintock

FRANKIE'S MIXED CAULIFLOWER SALAD

1 small head of cauliflower
2 ounces vinegar
4 ounces oil
1 teaspoon salt
1 tablespoon sugar
1½ teaspoons pepper

1 teaspoon garlic powder
small jar diced pimentos
4 ounces sliced mushrooms
6 ounces sliced onions
1 tablespoon tarragon leaves

Soak cauliflower in cold water for 15 minutes. Drain. Break cauliflower into small flowerettes. Mix remaining ingredients with cauliflower, toss and let stand 3 hours.

You can also use some green pepper. Mix now and then to get flavor through.

Donna Williford

FREEZER SLAW

¼ cup water
1 cup white vinegar
2 cups sugar
1 teaspoon celery seed
1 teaspoon mustard seed

1 teaspoon salt
1 medium cabbage
1 bell pepper
carrots, if desired

Boil first 5 ingredients for 5 minutes. Let mixture cool.

Chop, or shred, cabbage. Work in salt. Let set 1 hour in refrigerator. Drain well.

Add cooled mixture to cabbage with a chopped bell pepper; carrots too, if desired.

Press ingredients down so syrup covers. Keeps for 3 weeks in refrigerator after freezing.

Just before serving time, thaw, stir and serve.

Clara Hillenburg

FRESH TUNA FISH SALAD

1½ pounds boneless, skinless Black
    Fin Tuna fillet
water
salt
juice of one lemon
1 large onion, chopped
1 large tomato, chopped

¾ head lettuce
oregano
salt
pepper
green stuffed olives
olive oil
red wine vinegar

Cut fresh tuna into large chunks and cover with salted water to which lemon juice has been added. Cook until done, about 15-20 minutes on simmer. Remove from heat, drain and chill in refrigerator. Flake with a fork when chilled.

Tear bite-size pieces of lettuce into a large salad bowl, add cooked tuna, onion, tomato, olives, and sprinkle with oregano, salt and pepper to taste. Drizzle with olive oil and red wine vinegar. Toss well. Serve on a bed of lettuce leaves. Garnish with radish roses and lemon or lime slices.

Accompany with hot oven crisped crackers and fresh garlic butter.

Jeanne Crutchfield

FRUIT DELIGHT

1 can crushed pineapple, drained
1 can fruit cocktail, drained
1 large carton whipped topping

1 small carton cream cottage
    cheese
1 package strawberry gelatin OR
    any flavor desired

Mix cottage cheese and dry gelatin. Add fruit. Fold in whipped topping and refrigerate.

Any fruit can be used; also chopped nuts. Use on lettuce as a salad or serve in parfait glasses as a dessert.

Louise Gaines

FRUIT SALAD

½ cup blueberries, rinsed and
   drained
1 banana, sliced
¼ cantaloupe, diced

1 apple, peeled and cut
1 peach OR pear
juice from orange
2 tablespoons honey

Mix all cut up fruit. Slice banana just before serving. Pour orange juice mixed with honey over fruit. Mix gently.

Jean Finger

FRUITED CHEESE SALAD

YIELD: 8 servings

1 — 3 ounce package cream cheese
¼ cup mayonnaise
2 teaspoons lemon juice
⅛ teaspoon salt
⅓ cup chopped nut meats

1 — 8 ounce can drained pineapple
   tidbits
2 tablespoons chopped maraschino
   cherries
1 cup diced banana
½ cup heavy cream

Mash cream cheese, add mayonnaise, lemon juice and salt. Mix well. Add nut meats, pineapple, cherries, and banana. Whip cream until slightly thickened; fold in. Pour mixture into freezing tray and freeze until firm.

This recipe was given to me about 20 years ago by a lady in West Palm Beach who is the daughter of the minister who married my wife and me in the Presbyterian Church at the corner of Broad and Diamond Streets in Philadelphia, almost 50 years ago.

Bob Palmer

GELATIN SALAD

YIELD: 6-8 servings

1 small package lemon flavored gelatin
1½ cups hot water
¾ cup small marshmallows
½ small can crushed pineapple

1 small package cream cheese
½ cup pecans
1 apple with peeling
1 stalk celery
½ cup mayonnaise

Dissolve gelatin in hot water. Add all other ingredients but mayonnaise, which is added last. Refrigerate until set. Serve on lettuce leaves.

This salad is very rich and can be used when you have a light main course. It keeps very well.

Rachel H. Ryall

Since green leaves on the outside of lettuce contain more vitamins than the inside leaves, do not throw away any more than necessary.

GRANDMOTHER SHROPPIE'S
POTATO SALAD AND DRESSING

YIELD: 4 quarts/10-12 servings

6-8 hard cooked eggs
5 pounds potatoes, preferably
  Maine potatoes
1 large onion, or more if desired

Salad Dressing:
2 eggs, well beaten

½ cup sugar
½ cup vinegar
⅛ teaspoon dry mustard, optional
⅛ teaspoon salt
1½ tablespoons butter
celery seed
mayonnaise

Cook potatoes until done, but still firm. Cut into bite-size pieces. Chop onion and eggs. Make three recipes of salad dressing.

To make dressing, blend eggs and sugar together well. Add vinegar slowly. Mix all ingredients together. Place over medium heat and stir constantly. Allow mixture to cool. Then, while mixture is still warm, add 1 teaspoon celery seed.

Mix equal amounts of salad dressing and mayonnaise. In a large bowl, add ingredients together by layers; potatoes, onion, eggs, dressing, and repeat until all are used. Then mix very carefully.

I will not be responsible for the taste of this salad without the homemade dressing!

This dressing is delicious on cole slaw. Omit the celery seed and do not mix with mayonnaise. Use full strength.

This dressing will keep quite awhile in the refrigerator. It may be used on any salad or sandwich. Excellent on salmon, eggs, tuna. If the dressing is made ahead and is cold, just add hot water to celery seed to cover and let stand. Then add to the cold dressing for flavor to the potato salad.

This recipe came from Grandmother Shropshire; Grandmother Shroppie, as the family called her. Her family was originally from Shropshire, England, and was one of the first English speaking settlers in the southern New Jersey area. Grandmother Shroppie was my husband's maternal great grandmother; we judge that she was born about 1840.

Mrs. W. Allen Harris

To prevent salads from wilting, salt the greens just before serving.

HOT SPICED PEAR SALAD

OVEN: 350° 20 minutes

YIELD: 8 servings

1 — 29 ounce can Bartlett pear
  halves
1 — 17 ounce can apricot halves
1 — 17 ounce jar light sweet cherries
1 — 15¼ ounce can pineapple
  chunks
juice of one lemon

¾ cup combined fruit syrups
¼ cup brown sugar
¼ teaspoon nutmeg
¼ teaspoon cinnamon
⅛ teaspoon ground cloves
2 tablespoons butter
sour cream

Drain fruits, reserving ¾ cup of combined syrups. Arrange fruit in a 2 quart casserole and sprinkle with lemon juice. Combine syrup, brown sugar and spices and pour over fruit. Dot with butter and bake in 350° oven for 20 minutes.

Serve warm with sour cream. Sprinkle with a dash of nutmeg.

The chilled version makes a refreshing dessert.

Priscilla Haynes

ICE BOX SLAW

1 medium head green cabbage
1 medium head red cabbage
1 onion
1 cup salad oil

1¼ cups cider vinegar
⅞ to 1½ cups sugar, or to taste
1½ teaspoons celery seed salt, to
  taste

Grate or shred cabbages into large bowl. Slice or chop onion on top of cabbages. Sprinkle with salt to taste.

Combine salad oil, vinegar, sugar and celery seed in a saucepan and bring ingredients to a boil. While hot, pour over cabbages and onion. Do not stir. Cover bowl and place in refrigerator for 24 hours.Stir after 12 hours.

This slaw will stay crispy, fresh and good for a month.

Louise Gaines

IMPERIAL SALAD

3 ounces cooked pork OR chicken,
  slivered
½ head iceberg lettuce, shredded
¼ cup parsley, chopped
sesame seeds, lightly toasted, as
  needed

Sauce;
⅓ cup salad oil
⅓ cup red wine vinegar
1 tablespoon soy sauce, more to
  taste
1 teaspoon dry mustard
½ teaspoon seasoned salt
few dashes white pepper

Combine lettuce and parsley in a salad bowl. Cut pork or chicken into thin strips, about 1″ long. Add ingredients for sauce to a saucepan and bring to a boil; cook for about 1 minute. Add pork or chicken strips to sauce and heat through. Turn the very hot sauce into the salad bowl and toss quickly. Sprinkle sesame seeds over each serving.

Pat Raugh

ISLANDER SALAD

2 bunches fresh spinach, washed
  and shredded
1 cup thinly sliced celery
¼ cup thinly sliced green onion
1 chicken, cooked and diced
1 — 13¼ ounce can pineapple
  chunks, drained
1 — 4 ounce can water chestnuts
  drained

5 slices bacon, crumbled

Dressing:
1 cup salad oil
⅓ cup ketchup
⅓ cup sugar
¼ cup vinegar
2 teaspoons Worchestershire sauce
¼ teaspoon curry powder

Mix salad ingredients together.

Combine ingredients for dressing and cover; shake well to blend. Refrigerate salad and dressing separately until ready to serve, then apply dressing to salad and toss.

Nancy Davis

JELLO SALAD

1 large can crushed pineapple
1 can water
⅔ cup sugar
1 large package cream cheese
1 large package lime Jello

3 envelopes whipped topping mix
  OR 1 large container whipped
  topping
nuts, optional

Mix pineapple, water and sugar in a saucepan; boil for 5 minutes. Add cream cheese and jello to mixture and cool in refrigerator. Add nuts, if desired, and fold in whipped topping. Return salad to refrigerator until it sets.

Charline McClary

LAYERED SALAD

3 cups lettuce, shredded
1 cup Bermuda onion, sliced
1 cup fresh mushrooms, sliced
1 package frozen peas

1 cup mayonnaise
½ teaspoon sugar
1 teaspoon curry powder

Steam frozen peas for a few minutes, then cool. Layer first 4 ingredients in the order listed. Combine last 3 ingredients in a small bowl and spread over peas to seal. Refrigerate overnight if necessary.

Additional layers of chicken, water chestnuts, celery or ingredients of your choice may be added to make a main dish for a complete mean-in-one.

Jessie Perry

The leaves of a head of lettuce will separate easily by cutting the stalk out of the lettuce and pouring cold water forcefully into the opening for just a minute.

LIME GELATIN MOLD

2 — 6 ounce packages lime flavored gelatin
1 cup boiling water
2 cups cold water
2 cups creamed cottage cheese

⅔ cup mayonnaise
½ cup horseradish
2 tablespoons grated onion
parsley

Dissolve gelatin in boiling water. Add cold water and refrigerate. When mixture is syrupy, add cottage cheese, mayonnaise, horseradish and onion. Blend into syrup. Mold mixture and garnish with parsley.

Kathryn Burpo

LOW-CALORIE AMBROSIA

4 cups grapefruit sections
4 cups orange sections

1 — #2 can pineapple, packed in
own juice

Combine all ingredients, including juice and chill. For an added topping, blend cottage cheese in the blender.
This may be sweetened to taste with artificial sweetener.

Marguerite R. Brock

MANDARIN SALAD

YIELD: 8 servings

1 — 3 ounce package orange flavored gelatin
12 ounces cottage cheese
4 ounces whipped topping

1 can mandarin oranges
8 ounces crushed pineapple
½ cup slivered almonds

Drain all fruit. Pour dry gelatin over cottage cheese and mix thoroughly. Add fruit and mix. Then add topping and almonds. Refrigerate overnight.

Joan Kite

MARINATED VEGETABLE SALAD

1 medium can shoe peg white kernel corn
1 medium can French style green
beans
1 medium can English peas
1 cup finely chopped celery
1 cup OR ¾ cup chopped red onion

1 small jar pimentos chopped and
drained

Dressing:
½ cup salad oil
½ cup vinegar
6-8 tablespoons sugar
1 teaspoon salt
½ teaspoon pepper

Drain each can separately and rinse to remove liquid of can. Mix vegetables in a large bowl. Add chopped ingredients. Combine ingredients for dressing and taste-test before adding to vegetables. You may want to add more sugar to the dressing. Pour dressing over vegetables and stir several times before serving.
This salad may be made ahead. It is best when refrigerated.

Shirley Morgan

MEXICAN SALAD I

1 pound ground beef, browned and drained
1 can kidney beans
1 medium onion, peeled and chopped
2 tomatoes, coarsely chopped
8 ounces cheddar cheese, grated large
1 — 8 ounce jar taco sauce
¾ cup thousand island dressing
½ head lettuce, shredded
2 avocados, diced
1 — 5½ ounce bag taco-flavored tortilla chips, crushed

In a serving bowl, combine all ingredients except the lettuce and tortilla chips. Chill. At serving time, add lettuce and crushed chips and toss.

Mrs. Conrad Hardie, Jr.

MEXICAN SALAD II

1 onion, chopped
4 tomatoes, peeled and chopped
1 head iceberg lettuce, chopped
4 ounces cheddar cheese, grated
1 — 6½ ounce bag corn chips
1 avocado, sliced
1 pound ground round
1 can pinto beans
salt and pepper
thousand island dressing
1 jar chili sauce
½ cup sour cream
1 tablespoon dry parsley
½ cup mayonnaise
2 tablespoons chives
dash of tabasco

Fry meat and drain excess fat. Simmer pinto beans. Mix meat and beans with lettuce, cheese, chips, avocado and salt and pepper to taste; refrigerate.

Combine dressing, chili sauce, sour cream, parsley, mayonnaise, chives and tabasco in blender. Refrigerate.

Just before serving, mix meat, bean, lettuce, and chip mixture with blended liquids and toss to mix.

Serve with one jar of mild taco sauce served in a sauce boat.

Rhea Barrett

MOLDED AMBROSIA SALAD

⅓ cup sugar
½ cup chopped nuts
1 can flaked coconut OR fresh coconut
1 can mandarin orange sections
1 small can crushed pineapple
1 — 8 ounce carton sour cream
1 package orange flavored gelatin

Drain fruits and use juice to make 2 cups of liquid required for gelatin. Prepare gelatin using fruit juices for liquid. Add sugar and sour cream to gelatin mixture. Add drained pineapple and oranges along with coconut and nuts. Refrigerate.

I sometimes add fresh orange sections, about 2 oranges, to the mixture. If I add this, I also add about ½ package plain gelatin to the mixture.

Fresh grated coconut makes this salad much more tasteful.

Martha W. Rogers

QUICK COTTAGE CHEESE SALAD

1 large container cottage cheese
1 — 16 ounce can crushed pineapple

1 — 6 ounce package orange flavored gelatin
1 — 9 ounce container whipped topping

Drain pineapple until dry; with no syrup left. Mix pineapple with cottage cheese. Sprinkle dry gelatin mix over ingredients and combine. Fold in whipped topping and refrigerate.

Edie Stretch

QUICKIE SALAD

1 — 1 pound container cottage cheese
1 — 4½ ounce container whipped topping

1 small package any flavor gelatin
1 small can mandarin oranges
1 — 10 ounce can crushed pineapple

Drain fruits. Combine all ingredients and mix well. Chill and serve.

Annis Roberts

RASPBERRY-TOMATO GELATIN SALAD

1 — 16 ounce can stewed tomatoes

1 — 3 ounce package raspberry flavored gelatin

Place tomatoes in a saucepan and bring to a boil. Place mixture in blender and add gelatin. Mix well. Pour into mold and refrigerate until gelled.

C. F. Fawsett, Jr.

RUSTY PELICAN SALAD WITH HONEY DRESSING

iceberg lettuce
romaine lettuce
escarole
chickory
water cress
6 mushrooms
2 tomatoes
2 hard-boiled eggs
2 tablespoons chives
1 cup small shrimp, boiled with bay leaves

lemon juice
salt

Dressing:
5 ounces mayonnaise
2 ounces vegetable oil
2 ounces honey
1 ounce mustard
1 ounce scallion onion, finely chopped
1 pinch parsley, chopped
½ ounce lemon juice

Combine all salad ingredients in a large bowl. Blend ingredients for dressing. Chill salad and dressing separately; when ready to serve pour dressing on salad and toss lightly.

Eloise Tedder

SALMON MOUSSE

1 can (15½ oz.) salmon
2 envelopes unflavored gelatin
cold water
¼ cup lemon juice
½ cup peeled, seeded, and chopped
  cucumber

½ cup chopped celery
½ cup finely chopped onions
½ teaspoon salt
½ teaspoon fresh chopped dill
1 cup mayonnaise
1 cup heavy cream

Flake well-drained salmon; reserve liquid. Add enough water to liquid to make one cup. Place liquid in saucepan and soften the gelatin in it. Place over medium heat and stir until gelatin is dissolved. Pour into blender; add cucumber, onion, celery, and lemon juice. Blend until smooth. Add salmon, salt, and chopped dill; blend until well mixed. Remove one half of mixture and set aside. Add ½ cup of mayonnaise and ½ cup of heavy cream to mixture in blender; blend and remove from blender. Place remaining salmon mixture in blender; add balance of mayonnaise and cream and blend well. Remove from blender and chill mixtures until firm. Garnish with watercress and serve.

Lucinda Lauser

SHRIMP CHEESE MOLD

1 — 8 ounce package cream cheese
1 can tomato soup
1 cup mayonnaise
1 cup chopped celery
1 medium onion, chopped
⅛ cup green pepper, chopped

1-½ pounds fresh shrimp OR 2 cans
  shrimp
1 — 3 ounce package lemon flavored gelatin
¾ cup hot water

Heat soup and beat in cream cheese. Add mayonnaise, celery, onion and green pepper. Dissolve gelatin in water and blend with soup mixture. Cool mixture before molding. Pour into large mold and refrigerate. Serve as luncheon salad or appetizer with a salty cracker.

K. Prindible

SHRIMP MACARONI SALAD

¾ pound cooked, peeled, cleaned
  shrimp, fresh OR frozen
2 cups cooked shell macaroni
1 cup raw cauliflower, chopped
1 cup celery, sliced
¼ cup parsley chopped
¼ cup sweet pickle, chopped
½ cup mayonnaise OR salad dressing

3 tablespoons garlic French dressing
1 tablespoon lime OR lemon juice
1 teaspoon onion, grated
1 teaspoon celery seed
1 teaspoon salt
¼ teaspoon pepper
salad greens
1 hard-cooked egg, sliced

Thaw shrimp if frozen; cut large shrimp in half. Combine macaroni, cauliflower, celery, parsley, pickle and shrimp. Combine mayonnaise, French dressing, lime juice onion and seasonings; mix well. Add mayonnaise mixture to shrimp mixture and toss lightly; chill. Serve on greens; garnish with egg slices.

Ginger Hetrick Simmons

SHRIMP SURPRISE

YIELD: 1½ cups

¾ cup shrimp, chopped
¼ cup black olives, chopped
¼ cup black walnuts, chopped

1 tablespoon lemon juice
lettuce, chopped into bite-size
pieces

Combine all ingredients and blend well. Chill mixture thoroughly. When ready to serve, chop lettuce and toss with other ingredients.

Sandy Little

SPINACH SALAD I

YIELD: 8 servings

1 pound spinach
½ pound fresh mushrooms, thinly
sliced
¾ cup vegetable oil

1 tablespoon wine vinegar
1 teaspoon sugar
3 tablespoons lemon OR lime juice
1 orange, peeled and thinly sliced

Remove stems from spinach; wash leaves thoroughly and pat dry. Tear leaves into bite-size pieces. Combine spinach and mushrooms in a large bowl; set aside. Combine oil, wine vinegar, sugar and lemon juice; mix well. Toss spinach and mushrooms with dressing until well coated. Arrange orange slices on top.

Mrs. Noah Lybrand, Jr.

SPINACH SALAD II

1 package fresh spinach
¼ teaspoon cracked pepper
½ teaspoon Accent
½ teaspoon dry mustard
¾ teaspoon paprika
½ teaspoon salt
1 teaspoon sugar
2 teaspoons Worcestershire sauce
1 tablespoon A-1 Sauce

3 cloves garlic, chopped
3½ tablespoons wine vinegar
1 cup oil
¼ cup grated blue cheese
¼ cup bacon, fried crisp, then
crumbled
2 hard boiled eggs, chilled and
minced

Wash spinach and drain off excess water; let spinach drain well on a large towel, then place in a large plastic bag until ready to use. Mix next 11 ingredients in a jar and let stand for several hours. When ready to serve, tear spinach into small pieces and place in a large bowl; add egg, bacon and blue cheese. Toss ingredients together. Pour dressing from the jar over salad and toss again; serve.

Rose Anne Roche

In order to ripen an avocado, embed in a bowl of flour.

SPINACH SALAD WITH BEER DRESSING

Dressing:
½ cup mayonnaise
½ cup Dijon mustard
1 tablespoon horseradish
¼ cup beer

Salad:
fresh spinach
fresh mushrooms
cauliflower pieces
broccoli pieces
pecan halves

Mix mayonnaise and mustard together; add horseradish; gradually stir in beer. Blend until smooth.

Combine bite-size salad ingredients together in a bowl and pour dressing over salad; toss to mix. Serve.

Nancy Carlton

STUFFED-APPLE SALAD

6 big red apples
2 tablespoons lemon juice
¾ cup diced cheddar cheese
¾ cup coarsely chopped walnuts

¼ cup mayonnaise
¼ cup plain yogurt
6 lettuce leaves

Cut off the top third of one apple. Using a small, sharp knife and a large spoon, scoop out apple pulp, being careful not to puncture bottom of apple. Discard core. Dice remaining apple pulp; place immediately in a small bowl and toss with lemon juice to keep it from turning brown. Wrap apple shell in plastic. Repeat with remaining apples. Add cheese and walnuts to diced apple pulp. In a separate bowl, combine mayonnaise and yogurt; add to apple mixture. Toss until mixture is well coated. Line scooped out apple shells with the lettuce leaves. Fill shells with apple mixture; wrap each apple tightly in plastic wrap. Refrigerate until ready to serve.

Excellent for picnics. Use remaining apple mixture as a lunch salad; add raisins and chopped celery.

Debbie Jameson

TACO SALAD

1 pound ground OR very lean
  chuck
1 can red kidney beans, drained
⅛—¼ cup tabasco OR hot sauce
4 tomatoes, chopped
1 large head lettuce, shredded
½ cup green pepper, chopped

1 small can pitted black olives
  sliced
1 cup colby, longhorn, OR mild
  cheddar cheese, grated medium
1 large bag taco flavored corn
  chips, crumbled
1 large bottle creamy French
  dressing

Brown meat and drain well. Add kidney beans which have been drained and washed and hot sauce; heat until almost dry. Place lettuce, tomatoes, green pepper, and black olives in a large bowl. Add grated cheese and crumbled chips over this. Pour meat mixture over top of salad. Toss lightly and quickly with French dressing until well coated.

Green onion may be added to give an extra flavor. Serve with rolls, butter and beverage.

Barbara Kammeraad

TOMATO ASPIC

½ cup cold water
2 packages plain gelatin
3½ cups V-8 Juice OR tomato juice
¾ cup celery scraps and leaves, cut
　　into chunks
1 small onion, cut into chunks
6 whole cloves

1 large juicy lemon (to yield at
　　least 2 tablespoons)
1 teaspoon sugar
2-3 stalks celery, diced
½ to ¾ of one bell pepper, diced
½ cup sliced green olives

Mix gelatin and cold water together and set aside. Combine next 6 ingredients and simmer for 30 minutes; until flavors are mixed; then strain. Pour strained juice and gelatin together. Place into mold; add vegetables and chill.

Instead of green pepper, olives and celery, try artichoke hearts (packed in water), and chopped tomato pickles. You can make any number of recipes at one time.

Suzanne Varn

VEGETABLE SALAD

2 packages frozen baby lima beans
2 packages frozen green peas
2 cans yellow wax beans
packaged garlic OR herb dressing
oil vinegar
water

Dressing:
½ cup mayonnaise
½ cup sour cream
1 teaspoon salt
2 tablespoons mustard
2 teaspoons dry mustard
½ teaspoon pepper
½ cup onion, chopped
½ cup celery, chopped

Prepare packaged dressing mix with water, oil, and vinegar as package directs; set aside.

Drain yellow wax beans. Cook lima beans and peas as packages direct; drain. Combine limas, wax beans, and peas and chill. Marinate vegetables with ¼ cup garlic or herb dressing.

After 30 minutes drain any excess dressing from vegetables. Add onion and celery to vegetables.

Combine mayonnaise, sour cream and other dressing ingredients. Add to vegetables and blend well.

This recipe keeps well.

Libby Miller

To crisp up lettuce and celery, place in a container of cold water with slices of raw potato.

WINTER SALAD

YIELD: 6-8 servings

½ cup cider vinegar
½ cup sugar
¼ cup vegetable oil
1 teaspoon salt
½ teaspoon pepper
1 — 1 pound can sauerkraut

1 medium onion, chopped (to equal
 ½ cup)
1 green pepper, chopped
2 pimentos, chopped
½ teaspoon garlic salt
1 teaspoon celery seeds

Combine vinegar, sugar, vegetable oil, salt and pepper in a saucepan and bring to a boil, stirring to dissolve sugar.

Turn sauerkraut into a strainer and rinse under running water; drain well. Place kraut in a medium-size bowl. Pour hot vinegar mixture over kraut. Add onions, green pepper, pimentos, garlic salt and celery seed. Toss thoroughly. Allow salad to cool slightly; cover and chill for 4 hours before serving.

Crunchy sauerkraut, mellowed and seasoned, is so good with cold meats for Sunday suppers.

Jewell Hoyt

WIZ SLAW

3 apples, diced, but not pared
⅓ cup rose wine
4-5 cups shredded raw cabbage
 (one small head)
1 cup mayonnaise

1 cup raisins
1 tablespoon lemon juice
4 green onions, sliced
1 teaspoon celery seeds, optional

Pour wine over raisins and let stand for several hours. Then, dice apples and sprinkle with lemon juice; mix. Add wine-raisins, mayonnaise, onions, and apples to cabbage. Toss to mix; serve.

This goes great with ham, turkey, or roast pork.

Walt Wisnicky

YUM YUM SALAD

2 cups crushed pineapple and juice
juice of one lemon
½ cup sugar

1 package plain gelatin
¾ cup grated cheese
½ pint whipping cream, whipped

Heat pineapple, lemon juice and sugar. Soak gelatin in ½ cup cold water. Add gelatin to pineapple. Let mixture cool until it starts to set; add grated cheese and whipped cream. Refrigerate until firmly set.

Karen S. Hogan

Keep head lettuce wrapped in aluminum foil, it will keep longer.

A HONEY OF A SALAD DRESSING

¾ cup safflower oil
¾ cup corn oil
½ cup apple cider vinegar
1 tablespoon honey

1 teaspoon salt
½ teaspoon dry mustard
2 teaspoons salad herbs
1 large clove garlic

Pour oil into a 1 pint bottle. Simmer vinegar and herbs for five minutes to bring out flavor of herbs. Remove from heat; add honey, salt and dry mustard and stir until honey has dissolved. Peel garlic and make a few slits in it with a knife; but leave whole. Add vinegar mixture and garlic to oil and refrigerate.

Paul Mahan

AVOCADO DRESSING

½ avocado
½ cup French dressing
½ teaspoon lemon juice

½ teaspoon vinegar
dash of salt
dash of pepper

Mash avocado and slowly add dressing to avocado. Beat mixture until smooth. Then add lemon juice, vinegar and salt and pepper.

Dennis R. Nicewander, Ed.D.

BLEU CHEESE SALAD DRESSING

1 tablespoon vinegar
juice of one lemon
2 teaspoons seasoning salt
½ cup sour cream
¾ cup mayonnaise
¾ cup creamed cottage cheese

¾ cup oil
1 — 3 ounce package bleu cheese
¾ teaspoon garlic salt
dash of black pepper
dash of tabasco

Combine all ingredients and blend together well. Do not mix in a blender.

Pat Raugh

FAKE CAESAR SALAD DRESSING

1 package onion soup mix
1 can anchovy paste
6 eggs
½ teaspoon garlic powder
½ teaspoon curry powder

¼ teaspoon Worcestershire sauce
1½ cups mayonnaise
½ teaspoon dry mustard
1 cup grated Parmesan cheese
lemon

Combine all ingredients except lemon and place in a large bowl; blend until mixture is thick and smooth. If you like a saltier dressing, add more anchovies; whole ones may be used if they are smashed.

Place mixture in a large quart jar and refrigerate; use as needed. This will last for months.

When serving, remove portion to be used; add fresh squeezed lemon to taste to this portion.

Serve on romaine lettuce and add croutons.

I use all of the soup mix, but only half of the onions in it.

Lyn Jackson

FRENCH DRESSING I

YIELD: 2 quarts

2 cups oil
1⅓ cups sugar
2 cups ketchup
8 teaspoons A-1 Sauce

4 teaspoons paprika
4 teaspoons salt
4 small onions, grated
1 cup cider vinegar

Combine all ingredients and blend or shake well.

Pearl M. Wyse

FRENCH DRESSING II

½ cup sugar
½ teaspoon salt
small onion OR ½ medium onion

1 cup salad oil
½ cup chili sauce OR ketchup
½ cup vinegar

Place all ingredients in blender and blend until desired thickness is reached. This will keep for months under refrigeration.

Mrs. John D. Perdue

FRENCH DRESSING III

YIELD: about 2 cups

1 cup salad oil
½ cup ketchup
1 teaspoon salt
½ cup sugar

¼ teaspoon pepper
1 teaspoon dry mustard
½ cup plus 1 teaspoon vinegar
1 small onion, grated

Combine all ingredients in blender and blend for 2 minutes. Keeps in refrigerator for weeks.

Dorothy Klosterman

LAS VEGAS DRESSING

YIELD: 6 pints

2 quarts mayonnaise
½ cup sweet pickle relish
2 teaspoons black pepper
½ cup salad oil
4 tablespoons pineapple juice
½ cup sugar
4 tablespoons Worcestershire
 sauce
2 teaspoons celery salt

1 teaspoon garlic salt
2 teaspoons onion salt
1 teaspoon horseradish
2 teaspoons dry mustard
½ regular size bottle ketchup
¼ bottle chili sauce
4 hard boiled eggs, grated
4 tablespoons prepared mustard
1 onion, grated

Combine ingredients in a large bowl; mix or stir. This dressing will keep for six weeks if refrigerated. Use on salads, open face ham, chicken, or turkey sandwiches.

This recipe can easily be halved or quartered.

Mrs. Thomas P. Smythe

MILLIE'S SALAD DRESSING

1½ cups mayonnaise, do not use
  salad dressing
1 cup chili sauce

2 tablespoons finely grated sweet
  onion
¼ teaspoon ground red pepper
1½ cups whipped topping

Combine mayonnaise and chili sauce. Add grated onion and red pepper; mix well. Blend in whipped topping. Store dressing, covered, in refrigerator. This dressing keeps for 2 weeks.

This dressing is very light and has a delicate flavor. Serve on head lettuce or tossed green salad.

Mildred Brown Garrett

NO-COOK SALAD DRESSING

1 cup vinegar
1 cup oil
1½ cups sugar
½ teaspoon salt

2 teaspoons celery seed
½ teaspoon powdered mustard
½ onion, grated

Combine all ingredients in a tight-sealing jar and shake. Keep dressing refrigerated and shake before using.

Dot Gortner

POPPY SEED SALAD DRESSING

½ cup sugar
1 cup salad oil
1 teaspoon prepared mustard
1 teaspoon onion juice

¼ cup vinegar
¼ cup lemon juice
1 tablespoon poppy seeds

Combine all ingredients and whip with electric mixer. Store in pint container with lid in refrigerator. Use as needed on your favorite salads.

Fresh lemon juice is best.

I even use this dressing as a marinade for my potato salad. I marinate the salad for several hours in the refrigerator and all mayonnaise just before serving.

Wilda Worth

ROQUEFORT SALAD DRESSING

1 — 3 ounce package cream cheese
2 tablespoons cream
1 cup salad oil
3 tablespoons lemon juice
1 teaspoon sugar
1 teaspoon salt

¼ teaspoon onion powder OR ½
  small onion, chopped
½ teaspoon garlic powder
3 ounces Roquefort cheese
1 ounce blue cheese

Cream the cream cheese with a small amount of cream; add liquid and seasonings; mix well. Add crumbled cheeses and mix well. Mix well in blender or with electric mixer.

Peggy Prange

SALAD DRESSING I

½ cup sugar
1 teaspoon salt
1 teaspoon dry mustard
½ medium onion, cut fine

⅓ cup vinegar
1 cup oil
1 tablespoon celery seed

Mix sugar, salt and mustard together; add ½ of vinegar and ½ of oil. Beat thoroughly; add onions and remaining vinegar and oil; beat well. Add celery seed and beat again.

This dressing is a perfect complement to the best, garden-fresh salad.

R. Allan King

SALAD DRESSING II

1 lemon
1 lime
1 orange

1 cup sugar
1 egg

Juice lemon, lime and orange. Grate rind from lemon, lime and orange. Add rinds and juices to sugar and egg in a saucepan and bring mixture to a boil. Boil for 1 minute or until mixture is clear. Cool then refrigerate.

This may be used as any dressing, but this is very good on grapefruit early in season when they are not at their sweetest.

Rachel H. Ryall

SALAD DRESSING III

2½ cups white sugar
1 cup vinegar
1 cup ketchup
3 cups oil

1 tablespoon salt
1 tablespoon onion juice
1 tablespoon celery seed
1 tablespoon paprika

Mix all ingredients together and blend well with electric mixer or blender. This makes a nice sweet and sour dressing.

Judi Funnell

SANDY BEACHES

SANDWICHES

AVOCADO SANDWICHES

ripe avocado meat
salt
pepper

bran bread, thinly sliced
lime juice

Mash ripe avocado meat with a fork. Add salt and pepper and lime juice to season. Spread this mixture thickly between thin slices of bran bread.

The Committee

BAKED CHEESE SANDWICH

OVEN: 250° 1½ hours

16 slices sandwich bread
8 slices Old English cheddar
 cheese
5 eggs

3 cups milk
½ teaspoon dry mustard
salt
pepper

Grease pan large enough for 8 slices of bread. Butter one side of bread and place cheese between each 2 slices, buttered side out. Arrange in pan. In separate bowl, combine eggs, milk, mustard, salt and pepper. Mix well. Pour egg mixture over sandwiches on pan. Refrigerate pan and sandwiches overnight. Bake in 250° oven for 1½ hours. Slice diagonally and serve hot.

Dot Gortner

BEEF BARBECUE

2 pounds beef, cubed
½ cup vinegar
¼ cup sugar
1 can tomato soup
1 cup water

2 tablespoons Worcestershire
 sauce
salt
pepper
½ teaspoon A-1 Sauce

Mix all ingredients in heavy pan. Simmer for 3 to 3½ hours, until meat can be pulled apart. Add A-1 Sauce and cook for ½ hour longer.
Tasty to serve on a bun with cole slaw.

Mrs. Roy Green

For an easy and appetizing luncheon sandwich, top buttered rye toast with hard-cooked egg slices, add finely chopped onion to taste, cap with a slice of tomato and a slice of cheese, and place under broiler until cheese melts.

CHICKEN MAXIMUS

2 whole broiler-fryer chicken
  breasts
½ small onion, sliced
4 celery tops with leaves
½ carrot, sliced
1 chicken bouillon cube
1½ cups cold water
½ pound fresh mushrooms
4 tablespoons margarine

4 tablespoons flour
1 cup chicken broth
1 cup undiluted evaporated milk
1 tablespoon dry sherry
½ teaspoon salt
⅛ teaspoon pepper
8 slices white bread
3 tablespoons margarine
1 cup grated sharp cheddar cheese

Simmer first 6 ingredients, covered, for about 45 minutes; until chicken is done. Remove from heat and uncover. Allow chicken to cool while proceeding with recipe. Clean and slice mushrooms. Lift chicken from broth and set aside. Strain broth into a measuring cup. In the same pan used to cook the chicken, melt 4 tablespoons margarine and lightly sauté mushrooms. Blend in flour; gradually add broth and milk. Cook and stir until sauce reaches boiling point. Remove from heat and stir in sherry, salt and pepper. Remove chicken from bones and skin; slice meat. Lay bread slices in one layer on broiler pan. Toast one side; turn and toast second side. Spread margarine on one side of each slice. Arrange in pan, margarine side up in one layer. Spread chicken on toast and cover each open sandwich with mushroom sauce. Sprinkle each with grated cheese. Brown well under broiler, but do not have pan too close to heat source or browning will occur before sandwiches are heated through. Serve immediately.

This is an original recipe chosen by the National Chicken Cooking Contest as a semi-finalist for the 1972 Delaware Cook-Off.

Barbara Matuszewski

CHICKEN SANDWICHES

cold, finely chopped white chicken
  meat
finely chopped walnuts
finely chopped celery
lemon juice to taste

salt
pepper
mayonnaise dressing
lettuce
sourdough bread

Mix finely chopped chicken with walnuts, celery, salt and pepper and lemon juice with just enough mayonnaise to moisten. Spread mixture on crisp lettuce leaves and place between thin slices of buttered sourdough bread.

The Committee

Two tasty picnic sandwiches easy to pack are cream cheese, green onion and cucumber; and peanut butter and sliced bananas.

DRIED BEEF SANDWICH SPREAD

1 cup dried beef, finely chopped
1 cup grated sharp cheddar cheese
½ cup fresh green pepper, finely
  chopped

1 cup canned tomatoes, well
  drained
freshly ground pepper, to taste

In a saucepan, mix well the chopped dried beef, grated cheese, tomatoes, and ground pepper. Place on low heat for just a few minutes, stirring constantly, until the cheese is melted. Remove from heat and allow to cool. Spread on slices of natural wheat germ bread; add chopped green pepper, and serve.

Lucinda Lauser

GARDEN SANDWICH

1 pound cottage cheese
½ cup finely chopped, dry roasted
  peanuts
½ cup shredded carrot

4 tablespoons finely chopped radish
2 teaspoons minced onion
1 teaspoon Worcestershire Sauce
sliced bread
slightly softened butter

Thoroughly blend peanuts and cottage cheese. Cover and refrigerate until ready to use. Prepare other ingredients by combining all together. Spread bread with butter to the edges. Mix cottage cheese mixture with all other ingredients. Spread about ⅓ cup of the filling on each slice of bread.

One medium carrot will equal about ½ cup. One large radish will equal about 2 tablespoons.

Sandwiches may be frozen if radish is omitted. Sliced egg twist bread makes a delicious sandwich.

Millie Cook

HOT BROWN

4 slices of turkey OR chicken
  breast
4 slices of toast
4 slices bacon, cooked
4 slices tomatoes
1 cup cheese sauce

Cheese sauce:
2 tablespoons butter
1 cup milk
2 tablespoons flour
½ teaspoon salt
1 cup shredded cheddar cheese

To make cheese sauce, melt butter and add flour to make a paste. Add salt, milk, and cheese. Cook over moderate heat until thick and creamy. Keep hot.

For sandwiches, remove crusts from toast and cut toast into triangles. Lightly salt and pepper tomatoes. Place 4 triangles of toast to each oven-proof platter. Put slices of turkey or chicken on toast and pour hot cheese sauce over this. Place slices of tomato on top of sauce. Place platters under broiler and broil until tomato is done and sauce bubbles. Garnish with bacon.

If in a hurry, I sometimes use frozen Welsh rarebit instead of making the cheese sauce.

Mrs. Maltby F. Watkins

HOT HAM AND ASPARAGUS SANDWICHES

fried boiled ham
canned asparagus tips
cheese sauce
white bread

Cheese sauce:
3 tablespoons grated cheese
2 tablespoons butter
2 tablespoons flour
salt
pepper
1 cup hot cream

Place fried boiled ham on piece of thinly sliced white bread. Add 4 to 5 asparagus tips and cover with cheese sauce.

Cheese sauce: scald cream, melt butter in a saucepan over low heat. Remove from heat and add flour. Cook until bubbles form, then add all at once ⅔ cup of the hot cream, and gradually add the remainder of the cream. Add grated cheese, boil, stirring constantly until mixture thickens.

The Committee

HOT HAM SANDWICHES

OVEN: 350° 20 minutes   YIELD: 18 servings

18 hamburger buns, split
1½ pounds boiled ham, shaved
½ pound Swiss cheese, thinly sliced
½ pound butter, softened

2 tablespoons poppy seeds
3 tablespoons mustard
1 teaspoon Worcestershire sauce
½ small onion, minced

Equally divide the ham and cheese on the bottom half of each bun. Combine all remaining ingredients and beat well. Place dressing on top of each sandwich, top with lid of bun and wrap in foil. Bake in 350° oven for 20 minutes. Serve immediately.

With miniature buns, these would be excellent for a cocktail buffet.

The Committee

Sandwiches prepared in advance should be kept in a cool place, wrapped in a damp towel.

LUNCHEON SANDWICHES

YIELD: 4-6 sandwiches

tuna salad
egg salad
bread

pasteurized Neufachatel cheese
    spread with relish
8 ounces cream cheese
milk
sliced olives

Prepare your favorite tuna salad and egg salad. Cut bread in circles with a glass. On one layer of bread, spread egg salad, place a slice of bread on top and spread with tuna salad. Top with another slice of bread and spread with cheese spread with relish. Place another slice of bread on top. Soften cream cheese with enough milk to make it spreadable. Assemble remainder of bread circles with tuna and egg salad layers. Spread cream cheese/milk mixture over the top and sides of sandwiches.

It is best to prepare these the night before. Top sandwiches with slice of olive.

Serve with a molded or tossed salad.

Dixie Corrigan

SANDWICH LOAF

YIELD: 8-10 servings

1 loaf white bread, unsliced
1 cup cooked chicken
2 tablespoons diced celery
2 tablespoons chopped almonds
7-9 tablespoons salad dressing
1 — 6 ounce package frozen crab-
    meat
¼ cup diced cucumber, peeled
¾ cup grated cheddar cheese

2 tablespoons chopped olives
3 — 8 ounce packages cream
    cheese
1 tablespoon cooking sherry
salt
paprika
additional almonds and olives if
    garnish is added

Remove all crusts from bread. Cut horizontally into four slices, and spread each slice with butter to prevent fillings from soaking into bread.

Chicken filling: mix together diced chicken, celery, almonds and 3 tablespoons salad dressing. Season with salt.

Cheese filling: combine grated cheese with chopped olives. Add enough dressing to moisten.

Crabmeat filling: mix thawed crabmeat with cucumber, 2 tablespoons salad dressing and season with salt. Drain.

Frosting: combine softened cream cheese with sherry and enough salad dressing to make a frosting of spreading consistency. Season with salt and paprika.

To assemble loaf, spread chicken filling on one slice of buttered bread, cheese filling on second slice, crabmeat filling on third slice. Stack the three filled layers and cover with the fourth slice of bread, placing buttered side next to filling.

Frost top and sides of the stacked layers with cream cheese frosting. Garnish top (also sides if desired) with almonds and/or sliced olives.

Joyce Money

SUPER CORN DOGS

½ cup cornmeal
1½ cups flour
1 tablespoon baking powder
1 teaspoon salt

3 tablespoons sugar
milk
weiners
sticks

Mix all ingredients thoroughly using enough milk to make a thick batter. Insert sticks into ends of weiners and dip into batter. Fry in deep fat until brown.

Since I do not have a deep fryer, I use a deep Dutch oven pan with about 4 inches of fat heated to 350°-400°. I drop the corn dogs, sticks and all in and lift out with a pair of cooking tongs.

This is a favorite of all my children and their friends.

Wilda Worth

TUNA STACK-UPS

OVEN: 350° 20 minutes

15 thin slices bread, crusts removed
1 — 6½ ounce can tuna, flaked
1 — 2 ounce can mushroom stems
and pieces, drained
4 hard-cooked eggs, chopped
½ cup chopped ripe olives
¼ cup chopped green onions
½ cup mayonnaise

Sauce:
1 can condensed cream of chicken
soup
1 cup dairy sour cream
dash of Worcestershire sauce
¼ teaspoon dry mustard
dash of salt
dash of pepper

Butter both sides of bread slices. Combine tuna, mushrooms, eggs, olives, onions and mayonnaise. Spread on 10 slices of bread. Assemble 5 triple-decker sandwiches with remaining slices. Fasten corners with toothpicks and slice into two triangles. Butter edges of bread. Toast on baking sheet in 350° oven about 20 minutes or until lightly browned and crisp.

Sandwiches may be made ahead of time.

Heat sauce just until hot and spoon over hot sandwiches. Sprinkle slivered almonds over top if desired.

Kathryn Burpo

VEGETABLE SANDWICH

1 large cucumber
1 green pepper
1 medium onion
2 tomatoes, chopped fine
2 tablespoons gelatin

¼ cup cold water
1 cup mayonnaise
½ teaspoon dry mustard
1 teaspoon Worcestershire sauce
pinch of salt

Grind together cucumber, pepper and onion. Chop tomatoes very fine. Dissolve gelatin in cold water in a container set over pan of hot water. Add mayonnaise, mustard, Worcestershire sauce and salt to gelatin. Blend vegetables into this mixture. Chill.

The Committee

WELSH RABBIT

2 tablespoons butter OR margarine
1 pound grated sharp cheese
½ cup light beer OR milk
1 egg

½ teaspoon salt
½ teaspoon dry mustard
dash of cayenne OR black pepper
1 teaspoon Worcestershire sauce
toast slices

In medium saucepan, slowly heat butter. Add cheese and beer. Cook over low heat stirring frequently until cheese melts. Remove from heat. In small bowl beat egg with salt, mustard, cayenne and Worcestershire. Gradually add this to the cheese mixture, stir until well mixed. Stir over low heat until heated through and smooth, about 5 minutes. Serve over toast.

To keep warm, turn into top part of double boiler and let stand over hot water until ready to serve.

Sara L. Menge

NOTES

SAUCES

SAUCES

BARBECUE SAUCE I

1 large onion, cut up
2 tablespoons butter OR oleo
2 tablespoons vinegar
2 tablespoons brown sugar
4 tablespoons lemon juice
2 teaspoons prepared mustard

3 tablespoons Worcestershire
  sauce
1 cup water
1 cup ketchup
½ cup parsley, chopped
¼ teaspoon salt
⅛ teaspoon pepper

Brown cut up onion in butter. Add remaining ingredients and simmer 20 minutes. This sauce will keep a week in refrigerator or can be frozen for future use.

Gladys Grammer

BARBECUE SAUCE II

2½ pounds onions, cut up
3 pounds fresh OR 3 — 1 pound
  cans tomatoes
1 cup ketchup
1 cup smokey barbecue sauce
½ cup hot barbecue sauce
2 tablespoons liquid smoke

1 teaspoon mixed herbs
1 teaspoon oregano
1 tablespoon seasoned salt
1 tablespoon pepper
2 tablespoons prepared mustard
2-3 tablespoons bacon drippings

Sauté onions in bacon drippings until transparent, add tomatoes and cook on low or simmer for 1 hour. With potato masher, mash very fine; add other ingredients and cook on low until thick. Stir occasionally to prevent sticking to pan. Add more salt, if desired. Pour into sterilized jars while still cooking. I sometimes let it cool and put in blender, then re-heat for canning.

Carra Adams

BARBECUE SAUCE III

2 cups strained tomatoes
⅓ cup A-1 Sauce
2 garlic cloves, chopped
¼ cup lemon juice
¼ cup scallions, chopped

2 teaspoons prepared mustard
1½ teaspoons salt
1 teaspoon pepper
1 teaspoon dry mustard
dash of tabasco (optional)

Put the strained tomatoes and rest of ingredients in a blender, cover the container and blend the sauce thoroughly.

The Committee

Instant bearnaise sauce can be prepared quite easily by combining one cup mayonnaise with three tablespoons butter, two tablespoons tarragon vinegar, and one-eighth teaspoon tarragon in a sauce pan. On low heat, stir mixture with a whisk until smooth.

BARBECUE SAUCE FOR CHICKEN

½ cup peanut oil
½ cup lime juice

2 tablespoons onion, finely
  chopped
½ teaspoon dry tarragon
½ teaspoon tabasco

Combine all ingredients and blend thoroughly.

The Committee

BARBECUE SAUCE FOR HAM

1 cup brown sugar
½ cup vinegar
2 tablespoons prepared mustard

1 clove garlic, finely minced
1 cup pineapple juice

Combine all ingredients except pineapple juice in saucepan and bring to a boil and simmer for 3 minutes. Remove from heat and stir in pineapple juice.

The Committee

BASIC CHEESE SAUCE

3 tablespoons margarine, melted
4 tablespoons flour
1 cup evaporated milk
1 cup water

½ teaspoon salt
½ pound sharp American cheese,
  cut in small cubes
1 teaspoon lemon juice

Melt margarine in top of double boiler over direct heat. Stir in the flour. Blend water with evaporated milk. Gradually add this mixture with the margarine and flour. Cook over boiling water until thickened. Stir in cheese and stir until completely melted. Serve hot.

Ida C. Morgan

BLENDER BERNAISE SAUCE

⅓ cup minced onions
¼ cup white wine
¼ cup wine vinegar
1 teaspoon parsley
1 teaspoon tarragon

3 egg yolks
1 tablespoon fresh lemon juice
2 dashes salt
pinch of cayenne pepper
¼ pound hot, melted butter

Place onion, wine, vinegar, parsley, and tarragon in saucepan. Boil until almost all liquid has been evaporated. Put in blender and add egg yolks, lemon juice, salt and pepper. Blend at low speed for 5 seconds. Then add hot melted butter, slowly. Mixture may be thickened if necessary by heating slowly in double boiler for a few minutes.

Because of the lemon juice, this recipe can be made in multiple proportions and stored for several weeks under refrigeration. To use, heat amount needed in glass placed in hot water, stirring as the portion warms up. Left over egg whites are good for Ramos Gin Fizzes.

James W. Sneed, Jr.

BLENDER HOLLANDAISE SAUCE

3 egg yolks
1 tablespoon fresh lemon juice
2 dashes salt

pinch of cayenne pepper
¼ pound melted butter

In blender, place egg yolks, lemon juice, salt and pepper. Use very little pepper. While blending at slowest speed, slowly pour in butter.

Because of the lemon juice, this recipe can be made in multiple proportions and stored for several weeks under refrigeration. To use, heat amount needed in glass placed in hot water, stirring as the portion warms up. Left over egg whites are good for Ramos Gin Fizzes.

James W. Sneed, Jr.

CLAM SPAGHETTI SAUCE

¼ cup olive oil
½ cup butter
6 cloves garlic, chopped
¼ cup parsley, chopped
1 tablespoon sweet basil
3 tablespoons Parmesan cheese

1 pinch dry red pepper seeds
1 pinch black pepper, freshly
  ground
10-12 large clams
1 — 8 ounce can tomato sauce

Warm oil in saucepan, add butter and simmer until melted. Add all ingredients except clams and tomato sauce and bring to a boil. Add clams, clam liquid and tomato sauce and warm thoroughly.

Serve over cooked spaghetti.

I like to serve this with garlic bread and Key Lime Pie or Angel Pie. A Caesar Salad is also good.

Louise Sheward

COCKTAIL SAUCE FOR
SHRIMP AND CRAB FINGERS

1 cup tomato ketchup
½ cup chili sauce
1 tablespoon vinegar
1 teaspoon Worcestershire sauce

1 teaspoon horseradish, grated
juice of one lemon
¼ teaspoon celery salt, scant
5 drops tabasco

Mix all ingredients together thoroughly.

The Committee

HOLLANDAISE SAUCE

4 egg yolks
¼ pound soft butter, cut up
1 tablespoon lemon juice

2 tablespoons boiling water
salt
dash cayenne pepper

In blender combine yolks, butter, lemon juice and hot water. Cover and blend for 20 seconds. Empty blender into small saucepan and season mixture. Stir over hot water, or very low heat, until sauce is thick and smooth.

June Carlton Vest

ITALIAN SPAGHETTI SAUCE

1 pound ground meat
1 small pod garlic
4 stalks celery
1 small can tomatoes, chopped
3 medium onions
1 green pepper

1 small can tomato paste
3 tablespoons shortening
salt
pepper
1 teaspoon chili powder

Brown meat in shortening. Add chopped onion, celery, green pepper and garlic. Steam for 15 minutes. Add tomato paste and chopped tomatoes. Add salt, pepper and chili powder. Simmer for 2 hours, adding water as needed to prevent burning. Serve over spaghetti.

Ruth Minehan

MENUIERE SAUCE

2 tablespoons butter
1 tablespoon lemon juice

½ teaspoon chopped parsley

Melt butter in a pan; add lemon juice and parsley. Serve hot.
Especially good served with Pompano Almondine (see recipe).

Nick Midelis
Hilltop House

MUSTARD SAUCE

½ medium jar mustard
1 stick margarine
1 tablespoon Worcestershire sauce

3 tablespoons vinegar
¼ cup brown sugar

Combine all ingredients in saucepan and bring to a boil. Simmer about 10 minutes.
Delicious with ham, pork, or spareribs.

Shirley O'Haire

OKEECHOBEE BARBECUE
SAUCE FOR SPARERIBS

juice from a large bottle of sweet
  pickles
1 small bottle ketchup
½ bottle Worcestershire sauce

½ small bottle horseradish mustard
2 tablespoons mayonnaise
2 tablespoons melted butter
brown sugar, to taste, optional

Combine all ingredients and mix well. This mixture will keep indefinitely in refrigerator.
Baste ribs frequently either on charcoal grill or in a 325° oven.

Mrs. Burnett Bartlett

SAUCE ESPAGNOLE
OR BROWN SAUCE

OVEN: 475° 45 minutes

5 pounds veal bones, cracked
1 large onion, quartered
2 celery ribs with leaves, coarsely chopped
5 small carrots, peeled and quartered
½ teaspoon dried thyme
3 bay leaves

1 teaspoon peppercorns, crushed
3 garlic cloves, unpeeled
1 tablespoon salt
½ cup all-purpose flour
12 cups water
1¼ cups tomato puree
½ cup chopped leeks, green part
3 parsley sprigs

Preheat oven to hot, 475°. Combine bones, onion, celery, carrots, thyme, bay leaves, peppercorns, garlic and salt in open roasting pan. Bake for 45 minutes. Reduce temperature if necessary to keep bones from burning, but do not add any liquid to the pan.

Sprinkle bones with flour and stir with 2-pronged fork to distribute flour evenly. Bake for 15 minutes longer.

Transfer bones to large kettle. Add 2 cups water to the roasting pan and cook over moderate heat, stirring to dissolve brown particles on bottom and sides of pan.

Pour off liquid from pan into kettle with bones. Add tomato puree and remaining water. Add leeks and parsley and bring liquid to a rapid boil. Simmer for 2 hours. Add more liquid if necessary. Skim to remove fat and foam; strain.

Sauce may be frozen and defrosted as needed. Makes about 2 quarts.

There is nothing more French than the sauce that is known as Espagnole. It is one of the foundation sauces of French cuisine and is nearly as important as wine, shallots, butter and cream. Brown sauce is easy to prepare, but it is time consuming. It is used to enrich stews and ragouts and is frequently an accompaniment to grilled meats, poultry, and game.

Mrs. David S. Keen

SOUTHERN TOMATO GRAVY

YIELD: 4-6 servings

¼ cup grease; bacon, ham or beef
¼ cup flour
2 cups warm milk

salt
pepper
2 large ripe tomatoes

In skillet over medium heat, heat fat. Gradually add flour, stirring until smooth. Then, stirring constantly, slowly add warm milk and salt and pepper to taste. Cook until sauce reaches desired thickness, stirring constantly.

Dice tomatoes into approximately ½″ cubes and place in large bowl, pour gravy over tomatoes, mix and serve.

Best served over biscuits and baked ham.

Don D. Brown

SPAGHETTI SAUCE

2 seeds chili, no more
2 pinches thyme
1 can mushrooms OR ½ pound
   fresh mushrooms
2 small cans tomato paste
1 large can tomato juice

3-4 onions, chopped
garlic, to taste
1 green pepper, chopped
1 tablespoon granulated sugar
1 pound ground beef
1½ pounds spareribs, back ribs

Fry onions and garlic. Brown spareribs. Brown beef. Drain. Combine all ingredients in pan and simmer for several hours; the longer the better.

Serve over cooked spaghetti. Sauce may be frozen or kept in the refrigerator for 2-3 weeks.

Betty Durdy

SPECIAL TARTAR SAUCE

½ cup sour cream
½ cup real mayonnaise
1 tablespoon lemon juice

1 very small garlic clove, minced or
   crushed, optional
1 teaspoon coarsely grated onion
1-2 tablespoons dill pickle, finely
   minced

Combine all ingredients and mix well. Refrigerate until needed.

The Committee

STEAK SAUCE

2 tablespoons steak drippings
¼ cup onion, finely chopped
½ teaspoon mustard
1 teaspoon Worcestershire sauce

½ teaspoon salt
⅛ teaspoon pepper
½ cup boiling water
1 beaten egg

Place ingredients in saucepan, cover and simmer for 10 minutes. Strain sauce and pour it slowly, beating it constantly, over beaten egg. Stir and cook sauce for 1 minute over low heat. If desired, stir in strained drippings. Pour sauce over broiled steak.

Zelnith Y. Morris

SWEET AND SOUR SAUCE

2 chicken bouillon cubes
1 cup water
½ cup sugar
3 tablespoons cornstarch
½ cup pineapple juice

½ cup vinegar
3 tablespoons soy sauce
½ cup pineapple chunks
2 green peppers, cut in squares
3 stalks celery, cut diagonally

Mix cornstarch and sugar. Add water in which bouillon cubes are dissolved. Add vinegar, pineapple juice and soy sauce. Cook in saucepan until thick and clear. Just before serving add pepper, celery, and pineapple chunks and cook for about 3 minutes.

Very good with meat balls, cubed chicken or turkey.

Florence Banes

SOUPS

SOUPS

BAKED ONION SOUP

OVEN: 350°

½ cup butter
3 large onions, thinly sliced
1½ tablespoons flour
5½ cups seasoned meat stock
few drops tabasco sauce

salt
pepper
6 slices toast
6 slices provolone cheese, more if
  desired

Fry thinly sliced onions in butter until golden brown. Stir in flour, add stock and seasonings and simmer for 10 minutes. Pour soup into individual ovenproof dishes, lay a slice of toast, trimmed to fit, on top and cover with a thick layer of cheese. Bake in 350° oven until cheese is melted and bubbly.

Original recipe called for 4 ounces grated cheddar cheese, and was broiled for 3-4 minutes. I prefer to top it with provolone and bake it.

B. J. Nelson

CANADIAN CHEESE SOUP

YIELD: 2 quarts

¾ cup onion, finely chopped
¼ cup butter OR margarine
½ cup flour
4 cups milk
4 cups chicken broth
½ cup carrot, finely diced

½ cup celery, finely diced
⅛ teaspoon salt
dash paprika
1 cup sharp processed cheddar
  cheese, diced

Cook onion in butter until tender but not brown. Blend in flour. Add next 6 ingredients, cook and stir over medium heat until mixture thickens and bubbles. Reduce heat, add cheese, stir until cheese melts. Simmer for 15 minutes. Garnish with toasted bread, topped with olive slices.

Connie Wagers

For an exciting and exotic flavor, add freshly grated nutmeg to a cup of chicken soup.

CHICKEN BISQUE BARBARA

YIELD: 6 servings

1 — 3 to 3½ pound broiler-fryer
  chicken, cut up
1 cup celery, sliced with leaves
1 cup onion, coarsely chopped
½ cup carrots, thinly chopped
1 — 28 ounce can tomatoes OR 3½
  cups peeled, chopped fresh tomatoes
3 cups water
3 chicken bouillon cubes

2 tablespoons fresh parsley OR 1
  tablespoon dried parsley
4 whole cloves
6 whole peppercorns
1 small bay leaf
2 teaspoons salt
3 tablespoons converted raw rice
2 cups skim milk
2 tablespoons dry sherry
1 lemon, cut in paper-thin slices

Combine first 13 ingredients in a large Dutch oven. Cover and simmer 1 hour or until chicken is done. Take pan from heat and remove cover. Allow contents to cool slightly. Carefully lift chicken from broth, scraping any adhering vegetables and rice back into pot. Put meat on platter to cool enough for comfortable handling. Remove skin and bones from chicken and cut meat into bite-size pieces. Set aside.

Pour all contents of pot into container of blender in several batches. Puree until smooth. Return to Dutch oven and stir in milk, sherry, and chicken. Mix well and heat slowly. Do not allow soup to boil. Just before serving, garnish with parsley and lemon slices. Stir well. Ladle into warmed soup bowls.

If desired, this hearty, one-dish meal may be accompanied by hot biscuits and marinated cucumber slices.

Barbara Matuszewski

CLAM CHOWDER I

YIELD: 2 quarts

¼ pound salt pork, cubed
3 cups cubed potatoes
¾ cup chopped onion
2 cups water
salt

pepper
18 chopped clams and juice
1½ cups milk
4 tablespoons flour
½ cup milk

In heavy cooker, fry pork until brown. Add potatoes, onions and water. Add salt and pepper to taste. Cook until tender. Heat 1½ cups milk, do not boil, and add to potato mixture.

In small jar, place 4 tablespoons flour and ½ cup milk. Shake vigorously and then add to soup. Stir. Then add chopped clams and juice. Simmer for about 15 minutes. Do not boil.

Shirley W. Myers

To remove fat from soup, chill until the fat rises to the top and forms a thin layer, then remove.

CLAM CHOWDER II

1 pint fresh chopped clams with
juice
4 medium raw potatoes, cut in
cubes
1 medium onion, chopped

¼ pound salt pork, diced small
1 stalk celery, chopped
1 tablespoon cornstarch
1 quart water

Fry pork, add onion and celery. Cook for a few minutes but do not brown. Place potatoes in water and bring to a boil. Add other ingredients. Cook mixture until potatoes are tender. Thicken mixture with cornstarch which has been mixed with a small amount of water. For variations, a can of creamed corn or tomatoes can be added.

Peggy Hoskins

COLD BEET BORSHT

2 bunches beets, shredded
1 tablespoon salt
3 tablespoons sugar
2 lemons, juiced

1 teaspoon fresh ground pepper
2 eggs, beaten
sour cream

Choose small beets, if possible, cut off tops and roots and scrub skin well. Save tops. Shred beets with skins on, removing all rough skin from tops. Place in large kettle with cold water about 2 inches above beets. Boil 15 minutes. Skim when any scum appears. Set aside until lukewarm, then strain beets from liquid which is the soup. Add about 3 heaping tablespoons of beets back into the soup, reserve rest to make pickled beets.

Add salt, sugar, lemon juice, pepper and beaten egg to soup. Use one egg to each quart of soup. Chill well and serve cold with sour cream floating on top.

A small boiled potato, hot, may be added to the cold soup. Fresh beet tops may be cooked like spinach, add a little vinegar when adding butter when done.

This is a Russian recipe brought over by imigrants. There is also a borsht made with meat which is served hot.

Eden Gray

If soup is over-salted, simply peel a potato and place it in the soup. As the soup simmers the potato will absorb all the excess salt.

CONCH CHOWDER — INDIAN RIVER STYLE

2 pounds whole conch, usually frozen, fresh is best but hard to find
6 large potatoes, diced
4 large sweet onions, chopped
6 green peppers, diced
2 Cuban peppers, sliced
3 cloves fresh garlic, chopped
2 cans, peeled Italian tomatoes

12 peeled, fresh tomatoes, medium
size, sliced
3-4 quarts water
2 tablespoons freshly ground black
pepper
4 tablespoons hot sauce
4 tablespoons olive oil

Cut conch finely with sharp knife (no food processors, please!). Saute conch, onions, garlic and peppers in olive oil for 6 minutes. Mix with other ingredients and put all into large heavy pot. Bring to a boil and then simmer on low heat for 4 hours.

Refrigerate overnight and reheat for serving. This is an important step as it brings out all the flavor. Salt and pepper to taste and serve with hot sauce or tabasco on the side. Serve also with hot cornbread or corn muffins.

This chowder is a combination of Key West, Bahamian and Florida East Coast recipes dating from the 18th century. It's easy and always delicious.

M. L. Simmons, D.V.M.

CRAB BISQUE

1 onion, chopped
1 stalk celery
1 carrot
salt
pepper
1 cup white wine
2 cans chicken broth

1 pint medium cream
2 cups milk
½ stick butter
1 tablespoon ketchup OR tomato
paste
salt pork
fresh or canned crab

Sauté 2″ × 2″ chopped cube salt pork. Add onion, celery, and carrot. Sauté until brown. Add salt and pepper. After browning vegetables, add crab; while pan is still hot, add wine. This will be bubbly; simmer for 1 minute. Add chicken broth, cream and milk. All liquid ingredients should be added to your desired thickness. Add butter, ketchup or tomato paste. Season to taste.

Serve with warm French bread, unsalted butter, Caesar salad and ice cold chablis. Makes a wonderful romantic supper.

Lorraine Helms

When preparing soup, vegetables, spices, and salt should be added the last hour of cooking.

CRAB CHOWDER

4 large potatoes, diced
1 large onion, chopped
6 slices bacon, cut up
3 tablespoons flour

1 stick butter
2 cups crabmeat, cooked
1½ quarts milk
1 can evaporated milk

In large pot put potatoes in small amount of salted water. Cook until potatoes can be mashed. In frying pan, cook bacon and onions until brown and crisp. Add bacon and onions and bacon fat to mashed potatoes. Sprinkle flour and blend mixture. Add butter and milk, stirring constantly and heat almost to boiling. Add crabmeat and salt and pepper to taste. If too thick add more milk. Serve hot.

This is a splendid "supper" company meal to be served with salad and light dessert.

Mrs. Ralph Wilson

DELICIOUS CHICKEN SOUP

1 — 2 to 3 pound roasting chicken
2 carrots
2 onions
2 tomatoes
1 cup mushrooms
broccoli
1 cup white wine

4-5 cups water
1 tablespoon marjoram
1 bay leaf
1 can mushroom soup
salt
pepper

Roast chicken in a Romertopf oven with carrots, celery, onion, tomatoes, mushrooms and 1 flowerette of broccoli. Add white wine, and roast until chicken is tender. At this stage, enjoy legs and thighs for lunch.

Dump entire contents of Romertopf with all juices in large soup pot. Add water, marjoram, bay leaf, lots of salt and pepper, and soup. After simmering for ½ hour, remove all bones. Simmer for another 1½ hours. Cool.

Heat when ready to serve. Add noodles if desired.

Serve with warm French bread and glass of cold chablis.

Lorraine Helms

FISH CHOWDER

YIELD: 6 servings

2 pounds fish; bass, crappie,
  catfish, or saltwater fish
4 large potatoes, diced
1 bay leaf
2 tablespoons butter
freshly ground pepper

2 ounces salt pork, diced
2 onions, diced
1 cup celery, chopped
1 quart milk
1 teaspoon salt

Simmer fish in 2 cups water for 15 minutes. Drain, reserving broth. Remove bones from fish. Sauté diced pork until crisp, remove and set aside. Sauté onions in pork fat until golden brown. Add fish, potatoes, celery, bay leaf, salt and pepper. Pour in fish broth plus enough boiling water to make 3 cups liquid.

Simmer for 30 minutes. Add milk and butter and simmer another 5 minutes. Serve chowder sprinkled with diced pork.

Virginia Berger

FLORIDA CORN CHOWDER

YIELD: 6 servings

¼ pound salt pork, diced
1 medium onion, diced
½ cup celery, diced
2 cups potatoes, peeled and cut in
    ¼″ cubes
2 cups water
½ teaspoon salt
½ teaspoon sugar

¼ teaspoon pepper OR less
2 cups milk OR half & half
2 — 16 ounce cans whole kernel
    corn, white OR yellow
1 — 6½ ounce can minced clams
    (optional)
snipped parsley, chives OR paprika

Cook pork in large heavy kettle until crisp and brown. Add onions and celery and cook until tender, but not brown. Add potatoes, water, salt, sugar and pepper. Cover and simmer until potatoes are tender, about 20 minutes. Add milk, corn and clams, if used. Bring to a boil and remove from heat. Ladle into warm bowls and sprinkle with parsley, chives or paprika.

Paul Mahan

FRENCH ONION SOUP

OVEN: 325° 10 minutes

YIELD: 6 servings

2 tablespoons butter OR marga-
    rine
2 tablespoons oil
6 medium onions, sliced (about 1½
    pounds)
½ teaspoon sugar
3 tablespoons all purpose flour
3 — 10 ounce cans condensed beef
    bouillon

3 soup cans of water
1 cup dry red OR white wine OR
    use 1 cup water
1 bay leaf
½ teaspoon sage
1 cup grated Swiss cheese
1 cup grated Parmesan cheese
6 slices French or Italian bread,
    toasted, 1″ thick

Heat butter and oil in a heavy saucepan. Stir in onions, cover and cook over low heat 20 minutes, stirring occasionally. Uncover, add sugar and cook over medium heat for 20 minutes, stirring frequently until onions are golden brown. Reduce heat, blend in flour and cook for 2 minutes. Gradually stir in bouillon, water, wine, bay leaf and sage. Bring to a boil, reduce heat and simmer 30 minutes. Remove bay leaf. Combine cheeses. Ladle into individual oven-proof soup bowls. Top with toasted bread and grated cheese, using ⅓ cup cheese for each serving. Bake at 325° for 10 minutes, then broil 2 minutes until cheese is melted.

To toast bread, place on a baking sheet and bake at 325° for 10 minutes, turn and bake 10 minutes longer, until lightly browned and dry.

Marian Pearce

Sip a glass of chilled white wine with soup course.

HAMBURGER SOUP

1 pound ground beef, lean
1 cup chopped onions
1 cup cubed raw potatoes
1 cup sliced raw carrots
1 cup shredded cabbage
1 — #2 can tomatoes
1 small bay leaf, crushed

½ teaspoon dried thyme
¼ teaspoon dried basil
2½ teaspoons salt
⅛ teaspoon pepper
1½ quarts water
cubes of cheddar cheese, or grated
   for top of soup

Sauté beef and onion until slightly brown. Add tomatoes and simmer for about 45 minutes. Add all other ingredients, cover and simmer for 1 hour or until done.

Grated Parmesan cheese may be used instead of the cheddar cheese. Fruit for dessert will complete this light supper.

Kristin Wagers

HOMEMADE FRESH VEGETABLE BEEF SOUP

one large OR several small soup
  bones
2-3 pounds stew beef
water to cover OR ½ water and ½
  beef consomme
2 large carrots, chopped
½ small rutabaga, diced
1 small turnip, diced
2 roots parsnip, diced
4 big ears corn, cut off cob OR ¾
  cup frozen
8 red radishes, sliced
4 stalks celery, chopped
2 minced garlic cloves
2 large onions, chopped
½ package fresh OR frozen lima
  beans
½ package black-eyed peas, fresh
  OR frozen

1 pound (in shell) green peas OR 1
  cup frozen
¼ small head cabbage, shredded
½ head lettuce, shredded
½ pound snapped green beans, OR
  1 cup frozen
1 medium green pepper, chopped
¼ head cauliflower, chopped
¼ bunch fresh broccoli, OR ½
  package frozen
1 large cucumber, diced
10 small tomatoes, peeled and
  chopped
2 large zucchini squash, diced
2 large yellow summer squash,
  chopped
2 large potatoes, peeled and
  chopped
¼ bunch parsley OR 1 tablespoon
  parksley flakes
½ pound okra, fresh, OR ½ frozen
  package

Place bones and beef in 7 quart or larger pot. Bring to a boil then turn to medium-low while the remainder of vegetables are added in the order listed.

Simmer slowly for several hours until all vegetables are done. A dash of pepper sauce (hot peppers and vinegar) on top of each serving also adds a special flavor. Serve with fresh crisp crackers or hot Cuban bread with butter.

Jeanne Crutchfield

KING'S WESTERN BEEF CHOWDER

YIELD: 4 servings

1 pound ground chuck, lean
⅓ cup chopped onion
2 tablespoons shortening
2 — 10½ ounce cans cream of celery soup

1 soup can water
1 teaspoon salt
tabasco
½ teaspoon black pepper

Brown beef and onions in the shortening. Cut up tomatoes and add other ingredients. Salt to taste, and add about 4 drops of tabasco. Simmer about 20 minutes, stirring occasionally.

Cream cheese on your favorite breads will cap this cool weather favorite.

R. Allan King

LUISITA'S GAZPACHO

2 tablespoons salt
2 tablespoons olive oil
3 garlic cloves
1 lemon
1 medium onion
1 green pepper

1 large, fresh tomato
1 cucumber
1 rib celery
1 large can tomato juice
seasoned croutons

In a mortar, mash the garlic with salt and add oil and lemon juice and mix well. Chop onions, pepper, tomato, cucumber and celery. Place ½ cup of mixed chopped vegetables into a large serving bowl. Add garlic/lemon/oil mixture. With a heavy spoon, crush the vegetables and blend well. Add remaining ingredients. Stir and taste. Add more salt and lemon juice if needed. Chill. Serve cold with a few croutons in each soup plate.

Coni Harrison

A light meal begins with a heavy soup; a heavy meal begins with thin, clear or delicate cream soup; and jellied soups are usually served on hot summer days.

MANHATTAN CLAM CHOWDER

YIELD: 6 servings

½ pound bacon
4 medium onions, chopped fine
4 carrots, chopped fine
2 big stalks celery, chopped fine
2 tablespoons parsley, chopped
1 — 1 pound, 13 ounce, can tomatoes
1 pint clams with liquid

2 teaspoons salt
¼ teaspoon pepper
1½ teaspoon dried thyme
1 bay leaf
3 medium potatoes, diced
1 tablespoon sugar
1 tablespoon Worcestershire sauce
2-3 drops tabasco

Fry bacon in large skillet until almost crisp. Toss in onions and cook until they take on color. Next, stir in carrots, celery, and parsley and cook over low heat for about 8 minutes. Drain tomatoes, putting liquid into a measuring cup. Add tomato pulp to skillet.

Drain clams, mixing strained liquid to tomato liquid. Transfer all ingredients to large kettle (4 quart). Add enough water to the liquids to make 1½ quarts and pour into kettle. Season with salt and pepper, thyme, bay leaf, and cook to a boil. Reduce heat and simmer gently for 40 minutes. Add potatoes, cover and cook about 15 or 20 minutes. Finally, add clams, chopped fine, and simmer 15 minutes longer.

Gertrude Weh

MINESTRONE

1 pound onions
1 stalk celery
6 scallions
1 green pepper
¼ cup olive oil
2 cloves garlic
2 cups fresh tomatoes

2 teaspoons salt
½ teaspoon black pepper
½ teaspoon allspice
1 gallon rich beef stock
1 cup short type macaroni
1 cup lima beans
Parmesan cheese

Cut vegetables fine and sauté in olive oil until translucent. Add minced garlic, tomatoes and seasonings. Bring ingredients to a boil and add stock. Reduce heat and simmer for 1½ hours. Add macaroni and lima beans 20 minutes before cooking time ends. Serve with a spoonful of freshly grated Parmesan cheese.

Nick Midelis
Hilltop House

Garnish a bowl of cream soup by making roses of whipped cream, with a pastry tube, on melba toast rounds. Sprinkle with paprika and chopped parsley, and just before serving place on top of soup.

OYSTER STEW I

1 pint oysters, large; select on
  count
1 pint oysters, small, standard size
2 pints half & half cream
3 tablespoons butter
6-8 tablespoons medium dry sherry
½ teaspoon oregano OR thyme,
  crushed

heavy dash of Worcestershire
  sauce
light to medium dash tabasco
  sauce
½ teaspoon salt
2 tablespoons water
6-8 pats of butter

Place three or four large raw oysters in each of 6 or 8 soup bowls. Cover with sherry. Add small nugget of butter to each bowl and place bowls in warm (180°) oven.

Place 3 tablespoons butter, oregano or thyme, Worcestershire sauce, tabasco, salt and water in top of double boiler over boiling water.

Place all remaining oysters in a blender and reduce to a fine puree. Add to ingredients in top of double boiler and heat thoroughly.

In separate saucepan, over low heat, warm half and half just to below simmering point. As soon as the mixture in double boiler is hot add the heated cream to it.

Mix thoroughly, adjust seasoning if necessary, and pour over oysters in soup bowls. Serve with toast or hot bread and a salad.

These quantities will serve six as a main course or eight as a first course.

Lt. General Robert Taylor

OYSTER STEW II

¼ cup butter OR margarine
1 pint oysters and liquid
1 cup milk
1 pint half & half

¼ teaspoon celery seed
½ teaspoon salt
⅛ teaspoon pepper
1 teaspoon parsley

Melt butter in heavy saucepan. Add oysters with liquid and bring just to the boiling point, but do not boil. Slowly stir in half & half, milk, salt, pepper and celery seed. Keep on heat, stirring until edges of oysters curl. Add parsely. Serve immediately with crackers.

Gladys Grammer

PEANUT BUTTER SOUP

½ cup butter
1 small onion, diced
2 stalks celery, diced
3 tablespoons flour
2 quarts chicken broth

2 cups peanut butter
½ teaspoon celery salt
1 teaspoon salt
pepper to taste
1 tablespoon lemon juice

Melt butter in large pot. Add onion and celery. Sauté for 5 minutes, but do not brown. Add flour and mix well. Add hot chicken broth and cook ½ hour. Remove from stove, strain, and add peanut butter, celery salt, salt and lemon juice. If desired, sprinkle with ground peanuts before serving.

Although associated with Georgia and Virginia, peanut butter soup is certainly a delectable dish made with Florida-grown peanuts.

Mary-Frazier Palmore

PLAIN FISH CHOWDER

YIELD: 8 cups

2 — 10½ ounce cans condensed
  cream of potato soup
2 cups cooked, flaked fish
4 ounces whole kernel corn,
  drained

2 tablespoons butter OR margarine
dash of onion powder
dash of paprika
salt
pepper

Put soup in 3 quart saucepan and stir in milk. Add rest of ingredients and cook over low heat, stirring until well blended and completely heated. Do not boil.

Gladys Grammer

SCALLOP CHOWDER

YIELD: 4 servings

1 can condensed cream of potato
  soup
1 soup can of milk
2 — 8 ounce bottles clam juice
1 tomato, peeled, seeded, and cut
  up
½ large bermuda onion, minced
1 teaspoon Old Bay seasoning

2 strips bacon, cut small
1 tablespoon butter
2 teaspoons sherry
½-¾ pound scallops
Accent
parsley
paprika

Brown bacon, add onions and cook until soft. Add clam juice and soup, mix and simmer for 5 minutes. Add tomato pieces and simmer for 15 minutes. Add pepper, butter, scallops, milk, and Accent. Simmer for 10 minutes. Next, add sherry and Old Bay seasoning to taste. Simmer for 5 minutes more. Garnish with parsley and paprika.

Michael Grossman

Soup served in a meal acts in a two-fold manner: first, to stimulate the appetite, second, to provide nourishment.

SEAFOOD BISQUE

2 cans chopped clams, reserve liquid
1 pound frozen halibut OR cod
2 large raw potatoes, diced
2 large ribs celery, diced
1 onion, diced

1 small can evaporated milk
3 tablespoons butter
3 tablespoons flour
2 cups milk (or more)
thyme
salt to taste (optional)

Cook potatoes, celery and onion until tender. Drain. Do not reserve this liquid. Make a mixture of the butter and flour. Cook fish in simmering water for 10 minutes. Cut into bite-size pieces.

Add clam juice and evaporated milk to butter/flour mixture and stir until smooth. Add at least 2 cups milk and stir until liquid thickens into a light cream sauce.

Add clams and fish to cream sauce and season with thyme. Simmer for 10 minutes.

Vegetables and fish can be cooked ahead which makes it easier. If you want richer sauce, add cream. The amount of milk you use will depend on the consistency you want.

Mae Stubbs

SEAFOOD CHOWDER

Fresh:
1 pound shrimp, cleaned
1 pound scallops
1 pound grouper
1 pound lobster
1 pound canned crab claw meat

1 large onion, chopped
garlic salt, to taste
2 quarts half & half
1 quart whole milk
1 stick butter (no substitute)
pepper to taste

Sauté onion in butter and garlic salt with shrimp, scallops, grouper and lobster until white and almost done. Seafood should be added one at a time. Add milk and half & half, then crab meat. Cook until heated through, but do not let mixture come to a boil.

Serve with a salad and your favorite bread or crumbed crackers.

Cindi McCarty

SPANISH BEAN SOUP

1 quart water
1 small ham hock, split in half
1 medium onion, minced
1 clove garlic, minced
2 medium potatoes, each cut into six pieces

1 — 8 ounce can garbanzo beans
2 links chorizo Spanish sausage, sliced
½ small head cabbage, chopped
1 large carrot, sliced

In a 3 quart saucepan, cover ham hock with water, then add balance of ingredients except for sausage and beans. Cook until potatoes are almost done. Then add sausage and beans and simmer 20 minutes. Season to taste with salt and pepper.

Rosaila Maggiacomo

SPANISH BLACK BEAN SOUP

2 cups black beans
10 cups water
1 — 2" cube salt pork
½ cup chopped onions

1 cup chopped celery with leaves
1 clove garlic
1 bay leaf
1 teaspoon sugar

Pour beans into a tray and pick them over carefully. Foreign objects get into packages of beans; especially rocks.

Then place all ingredients into a large pot. Bring mixture to a boil; reduce heat and simmer for at least 3 hours, until beans are tender. Remove garlic and bay leaf and pork. Soup may be cooled and put through a food mill, or it may be served as it comes from the kettle. It may be served with chopped onion; 1 tablespoon per cup; or thinly sliced lemon on top. It may also be served over rice. A jigger of dry sherry may be added to the cup before pouring the soup in.

The Ocean Grill

SPINACH SOUP I

2 tablespoons butter
2 tablespoons onions, chopped
2 cups chicken broth

1 package frozen spinach
dash nutmeg (optional)

Thaw, drain, and squeeze the spinach. Melt butter and sauté onions until translucent. Add chicken broth and bring to a boil. Add spinach and cook for 5 minutes. Then place mixture in blender for several seconds. Serve very hot with a dash of nutmeg on top.

Mae Zuver

SPINACH SOUP II

2 quarts strong chicken stock
2 cups fresh spinach OR 1 package
  frozen spinach
1 can split pea soup, undiluted

½ cup onion, chopped
1 garlic clove
salt

Add split pea soup to chicken broth and let simmer. Place all other ingredients in blender and blend until smooth. Add blended ingredients to broth and simmer for 6 minutes. If liquid is too thick, add more stock. Serve in small soup bowls or cups and add a dash of sherry at the table for added flavor.

This is good with chicken salad or any fruit salad. Be careful not to overcook so that the beautiful spinach color will not darken.

Jean Varn

Drop ice cubes into the soup pot, and as you stir, the fat will cling to the cubes. Be sure to discard the ice cubes before they melt.

SURPRISE SOUP

8 medium zucchinis
salt
pepper

butter
1 large package cream cheese

Clean, slice and cook zucchinis in small amount of water until tender but do not overcook. Drain and season with salt, pepper and butter. Combine with cream cheese in a blender. Whip until very foamy. Serve hot in cups before dinner.

Especially good with barbecued beef or chicken, a green salad, and hard rolls or bread.

The Committee

TASTY CONCH SOUP

3 pounds conch meat
2 quarts water
1 can stewed tomatoes

1 can tomato sauce
mixed vegetables (optional)

Pressure cook conch for 4 hours on fifteen pounds pressure. Take out and cut off tough skin, then cut into small chunks. Put back into cooker with water and add stewed tomatoes and tomato sauce.

If you don't use stewed tomatoes, add one cup diced celery and at least one diced onion.

If you prefer, add mixed vegetables to pot, using one package frozen mixed vegetables. Add ¾ cup rice or several diced potatoes and cook for one half hour more.

This is a real prize homemade meal.

Mrs. George Blanton

TRADITIONAL SWISS CHEESE SOUP

YIELD: 6 servings

2 large onions
6 cups beef broth
1 cup dry French bread crumbs
2 cups (8 ounces) grated Swiss OR
  Gruyere cheese

1 tablespoon flour
salt
pepper
¼ cup butter
¼ cup dry sherry (optional)

Chop one of the onions and add to beef broth. Heat broth until boiling. Stir in bread crumbs. Pour mixture into blender and whirl until smooth. Replace in saucepan and heat until just simmering. Mix cheese and flour. Drop cheese by small handfuls into soup, stirring each time cheese is added until cheese is melted. Season to taste with salt and pepper. If necessary, thin soup to desired consistency with additional broth. Slice remaining onion thinly and saute in hot butter until golden brown. Serve soup in bowls topped with sauteed onions.

To elevate this soup to a gourmet dish, stir in sherry before serving.

The Committee

U.S. SENATE BEAN SOUP

2 pounds Michigan navy beans   1½ to 2 pounds smoked ham hocks
4 quarts hot water   1 onion, chopped

Wash and rinse beans through hot water until beans are white. Put on the fire with 4 quarts of hot water. Take ham hocks and boil slowly for 3 hours in a covered pot. Braise one onion, chopped, in a little oil or butter and, when tender, add to soup. Remove ham hocks and let cool, dice and return to soup. Remove 2 cups of beans, puree, and return to soup. When ready to serve, season with salt and pepper.

A green salad and cornbread are so good with this. Apples and cheese wedges for dessert complete meal.

Connie Wagers

NOTES

VEGETABLES

VEGETABLES

ARTICHOKE CASSEROLE

OVEN: 350° 65 minutes

1 package frozen artichokes, do
not thaw
2 packages frozen peas
4 ounces canned mushrooms

¼ cup oil
seasoned bread crumbs
grated cheese
⅓-¼ cup oil

Place oil in casserole dish. Place frozen peas in bottom of dish, then add mushrooms on top of peas; then add frozen artichokes on top of mushrooms. Cover with seasoned bread crumbs and sprinkle with cheese. Pour ⅓-¼ cup of oil over the top of all ingredients. Cover casserole with foil and bake for 45 minutes in 350° oven; uncover and bake for 20 minutes longer.

Leila Fries Darress

ASPARAGUS ANGELIQUÉ

OVEN: 400° 15 minutes   YIELD: 6-8 servings

2 pounds fresh asparagus OR 2
boxes frozen asparagus
4 tablespoons butter
6 tablespoons bread crumbs
½ teaspoon salt
¼ teaspoon pepper

3 egg whites
¾ cup pancake batter
2 tablespoons grated cheddar
cheese
2 tablespoons grated Parmesan
cheese

Parboil asparagus. Cut cooking time down to allow for time in oven. Preheat a shallow baking dish with butter. Dish may be 10 x 5" oblong or 10 x 1-½" round. When butter is melted, add bread crumbs. Beat egg whites stiff, but not dry. Stir cheeses and salt into pancake batter. Fold in egg whites. Spread mixture over asparagus in dish and bake at 400° for 15 minutes.

Substitute other vegetables for asparagus. For advance preparation, do everything up to, but not including, beating the egg whites. Twenty minutes before serving, take three minutes in the kitchen to complete the recipe.

Arlene Rossway

Cut tops off of carrots, beets, turnips, and parsnips before storing in refrigerator. If left on, the tops will draw off moisture and some of the food value of the roots.

ASPARAGUS CASSEROLE I

OVEN: 350° 35 minutes

2 large #2 cans asparagus
1 small box cheese flavored round
  snack crackers
⅓ cup blanched, slivered almonds
2 cans mushroom soup

grated cheese to taste
salt
pepper
butter

Drain asparagus. In a greased dish, place a layer of crackers, then asparagus, add soup and cover with a layer of crackers. Add grated cheese and dot heavily with butter. Bake at 350° for 35 minutes.

Sara R. Whitacre

ASPARAGUS CASSEROLE II

OVEN: 350° 25 minutes

1 can asparagus, drained
3 hard-boiled eggs, sliced
1 small can English peas

1 can cream of mushroom soup
canned onion rings

Arrange asparagus, peas and egg slices in a casserole dish. Pour soup over ingredients and sprinkle with onion rings. Cover with foil. Heat in 350° oven for 25 minutes, removing cover the last few minutes so onion rings can brown.

Frances Harper

BAKED ASPARAGUS

OVEN: 325°-350° 20 minutes

1 — #2 can asparagus
1 pimento, chopped, optional
2-3 hard-cooked eggs
1 small onion, chopped

1 cup grated American cheese
1 cup medium white sauce
fine cracker crumbs
paprika

Place half of asparagus in a casserole; top with pimento, eggs, onion and cheese. Arrange remaining asparagus over cheese. Pour white sauce over asparagus and sprinkle with cracker crumbs. Garnish with paprika. Bake at 325°-350° for 20 minutes.

Barbara Wells Steele

Asparagus, if wilted, can be refreshed, if stems are set in cold water.

BAKED BLACK BEANS

OVEN: 350° 2 hours

1 pound dried black beans	1 bay leaf
¼ pound salt pork, cut	1 teaspoon dried thyme
2 celery stalks, with leaves,	1 teaspoon salt
chopped	1 cup white wine
1 carrot	¼ teaspoon pepper
1 onion, stuck with 2 whole cloves	2 tablespoons parsley
2 garlic cloves	½ pint sour cream
1 dried chili pepper	

Soak beans overnight in water to cover. Cook beans until tender with salt pork, celery, carrot, onion, garlic, dried chili pepper, and bay leaf. When tender, drain, reserving 1 cup of liquid. Place beans in a casserole dish or bean pot. Mix 1 cup of bean broth with salt, pepper, thyme and white wine; pour over beans. Bake for 2 hours at 350°. Mix parsley with sour cream and serve on top of beans.

Crumbled bacon may be added to sour cream, if desired.

A. R. Trottier

BAKED ONION

OVEN: 350° 1 hour

large Spanish onion	Parmesan cheese

Cut large onion into 8 wedges, keeping together at bottom of onion. Wrap onion securely in foil and bake for at least 1 hour in 350° oven, depending on size of onion. When tender, remove foil and place in serving dish, opened petal style, and sprinkle generously with Parmesan cheese.

Mrs. Leroy E. Oakes

BAKED POTATO SLIMS

OVEN: 400° 30-35 minutes

¼ cup water	6 potatoes
2 tablespoons oil	1 package poultry coating mix
½ teaspoon tabasco sauce	¼ cup grated Parmesan cheese

Combine water, oil and tabasco sauce together. Cut potatoes into ½" strips, as for french fries. Toss potato strips in tabasco mixture, then toss with poultry coating mix which has the Parmesan cheese added to it. Place potatoes in a single layer on a cookie sheet lined with foil. Bake in preheated 400° oven for 30-35 minutes.

Frozen pototoes may be used; if so, bake about 20-25 minutes.

Mary M. Hardee

BAKED TOMATOES STUFFED WITH MUSHROOMS

OVEN: 400° 10 minutes

4 large firm tomatoes
1 tablespoon salad oil
1 tablespoon oleo OR butter

½ pound fresh mushrooms, sliced
thin
½ teaspoon flour
½ teaspoon salt
pinch of savory

Put tomatoes in enough boiling water to cover for about 10-12 seconds; remove quickly and peel. Remove pulp and seeds, leaving a ½" outside edge so the tomato will be substantial enough to hold the filling during baking.

Melt the butter and salad oil; sauté mushrooms for 5 minutes; sprinkle flour over this and add remaining ingredients. Fill each tomato with the mushroom mixture and bake in a greased dish for 10 minutes at 400°.

Connie Wagers

BAKED WINTER SQUASH WITH RAISINS

OVEN: 375° 1 hour   YIELD: 4-6 servings

1 Hubbard, yellow squash OR 2
acorn squash
4 tablespoons brown sugar OR
honey

2 tablespoons butter OR vegetable
oil
2 cups applesauce
½ cup raisins
2 teaspoons lemon juice
1 teaspoon cinnamon

Cut squash in half lengthwise; remove seeds and membranes; sprinkle with salt. Mix the rest of the ingredients in a bowl and spoon mixture into the squash hollows. Bake at 375° in a pan with sides, covering squash with foil for the first 30 minutes; remove foil and bake uncovered another 30 minutes or until the squash is tender.

This is a colorful and healthy dish.

Eden Gray

Do not wash vegetables until just before using them. Moisture that may remain after washing encourages mold and rot.

BLACK BEANS AND RICE

3 cups dry black beans
2 large onions, peeled and halved
¼ cup olive oil
2 large green peppers, halved and seeded
2 bay leaves
1 teaspoon salt
3 peppercorns
6 whole cloves
1 clove garlic

1 can Italian-seasoned tomato sauce (about 1 cup)
½ cup olive oil
¼ pound diced, cooked ham OR meaty ham bone OR 3-4 slices bacon, diced OR ¼ pound diced salt pork
¼ cup dry white wine
2 tablespoons wine vinegar
2 tablespoons sugar
salt to taste

Soak beans in water to cover overnight. Cook beans in the same water for 40 minutes in pressure cooker at 15 pounds pressure. If beans look dry, add more water before cooking. Cool pressure cooker under cold running water immediately. Add remaining ingredients and cook for 45 minutes at 15 pounds pressure; cool the same way.

Fry onions and green peppers in olive oil after chopping. Add ¼ pound diced, cooked ham or a meaty ham bone, 3-4 slices bacon, diced or ¼ pound diced salt pork, cook until meat is browned.

Add onions, peppers and meat to pressure cooker with wine, wine vinegar, sugar and salt to taste. Cook for 45 minutes in pressure cooker at 15 pounds pressure. Cool as before. Serve over hot fluffy rice. If you like, cook 1 clove minced garlic in ¼ cup olive oil and stir into rice.

The Committee

BOSTON BAKED BEANS PRESSURE COOKER STYLE

2 cups dried navy beans
6 tablespoons sugar (½ cup)
⅓ cup molasses
2 teaspoons salt

2 teaspoons mustard
1 medium onion, diced
6 ounces ketchup
2 cups water, approximately

Soak beans overnight. Par-boil for ½ hour until beans are soft. Place beans in pressure cooker and add remaining ingredients. Cook for 12 minutes; and let pressure drop of its own accord.

One cup crushed pineapple may be added to beans after they are cooked for a different flavor.

Peg Beaudoin

Heat a few thin slices of garlic in butter; remove the garlic and season vegetables with the butter — very tasty.

BRANDIED ORANGE SWEET POTATOES

OVEN: 350°   YIELD: 8 servings

6 medium sweet potatoes
½ cup melted butter
1 cup firmly packed brown sugar
½ cup orange juice
½ teaspoon salt

½ cup chopped pecans
⅓ cup apricot brandy
1 — 6½ ounce bag miniature
    marshmallows

Scrub potatoes and boil until tender; drain, whip until fluffy. Add other ingredients, reserving a few marshmallows for topping. Place ingredients in a 2 quart casserole and top with marshmallows. Bake at 350° until bubbly and marshmallows are browned. May be made ahead and refrigerated until time to bake and serve.

Canned potatoes may be used.

Mrs. Noah Lybrand, Jr.

BROCCOLI AND RICE CASSEROLE

OVEN: 350° 30 minutes

2 packages frozen chopped broc-
    coli
1 cup minute rice
1 small jar pasteurized, processed
    cheese spread

1 — 10¾ ounce can cream of
    chicken soup
⅔ stick of butter
½ cup chopped onion

Sauté onion in butter; add all other ingredients and place in a greased casserole dish. Bake at 350° for 30 minutes.

Wanda L. Collins

BROCCOLI CASSEROLE I

OVEN: 350° 20-25 minutes   YIELD: 8-10 servings

2 packages frozen broccoli spears
1 cup sour cream
1 cup onion dip (comes in metal
    container already mixed)

1 can mushroom soup, undiluted
½ cup sliced almonds
1 cup soft buttered bread crumbs

Broil broccoli as directed on package until almost done; drain well. Chop broccoli and place in bottom of buttered casserole dish. Mix sour cream, onion dip, and soup together; pour over broccoli. Butter both sides of 4-5 slices of bread and remove crust; tear bread into very small pieces and sprinkle on top of casserole. Sprinkle sliced almonds on top of bread crumbs. Bake for 20-25 minutes at 350°. If necessary, turn heat up to 400° the last 3-4 minutes to brown.

Ruth Huggins

BROCCOLI CASSEROLE II

OVEN: 350° 45 minutes

⅓ cup butter
1 medium onion, chopped
2 packages frozen broccoli,
  chopped
1 can cream of mushroom soup
½ cup mayonnaise
1 egg, beaten

1 cup sharp cheddar cheese, shredded
½ teaspoon salt
¼ teaspoon lemon pepper seasoned
  to taste
1 cup seasoned bread crumbs

Sauté chopped onion in melted butter in a skillet. Cook frozen broccoli according to package directions and drain in a collander. In a decorative casserole dish, mix egg, soup and mayonnaise with salt and pepper. Add cooked onion and broccoli and mix well. Sprinkle cheddar cheese over the top. Follow by
sprinkling bread crumbs over the cheese. Bake at 350° in a pre-heated oven
for 45 minutes or until cheese melts and bread crumbs are brown.

Elizabeth E. Mayer

BROCCOLI CASSEROLE III

OVEN: 350° 30-35 minutes

1½ pounds fresh broccoli
1 — 10-¾ ounce can condensed
  cream of chicken soup
1 tablespoon flour
½ cup sour cream
¼ cup grated carrot

1 tablespoon grated onion
¼ tablespoon salt
⅛ teaspoon pepper
¾ cup herb stuffing mix
2 tablespoons melted butter

Cube broccoli stalks and cook in boiling water for 5-8 minutes; add flowerettes and cook 5 minutes more; drain. Separately blend soup and flour; add
sour cream, carrot, onion, salt and pepper. Stir in broccoli. Place mixture in a
casserole dish. Combine stuffing mix and butter and sprinkle around edges of
casserole. Bake in 350° oven, uncovered, for 30-35 minutes.

Berta Hayes

BROCCOLI PIEDAD

OVEN: 350° 20 minutes   YIELD: 8 servings

2 packages frozen broccoli spears
2 packages cheese sauce mix
3 ounces almond pieces

salt
½ cup dry sherry
1½ cups milk

Prepare broccoli according to package directions, salting to taste. Meanwhile, prepare cheese sauce as package directs, but use ¼ cup sherry and ¾
cup milk per package as substitutes for liquids specified on package. Heat
sauce to boiling, but do not boil. Place drained broccoli in a flat baking dish,
about 2 quart size. Pour cheese sauce over broccoli and sprinkle almonds over
cheese. Cover and bake at 350° for 20 minutes or until sauce bubbles.

Millie Cook

BROCCOLI REGIS

OVEN: 350° 45 minutes

3 packages frozen chopped broccoli
1 stick butter
1 can cream of mushroom soup

1 — 8 ounce package cream cheese,
at room temperature
1 medium-size onion, chopped
16 round snack type crackers,
crushed

Cook broccoli as directed on package. Drain water and place broccoli in a casserole dish.

Melt half of the butter in a saucepan and add chopped onion; cook until onion is soft and light brown. Remove from heat and add soup and cream cheese. Blend together until smooth. Pour over broccoli and mix until well distributed. Melt remaining butter and add crushed crackers; spread mixture over broccoli. Bake at 350°, covered, for 45 minutes.

R. Dale Trefelner

CABBAGE AND BACON

1 head cabbage
½ pound bacon

1 package small noodles
1 large OR 2 small onions

Fry bacon and chopped onion together. Drain some of the grease from the pan. Shred cabbage and wilt it slightly by leaving it a few minutes in boiling water. Drain. Cook noodles until done according to package directions. Drain noodles. Add wilted cabbage and noodles to bacon and onion mixture and fry over medium heat in frying pan; turn occasionally to prevent burning. Fry until slightly browned.

Leila J. Komara

CALICO CASSEROLE

OVEN: 325° 40-60 minutes   YIELD: 5-6 servings

White Sauce:
¼ cup flour
¼ teaspoon salt
1½ cups milk
dash of pepper, OR to taste
½ teaspoon dry mustard OR prepared mustard
1 tablespoon Worcestershire sauce
4 tablespoons margarine

Casserole Ingredients:
¼ medium-sized onion, grated
⅓ cup cheddar cheese, broken into
marble size chunks
1 heaping cup diced ham
1 package frozen mixed vegetables
1 cup cubed bread, browned in
margarine

Do not cook or thaw vegetables.

Combine ingredients for white sauce and mix well. Add other ingredients to white sauce and pour into a greased baking dish and refrigerate for 24 hours. Remove from refrigerator at least 1 hour or longer before baking. If desired, sprinkle crushed potato chips on top of casserole ingredients that have been placed in casserole dish. Bake for 40 minutes to 1 hour at 325°.

Joanne W. Bolton

CANDIED SWEET POTATOES

OVEN: 375° 45 minutes   YIELD: 6 servings

6 peeled, cooked, medium-size   ¼ cup water
   sweet potatoes   ½ teaspoon salt
1 cup brown sugar, firmly packed 3 whole cloves
¼ cup butter OR margarine   1 stick cinnamon

Arrange potatoes, which have been cut in halves, lengthwise, in an uncovered baking dish.

Meanwhile, combine remaining ingredients and simmer for 10 minutes.

Pour mixture over potatoes and bake in a 375° oven for 45 minutes, basting occasionally.

Ethel Kicliter

CARROTS A LA ORANGE

8-10 carrots, sliced OR cut into   3 tablespoons butter
   strips the size you prefer   ⅓ cup brown sugar
½ cup orange juice   ⅛ teaspoon nutmeg OR mace

Cook carrots as usual in slightly salted water; drain. Add rest of ingredients and simmer until carrots are glazed. Garnish with orange slices.

Blanche Hunt

CARROTS SUPREME

1 bunch carrots   2 tablespoons butter OR marga-
3 onions   rine
1 chicken bouillon cube   ¼ cup flour
                                   ½ cup water

Cut carrots julienne style. Place a small amount of water with bouillon cube in a saucepan and cook carrots until tender. Meanwhile, in a frying pan, sauté onions in the butter, until tender. When done, sprinkle flour over onions until flour disappears; then add water and cook until mixture thickens. Do not drain carrots. Combine the two mixtures together and serve.

Emily Johnson

CAULIFLOWER SUPREME

OVEN: 425° 15 minutes   YIELD: 6 servings

1 head cauliflower, boiled until   ⅓ cup grated Parmesan cheese
   tender and drained   ¼ cup crushed soda crackers
⅔ cup shredded Swiss cheese   ¼ cup melted butter

Place cauliflower in a 9″ square baking dish. Combine remaining ingredients; sprinkle cheese mixture evenly over the top. Bake at 425° for 15 minutes or until golden brown.

Kim Lybrand

CELERY CASSEROLE

OVEN: 300° 30-40 minutes

4 cups cut up celery
1 can cream of chicken soup
1 can water chestnuts, sliced
½ jar chopped pimentos

½ cup sliced almonds
½ cup bread crumbs
2 tablespoons butter OR margarine

Cook celery in water; do not cook too long as it will cook more while in the oven. Celery should measure 4 cups after cooking.

Combine soup with water chestnuts, pimento and celery in a casserole dish. Sauté bread crumbs in the butter and add sliced almonds. Sprinkle mixture over casserole. Bake at 300° for 30-40 minutes.

Estelle Glillon

CHEESE BROCCOLI I

OVEN: 350° 30 minutes   YIELD: 6 servings

1 — 8 ounce package fine spaghetti, cooked
2 packages chopped broccoli

1 cup half & half cream
1 pound processed cheese
1 onion, chopped fine

Brown onions; add broccoli and cover pan; allow 5 minutes to thaw broccoli. In a casserole, layer spaghetti, broccoli, onion and cheese. Cover with buttered bread crumbs and bake, uncovered, at 350° for 30 minutes.

June Carlton Vest

CHEESE BROCCOLI II

OVEN: 350° 30 minutes

2 — 10 ounce packages frozen broccoli
3 cups cooked rice

1 — 8 ounce jar pasteurized, processed cheese spread
1 chopped onion
butter

Cook broccoli according to package directions. Cook rice. Sauté onion in butter or bacon drippings. Add rice and cheese spread. Combine broccoli, rice, cheese spread and onion mixture in a casserole dish; bake in 350° oven for 30 minutes or until cheese is well melted.

I like to use a large jar of the cheese spread and more broccoli with the same amount of rice.

Betty Lopes

Do not overcook tender sweet corn. Drop the corn into enough boiling water to cover the ears. Add one teaspoon sugar per quart of cooking water. Cover and cook rapidly, just until milk is set, about five to six minutes for young corn, ten minutes for the more mature ears.

CHEESE CORN SOUFFLÉ

OVEN: 350° 45-50 minutes   YIELD: 5-6 servings

¼ cup butter OR margarine
1 — 1 pound can yellow cream style
   corn
¼ teaspoon salt
¼ cup flour
⅓ cup milk

⅛ teaspoon garlic salt
½ cup grated provolone cheese
½ teaspoon Worcestershire sauce
5 large eggs, separated
1½ cups shredded Cheddar cheese

Melt butter and stir in flour until smooth. Add corn, milk, salt, garlic salt and Worcestershire sauce. Stir until thick. Add cheese and stir until cheese is melted. Beat egg yolks slightly. Blend into cheese mixture. Cool slightly. Beat egg whites stiff. Gently stir ¼ of the egg whites into the cheese sauce. Carefully fold in the remaining egg whites until just blended. Pour mixture into an ungreased 2 quart casserole. Bake at 350° for 45-50 minutes. Serve at once.

Mary Ann Bryant

CHEESED ZUCCHINI EN CASSEROLE

OVEN: 375° 35 minutes

6 medium zucchini, quartered
3 ripe tomatoes, sliced
sliced onions
shredded mozzarella cheese
bacon

salt
pepper
oregano
garlic powder

Oil a 2 quart shallow baking dish lightly. Place zucchini in baking dish and sprinkle with seasonings. Place sliced tomatoes over zucchini and season the same as squash. Slice enough onions to make a layer over the tomatoes; season as before. Place a layer of shredded cheese over onions; top with a layer of bacon cut into squares. Cook, uncovered, for 35 minutes at 375°.

This is the perfect vegetable to serve with Chicken Oriental as they cook at the same oven temperatures.

Rosaila Maggiacomo

CHICK'S FRENCH-FRIED ONIONS

1 cup flour
¼ teaspoon salt
½ cup evaporated milk
2 tablespoons salad oil

1 egg
6 tablespoons water
2-3 large onions, peeled and sliced
   about ¼" thick

Mix flour, salt, milk, oil and egg together; beat until smooth. Add water to make a medium thin batter. Separate onion slices into rings and dip into the batter until each ring is covered. Drop rings, a few at a time, into deep fat, heated to about 375°. An electric frying pan will do nicely for this; fry rings until they are golden brown. Drain on paper towels and sprinkle with salt. Serve hot.

Antoinette Pope

CHINESE BROCCOLI SCALLOP

OVEN: 350° 20 minutes   YIELD: 6 servings

1 bunch (2 pounds) trimmed broccoli, cooked until tender
2 tablespoons butter OR oleo
1½ teaspoons salt
¼ teaspoon dry mustard
1½ tablespoons flour

⅛ teaspoon pepper
2 cups milk
6 sliced water chestnuts, canned
½ cup grated cheese
½ cup buttered soft bread crumbs

Melt butter in a small saucepan. Remove from heat and blend in flour, salt, mustard and pepper. Slowly blend in milk and cook mixture until it thickens; boil for 1 minute. Add broccoli with chestnuts. Fill a buttered baking dish with mixture and top with crumbs and cheese. Bake at 350° for 20 minutes.

I have always used Romano cheese but any grated cheese is acceptable, depending on individual taste.

Terese Burke

CONFETTI RICE

1 cup sliced mushrooms
½ cup chopped onion
⅓ cup butter
3 cups hot cooked rice

1 — 10 ounce package frozen peas,
  cooked and drained
1 teaspoon salt
¼ teaspoon pepper
¼ teaspoon crushed rosemary
¼ cup sliced almonds, toasted

Cook mushrooms and onion in butter until tender. Add rice, peas and seasoning. Reheat with almonds and serve.

May be frozen for future use. Very good served with Chicken Jubilee.

Mrs. Roger Keilholtz

COOL CARROTS

2 bunches carrots
1 green pepper
1 small jar pickled onions
1 can condensed tomato soup

½ cup cooking oil
¾ cup vinegar
1 cup sugar

Peel and slice carrots fairly thin; cook for 10 minutes; drain and cool. Finely chop green pepper; slice onions thinly. Combine peppers and onions in a large bowl. Combine soup, oil, vinegar, sugar and mustard in a saucepan and heat just to below boiling point and until sugar is completely melted. Pour hot mixture over onions and peppers; stir well and add cooked carrots, mixing well. When cool, pour into a large covered container and allow to marinate in refrigerator at least 24 hours before serving. Will keep for weeks.

Mrs. Arthur Causier

COPPER PENNY CARROTS

2 pounds carrots, washed and
   sliced
1 small green pepper, thinly sliced
1 medium onion, thinly sliced
1 — 10¾ ounce can condensed tomato soup
½ cup vegetable oil

1 cup sugar
¾ cup vinegar
1 teaspoon prepared mustard
1 teaspoon Worcestershire sauce
salt
pepper

Cook carrots in salted water until medium done. Rinse in ice water. Arrange layers of carrots, green pepper and onion in a bowl or container. Combine all remaining ingredients in a saucepan and bring to a boil, stirring until thoroughly blended. Pour over carrots and refrigerate until flavor is absorbed.

Keeps for weeks in refrigerator.

Betty Morse Hendershott

COTTAGE POTATOES

OVEN: moderate heat 15-20 minutes

YIELD: 6-8 servings

6-8 medium potatoes, peeled
1 cup cottage cheese
¼ cup chopped onion, very fine
1 teaspoon salt

white pepper to taste
¾ cup milk
1 teaspoon dry parsley
grated cheese

Dice potatoes and cook in boiling salted water until tender. Drain and place in a buttered 2 quart casserole. Combine cottage cheese, onion, salt, pepper, milk and parsley together. Add to potatoes in casserole. Sprinkle grated cheese, your favorite kind, over the top and bake for 15-20 minutes in moderate oven until light brown.

The Committee

EASY BAKED EGGPLANT

OVEN: 350° 1 hour

1 large eggplant
1 envelope onion soup mix
1 can mushroom soup

1 soup can water
½ pint sour cream
2 tablespoons salt

Cut eggplant in ½ rounds; leave skin on. Place in a large pot and cover with water; add salt and let soak for 1 hour. Pour off water and place eggplant in a baking dish. Put soup on each piece of eggplant; add 1 soup can of water; sprinkle onion soup mix over eggplant and bake in 350° oven for 1 hour or until tender. Just before serving, put about 1 tablespoon of sour cream on each slice of eggplant.

Louisa Christen

EASY CREAMED SQUASH

1½ to 2 pounds yellow squash
  sliced ¼" thick
2 tablespoons butter

½ cup coffee creamer, powdered
1 small diced onion

Cook squash and onion until tender; 20-25 minutes. Drain all water off and add butter. Stir in powdered coffee creamer; mixture will be soupy. Season with salt and pepper to taste.

Dorothy A. Bishop

EGGPLANT CASSEROLE I

OVEN: 350° 45 minutes

3 cups cooked eggplant
3 slices bread, softened in water
  from eggplant
1 tablespoon bacon drippings
2 tablespoons butter OR oleo

1-2 eggs, optional
seasoned salt
pepper
grated sharp cheese

Peel, slice and cook eggplant in 1-½ cups water until tender. Drain; reserve water to soak bread; add other ingredients to eggplant and place in baking dish; bake in 350° oven for about 45 minutes. Top with grated cheese. Do not return to oven.

Carra Adams

EGGPLANT CASSEROLE II

OVEN: 350° 1 hour

1 large eggplant
1 medium can tomatoes
1 small onion
crackers

cheese
salt to taste
pepper to taste

Peel eggplant and dice; dice onion and brown with eggplant in small amount of butter. Grease a casserole and place layers of eggplant and onion; crumble crackers over eggplant, and pour part of tomatoes over crackers. Salt and pepper each layer. If using whole tomatoes, chop them up. Repeat layers using all ingredients. Grate cheese over the top and bake in 350° oven for about 1 hour.

Joan Schroeder

To prevent canned asparagus tips from breaking off, open the can and remove the vegetable from the bottom instead of the top.

EGGPLANT ITALIAN STYLE

OVEN: 350° 30 minutes

Frying Batter:
3 eggs
¼ cup water
½ cup flour
¼ cup Parmesan cheese
salt
pepper
dash of nutmeg
eggplant

Other Ingredients:
1 cup spaghetti sauce
chopped ham OR sautéd hamburger
grated Parmesan cheese
grated Mozzarella cheese

For frying batter, beat eggs and water together, mix flour, and cheese; add to egg; add salt pepper and nutmeg. Peel eggplant, slice lengthwise into thin slices; soak in salt water for about 30 minutes; remove from water and dry between paper towels. Dip eggplant in batter and fry in about 2″ of fat until lightly brown.

To assemble casserole, pour about ½ cup spaghetti sauce into the bottom of baking dish; layer fried eggplant over sauce and sprinkle ham or hamburger over eggplant. Top meat layer with grated mozzarella cheese and Parmesan cheese. Repeat layers until all eggplant is used. Pour more spaghetti sauce on, almost covering top. Sprinkle on more Parmesan cheese and bake at 350° for about 30 minutes.

Helen Schulz

EGGPLANT PARMIGIANA

OVEN: 350° 20 minutes

1 eggplant, about ¾ pound
2 eggs, beaten
¾ cup olive oil
1 cup flour

1 — 14 ounce jar tomato sauce
6 ounces Mozzarella cheese
½ cup grated cheese
seasoning to taste

Cut eggplant into ½″ slices. Dip slices into egg; then into flour. Sauté eggplant in hot oil for about 2 minutes on each side until light brown. Drain, then start layers of ingredients in a baking dish. Begin with eggplant, then mozzarella cheese, sauce, grated cheese; repeat layers until ingredients are used. Bake in hot oven, about 350°, for about 20 minutes.

Grace Barrie

Cucumber cups are easily shaped from large cucumbers. Peel, score, and cut into one and one-half inch slices. Hollow out the center with a melon ball cutter. Fill with a choice stuffing.

EGGPLANT SPECIAL

1 eggplant
1 egg, beaten
1 tablespoon milk
1 cup dry bread crumbs
½ cup diced green pepper
1 onion, chopped

½ cup milk
1 can cream of chicken soup
½ teaspoon salt
1 cup grated sharp cheddar cheese
⅓ cup shortening

Peel eggplant and cut into ¾" slices. Dip slices in egg, combined with milk; then dip into crumbs. Brown slices in shortening and remove. Brown green pepper and onion. Add soup, milk and salt and ⅔ of cheese. Arrange slices in a baking dish; pour sauce over top and sprinkle on remaining ⅓ cup of cheese and remaining bread crumbs. Bake until cheese melts.

May also be cooked in same skillet on top of stove.

Eva Mae Williams

ESCALLOPED ONIONS

OVEN: 350° 30-45 minutes

6 medium onions
2 cups soft bread crumbs, cubed
salt to taste

pepper to taste
½-¾ cup cream
4 tablespoons butter

Slice onions as for frying; cook by placing in cold water and bring water to a boil; discard water and repeat. Boil until onions are tender; drain. Place a layer of onions then a layer of bread cubes in a shallow baking dish; alternate layers until ingredients are used and bake in 350° oven until brown on top; approximately 30-45 minutes.

This recipe was my Grandmother's. She came from Butler Co., Pennsylvania, but lived most of her life in southern Ohio.

Mrs. Parker Henry

FANTASTIC POTATO KUGEL (PUDDING)

OVEN: 350° 40 minutes

5 eggs, separated
3 cups grated Irish potatoes
½ cup grated onion
1 tablespoon minced fresh parsley

1 tablespoon oil
1½ teaspoons salt
pepper

Beat egg yolks until thick and lemon-colored; add grated potatoes, onion, oil, salt, pepper and parsley. Mix lightly but well, fold in egg whites that have been beaten stiff, but not dry. Pour into oiled casserole or souffle dish; 1½ quart size. Bake in 350° oven for 40 minutes.

If you have a processor, grate onions and potatoes and blend in other ingredients, add egg whites beaten separately.

Peggy Berg

FAR EAST CELERY

OVEN: 350° 35 minutes   YIELD: 6 servings

4 cups diced celery
1 can cream of chicken soup
1 — 15 ounce can water chestnuts,
  sliced

¼ cup diced pimentos
½ cup bread crumbs
¼ cup slivered, toasted almonds
2 tablespoons melted butter

Cook celery for 8 minutes and drain well. Mix soup, water chestnuts and pimento with celery and place in a casserole.

Combine bread crumbs and almonds and sprinkle over casserole. Bake for 35 minutes at 350°

Mary Klueppelberg

GUINEA SQUASH PIE
(Eggplant)

OVEN: 350° 25 minutes

1 eggplant
1 dozen soda crackers
milk
2 eggs, beaten slightly

1 onion, chopped
3 tablespoons butter
sharp cheddar cheese
paprika

Peel and boil eggplant in salted water for 10 minutes. Drain. Sauté onions in butter until translucent. In a casserole, soak crumbled crackers in milk; and beaten eggs, eggplant which has been cubed, and onions. Mix. Top with grated cheddar cheese; sprinkle with paprika. Bake for 25 minutes in 350° oven.

Marilyn Carlton

HERBED POTATO BAKE

OVEN: 425° 15 minutes   YIELD: 6 servings

5 cups boiled, cubed potatoes
2 tablespoons instant minced onion
6 tablespoons butter, divided
1 — 8 ounce can tomato sauce
2 tablespoons basil leaves
½ teaspoon marjoram leaves

⅛ teaspoon black, coarse ground
  pepper.
1 cup soft bread crumbs
2 tablespoons Parmesan cheese
1 tablespoon parsley flakes

Melt 4 tablespoons of butter in a skillet; sauté onions for 5 minutes; add tomato sauce, salt to taste, and spices. Pour mixture over potatoes. Spoon mixture into a buttered 1 quart casserole. Melt remaining butter and stir in bread crumbs, cheese and parsley flakes. Sprinkle mixture over potatoes and bake in preheated 425° oven for 15 minutes or until crumbs are browned and potatoes are hot.

One young guest remarked, "Gee, Aunt Helen, this is almost as good as pizza." High praise!

Helen George

IMAM BAELDI

1 eggplant, sliced
2 onions, sliced
1 — 16 ounce can tomatoes OR 4
   fresh tomatoes

1 clove garlic
2 tablespoons olive oil OR vegetable oil

Heat olive oil in frying pan; add sliced onion and simmer until nearly done; add sliced garlic and then tomatoes. Simmer for 5 minutes. Slice eggplant lengthwise into eighths and cut crosswise. Add eggplant to simmering ingredients, and simmer covered for ½ hour until eggplant is done. Salt and pepper to taste.

Imam Baeldi may be served hot as a vegetable or cold as a salad. Zucchini can be prepared this same way.

This is a Turkish or Armenian dish. Imam is the head man or priest of a community and baeldi means the beautiful dish fit for such an exalted person.

Eden Gray

IOWA CABBAGE CASSEROLE

OVEN: 350° 50 minutes

6 slices partly cooked bacon
1 medium head cabbage, shredded
   fine, do not grate
1 cup cream OR 1 cup undiluted
   evaporated milk

1 teaspoon sugar
1 teaspoon salt
2 tablespoons flour
¼ teaspoon pepper

Partly cook bacon. Grease a 1-½ quart casserole and place shredded cabbage in casserole.

Combine flour, sugar, salt and pepper with the cream or milk and make into a nice smooth paste.

Pour paste over cabbage and top with strips of bacon. Cover and bake at 350° for 40 minutes. Remove cover and bake another 10 minutes to fully cook the bacon and turn the delicacy to a toasty brown.

Isabelle Dorland McClintock

Chinese or celery cabbage adds crispness to menus. It may be shredded and made into cole slaw. It may also be cooked and served in any of the methods given for cabbage. An added advantage in using Chinese cabbage is that it does not have a strong odor while cooking.

ITALIAN EGGPLANT-SAUSAGE CASSEROLE

OVEN: 350° 30 minutes

2 large eggplants
1½ pounds ground sausage
½ cup chopped spring onion
1 clove garlic, minced
¼ cup chopped parsley
¼ teaspoon fennel seed
¼ teaspoon oregano
1 small can tomato paste

1 small can sliced mushrooms
½ cup white wine
olive oil
grated Romano cheese
shredded mozzarella cheese
salt
pepper

Slice eggplant ½" thick and fry in olive oil until lightly browned. Drain on paper towels. Place eggplant overlapping in a large casserole dish. Fry sausage, onion, garlic, parsley, fennel seed and oregano until browned; salt and pepper to taste. Add tomato paste and mushrooms with liquid and simmer gently, 10 minutes. Add wine. Spread meat sauce on top of eggplant slices, sprinkle with Romano cheese. Repeat layers of eggplant, meat sauce and cheese. Top with shredded mozzarella cheese. Bake in 350° oven until bubbly, about 30 minutes. Cut in squares to serve. Serve hot with garlic bread and tossed green salad. This recipe is one handed down by my mother, who was born in the province of Aburzzi in Italy.

Julie Livesay

JESSIE'S CELERY CASSEROLE

OVEN: 350° 35-40 minutes

4 cups celery diced 1½" thick
1 can cream of chicken soup
1 can water chestnuts, sliced

¼ cup chopped pimento
¼ cup slivered almonds
½ cup browned, buttered crumbs

Combine celery, cream soup, water chestnuts, pimentos and almonds in a 2 quart casserole. Top with buttered crumbs and bake in 350° oven for 35-40 minutes.

Better double this recipe if you have a family of more than six; everyone loves it!

Jessie Backus Guhse

LIBBY'S CELERY CASSEROLE

OVEN: 350° 20 minutes

4 cups celery
1 can cream of mushroom soup
1 small can water chestnuts, sliced
1 small jar pimentos

4 slices bread, made into crumbs
¼ stick butter OR margarine,
melted

Cut celery in ½" slices; cover with water and boil until soft. Meanwhile, mix soup, water chestnuts and pimento. When celery is cooked, drain well and mix with soup mixture. Place in a casserole dish and top with bread crumbs that have been tossed with melted butter. Bake in 350° oven for 20 minutes.

Mrs. Robert P. Fletcher

MASHED POTATO CASSEROLE

OVEN: 350° 40 minutes   YIELD: 10 servings

4 cups hot mashed potatoes
1 — 8 ounce package cream cheese
1 egg
2 tablespoons chopped onions

1 tablespoon chives
1 tablespoon chopped pimento
shredded sharp cheese

Combine all ingredients except cheese and mix together well. Place in a buttered baking dish and bake for 30 minutes at 350°. Remove from oven and cover top with shredded cheese; return to oven and bake for 10 minutes longer. Serve hot.

This is very easy and good.

Olive Smith

MEXICAN ZUCCHINI

OVEN: 400° 20 minutes

8 medium zucchini, washed and
  sliced
2 tablespoons butter
1 — 4 ounce can mushrooms, sliced
  and drained

1 small can green chilies, chopped
1 — 8 ounce jar processed cheese
1 small jar chopped pimento
1 small can evaporated milk
12 round snack crackers, crushed

Cook zucchini in boiling, salted water until done; about 8 minutes. Drain very well. Simmer mushrooms and chilies in butter; add cheese, pimento, and evaporated milk. Stir until cheese melts. Place zucchini in rectangular casserole or baking dish. Pour cheese sauce over zucchini and sprinkle crushed crackers on top. Bake in 400° oven for 20 minutes.

If ingredients are cold, add a few more minutes to baking time.

Shirley DeCarlo

MUSHROOM ASPARAGUS CASSEROLE

OVEN: 350° 40 minutes   YIELD: 8-10 servings

4 cups fresh mushrooms, halved
1 cup chopped onion
4 tablespoons butter
2 tablespoons all-purpose flour
2 chicken bouillon cubes
¼ cup chopped pimento
1½ teaspoons lemon juice
½ teaspoon salt

dash of pepper
½ teaspoon nutmeg
1 cup milk
2 — 8 ounce packages frozen asparagus, slightly thawed
¾ cup crushed herb stuffing mix
1 tablespoon butter, melted

Cook mushrooms and onions, covered, in 4 tablespoons butter until slightly tender. Remove and set aside, leaving butter in skillet. Blend in flour, bouillon cubes, salt, pepper and nutmeg. Add milk and cook, stirring until bubbly and slightly thick. Stir in mushrooms, onion, pimento and lemon juice. Arrange asparagus in a 1-½ quart baking dish and pour mushrooms mixture over asparagus; mix lightly. Combine stuffing mix, crushed, with melted butter and sprinkle over top of casserole. Bake for 40 minutes at 350°.

Teresa Eidson

MUSHROOM CASSEROLE

OVEN: 375° 15 minutes   YIELD: 6 servings

½ cup chopped onion
½ cup margarine
2 — 6 ounce cans mushroom
  crowns, drained
¼ cup flour
½ teaspoon dried marjoram,
  crushed

1 — 10½ ounce can condensed
  beef broth
2 tablespoons dry sherry
2 tablespoons snipped parsley
½ cup coarse cracker crumbs
2 tablespoons grated Parmesan
  cheese
1 tablespoon margarine, melted

Cook onion in butter until almost tender; add mushrooms and cook lightly. Blend in flour and marjoram; add beef broth soup all at once; cook and stir until mixture thickens and bubbles. Remove from heat; stir in wine and parsley. Pour into 1 quart casserole. Combine cracker crumbs, Parmesan cheese and melted butter; sprinkle over casserole and bake in 375° oven for 15 minutes or until hot and bubbly.

Connie Montuoro

NANNY'S SQUASH CASSEROLE

OVEN: 325° 1 hour

8-10 yellow squash
6-8 crackers
½ cup milk
2 eggs
1 onion
1 bell pepper

½ cup longhorn cheese
½ stick butter OR oleo
1 teaspoon sugar
salt to taste
pepper to taste

Parboil squash in salted water until tender. Drain and mash well. Add crackers that have been crushed fine. Beat milk and eggs together and add to squash. Grate onion, pepper and cheese; add to squash. Add butter and sugar; salt and pepper to taste. Pour mixture into buttered casserole and top with additional cracker crumbs; bake for 1 hour at 325°. When casserole is almost done, add additional shredded cheese and leave in oven long enough to melt cheese.

Julia Hall

Boil zucchini with sliced onions; drain, add melted butter and a dash of garlic powder with a dash of Parmesan cheese — simply delicious.

NEW ORLEANS BEANS AND RICE

2 pounds dried beans, your choice
dry salt bacon
ham chunks
smoked sausage
2 large onions

1 large bell pepper
dash of hot sauce
salt
pepper

Cook beans and dry salt bacon for about 3 hours in about 3 cups of water. As water cooks out it may be necessary to add more.

In a skillet, with about 2 tablespoons bacon drippings, add chopped smoked sausage, ham pieces, chopped bell pepper, chopped onion and hot sauce. Cook in hot drippings until onion is clear. Add to the cooked beans and allow to cook together until all seasoning has cooked through the beans. Serve over cooked rice with skillet cornbread and a green salad.

By skillet cornbread, I mean cornbread cooked in an iron skillet. It gives the cornbread a crust that is chewy and good. Do not salt beans while cooking as it will harden the water and take the beans longer to cook. Our preference of beans is pinto or large butter beans.

Lucy Gant

OLD FASHIONED CORN PUDDING

OVEN: 350° 1 hour

6 ears corn, scraped
¾ cup milk
3 tablespoons sugar
3 tablespoons melted butter

1 teaspoon cornstarch
½ teaspoon salt
2 eggs
½ cup cheese, in small pieces

If using canned corn, use 2 cans and use ½ cup milk.

Dissolve cornstarch in milk.

Combine all ingredients except corn and mix well. Then add to corn and place in a casserole dish and bake in moderate, 350° oven for 1 hour.

Ruth Reiff

ONION PIE

OVEN: 350° 30 minutes

1 stick oleo
1 cup crushed round snack crackers
3 cups sliced onions
¾ cup milk

2 eggs
1 teaspoon salt
2 dashes black pepper
¾ cup grated cheddar cheese

Melt ½ stick oleo in a 9" pie pan. Then add cracker crumbs and toss around in oleo until they are coated. Press crumbs to bottom and sides of pan.

Sauté sliced onions in remaining ½ stick oleo until barely tender, then place in pie shell. Beat together milk, eggs, salt and black pepper. Heat this mixture until hot, but not boiled. Pour over onions in pie shell. Sprinkle with grated cheese. Bake for 30 minutes at 350°.

Glenda H. Shelfer

P. J.'S SPINACH CASSEROLE

OVEN: 350° 30 minutes

YIELD: 6-8 servings

2 packages frozen chopped spinach
minced onion
nutmeg to taste
salt to taste

pepper to taste
1 stick melted butter
2 large package cream cheese
½ package (small) dressing

Cook spinach according to package directions with minced onion, nutmeg, salt and pepper. Drain. Mix ½ stick melted butter and cream cheese together; add to drained spinach. Prepare topping by blending dressing and remaining melted butter. Sprinkle over spinach mixture in casserole dish and bake in 350° oven for 30 minutes.

Nancy Carlton

POMMES DE TERRÉ GRATINEÉS

OVEN: 325° 1 hour

6 baking potatoes, peeled and
   sliced thin
2 tablespoons butter
1 cup milk
1 cup heavy cream
½ cup Swiss cheese, grated

¼ cup grated Parmesan cheese
2 cloves garlic, crushed
½ teaspoon salt
black pepper, freshly ground
dash of nutmeg

In a small saucepan, place milk, cream, butter, garlic and nutmeg. Simmer about 10 minutes until slightly thickened. Arrange ⅓ of potatoes in bottom of baking dish; cover with ⅓ of cheeses; salt and pepper. Repeat, making 3 layers of all ingredients; dot with butter and add cream mixture. Cover dish and bake about 1 hour in 325° oven.

Do not substitute Swiss cheese, please. This is excellent with beef roast.

Louise Hayes

To bake potatoes in half the normal time, parboil the potatoes for five minutes before baking. Drain and dry with paper towel before placing in oven.

POTATO CASSEROLE

OVEN: 350° 45 minutes

YIELD: 15-20 servings

2 pound package frozen hash
  browns, partially thawed
½ cup melted butter
1 teaspoon salt
¼ teaspoon pepper
½ large onion, chopped
2 cans cream of mushroom soup,
  undiluted

1 pint sour cream
2 cups grated sharp cheddar
  cheese

Topping:
¼ cup melted butter
2 cups crushed flaked corn cereal

Combine hash browns with ½ cup melted butter, salt, pepper, onion, soup, sour cream and cheese. Mix together well and spread in a 9 x 13 cake pan. Combine ingredients for topping and spread over mixture in pan. Bake at 350° for 45 minutes. Bake longer if potatoes are not thawed.

This recipe has been passed over the entire county and even into Palm Beach County and as far north as West Virginia.

Mary Ann Holt

POTATO DUMPLINGS

YIELD: 10-12

8 pounds potatoes, ⅔ raw potatoes
  and ⅓ cooked potatoes
2 eggs

2 slices bread, diced and roasted
1 tablespoon salt

Peel and grate potatoes; press through a cheesecloth; remove all liquid; add eggs, salt and mashed potatoes. Also add the starch settled from raw potato-water and mix well. This makes a soft dough. Form dumplings about the size of golf balls by taking several pieces of roasted, diced bread for the inside of each dumpling and press to make firm balls.

Bring about 8 quarts of water to a boil; add 2 tablespoons salt and drop dumplings into boiling water. Bring water to a boil again and boil for about 20 minutes. Remove dumplings from water at once and serve. Bread crumbs may be sprinkled over dumplings if desired.

Louise Beerhalter

When boiling field peas the addition of a teaspoonful of sugar will be found to make them almost equal to "garden peas."

PRALINE SWEET POTATOES

OVEN: 350° 30 minutes

1 large can sweet potatoes
2 eggs
⅔ cup sugar
½ stick butter OR oleo
1 teaspoon vanilla
¼ teaspoon salt

Topping:
1 cup brown sugar
½ stick oleo
⅓ cup flour
1 cup chopped pecans

Drain and mash potatoes; add other ingredients and pour into a buttered casserole. Mix brown sugar, flour and butter until crumbly; add pecans and sprinkle over top of potatoes. Bake in 350° oven until topping is bubbly; about 30 minutes.

May be made ahead, frozen and baked later.

Mary Klueppelberg

RATATOUILLÉ

OVEN: 350° 15-20 minutes

YIELD: 6 servings

1 medium eggplant, unpeeled, and
  cut into 1½ inch cubes
3 medium zucchini, quartered, and
  cut into 1 inch lengths
6 tablespoons olive oil
salt, to taste
freshly ground pepper, to taste
3 onions, chopped
3 green peppers, cored, seeded and
  chopped

1 clove garlic
1 bay leaf
2 pounds tomatoes, peeled, and cut
  into 1 inch cubes
½ cup fresh parsley, finely chopped
1 tablespoon fresh basil, finely
  chopped
1 tablespoon fresh thyme, finely
  chopped
lemon slices

Preheat oven to 350°. In a large skillet heat three tablespoons olive oil; add chopped onion and green peppers. Chop garlic and bay leaf together to make a paste. Add to onion mixture. Remove from heat. In second skillet, heat remaining olive oil; add eggplant, zucchini, salt and pepper. Remove from heat. Add tomatoes to skillet containing onion, green pepper, garlic and bay leaf mixture; simmer, stirring occasionally, for ten minutes. Add eggplant and zucchini mixture; stir in parsley, thyme, and basil. Remove from heat and place into a casserole; cover and bake fifteen to twenty minutes or until vegetables are fork tender. Garnish with twisted slices of lemon.

Lucinda Lauser

Potatoes will keep for several weeks if properly stored. Place in a cool dark humid place. It is far better to keep them at room temperature than in the refrigerator. Under refrigeration the potatoes become sweet.

RED CABBAGE

1 medium-size head red cabbage
2 tablespoons lard OR bacon fat
1 tablespoon salt
2 tablespoons vinegar

1 cup water
1 teaspoon sugar
2 tablespoons flour
1 cup red wine

Simmer shredded cabbage in hot fat; add water, vinegar, salt and sugar gradually and simmer in a covered pot for about 2 hours; add red wine mixed with flour and simmer for another 30 minutes.

Louise Beerhalter

SCALLOPED CABBAGE

OVEN: 350° 40 minutes   Yield: 6 servings

1 small head cabbage
1 cup thinly sliced celery
1 cup boiling water
½ teaspoon salt
1 can cream of celery soup
⅓ cup milk

4 teaspoons soy sauce
1 tablespoon minced onion
dash of tabasco sauce
½ cup crushed saltines
2 tablespoons butter

Shred cabbage to make 4 cups; bring cabbage, celery, water and salt to a boil for 5 minutes; drain; place in casserole with remaining ingredients except butter and crackers. Melt butter and add crackers; sprinkle on top of casserole. Bake at 350° for 40 minutes.

Marge Dunklee

SOUTHERN DELIGHT

OVEN: 325° 1 hour

15 ounces tomato puree
5 ounces water
1 pound dark brown sugar

7 slices white bread, diced
¾ pound oleo OR butter, melted

Combine puree, water and brown sugar in a saucepan and cook for 5 minutes. Pour melted butter over diced bread; place bread in a casserole dish and pour puree mixture over buttered bread. Bake, covered, for 1 hour at 325°.

James S. Foster

There are lots of delicious ways to cook greens. Cook them with ham scraps. Add onion, chives or fresh parsley. Dress them up with sour cream or cottage cheese and a teaspoon of curry powder. Serve them as a hot salad with a tart french dressing.

SPANAKOPETA
(Spinach Pie)

OVEN: 350° 1 hour

3 packages frozen, chopped spinach OR 2 pounds fresh spinach
1 pound strudel pastry sheets
1 pound feta cheese (white Greek
goat cheese), crumbled
1 pound dry cottage cheese

6 tablespoons grated cheese
7 eggs
1 stick butter (for filling)
2 sticks butter, melted (for brushing pastry sheets)

Grease a 9 x 13 pan and place 7 sheets of pastry into the pan; brushing each sheet with melted butter. Combine spinach, goat cheese, cottage cheese, grated cheese, eggs, and 1 stick butter together in a large mixing bowl. Spread spinach mixture evenly on pastry sheets and cover with 7 individually buttered pastry sheets. Bake in 350° oven for approximately one hour or until top is golden brown.

Cut into squares and serve hot or cold.

Irene Crist

SPINACH CASSEROLE I

OVEN: 350° 30 minutes

2 packages frozen spinach OR
fresh spinach
4 tablespoons butter
2 tablespoons flour
1 teaspoon Worcestershire sauce
2 tablespoons minced onion

¾ teaspoon celery salt
⅓ teaspoon garlic salt
4 ounces jalapeno pepper cheese,
sliced
bread crumbs

Cook frozen spinach as directed on package. If fresh, bring to a boil and cook about 7 minutes.

Drain spinach, reserving ½ cup liquid. Melt butter in pan, adding flour and onion. Cook slowly and add spinach liquid, stirring until smooth; add seasonings and cheese. When cheese melts add spinach. Put in a shallow 1 quart casserole and cover with buttered bread crumbs. Bake uncovered for 30 minutes at 350°.

Can be made the day before and refrigerated until baked.

Hazel N. Crews

SPINACH CASSEROLE II

OVEN: 350° 20-30 minutes

2 packages spinach, cooked
½ cup chopped onion
½ stick butter

8 ounces cream cheese
bread crumbs

Cook spinach and onion together; drain and add butter and cream cheese. Pour into baking dish and cover with bread crumbs. Bake for 20-30 minutes at 350°.

LeVan N. Fee

SPINACH MORNAY

OVEN: 350° 20 minutes   YIELD: 8-10 servings

4 — 10 ounce packages frozen
  chopped spinach
salt
pepper
4 tablespoons butter
3 tablespoons flour
dash of salt
dash of cayenne pepper

1½ teaspoons Dijon mustard
1 teaspoon dry mustard
1 cup milk
4 tablespoons grated Swiss cheese
½ cup grated Parmesan cheese, reserve some for top
4 tablespoons light cream

Cook and thoroughly drain spinach; season with salt and pepper; set aside.
Melt butter and remove from heat; add flour; season with salt and cayenne pepper, Dijon mustard and dry mustard. Blend in milk and stir over low heat until mixture boils; add Swiss cheese, Parmesan cheese and light cream. Simmer for 5 minutes. Combine with spinach and refrigerate or freeze. To serve, bring to room temperature and heat thoroughly at 350° for about 20 minutes. Five minutes before serving, remove from oven and sprinkle remaining Parmesan cheese over the top. Return to oven for last 5 minutes cooking.
If you do not have cayenne pepper, use regular pepper.
A delicious and very attractive dish if baked in tomato cases, but remember, tomatoes are not freezable.

Arlene Rossway

SPRINGTIME POTATOES

1½ pounds small, new potatoes
⅓ cup chopped cucumbers
1½ tablespoons green onions
2 tablespoons chopped green peppers

2 tablespoons sliced radishes
1 teaspoon salt
dash of pepper
½ cup sour cream

Scrape potatoes and cook until tender in salted water. Combine all ingredients with potatoes except sour cream and heat with potatoes.
Heat sour cream separately and pour over hot potatoes.

June Carlton Vest

SQUASH CASSEROLE I

OVEN: 350° 25 minutes

1 pound yellow squash
1 egg, beaten
⅓ — ½ cup evaporated milk
2 tablespoons finely chopped onion
1 teaspoon sugar

salt
pepper
2 tablespoons butter
buttered bread crumbs

Wash, slice and cook squash until tender in a small amount of water. Drain and mash; add other ingredients except bread crumbs and pour into buttered casserole. Top with bread crumbs and bake in moderate 350° oven until brown, about 25 minutes.

Ethel Kicliter

SQUASH CASSEROLE II

OVEN: 350° 30-35 minutes   YIELD: 6 servings

2 pounds yellow squash
1 medium onion, chopped
1 — 8 ounce can water chestnuts,
   sliced thin
1 can celery soup, undiluted

½ cup sour cream
salt
pepper
1 cup herb stuffing

Cut squash in rounds; add chopped onion, salt and pepper to taste. Boil in small amount of water until almost done, pour into a strainer and drain very well. Mix soup, chestnuts and sour cream together; add drained squash and mix well; pour into buttered casserole and spread stuffing on top. Bake for 30-35 minutes at 350°

Ruth Huggins

SQUASH CASSEROLE III

OVEN: 350° 20 minutes   YIELD: 4-6 servings

2 cups mashed Hubbard squash
4 tablespoons butter, melted
3 tablespoons brown sugar
1 tablespoon prepared mustard

1 egg
salt
pepper
½ cup crushed flaked corn cereal

Mix squash with 2 tablespoons each of butter and brown sugar. Add mustard, egg, salt and pepper. Place mixture in a shallow 1 quart baking dish. Mix remaining butter and brown sugar with cereal crumbs and sprinkle over top. Bake in 350° oven for 20 minutes.

Nancy Gollnick

SQUASH CASSEROLE IV

OVEN: 350° 25 minutes

2½ to 3 pounds yellow squash
1 pint sour cream
1 can cream of chicken soup
onions to taste

salt to taste
pepper to taste
1 small package stuffing
2 tablespoons butter

Cook squash and onions in salted water until tender; stir together with butter, soup, sour cream, salt and pepper. Sprinkle half of stuffing evenly on bottom of an oblong baking pan. Spread squash mixture over stuffing and sprinkle remaining stuffing mix on top. Bake at 350° for about 25 minutes.

Kathy Sayers

To keep onions from making eyes tear, place a small chunk of bread on the end of paring knife. The bread will absorb the juices and fumes of the onion.

SQUASH SOUFFLÉ

OVEN: 350° 45 minutes

2½ cups cooked yellow squash,
  about 2 pounds
2 cups grated sharp cheese
3 whole eggs
7 tablespoons butter

6 tablespoons flour
1 cup milk
buttered bread crumbs
slivered almonds

Drop eggs into warm, cooked squash; mix with an egg beater.

In a heavy saucepan, make a cream sauce of butter, flour and milk; then add cheese. Stir together sauce and squash; pour into a buttered 3 quart flat oven-proof baking dish; top with bread crumbs and almonds. Bake in preheated oven at 350° for 45 minutes or until brown and set.

Squash should be cooked with very little water and do not drain.

This is a marvelous "party" recipe and always gets compliments.

Mrs. Charles R. P. Brown

SUMMER SQUASH CASSEROLE

OVEN: 350° 25-30 minutes   YIELD: 6 servings

2 pounds yellow summer squash,
  sliced to yield 6 cups
¼ cup chopped onion
1 can condensed cream of chicken
  soup

1 cup dairy sour cream
1 cup shredded carrot
1 — 8 ounce package herb-
  seasoned stuffing mix
½ cup butter OR oleo, melted

In a saucepan, cook squash and onion in boiling salted water for 5 minutes. Drain. Combine soup and sour cream; stir in carrot; fold in drained squash and onion. Combine stuffing mix and butter or margarine. Spread half of stuffing on bottom of 12 x 7-½ x 2" baking dish. Spoon vegetable mixture on top and add remaining stuffing over vegetables. Bake at 350° for 25-30 minutes.

You may wish to use less stuffing. If so, reduce amount of butter or margarine accordingly.

Priscilla Haynes

SUNBEAM CUSTARD

OVEN: 350° 45-50 minutes   YIELD: 4-6 servings

4 eggs
2 cups fresh corn, about 4 ears
1 can evaporated milk, 13 ounce
3 tablespoons finely chopped onion

1½ tablespoons butter OR margarine, melted
2 teaspoons sugar
1½ teaspoon salt
¼ teaspoon nutmeg
⅛ teaspoon pepper

In a medium bowl, beat eggs with undiluted milk; add corn, onion, butter, sugar, salt, nutmeg and pepper. Mix well. Turn into a greased, shallow 1-½ quart casserole and place in large pan with 1" boiling water in pan. Bake in 350° oven for 45-50 minutes or until tip of knife inserted in center comes out clean.

Jean Finger

SWAMP CABBAGE I

1 swamp cabbage
½ cup salt pork, diced
4 tablespoons flour

1 teaspoon salt
pepper
2 — 13 ounce cans evaporated milk

Cut up cabbage using only tender parts; cook in water until tender but firm; drain; set aside.

In a large frying pan, fry salt pork until brown; remove pork from fat, add flour, salt and pepper to fat and stir until well blended. Gradually stir in milk and return to medium heat; cook, stirring constantly until thick and smooth. Add sauce to cabbage; salt and pepper to taste and simmer for about 15 minutes, covered. Add more sauce if cabbage is larger; if sauce is too thick, add a little water.

Mr. and Mrs. Ewell E. Menge

SWAMP CABBAGE II

2 cabbages from cabbage palm
  tree

½ pound salt pork
salt to taste

Cut cabbage palm tree, boot it, and use tender part of bud; cut bud into 2 small pieces — 2 cabbages. Cut cabbage into small pieces and place in a large kettle.

Cut 2 trees for a family of six people.

Score ½ pound piece of salt pork criss-crossed and place in pot with cabbage; salt to taste and cover with water. Boil until tender. Do not overcook.

Addie Holmes Emerson

SWAMP CABBAGE III

swamp cabbage
bacon bits and drippings
salt

dash of pepper
1 tablespoon sugar

Cut cabbage palm down below first row of dead fronds. Peel fronds of cabbage until white tender appears. Remove all bitter parts. Cut cabbage into chunks and place in a large pot and add water, bacon bits and drippings, salt, pepper and sugar. Begin to cook immediately. Bring to a boil, reduce heat, cover and simmer until tender.

Swamp cabbage is much better if not over-cooked. It should be tender but not mushy.

Earl Raulerson

One pound of tomatoes consists of three medium or four small tomatoes.

SWEET POTATO CASSEROLE

OVEN: 350° 25 minutes

1 large can sweet potatoes, drained
⅔ cup sugar
⅓ cup milk
2 eggs
1 teaspoon vanilla
¼ teaspoon nutmeg
¼ teaspoon cinnamon
¼ teaspoon allspice
1 stick margarine

Topping:
1 stick margarine, melted
½ cup flour
⅔ cup light brown sugar
½ teaspoon cinnamon
1 cup nuts, optional

Combine potatoes, sugar, milk, eggs, vanilla and spices with margarine; beat with mixer until mixture is smooth. Pour into a 2 quart casserole.

Blend together melted margarine, flour, brown sugar, cinnamon and nuts for topping. Blend well and spread over mixture in casserole. Bake in 350° oven for 25 minutes.

Judie England

SWEET POTATO SOUFFLÉ I

OVEN: 375° 25 minutes

3 cups mashed sweet potatoes
½ cup sugar
¾ cup margarine
1 cup milk
2 eggs
1 teaspoon vanilla
1 teaspoon cinnamon

Topping:
1 cup light brown sugar
1½ cups flour
¾ cup margarine
¾ cup broken pecans

Combine mashed sweet potatoes with sugar, margarine, milk, eggs, vanilla and cinnamon. Blend well and pour into a flat dish. Blend together brown sugar, flour and butter. Sprinkle mixture over casserole. Sprinkle broken pecans over topping.

Bake at 375° for 25 minutes.

The Honorable R. Dale Patchett
The Florida State House
of Representatives,
District 48

Revive wilted or blemished vegetables by sprinkling them with cool water then wrapping in a towel and refrigerating for about one hour.

SWEET POTATO SOUFFLÉ II

OVEN: 350° 30-45 minutes

3 cups mashed, fresh sweet potatoes
2 eggs, beaten slightly
⅓ cup milk
1 cup white sugar
½ teaspoon salt
1 tablespoon vanilla

Topping:
1 cup brown sugar
⅓ cup flour
⅓ cup butter
1 cup chopped nuts

Combine mashed potatoes with eggs, milk, white sugar, salt and vanilla.
Mix together well and pour into a 13 x 9 x 2-½″ pan.
Combine brown sugar, flour, butter and nuts and blend well.
Sprinkle mixture over sweet potatoes in pan and bake in 350° oven for 30-
45 minutes.

Onnie Jean Walker

SWEET POTATO SOUFFLÉ III

OVEN: 350°

2 cups cooked, mashed sweet potatoes
1 cup hot milk
½ teaspoon salt
2 tablespoons sugar
2 eggs

2 tablespoons butter
¼ cup raisins
¼ cup chopped nuts
1 teaspoon nutmeg
marshmallows

Heat milk and dissolve sugar and salt in it. Add butter, stirring until
melted. Add this mixture to mashed sweet potatoes and mix well. Separate
eggs and beat yolks; add yolks to potato mixture. Add nutmeg.
Beat egg whites until stiff then fold lightly into potato mixture. Pour mixture into a buttered baking dish. Arrange marshmallows on top and place in
350° oven. Bake until heated through and brown on top.
This is my Mother's original recipe. To it I have added about 1 teaspoon
grated, dried orange rind for additional flavor.

Betty Peterson

Bake potatoes in a muffin pan for easier removal from the oven.

SWEET POTATOES AND WALNUTS

OVEN: 400° 30 minutes YIELD: 8-10 servings

3 pounds sweet potatoes
2 tablespoons brown sugar
3 tablespoons butter OR margarine
½ teaspoon cinnamon
½ teaspoon nutmeg

salt to taste
1 cup milk
½ cup brandy
1 cup broken walnut meats, English or black

Cook, drain, peel and mash potatoes. Combine potatoes with remaining ingredients and mix well; spoon mixture into a greased 2 quart casserole. Refrigerate or freeze, if desired.

To serve, return to room temperature and bake at 400° for 30 minutes or until heated through.

The original recipe called for ¾ cup granulated brown sugar.

The Committee

TANGY GREEN BEANS

YIELD: 6 servings

2 tablespoons prepared mustard
2 tablespoons sugar
⅓ cup butter
¾ teaspoon salt

2 tablespoons lemon juice
2 tablespoons vinegar
3 cups hot cooked green beans

Combine mustard, sugar, butter and salt together in a saucepan. Heat slowly, stirring constantly. Stir in lemon juice and vinegar. Pour mixture over beans and heat thoroughly.

Mrs. K. W. Filbert

TANGY YELLOW SQUASH

YIELD: 10 servings

5 medium-size yellow squash,
thinly sliced
½ cup green onion, thinly sliced
½ cup green pepper, chopped
½ cup celery, sliced
2 tablespoons wine vinegar

¾ cup sugar
1 teaspoon salt
½ teaspoon pepper
⅓ cup salad oil
⅔ cup cider vinegar
1 clove garlic, minced

Combine squash, green onion, green pepper, and celery in a large mixing bowl; toss lightly. Combine wine vinegar, sugar, salt, pepper, salad oil, cider vinegar and garlic together; stir well and spoon over vegetables. Chill for about 12 hours, stirring occasionally. Drain and serve.

Audrey Park

TURNIP CASSEROLE

OVEN: 350° 30 minutes

2 cups cooked, mashed turnips
½ stick butter, OR less
1 teaspoon salt
1 teaspoon pepper

1 cup soft bread crumbs
2 eggs slightly beaten
2 tablespoons sugar

Combine mashed turnips with remaining ingredients and mix together well. Place in a greased baking dish and bake for 30 minutes at 350°.

Mrs. John P. Turk

TURNIPS BAKED IN SOUR CREAM

OVEN: 375° 20 minutes   YIELD: 6 servings

6 young white turnips
½ teaspoon caraway seeds
4 tablespoons sour cream
½ teaspoon sweet basil

salt
paprika
2 tablespoons lemon juice

Parboil turnips for 10 minutes in boiling water with caraway seeds added to water. Drain, peel, and dice quite small. Place diced turnips in a small greased casserole. Stir in sour cream and basil. Cover and bake at 375° until tender, about 20 minutes.

Check seasoning before serving, and if necessary, add a little salt. Sprinkle with paprika and dribble lemon juice over casserole before serving.

Kathryn Burpo

VEGETABLE MEDLEY

2 cups carrots
1 package frozen wax beans
1 package frozen green beans
½ pound fresh mushrooms
1 large onion
¼ cup butter OR margarine
1 teaspoon Accent
½ teaspoon garlic powder

1 teaspoon salt
¼ teaspoon white pepper
½ teaspoon marjoram

Glaze:
1 tablespoon cornstarch
1 can clear chicken broth
2 tablespoons water

Prepare glaze by mixing water and cornstarch together; add to broth in a saucepan and heat, stirring mixture until it reaches simmering point.

Cut carrots into diagonal strips about ¼″ thick; cut onion in long slices, about ¼″ thick; cook beans and carrots until tender. Drain vegetables. Allow butter to become hot, then saute onions and mushrooms for about 3-4 minutes; add onions, mushrooms, beans and carrots to the glaze. Combine seasonings and mix well.

Fresh or canned beans may be substituted for frozen beans.

Jean Rusnak

VEGETABLES IN ITALIAN BEER BATTER

YIELD: 3 cups batter

1¼ cups beer
1⅓ cups sifted all-purpose flour
2 tablespoons grated Parmesan
cheese
1 tablespoon snipped parsley
1 teaspoon salt
dash of garlic powder
1 tablespoon olive oil
2 beaten egg yolks

2 egg whites, stiffly beaten
1 — 9 ounce package frozen artichoke hearts, cooked and
drained
1 medium zucchini, sliced
1 small cauliflower, broken into
buds
1 green pepper, cut into strips
cooking oil

Let beer stand at room temperature for 45 minutes or until flat. In a mixing bowl, combine flour, cheese, parsley, salt and garlic powder. Stir in olive
oil, egg yolks and the flat beer. Beat mixture until smooth. Fold in stiffly
beaten egg whites.

Dip vegetables into batter and fry in deep hot fat, 375°, a few at a time, until golden, about 2-5 minutes. Drain on absorbent paper; serve immediately.

Vegetables may be frozen and reheated at 375° for 8 minutes.

Emily Gasper

VEGETARIAN CHILI

OVEN: 350° 20 minutes

YIELD: 6 cups

1 pound dried pinto beans
8 cups water
1 tablespoon PLUS 1½ teaspoons
salt
¼ cup salad oil
1 cup chopped onion
½ cup chopped green pepper

3 garlic cloves, chopped
4 teaspoons chili powder
2 teaspoons Worcestershire sauce
2 cups (8 ounces) shredded sharp
cheddar cheese
¼ teaspoon pepper

Wash beans; drain and place in a large saucepot. For quick soak method,
combine beans and water; bring to a boil; boil 2 minutes; remove from heat,
cover, and let stand for 1 hour, OR cover with water and soak overnight. Then
simmer, covered for 1 hour in soaking liquid. Add 1 tablespoon salt and continue cooking for ½ hour or until tender. Reserve 1 cup bean liquid, discard
the rest. Preheat oven to 350°.

In a medium skillet heat oil; add onion, green pepper, garlic, chili powder
1½ teaspoons salt and pepper; sauté, stirring often, until onion is tender. In
blender container place 1 cup cooked beans 1 cup bean liquid and Worcestershire. Cover and blend until pureed. Stir into remaining beans with the sautéed vegetables.

Spoon mixture into a lightly greased 8″ square baking dish and cover with
foil. Bake for 20 minutes. Recipe can be prepared in advance, covered and refrigerated up to 24 hours. Then reheat, covered, in 350° oven for 30-40 minutes, until completely heated through.

Remove foil, sprinkle cheese on top and bake for 5 more minutes, or until
cheese melts.

The Committee

YELLOW SQUASH WITH PEAS

OVEN: 350° 15-18 minutes

6-8 small yellow squash
10 ounces shelled, green peas
2 tablespoons butter
1 teaspoon salt
⅛ teaspoon white pepper

2 tablespoons light cream
1 teaspoon sugar
2 tablespoons fresh bread crumbs
2 tablespoons Parmesan cheese

Parboil squash until tender; about 5 minutes; drain, cut in half lengthwise and form a cavity by scooping out seeds.

Cook peas, and place in blender with butter, salt, pepper, cream and sugar. Blend. This mixture should be soft but still hold its shape. Add more cream if mixture is too stiff.

Fill cavities with puree and place squash in greased casserole. Top each one with bread crumbs and cheese. Bake at 350° for 15-18 minutes.

This recipe may be prepared the day before using.

Mrs. Edward Jackson, Jr.

ZUCCHINI AND MUSHROOMS

YIELD: 6-8 servings

1 — 2 pound zucchini
1 large bell pepper
8 ounces fresh mushrooms
1 tablespoon vegetable oil

salt to taste
pepper to taste
2 tablespoons water

Slice zucchini in rounds ¼″ thick. Slice bell pepper lengthwise 1/16″ thick. Slice mushrooms ¼″ thick.

Heat oil in wok or frying pan and add vegetables and mushrooms. Cook about 1 minute. Add approximately 2 tablespoons water, salt and pepper to taste, cover and cook for 7 minutes.

Vegetables should be crisp, but may be cooked longer if you like soft vegetables. This recipe is great done either way.

Doris Barnes

ZUCCHINI BISQUÉ

2 — 10½ ounce cans condensed
   chicken broth OR home-made
1 cup water
2 cups zucchini, thinly sliced
¼ cup chopped onion
3 tablespoons long cooking rice

1 tablespoon curry powder
½ teaspoon ginger
½ teaspoon dry mustard
salt
pepper
1½ cups half & half OR milk

Cook all ingredients except half & half or milk in a 3 quart covered saucepan for 20 minutes. Place in blender and adjust seasonings. Chill overnight if possible. Just before serving, stir in half & half or milk. Garnish with sour cream or whipped cream, parsley or stuffing or croutons.

This can be served hot or cold but we much prefer it as a cold soup. If you don't worry about calories, use half & half. You will have repeat orders on this. It is great for the freezer too.

Louise Sheward

ZUCCHINI CASSEROLE

OVEN: 350° 25-30 minutes

6 cups zucchini OR yellow squash	1 cup shredded carrots
¼ cup chopped onion	1 — 8 ounce package herb-
1 cup cream of chicken soup	seasoned stuffing mix
1 cup sour cream	1 cup melted butter

Cook squash and onions in a small amount of water for 5 minutes; drain.

Mix soup and sour cream together then stir in carrots; then fold in squash and onions. Blend well. Combine stuffing mix with butter and spread half of stuffing in the bottom of a 9x12 pan. Cover with cooked vegetable mixture and place remaining stuffing over vegetables. Bake in 350° oven for 25-30 minutes.

Rose Becker

ZUCCHINI CORN CASSEROLE

OVEN: 375° 40 minutes   YIELD: 10 servings

6 slices white bread, buttered and crusts removed	2 cups shredded Monterey Jack cheese
1 — 1 pound can corn, drained	4 eggs
2 cups sliced zucchini	2 cups milk
1 can chopped green chilies	salt
	pepper

Place buttered slices of bread, crusts removed, buttered side down in a 9x13 baking pan. Distribute corn, zucchini, chilies and cheese over bread slices. Beat eggs and add milk; pour mixture over casserole and refrigerate at least 4 hours or overnight. Bake at 375° for 40 minutes, uncovered.

Mrs. M. C. Minella

Slice tomatoes lengthwise rather than crosswise for much firmer slices.

ZUCCHINI SKILLET CASSEROLE

YIELD: 2-4 servings

1 pound ground beef
1 large onion OR 2 medium onions
1 clove garlic
½ teaspoon oregano
¼-½ teaspoon Jane's crazy mixed
 up salt

pepper to taste
1 — 4 ounce can tomato sauce
2 large OR 4 medium zucchini,
 sliced
1 cup corn, optional

Brown meat; add onions and sauté until transparent; add garlic, whole or diced; add oregano, salt and pepper. Add tomato sauce and zucchini. Cover and simmer over low heat until zucchini is just tender, or cook to desired doneness.

Other spices can be substituted or added according to taste preference.

Do not add water as tomato sauce and other ingredients draw enough juices.

Can be served over rice or as is. Ideal with corn muffins, or add corn to recipe.

This is an original recipe which I consider one of my "quickies."

Hilda N. Perkins

ZUCCHINI-TOMATOES
(Fat Free)

1 can stewing tomatoes, #2
½ cup diced bell pepper
½ cup diced onion
2 chicken bouillon cubes

2 teaspoons sugar, or more
pepper, optional
3 medium zucchini, sliced

Combine all ingredients except zucchini and simmer for 30-45 minutes. Add zucchini and cook about 10 minutes, until just tender.

It is better to be a little sweet; recipe will be soupy and is good for a side dish; it is delicious cold.

Mabel Burry

Buy frozen vegetables that come in clear plastic bags rather than cartons. This way the contents can be seen. Remember — pick out frozen foods just prior to going to the checkout counter; they will be less likely to defrost.

NOTES

INDEX

NOTES

Indian River Cuisine
Indian River Community College
3209 Virginia Avenue
Fort Pierce, Florida 33450
Attention Director of Development

Please send _____ copies of **Indian River Cuisine** at $12.95 per copy plus $1.50 for postage and handling for each copy. Florida residents please add $.36 sales tax per copy.

Name_____
Address_____
City_____State_____Zip_____

Make checks payable to **Indian River Cuisine**

Indian River Cuisine
Indian River Community College
3209 Virginia Avenue
Fort Pierce, Florida 33450
Attention Director of Development

Please send _____ copies of **Indian River Cuisine** at $12.95 per copy plus $1.50 for postage and handling for each copy. Florida residents please add $.36 sales tax per copy.

Name_____
Address_____
City_____State_____Zip_____

Make checks payable to **Indian River Cuisine**

Indian River Cuisine
Indian River Community College
3209 Virginia Avenue
Fort Pierce, Florida 33450
Attention Director of Development

Please send _____ copies of **Indian River Cuisine** at $12.95 per copy plus $1.50 for postage and handling for each copy. Florida residents please add $.36 sales tax per copy.

Name_____
Address_____
City_____State_____Zip_____

Make checks payable to **Indian River Cuisine**

Indian River Cuisine
Indian River Community College
3209 Virginia Avenue
Fort Pierce, Florida 33450
Attention Director of Development

Please send _____ copies of **Indian River Cuisine** at $12.95 per copy plus $1.50 for postage and handling for each copy. Florida residents please add $.36 sales tax per copy.

Name_____
Address_____
City_____State_____Zip_____

Make checks payable to **Indian River Cuisine**

Indian River Cuisine
Indian River Community College
3209 Virginia Avenue
Fort Pierce, Florida 33450
Attention Director of Development

Please send _____ copies of **Indian River Cuisine** at $12.95 per copy plus $1.50 for postage and handling for each copy. Florida residents please add $.36 sales tax per copy.

Name_____
Address_____
City_____State_____Zip_____

Make checks payable to **Indian River Cuisine**

Indian River Cuisine
Indian River Community College
3209 Virginia Avenue
Fort Pierce, Florida 33450
Attention Director of Development

Please send _____ copies of **Indian River Cuisine** at $12.95 per copy plus $1.50 for postage and handling for each copy. Florida residents please add $.36 sales tax per copy.

Name_____
Address_____
City_____State_____Zip_____

Make checks payable to **Indian River Cuisine**